Political Ethics and
the United Nations

GW00544372

Based on a wealth of sources, files and interviews, and including previously unpublished material, this book explores the foundations of the political ethics of Dag Hammarskjöld, the second Secretary-General of the United Nations, and examines how they influenced his actions in several key crisis situations.

Hammarskjöld's political innovations, such as the creation of peacekeeping forces, the use of private diplomacy and the concept of the international civil service, were bold attempts at translating the aims and principles of the UN charter into concrete thought and action. Kofi Annan described Hammarskjöld's approach as a useful guideline to dealing with the problems of a globalised world. Offering a topical perspective on a subject that has not recently been explored, this book analyses Hammarskjöld's successes and failures in a way which offers insights into contemporary problems, and in doing so provides a significant and original contribution to UN studies.

This book will be of interest to students of the United Nations, Peace Studies, and International Relations in general.

Manuel Fröhlich is Junior Professor for Political Science at the Friedrich-Schiller University of Jena.

The Cass Series on Peacekeeping
ISSN 1367–9880
General Editor: Michael Pugh

This series examines all aspects of peacekeeping, from the political, operational and legal dimensions to the developmental and humanitarian issues that must be dealt with by all those involved with peacekeeping in the world today.

Political Ethics and the United Nations

Dag Hammarskjöld
as Secretary-General

Manuel Fröhlich

Routledge
Taylor & Francis Group

LONDON AND NEW YORK

Transferred to digital printing 2010

First published 2008
by Routledge
2 Park Square, Milton Park, Abingdon, Oxon OX14 4RN

Simultaneously published in the USA and Canada
by Routledge
270 Madison Ave, New York, NY 10016

*Routledge is an imprint of the Taylor & Francis Group, an informa
business*

© 2008 Manuel Fröhlich

Typeset in Times by
HWA Text and Data Management, Tunbridge Wells

British Library Cataloguing in Publication Data
A catalogue record for this book is available from the British Library

Library of Congress Cataloging-in-Publication Data
Fröhlich, Manuel
[Dag Hammarskjöld und die Vereinten Nationen. English]
Political ethics and the United Nations: the political philosophy of Dag
Hammarskjöld / Manuel Fröhlich.
     p. cm.
Translated from German.
Includes bibliographical references and index.
1. Hammarskjöld, Dag, 1905–1961. 2. United Nations–Biography.
3. Political ethics. 4. World politics–1955–1965. I. Title.
D839.7.H3F76 2007
341.23092–dc2
[B]   2007015927

ISBN10: 0–415–44532–9 (hbk)
ISBN10: 0–415–58833–2 (pbk)

ISBN13: 978–0–415–44532–0 (hbk)
ISBN13: 978–0–415–58833–1 (pbk)

Contents

Foreword to the English edition

This book is a revised and updated version of *Dag Hammarskjöld und die Vereinten Nationen: Die politische Ethik des UNO-Generalsekretärs* published in 2002 by Ferdinand Schöningh Verlag. The text, especially the references with further material and quotations, have been substantially shortened while a number of recent events concerning the tenure of Kofi Annan and his place in the tradition of Dag Hammarskjöld have been integrated into the book. These changes, however, have not altered but rather reinforced the general conclusions drawn in 2002.

The realization of this book would not have happened without the invaluable support and help of many people. I should like to thank Prof. Dr. Klaus Dicke (University of Jena) for his academic inspiration. I am deeply indebted to Sir Brian Urquhart whose unequalled experience both in UN affairs and as Hammarskjöld's first biographer repeatedly opened up new perspectives in my work. My thanks also go to the various interview partners who provided a number of insights not available in other sources and to Sibyl Stokar for a continuous dialogue on various aspects of Hammarskjöld's life and work. Last, but not least, I am grateful for the assistance of Prof. Michael Pugh and his offer to include the book in the Cass Series on Peacekeeping. My thanks go also to the anonymous reviewers of the manuscript.

The English translation of the book has come about due to the excellent work of John Richardson. Dr. Klaus Kübel (University of Jena) provided crucial help in finding the resources needed to fund such an endeavour. Preparing the text for publication, proof-reading and research on literature was quite a tremendous task and I am grateful for the invaluable support of Sylvia Lenke, Stefan Ipach, Martin Wieczorek, Jochen Moss, Christoph Sperfeldt, Ricky Wichum, Roger Lipsey and Jonathan Lowell Gibbs who in different stages of the project were engaged in its realization. Wherever possible, I have tried to quote primary sources from the relevant English editions. When that was not possible, I decided on a translation of German texts not available in English.

Since this book for a huge part relies on archival material I cannot thank enough Marilla Guptil of the United Nations Archive in New York and Jack Zawistowski of the Royal Library in Stockholm for their assistance. I am also indebted to the Dag Hammarskjöld Foundation and Olle Nordberg, its chairman, for countless stimuli and unflagging support. My parents Fred and Christa as well as my siblings Anna-

Cathérine and Alexander have each in their own way accompanied the book. Once more, it would not have been possible without the patience, support and love of Anette.

Manuel Fröhlich

Preface

Sir Brian Urquhart

Dag Hammarskjöld was an unusual and fascinating public figure. As the second Secretary-General of the United Nations, he provided the most dynamic and striking leadership that organization has ever had. He personified the ideals of the UN Charter in action in a way that made a profound impression on hundreds of millions of people all over the world. He also developed a variety of new instruments of multilateral preventive action – peacekeeping, United Nations 'presences', and various effective experiments in good offices and quiet diplomacy. As the contemporary slogan: 'leave it to Dag', indicated, Hammarskjöld gave the concept of international service a new involvement and meaning. Perhaps most important of all, he showed that one man, if sufficiently courageous, could stand up for principle against even the greatest powers in a way that could sometimes influence important events.

The source of Hammarskjöld's strength was not conventional power, of which the UN Secretary-General has none. His achievements rested rather on a strong inner discipline and an unassailable integrity, not only in the sense of purity and honour, but also of seeing life as a consistent whole, subject in all its parts to the same rules of conduct and standards of performance. As his friend the English sculptor Barbara Hepworth put it, 'Dag Hammarskjöld had a pure and exact perception of aesthetic principles, as exact as it was over ethical and moral principles. I believe they were, to him, one and the same thing.' Although he was a shy and rather solitary person, he had that imponderable quality of 'charisma', through which his purposes and his ideals were communicated to an extraordinarily wide international public.

Manuel Fröhlich has undertaken the formidable task of concording the ethical and spiritual side of Hammarskjöld's personality with his public and political achievements. No previous writer has attempted this task on as wide or well-researched scale, and the results are both impressive and illuminating. He has written a penetrating and comprehensive analysis of the way in which a dedicated leader can translate personal beliefs and principles into political action.

Hammarskjöld's constant companion and guide during his time at the United Nations was the UN Charter, and Fröhlich rightly starts his book with a study of the Charter and Hammarskjöld's understanding of it, especially in relation to the office of the Secretary-General. This is a matter of the utmost relevance to the understanding both of Hammarskjöld's actions and of the principles underlying those actions. In Hammarskjöld's later years, his interpretation of his duties as Secretary-General was to become a source of profound disagreement with the Soviet Union and with President de Gaulle of France.

Hammarskjöld was, to the end of his life, first and foremost a Swede raised in the very distinctive tradition of his own country. At the United Nations his conduct was ruled by the Swedish concept of a neutral and objective civil service. He was also the heir to the austere code of conduct and international beliefs of his own father, an august and conservative figure who had been both prime minister of Sweden and governor of Uppsala. In Hammarskjöld's youth Uppsala, under the influence of Archbishop Nathan Söderblom, had been an important centre of enlightened religious discussion. These family and national threads formed the basis of Hammarskjöld's ethic of public service. To them he added his own findings on international conduct and also the growing force of a very personal mysticism, which can be sensed in some of the passages of his posthumously published 'spiritual diary', *Markings*.

Hammarskjöld gave a great deal of thought to the nature of the fledgling international civil service of which he was the head. He was strict in enforcing the standards of behaviour that he considered essential for the international secretariat, but he also thought a great deal about the practical contradictions between the concept and the reality of the international civil service. In his last years, the often vitriolic attacks of Khrushchev and de Gaulle spurred him to a forceful defence of the independence and integrity of the secretariat. In one of his last speeches, at Oxford, Hammarskjöld set out the political and ethical dilemmas which he and his secretariat colleagues had to face in the highly politicized world of the Cold War. In the last analysis, he said, the correct reaction to them was 'a question of integrity or [...], if you please, a question of conscience.'

When I wrote a biography of Hammarskjöld nearly thirty years ago, I tried, in the epilogue, to foresee the probable nature and durability of Hammarskjöld's legacy. Only ten years after his death it proved impossible to write much more than a series of rhetorical questions. Manuel Fröhlich, in a masterly chapter on, 'The Hammarskjöld Tradition', has gone a long way to answering some of the questions I raised so ineffectively thirty years ago. In fact, his chapter title already foreshadows the answer. Dag Hammarskjöld, through his vision, personality, courage and integrity, not only put the United Nations on the map as an agency for keeping the peace; he also set a new, and as yet unmatched, standard for international service and leadership.

Abbreviations

AC	Advisory Committee
AR	Annual Report
CF	Andrew Cordier and Wilder Foote
CH	Andrew Cordier and Max Harrelson
CIA	Central Intelligence Agency
DTV	Deutscher Taschenbuch-Verlag
ES	Emergency Session
FN	Footnote
GA	General Assembly
GAOR	General Assembly Official Records
KB DHS	Kungliga Biblioteket Dag Hammarskjöld Samling
NATO	North Atlantic Treaty Organization
NGO	Non-Governmental Organization
NPL	Neue politische Literatur
OEEC	Organization for European Economic Co-operation
ONUC	Organisation des Nations Unies au Congo
ORCI	Office of Research and the Collection of Information
PC	Press Conference/Preparatory Commission
SC	Security Council
SG	Secretary-General
SZ	Süddeutsche Zeitung
TLS	Times Literary Supplement
UN	United Nations
UNA	United Nations Archives New York
UNEF	United Nations Emergency Force
UNISCAN	United Kingdom – Scaninavia Free Trade Project
UNITAR	United Nations Institute for Training and Research
UNO	United Nations Organisation
UNTSO	United Nations Truce Supervision Organization
USA	United States of America
USG	Under Secretary-General

1   Introduction

After Dag Hammarskjöld, the second Secretary-General of the United Nations, was killed in a plane crash near Ndola on 17 September 1961, two of his colleagues began to sort out his estate and personal papers in New York prior to depositing them in a private archive at the Royal Library in Stockholm. In the course of their work they made two discoveries. In Hammarskjöld's apartment, Per Lind, a staff member of the Swedish foreign ministry who Hammarskjöld had taken with him to New York in 1953, found a manuscript that contained a diary of sorts, together with a covering letter to Leif Belfrage, a former colleague of Hammarskjöld at the foreign ministry. This manuscript, subsequently published as *Markings*, provided a completely new insight into Hammarskjöld's personality. Brian Urquhart, who divided the Secretary-General's personal documents between the UN archive in New York and the private archive in Stockholm, made a second discovery: 'His papers were arranged in a way as if he wanted to write a moral book on politics' (Interview 1997).

Indeed, the private archive in Stockholm does contain various preparations for such an undertaking which up to now have not been systematically evaluated. Hammarskjöld would not have been interested in recording just facts and events. In a letter to a friend in 1960 he wrote:

> The mission and formula for our generation – I think I know them, perhaps I even live them. But I could not formulate them in a way that would help others. Perhaps I shall be able to do so one day when I can see what I experience every day in a more neutral perspective.
>
> (quoted in Lindegren 1971: 1)

Hammarskjöld never got to write such a book, which he occasionally mentioned as a project for the time after his retirement as Secretary-General (Beskow 1969: 17). Even during his lifetime it was obvious that the man whose innovations, such as the reorganization of the Secretariat and the first deployment of blue helmets during the Suez Crisis, shaped the UN during its formative years was always at pains to reflect on the actions, functions and objectives of the United Nations in international politics. C.V. Narasimhan, his former executive assistant, also emphasizes Hammarskjöld's exceptional ability to combine practical and theoretical concerns:

> A man who is a good negotiator and who is able to find a solution for every problem that comes along that he meets in the course of solving a political problem need not necessarily have a deep political philosophy, or a contribution to political theory. But Hammarskjöld had that also. He was not just content to solve problems as they came along. He had a whole vision of the United Nations, not just of the conference machinery but of the means for instilling in all nations a respect for international law and order, as a means for avoiding potential conflicts, as a means for providing an additional tool of diplomacy, as a means for maintaining the peace, aside from what you might call the balance of terror, of nuclear power. [...] And he practised it.
>
> (Interview Narasimhan 1973: 27)

Hammarskjöld's particular way of approaching his task appears to have had considerable success. U Thant, his successor, sums it up as follows: 'In the eight years in which he served the United Nations, he brought to the office of the Secretary-General new meaning and new standing in international life' (Thant 1971: 154). Pak draws a similar picture: 'Hammarskjöld's personal leadership was the most important single factor contributing to the growth of the role [of the United Nations]' (1963: 221). This assessment is also shared by people who are not known to be unconditional supporters of the United Nations, e.g. Hans Morgenthau:

> The late Mr. Hammarskjöld's tenure of office shows impressively how dependent the peace-promoting functions of the Secretary-General are upon the intellectual and moral qualities of the holder of that office. Only a man of Hammarskjöld's personality could have tried to do what he did in this respect, and have achieved what he achieved.
>
> (1973: 486)

Hammarskjöld's death in Ndola, however, coincided with the climax of the Congo Crisis and the concomitant conflict over the role of the United Nations. In the confusion of the superpowers' conflicting interests in what was the largest UN operation ever undertaken in a civil war situation up to that time (and which in some ways foreshadowed the intrastate conflicts since the 1990s) Hammarskjöld had become a target of heavy criticism. This development points to a significant aspect in the understanding of the work of the United Nations that goes well beyond Hammarskjöld: in its problems and opportunities, successes and frustrations, the organization reflects fundamental trends and developments in global politics. In this regard, the office of the Secretary-General is often the symptomatic focus of the challenges and hopes as well as the expectations and disappointments in international politics. From his own experience, Javier Pérez de Cuéllar describes this state of affairs as follows: 'To understand correctly the role of the Secretary-

General is to appreciate the whole mission of the United Nations. And that, in turn, is central to the way international life is organized' (1995: 125).

The challenge of 'international leadership'

This relationship has been particularly apparent since the end of the Cold War. The demise of the East–West conflict led to a promising rediscovery of the United Nations and the vision of a new era of multilateralism. This change in turn was reflected in attitudes towards the office of the Secretary-General. The permanent members of the Security Council charged him with the task of drawing up an 'Agenda for Peace' with a view to strengthening the United Nations' prospects of maintaining peace in the international system. The end of the rivalry between political systems for pre-eminence in international politics appeared to clear the way for a factual, problem-oriented approach to major global challenges. Ideologically coloured debates gave way to a fresh perspective on the obligations, possibilities and limits of responsibly shaping world politics.

In this context there have been calls for international or global leadership to promote such a new agenda.[1] The difference in adjectives alone is revealing: whereas 'international' takes individual nations or states as the point of reference for such leadership, the adjective 'global' stands for the transformation in international relations and the introduction of new actors and problem areas. Above and beyond these terminological distinctions, the concept serves to express a unifying idea: instead of ready-made blueprints for an established 'order' or a 'system' of international relations, the concern here is for a more flexible concept focused on identifying international problems, framing suitable guidelines and standards as well as bundling the appropriate resources. The idea of a uniform international 'system' that strives for equilibrium on the basis of incommutable rules, causes and effects appears inadequate for coping with the demands of redimensioned space and time in a globalized as well as regionalized world (Hubel 1995; Buzan 1991; Singer and Wildavsky 1993). In this sense, the report of the 'Commission on Global Governance' (1995) identifies global leadership as the crucial challenge and necessity for international affairs. But who should lead? Brian Urquhart and Erskine Childers, in their study on the UN's leadership capacity emphasize the special role of the United Nations Secretary-General:

> Developing an active consensus about the world agenda and the UN system's part in it should be a central task for the Secretary-General and his or her colleagues in the UN system. Without the Secretary-General's leadership such a consensus is unlikely to emerge.
>
> (1996: 13)

In a certain sense, Boutros Boutros-Ghali took charge in the debate on the leadership capacities of the United Nations. He left no doubt that in his mind the Secretary-General of the United Nations was a crucial factor in international relations:

Today and for the foreseeable future, the Secretary-General must operate within the context of both the world dialectic of globalization and fragmentation and the U.N. dialectic of an increasing burden and decreasing resources. If the United Nations is to serve the new range of requirements of member states and their peoples, the role of the Secretary-General must be created anew. Faced with these obstacles, what is the role of today's Secretary-General? What can the Secretary-General do? I believe a great deal can be done. I believe the Secretary-General can be crucial.

(1996a: 88)

These and similar remarks that Boutros-Ghali self-consciously published under the heading 'global leadership' did not meet with unanimous approval (Helms 1996: 3–7). Indeed, the experiences of the crises in Somalia and the former Yugoslavia soon raised questions about the ability of the United Nations to assume pivotal responsibility for international security (Link 1999: 114–21). As the example of Yugoslavia showed, an organization of collective defence such as NATO was held to be more reliable and effective in peace-making and peace-keeping. In this perspective, 'leadership' fell to the 'sole superpower', the USA (Nye 1991). This difference was certainly one of the reasons why the Clinton administration vetoed Boutros-Ghali's re-election, since his claim to 'global leadership' could be interpreted as an affront against the United States. Despite the influence of domestic political considerations, this event, too, confirms the connection between developments in international relations, the importance of the United Nations and the role of the Secretary-General, whose office reflects, as it were, the ambitious search and set-backs of a 'new world order'.[2]

Boutros-Ghali's successor, Kofi Annan, inherited his predecessor's expectations and frustrations (Fröhlich 1997b). Great expectations collided with great criticism of the UN's effectiveness in promoting international security (as for example in the context of the Iraq war of 2003) and its efficiency in handling new tasks and challenges (as for example in the Oil for Food Programme). These recent debates, which will be dealt with in Chapter 5, prolong a tradition of fundamental doubt about the general usefulness of the UN (Touval 1994; Lefever 1993; Righter 1995). Are the United Nations and its Secretary-General in a position to exercise leadership? The decision to replace Boutros-Ghali highlighted the extremely fragile position of the office: '[T]raditional power politics models of leadership are simply not applicable to the United Nations Secretary-General' (Trachtenberg 1982: 615). Against this background, Gordenker more narrowly defines leadership as it pertains to the Secretary-General:

Leadership by the Secretary-General consists of projecting values, policies, and procedural approaches on defined issues related to acknowledged organizational functions. Further, it includes stimulating, overseeing, and sometimes directing the execution of adopted policies.

(1993a: 268)

This definition, which comes close to what Urquhart and Childers call 'intellectual leadership' (1996: 18), refers again to the ethical implications of such leadership, which has become even more topical due to the growing relevance of ethical standards in coping with new crisis scenarios. Gordenker, as well as Urquhart and Childers, offers one specific example of successfully realized, ethically based, international leadership: Dag Hammarskjöld. In this vein, the debate about international leadership drew attention to the second Secretary-General again, and there were even calls for a 'new Hammarskjöld' needed to exercise leadership for the United Nations in an increasingly globalized world with all its contradictions (Meisler 1995: 189–97; Urquhart 1987b: 10). In this sense, the Report of the Commission on Global Governance introduced Hammarskjöld as an example of the kind of 'leaders made strong by vision, sustained by ethics, and revealed by political courage' (1995: 353) that international politics urgently needs. These references presume that Hammarskjöld is not just an historical example, but that his example may shed light on the conditions that will enable the Secretary-General of the United Nations to provide international leadership (Jones 1994).

This presumption brings us back to Hammarskjöld's 'unfinished' book project and his 'theory' of the UN. Owing to his early death, many of his views and his reflection on his work with the necessary detachment are irretrievably lost. Yet, in his active years as Secretary-General he left an abundance of evidence that contains essential elements of his 'theory' of the United Nations (see also Zacher 1983: 111). The following study will attempt to reconstruct Hammarskjöld's contribution to the debate on ethically motivated international leadership. To do this, the analysis must combine Hammarskjöld's theoretical and practical political achievement.

At this point, the concept of political ethics needs to be defined more closely (Sutor 1991; Buchheim 1991; Riklin 1994: 105–20; Anzenbacher 2001). The common argument is that the sphere of politics and the sphere of ethics have to be distinguished from each other; at the same time, they can not be separated (Valdés 1987: 92–5). Every concept of morality that seeks to become a socially binding force depends on the mediation of politics. Conversely, one of the striking features of politics is its frequent use of moral arguments and purposes – whether just rhetorical or factual – to legitimize itself. Dorothy V. Jones describes the ideal case of the interrelation between politics and ethics as follows: 'Ideally, politics keeps ethics from becoming so abstract that it is of no use in the real world, and ethics keeps politics from becoming nothing more than an amoral contest of force and guile' (1991: 163). On the other side we find the mere instrumental use of morality in politics expressed in Kant's distinction between the moral politician and the political moralist: 'I can actually think of a moral politician, i.e., one who so interprets the principles of political prudence that they can be coherent with morality, but I cannot think of a political moralist, i.e., one who forges a morality to suit the statesman's advantage' (Kant 1795: 128; Gerhardt 1995: 146–85).

Further differentiating the concept of political ethics, Alois Riklin (1994: 105) distinguishes three dimensions of political ethics, namely the dimension of the politician as a person, the political institutions and, finally, the political results.

Ideally, all three dimensions form a symbiosis. Political ethics in this sense can then function simultaneously as a standard and motivation of politics. In the final analysis, politics and morality cannot be identical, as each occupies its own sphere with its own functionality and logic. It is precisely this insight that feeds Max Weber's distinction between the ethics of conviction and the ethics of responsibility (1989: 54–55). According to Weber, any political ethics has to recognize the special characteristic of political power – and this recognition distinguishes political ethics from the ethics of other areas of human life. Any ethics of conviction that disregards the inherent rationale of politics and the politician's resultant responsibility may (despite best intentions) lead to catastrophic results. However, Weber himself points out:

> One can see now: the ethics of conviction and the ethics of responsibility are not absolute opposites, but rather they complement each other and together they mould the authentic human beings who then may show a 'vocation for politics'.
>
> (1989: 63)

From that point of view, enduring and coming to terms with this insoluble strained relationship is the actual challenge of political ethics: 'The moral impulse must be transformed into political rationality …' (Sutor 1991: 68). In this light, Dicke, referring to Weber and Kant, describes the task of political science as the attempt 'to trace normative rules in practice, without falling into moralizing mysticism on the one hand or an empiricism that defines normativity only in terms of reality on the other' (1993: 10). Political ethics understood in this way fulfils a genuinely critical function in the assessment of political reality. It is particularly relevant in crisis situations in which familiar guidelines for social processes and political actions no longer hold. In such situations, political ethics is more than a motivational source, a standard and a frame of reference for political actions; it is also an orientation guide amidst confusing and contradictory developments in political reality.

With regard to international politics the situation is particularly difficult, as the pluralism of national traditions as well as philosophical frameworks of ethical thought and action is multiplied. Against this background, it is difficult to establish a uniform definition of international ethics; at any rate they cannot be decreed (Huber 1955: 352–82). On the other hand, respect for international law and the performance of international cooperation largely depend on as broad a consensus on fundamental ethical rules as possible (Tomuschat 1986: 129). Any attempt to speak of political ethics in international affairs has to take into account specific people, institutions or situations.

The topic of this work is Dag Hammarskjöld's political ethics. One of the peculiarities of this study lies in the fact that Hammarskjöld's political ethics was not applied to politics from the outside, but developed in the course of his efforts to come to terms with the experience of political reality. An active politician articulating ethical concepts and positions is unlikely to meet the terminological, scientific distinctions outlined so far. Nevertheless, this work will attempt to explain Dag Hammarskjöld's political ethics on the basis of three central questions that at the same time refer to the three dimensions of political ethics introduced above:

1   What value is accorded to political ethics in the work of the United Nations? How can it be pinpointed in an analysis of the office of the Secretary-General of the United Nations? (*institutional ethics*)
2   What are the fundamental biographical and philosophical elements that formed Dag Hammarskjöld's political ethics? What are the characteristics of his political ethics? (*personal ethics*)
3   In which way did Hammarskjöld's political ethics influence his actions and political concepts? How did he implement his ethical ideas and what is the relevance of his method today? (*applied ethics*)

The topic in literature

An analysis in this form can build on insights gained in several fields of research that have gained in significance during recent years: the renaissance of political biography (e.g. Thaysen 1996), studies in political leadership (e.g. Hermann and Hagan 1998), ideas and international politics (e.g. Goldstein and Keohane 1993a) as well as morality in international relations (e.g. Nardin and Mapel 1992).[3] Although these trends do not form a coherent line of argument, there are some recurring results and foci that do inform the present analysis. Byman and Pollack (2001) under the subtitle of 'Bringing the Statesman Back in' have pointed out that the analysis of international relations should not neglect individual personalities and their actions. In order to evaluate their role and impact, leadership studies make use of political psychology as well as theories of information processing, cognition and perception (Vertzberger 1990; George and George 1964; Holsti 1970; Hermann and Milburn 1977). Their interest lies in identifying 'cognitive maps' (Axelrod 1976b) using the analysis patterns of an 'operational code' (Leites 1953). While there are obvious limits to a mathematical translation of fundamental motivations and ideas, the focus on situations of crisis and the influence of personal and close advisors will be adopted in parts of the examination. This ties in with an emphasis on ideas in the sense that Goldstein and Keohane outlined:

> Our argument is that ideas influence policy when the principled or casual beliefs they embody provide road maps that increase actor's clarity about goals or ends-means relationships, when they affect outcomes of strategic situations in which there is no unique equilibrium, and when they become embedded in political institutions.
>
> (1993b: 3)

Such an emphasis on actors, ideas, values and norms is often connected to what has been labelled a constructivist approach (see Onuf 1989; Chekel 1998; Finnemore and Sikkink 1998; Boekle *et al*. 1999). The scope of this work, does however, not seek to identify intersubjective attitudes and expectations but concentrates on one person as an 'exceptionally-situated individual actor' (Murphy 1970: 165). Some of the findings, e.g. on the normative basis of international organization, may nonetheless prove interesting in the constructivist sense. A similar relationship can be seen between this analysis and the research concerns of the 'English School' (Wight 1992; Dunne 1998). The study of the very sources of ideas and actions as well as a concentration on political ethics in that context informs various studies within that tradition, and its concept of the UN inevitably deals with the central question of the conditions and limits of international society. As far as international ethics are concerned Brown (1994) discusses the question whether it could be established as a discipline of its own and Booth passionately argues for restructuring international relations as a 'global moral science' (1995: 109–10). A lot of studies do, however, deal with mere postulations of various norms and values. The question of how these ideals translate into action and how they can be measured against the 'reality' of politics has received far less attention. In this context, Rosenthal writes in his foreword to a collection of case studies by Nolan (1995: xi): 'There are few more compelling sources for the study of ethics and international affairs than the true stories and historical experiences of statesmen who made hard choices in reconciling principle and power'. Among those exemplary case studies one can find a chapter on Dag Hammarskjöld (Jones 1995).

The office of the Secretary-General of the United Nations is the subject of a vast number of studies, usually from the perspective of international law (see also 'The position of the Secretary-General according to the Charter' in Chapter 2). They all struggle with the complexity of this office, its defining qualities and the political prerequisites for its effectiveness. Newman's study comes to the conclusion: 'The Office remains an anomaly, a political chimera' (1998: 201). Any attempt to study this chimera leads to the personality of the incumbent. In his classic 1967 study on the Secretary-General Gordenker sums up: 'No matter how dispassionately or scientifically the office of Secretary-General is studied, it is still occupied by a human being with a will. The human qualities of the Secretary-General contribute to his influence' (1967a: 320; Claude 1993: 255). In a similar vein, Tapio Kanninen, former assistant to Secretary-General Pérez de Cuéllar, argued that the question of the values underlying the Secretary-General's political leadership was still a desideratum:

> [The] discussion of the previous chapters has left one dimension of leadership unanswered, that of the permanent inner values (overarching fundamental beliefs) of the leader and how particular values of the highest order affect the decisions taken, if at all.
>
> (1995: 261)

Such a systematic analysis of the personality, political views and values of the Secretary-General and their effect on his political leadership has been called for by Cox who already in 1969 argued that '[t]he quality of executive leadership may prove to be the most critical single determinant of the growth in scope and authority of international organization' (1969: 205). But Cox also warns against overemphasizing personality: 'The executive head, in this vision, is cast in a role comparable to that of the proletariat in a better-known dialectical proposition – a heavy load of historical expectations for a rather lonely figure to bear' (ibid.: 207). In order to test his theory of the importance of the personality factor in the growth of international organizations, Cox heavily draws from the example of Dag Hammarskjöld.

Turning to biographical studies about Hammarskjöld, one can observe a variety of texts from books for young readers, through historical appreciations of his term of office, to critical discussion of his political achievements and personality.[4] The opinions and priorities vary enormously, which prompted Urquhart to conclude: 'It is difficult to appreciate a man so strange and so important without either descending into cheap and impertinent analysis or getting lost in admiration' (1964: 232–44). The main body of literature appeared in the period from the early 1960s – starting with Lash's biography completed shortly before Hammarskjöld's death – to the early 1970s, when Brian Urquhart's standard work (1972) was published for the first time. After that, writings on Hammarskjöld appeared only sporadically, e.g. on the anniversary of his death. With the end of the Cold War and the revival of the influence of the United Nations and the discussion about the person and administration of Boutros-Ghali, there was a brief flurry of articles on and references to Hammarskjöld (Meisler 1995; Birnbaum 1997). In this context, particular mention must be made of Kofi Annan's reference to Dag Hammarskjöld (see also Chapter 5).

The literature on Hammarskjöld can be divided into two areas: articles and books tend to focus either on Hammarskjöld the politician[5] or on Hammarskjöld the Christian mystic and writer.[6] As representative of these two 'camps' we can mention Urquhart's biography for a detailed account of Hammarskjöld the Secretary-General, on the one hand, and van Dusen's study (1969) of Hammarskjöld's faith on the other hand. As Hammarskjöld's assistant for many years, Urquhart is a contemporary witness; for his political biography he was able to evaluate a mass of official and private records to which he had access even before the period of official secrecy expired. The only limitation was the fact that at the time of publication Urquhart was still working for the United Nations; thus, the description and evaluation of specific facts in his publication were subject to certain restrictions. Van Dusen also had access to official documents and private records, primarily from Hammarskjöld's personal correspondence. Over and above this, Hammarskjöld's family put him in touch with many friends, acquaintances and colleagues from different phases of the life and career of the later Secretary-General. Of particular interest for the work at hand is the fact that van Dusen does not only deal with Hammarskjöld's faith, but also with the influence of Albert Schweitzer and Martin Buber – even if only in two short digressions (Dusen 1969: 215–23).[7] By constructing a calendrical synopsis of important entries in Hammarskjöld's spiritual diary and official appointments as Secretary-General, van Dusen presents evidence of reciprocal influence between Hammarskjöld's private and official lives. At the same time he emphasizes that political issues go beyond the scope of his study (1969: 105).

In the rest of the literature, there is often a remarkable parallelism in the treatment of these two qualities and the two 'camps' do not benefit from each other as they probably could. This is partly owing to the apparent irreconcilability of what Cordier calls 'the two Hammarskjölds': 'Hammarskjöld, the religious mystic, and Hammarskjöld, the man of action' (1972: 3). Henderson had already concluded his biography with a call to combine these two aspects (1969: 131).

However, the thesis that knowledge of the private person is indispensable for an understanding of the politician has not met with complete approval. Hammarskjöld's colleague, the former Assistant Secretary-General for Economic and Social Questions, Philippe de Seynes, declared: 'His public life and his private life ... were in my view quite separate' (1983: 65–75). With reference to Hammarskjöld's spirituality and its connection with his political achievements, a Swedish article that appeared on the occasion of the posthumous publication of Hammarskjöld's diary noted: 'Hammarskjöld was a dutiful office-bearer and a skilled diplomat. But that was not a result of his mysticism, but independently thereof' (cited in Kranz 1973b: 23). Yet in his review of Hammarskjöld's diary, Erich Goldman, an American historian, asserted: 'It cannot be denied that his deep religiousness made a major contribution to his sweeping effectiveness as Secretary-General of the UN' (ibid.). To investigate the connection between the private and the public man more closely, sources other than published literature on Hammarskjöld have to be considered.

Line of argumentation and sources

Different sources involve different styles and levels of abstraction. Each has its own particular content and, thus, its own validity. As we learn from leadership studies, the wider context of published speeches and statements needs to be examined in two respects. First, to establish the authenticity and authorship of official comments it is necessary to clarify the administrative channels and the role of close advisors (Holsti 1976: 27–9). Second, particular attention must be paid to spontaneous and unfiltered comments of the person in question, which can be reconstructed from protocols or minutes of internal meetings (ibid.: 43–5). Just as leadership research constantly emphasizes the value of such sources, it also complains that it is very difficult to gain access to such sources. In Hammarskjöld's case, however, it is possible to locate and evaluate various sources of this nature.

1. The Secretary-General's public papers

These are the sum of Hammarskjöld's official oral and written contributions. The four volumes covering Hammarskjöld's period of office were edited and published by his former colleagues Andrew Cordier and Wilder Foote (1972–5, hereinafter cited as CF II, III, IV, and V). They offer a truly comprehensive documentation of Hammarskjöld's public texts and documents: approximately 150 statements, comments and speeches in various UN fora, more than 60 comprehensive reports of the Secretary-General on different topics, excerpts and minutes of more than 70 press conferences, about as many letters, telegrams, journal articles and memorandums and last, but not least, more than 50 major speeches and addresses on occasions inside and outside the world organization. As shall be shown below, the authenticity and importance of Hammarskjöld's speeches and reports is particularly significant because he wrote an unusually large number of them himself (Chapter 2 and 4).

2. Markings

The entries, poems and texts in Hammarskjöld's diary (1964),[8] which he termed 'a kind of white book of my negotiations with myself – and with God',[9] are of a very different nature from his official comments. But despite the difference in style and abstraction, the diary is indispensable for any study of Dag Hammarskjöld. In a letter to his friend Leif Belfrage, Hammarskjöld wrote: 'These entries provide the only true "profile" that can be drawn' (*Markings*: v). The revelation of his weaknesses and self-doubt adds depth to the image of Hammarskjöld the politician, and discloses a very specific view of his personality. W. H. Auden, who was acquainted with Hammarskjöld, translated and edited the diary in English. He concludes: 'It is also an historical document of the first importance as an account – and I cannot myself recall another – of the attempt by a professional man of action to unite in one life *the via* [sic] *activa* and the *via contemplativa*' (1964: xx).

3. Papers in the private archive and the archive of the United Nations

The two most important archives on Hammarskjöld are the main archive of the United Nations in New York and the Hammarskjöld Collection of the Swedish Royal Library in Stockholm. Whereas the holdings of the New York archive are mainly records from the Executive Office of the Secretary-General, the Stockholm Collection has comprehensive holdings of 'private' records. In this connection, special mention must be made of Hammarskjöld's almost complete correspondence (as a rule in English) with a number of eminent personalities in different fields.[10] It should be noted that in most cases both sides of the correspondence have survived, largely a feat of Hammarskjöld's nephew Peder, who, when building up the archive with Hammarskjöld's former colleague Per Lind, tried to gather as many documents as possible from acquaintances and confidantes. In his often very long letters with leading statesmen such as David Ben Gurion and Anthony Eden, with writers such as Saint-John Perse, John Steinbeck and Djuna Barnes, artists such as Bo Beskow and Barbara Hepworth and, not least, thinkers such as Martin Buber and Albert Schweitzer, Hammarskjöld also expressed his opinions on the moral and political problems of his office. Some of the self-interpretations and reflections in these sources are indispensable for any analysis of his political ethics (see Lash 1957: 233–42).

Hammarskjöld's private library, which still exists, is also of particular interest. An analysis of the contents reveals which works he at least owned and probably studied more intensively. Furthermore, the Stockholm archive also contains some of Hammarskjöld's political records in the narrower sense, which complement the holdings in New York. These include almost all drafts of his speeches.

4. Interviews with former colleagues and experts

Another source is interviews with former colleagues and acquaintances of Hammarskjöld as well as experts related to the United Nations.[11] These interviews provided information that could not be obtained from other sources. They proved especially useful in respect of the patterns of work in the Secretariat and the link between theory and practice. Personal interviews with most of Hammarskjöld's close colleagues were no longer possible. However, access to three collections of interviews was able to considerably redress this shortcoming. These holdings included: first, interviews from a project of the Oral History Research Office of Columbia University from the 1960s and 1970s; second, interviews made under the United Nations Oral History Programme in the course of the 1980s; and, finally, interviews conducted as part of a Yale University interview series on Dag Hammarskjöld.

By the standards of leadership research, this variety of sources constitutes a remarkable body of information. These sources will be used to investigate one of the dimensions of political ethics in each of the Chapters 2 to 5. Chapter 2 will deal primarily with institutional ethics, Chapter 3 with personal ethics, and Chapters 4 and 5 with applied ethics. These dimensions cannot be sharply separated from one another. Rather, they offer interconnected approaches to Dag Hammarskjöld in the sense of a 'hermeneutic circle' (Heinrich 1989: 74–5; Gadamer 1972: 325–44). The individual steps of the investigation are as follows:

Chapter 2 will start by explaining the position of the Secretary-General of the United Nations as laid down in the organization's Charter. After analysing the relevant legal provisions, the examination will focus on the question of the political functions and, finally, the political power of the Secretary-General. By sifting through these considerations, essential determinants of the office shall be established. This is followed by a content analysis of the introductions to Hammarskjöld's annual reports to the General Assembly, which will form the basis of an initial approximation of his understanding of the office and his 'philosophy' of the United Nations. With the aid of Hammarskjöld's statements in the annual reports, 'political ethics' will be included as a factor among the determinants of the office. Hammarskjöld's understanding of the role of the United Nations will be examined more closely with reference to Henri Bergson's philosophy of life and the categories of Maurice Hauriou's theory of institutions. Finally, the question of the Secretary-General's political power will be defined more closely by applying Hannah Arendt's concept of power.

Chapter 3 reconstructs the history of the ideas, the various elements and the factors that influenced the development of Dag Hammarskjöld's political ethics. The selection is based on the factors and personalities that he himself mentions, though extended in places. Among the factors mentioned are biographical influences, medieval mysticism, Albert Schweitzer and his ethics, Martin Buber and his philosophy of dialogue as well as a series of other personalities and concepts. These influences cannot be treated as separate from one another, but must be considered in the light of their interdependence and interaction. The investigation in each of the sub-chapters takes place in three stages. First, Hammarskjöld's own mention and weighting of the different influences are presented, then the content of each is more closely defined, and, finally, examples are chosen to illustrate how these influences permeate his thoughts and speeches.

Chapter 4 will elucidate the effects and implementation of Hammarskjöld's ethics in the practice of politics – illustrated by examples of political, organizational and legal innovations initiated by Hammarskjöld. The framework for this task is provided by a description of the work flow in the UN Secretariat. Building on that framework, three case studies have been chosen according to an insight from research on 'cognitive maps', namely that a politician's fundamental convictions are most clearly manifested in unprecedented situations of structural uncertainty (Holsti 1976: 30). This criterion applies to all three case studies. Moreover each represents an important instrument of Hammarskjöld's political practice: the negotiations to free American pilots from Chinese captivity in 1955 (private diplomacy), the creation of the first UN peacekeeping force during the Suez Crisis (UN presence in the form of blue helmets), and, finally, the 1960–1 debate on the Soviet Union's troika proposal to replace the office of the Secretary-General (international civil servant). Each analysis consists of three parts: a description of the conflict situation, an analysis of Hammarskjöld's reactions, and the connection with basic elements of his political ethics. As in the discussion of the basic elements of Hammarskjöld's political ethics, here, too, the fact is emphasized that the aforementioned concepts are not independent of one another, but are closely interconnected.

Chapter 5 discusses the relevance as well as the deficits and weaknesses of the concepts based on Dag Hammarskjöld's political ethics. By reviewing the successors' reception or non-reception of his views and the continued application of the instruments he developed, it is possible to trace the development of a 'Hammarskjöld tradition'. Finally, the question of whether and to what extent the historical example of Hammarskjöld and his particular 'style' can be applied to current contexts and can still point to the future is discussed. This applies to both the political challenges facing the United Nations and the theoretical considerations about the work of the world organization.

Through this approach, the study combines classic questions of biography with the reconstruction of the thoughts behind fundamental positions of political ethics, case-oriented history of diplomacy and an analysis of the function and mode of operation of the United Nations. At the same time, it can also be seen as an attempt to elaborate the topos of the UN's moral force in international relations. Hence, the investigation must of necessity be interdisciplinary. Apart from the insights of political science in the narrower sense, the study includes insights from the fields of theology and philosophy. In the course of this 'archaeology' of the ethical foundations of Dag Hammarskjöld's activities as Secretary-General of the United Nations, different facets of Hammarskjöld will be unearthed. The overall picture includes seemingly contradictory images of the hands-on crisis manager and the resigned loser; the impression of a mystic grappling with his feelings and experiences stands alongside that of the cool, calculating intellectual; the isolated loner contrasts with the constantly motivated organizer of the UN administration. A tension will emerge between the youthful, vital Secretary-General and the man for whom thoughts about death and the meaning of life have been constitutive. Urquhart is not the only one to point out that the different aspects of Hammarskjöld's personality strike people as irreconcilable: 'Hammarskjöld was in many ways a paradoxical man – shy but proud, personally modest but highly ambitious for his office, intellectually brilliant but in some ways naive, given to mysticism but severely pragmatic in political arrangements, aristocratic but informal, highly motivated but deeply sceptical.' (Urquhart 1983: 133–4) This analysis of Dag Hammarskjöld's political ethics is intended to establish the relationship between these contradictions and reveal whether (and if so to what extent) this special mix of different influences on and facets of Hammarskjöld's personality directly informed his work as UN Secretary-General and the work of the UN in general.

2 The office of the UN Secretary-General

Dag Hammarskjöld was received by his predecessor Trygve Lie at Idlewild Airport in New York with a warning: 'The task of the Secretary-General is the most impossible job on earth' (1954: 417). Lie's words carry an unmistakeable tone of bitterness at having to retire. Above all, this half-joking, half-serious sentence sums up one man's experience of a seven-year term in a unique post. The complaint about the most impossible job on earth has often been repeated. This complaint usually goes hand in hand with the remark that it is also one of the most difficult political offices to understand and analyse.[1] Max Jacobson, a Finnish diplomat, described the ideal Secretary-General as 'a communicator like Reagan, a reformer like Gorbachev, a diplomat like Kissinger, and a manager like Iacocca' (quoted in Rivlin 1994: 53). It seems impossible to sketch the demands and scope, the laws and determinants of this office in just a few strokes. These difficulties arise partly from the circumstance that – as already indicated – the analysis of the office inevitably implies a discussion about the mission, functioning and nature of the United Nations (Dicke 1998). The Secretary-General is the personification of the UN *per se*. As Boutros-Ghali put it:

> [L]e Secrétaire-Général est, qu'il le veuille ou non, l'incarnation de l'organisation mondiale. C'est à lui, à titre principal, que l'opinion publique internationale demande des comptes. C'est sur sa personne que se concentrent les critiques ou les frustrations de la communauté internationale.
>
> (1996b: 408)

The dry legal provisions of the United Nations Charter do not give much orientation (Tinker 1992: 310). Only the interplay of several factors gives an approximate sense of the possibilities and limits of the office. This chapter will deal with the question of the Secretary-General's as yet unspecified 'power', and simultaneously attempt to pinpoint the role of political ethics in this context. For this purpose the legal principles of the office will be considered and its political powers clarified on that basis. These general insights can then be supplemented by a first approximation of Dag Hammarskjöld's understanding of the Charter, office and organization.

The position of the Secretary-General according to the Charter

The Secretary-General of the United Nations is not only the highest administrative officer of an international organization as was already the Secretary-General of the League of Nations, he also has explicit political powers.[2] The standing of the office evolved out of the tension between primarily administrative and primarily political concepts of managing an international organization. Sir Eric Drummond, the first Secretary-General of the League of Nations, embodied the administrative concept. Although he also achieved considerable political success, he was, as a product of the British civil service, almost completely self-effacing and usually acted behind the scenes.[3] Albert Thomas, the first director of the International Labour Organization, was by contrast the embodiment of the political concept. He stressed the exercise of political leadership by taking the initiative and public stands.[4] Both traditions influenced the formulation of the provisions of the Charter that govern the office of the Secretary-General. In the end, neither of the concepts was favoured over the other. The tension is illustrated by different titles that were discussed as alternatives to Secretary-General: 'Director-General' did not go far enough for most, whereas 'World's Moderator' (proposed by Roosevelt, who was said to have been interested in the office after his presidency) went too far (Schwebel 1952: 18). Dicke describes the eventual compromise and political practice in short words: 'They followed Drummond and got Thomas' (1998: 71).

The office as an innovation in international law

The combination of administrative and political powers in the office of the Secretary-General is reflected in the deliberately vague formulations of the relevant provisions of the Charter, which nonetheless represent a significant innovation in international law.[5] The restraint in the wording of the provisions reflects the insight of the founding fathers and mothers that the office of the Secretary-General as a political office had to be established and developed in the context of political practice.[6] Seen in this way, the provisions of Chapter XV of the UN Charter, i.e. Articles 97 to 101,[7] initiated an experiment whose success depended on the performance of the individual incumbents. The title of Chapter XV is 'Secretariat', and hence goes beyond the person of the Secretary-General, as is made clear in Art. 97:

> The Secretariat shall comprise a Secretary-General and such staff as the Organization may require. The Secretary-General shall be appointed by the General Assembly upon the recommendation of the Security Council. He shall be the chief administrative officer of the Organization.

The provisions of Chapter XV identify the Secretariat as one of the principal organs of the United Nations. *De jure*, the Secretary-General is not a principal organ of the United Nations; *de facto*, though, his position as the chief administrative officer and personification of the UN (Sutterlin 1993) lends his actions considerable legitimacy. Accordingly, Ramcharan (1982: 135) distinguishes between the procedural and the substantial significance of Art. 97 for the office of the Secretary-General: procedurally, the Secretary-General is obliged to support the other principal organs of the UN in implementing resolutions and decisions; substantially, however, he, like all other principal organs, is obliged by Art. 97 to promote through his actions the realization of the goals and principles of the organization as a whole. Such a general mission makes possible a certain scope of action for the Secretary-General. In this perspective the roles of the Secretariat and the Secretary-General coincide: 'The Secretariat exists only in the office of the Secretary-General, for, although the Charter speaks of the Secretariat as a principal organ of the United Nations, it proceeds to lay obligations upon the Secretary-General personally as a specific official' (Davies 1953: 135). It has rightly been pointed out that the position of the Secretary-General is qualified by the fact that Art. 97 provides for his '*appointment*', not 'election', by the General Assembly. The latter might have given the office even greater legitimacy (Dicke 1998: 73). But still, just as the Secretary-General benefits from the position of the Secretariat as a principal organ of the UN, the Secretariat as a whole benefits from the political authority of the Secretary-General, that results in work going beyond the traditional administrative tasks of an international organization (James 1985; Fiedler 1994: 1021). Before we turn to these political competences, it has to be said that the Secretary-General fulfils a series of representative and administrative functions.[8] However, all these functions often merge with one another and are difficult to keep apart.[9]

Political competences

This section shall deal with the political competences of the Secretary-General in the narrower sense. They derive from Art. 99 of the UN Charter:[10]

> The Secretary-General may bring to the attention of the Security Council any matter which in his opinion may threaten the maintenance of international peace and security.

This article directly associates the Secretary-General with the UN organ that, according to the Charter, bears primary responsibility for maintaining peace and international security, the Security Council. In this context, three formulations deserve special attention: first, the Secretary-General may introduce any '*matter*' (not only a specific kind of event); second, the criterion for assessing whether there is a threat to international peace and security is left to the discretion of the Secretary-General ('*in his opinion*') – two formulations deliberately chosen to allow the Secretary-General some leeway in making political decisions.[11] This intention is underscored by the third provision that the Secretary-General '*may*' bring such matters to the attention of the Security Council. The Secretary-General is by no means obliged to bring all potential cases to the attention of the Security Council. Not invoking Art. 99 may also be an eminently political action (Bourloyannis 1990: 659). The wording of Art. 99 is very unspecific; at first glance it offers only a flimsy basis for concrete political action. However, as a principle, the more general the wording of the Charter, the more potential and scope it offers to the Secretary-General. In this vein Boutros-Ghali calls the openness in the provisions of the Charter 'not a liability but an asset' (1996a: 86). Regarded superficially, the effects of Art. 99 in practice seem to be negligible: officially Art. 99 has been applied in very few cases.[12] Hammarskjöld himself explicitly referred to Art. 99 only once, early in the Congo Crisis. The potential of this article, however, lies not in the direct appeal to its legal wording, but in its implications (Nayar 1974: 59; Wege 1976: 360; Fiedler 1994: 1048; Franck 1984: 491). The UN Secretary-General's political effectiveness does not stem from admonition and standing on legal principles, but in lending his personal authority to political actions and in the more or less tacit respect accorded to him by the other principal organs of the United Nations. Two examples may serve to illustrate the derivation of political competences from Art. 99: the competence to carry out fact-finding missions and the competence to employ the good offices of the Secretary-General. Neither is mentioned in, but both arise out of Art. 99.

'Implied powers': 'fact-finding missions' and 'good offices'

Fact-finding missions (Partsch 1981: 61–2; Bourloyannis 1990; Boudreau 1991: 17–19) are efforts to impartially investigate and establish the situation and actual developments of a conflict. As such, they are part of the classic repertoire of international mediation and may be conducted by a number of 'impartial' authorities. A statement by Secretary-General Trygve Lie in September 1946 is generally regarded as the origin of the Secretary-General's independent right to appoint fact-finding missions. In connection with the Greek question, the American delegation had demanded the appointment of a fact-finding mission. Even before this proposal was voted on Lie delivered a terse speech setting out his competence:

> Just a few words to clear my position as Secretary-General and the rights of this Office under the Charter. Should the proposal of the United States not be carried out, I hope that the Council will understand that the Secretary-General may reserve his right to make such inquiries or investigations as he may think necessary, in order to determine whether or not he should consider bringing an aspect of this matter to the attention of the Council under the provisions of the Charter.
>
> ('Statement in the Security Council 20 September 1946', in CFI: 46–7)

The argument is brilliantly simple: to do his job as required by Art. 99 the Secretary-General must of necessity be able to inform himself carefully so that he can take all aspects of a problem into account in making his decision on whether to bring the matter to the Security Council. It follows from the 'subjective discretion' (Fiedler 1994: 1047) of the Secretary-General that '... Article 99, by necessary implication, gives him [the Secretary-General] an investigating and exploratory power' (Nayar 1974: 50). In other words, Art. 99 has preconditions, which Lie spelled out. Significantly, no objections were raised; indeed, the Soviet representative supported Lie's words (Elaraby 1987: 190; Schwebel 1951: 379–80). As subsequent Secretaries-General appointed fact-finding missions, it was finally accepted as their right to do so (even if viewed critically by member states). Although there is no explicit mention in the Charter the Secretary-General may therefore invoke the 'implicit investigative powers under Article 99' (Bourloyannis 1990: 650). Significantly, no distinction is drawn between 'technical' fact-finding and the Secretary-General's active, independent efforts to mediate and arbitrate in conflicts (Partsch 1981: 61).

Another political competence is the exercise of 'good offices' by the Secretary-General, an ideal combination of a legal basis open to interpretation and the Secretary-General's potential for action. Franck goes as far as to state that the label 'the UN's good officer' (1995: 360) expresses the Secretary-General's main mission. Indeed, Pérez de Cuéllar referred to himself in this way several times (Jensen 1985: 347). This concept, too, belonged to the repertoire of international mediation before the formation of the UN. Pechota defines the function of good offices as 'a specific third-party procedure designed to keep the diplomatic process alive and fill gaps in available procedure so that conflict does not break loose from the orbit of pacific settlement and can be channelled through the path of negotiation' (1976: 192). Good offices thus form a concept closely related to that of preventive or behind-the-scenes diplomacy (ibid.: 199). Good offices must be distinguished from mediation in the narrower sense; as a rule, the use of good offices does not involve any concrete proposals (Simmonds 1959: 335). Although it is easier than in the case of fact-finding missions to distinguish between technical (organizational, logistic support for conferences, etc.) and political good offices (direct appeals, offers of implementation, etc.) (Bindschedler 1981: 67), in practice the boundary between the two is blurred (Pechota 1972: 13). Schachter underlines this lack of precise definitions and asserts that the practical implementation is 'more of an art than a science' (1972: i). Franck and Nolte believe that the exercise of good offices 'has always been the most crucial indicator of the Secretary-General's evolving constitutional role within the UN system' (1995: 144).

The examples of fact-finding missions and good offices illustrate that the Secretary-General's crucial 'prerogative powers' (Franck 1987) result from these 'implied powers' (Fiedler 1994: 1053) or 'inherent powers' (Lavalle 1990). And that is important for the interaction with the other UN organs. Thus, the Secretary-General is almost a '16th member of the SC, without voting or veto rights' (ibid.: 1046). This can be taken almost literally as in the meantime it is acceptable for the Secretary-General, in extension of the provisions of Art. 99, to convene the Security Council even in the absence of a clear threat to peace (Franck 1984: 481). The question first raised by Kelsen of whether the creation of powers such as that of independent fact-finding was intended by the authors of the Charter (1964: 304) has lost its relevance. There are good reasons to believe that this development is fully in line with the intention of the founders of the United Nations. Even during the consultations in the Preparatory Commission, the 'dynamic interpretation' (Fiedler 1994: 1052) and the 'implied powers' of what came to be Art. 99 were raised in the discussion of the 'quite special right' of the Secretary-General. Of course there are instances in which the concept is stretched too far and the legal basis gets very thin. Lavalle offers a compromise formula by observing that the development of the office has taken place 'on the margin of the Charter' (1990: 35), but ultimately does not violate it. In addition to the legal basis, the intentions of the authors of the Charter and the reference to precedent, the successful application of the Secretary-General's implied powers is obviously dependent on a political mechanism.

The political mechanism: a spiral of trust

The reference to precedent presumes that at least some of the respective activities of the Secretary-General must have been successful. The first official acts of hitherto relatively unknown Secretaries-General can become the 'litmus test' for their entire period in office. An early personal success will secure the incumbent's position. And with that, the second option in the Charter on the political functions of the Secretary-General gains traction: Art. 98, according to which the Secretary-General performs all functions entrusted to him by the principal organs of the UN:

> The Secretary-General shall act in that capacity in all meetings of the General Assembly, of the Security Council, of the Economic and Social Council, and of the Trusteeship Council, and shall perform such other functions as are entrusted to him by these organs. The Secretary-General shall make an annual report to the General Assembly on the work of the Organization.

Once again, one is struck by the vagueness of '*such other functions as are entrusted to him by these organs*'. A glance at UN practice shows that these are not limited to administrative and supporting functions, but can, on the contrary, include highly political tasks and authority with broad latitude for the Secretary-General.[13] In this connection, Fiedler speaks of a 'true political dimension of considerable weight' (1994: 1023), that by way of Art. 98 permeates the work of the Secretary-General. The provision obliging the Secretary-General to present an annual report to the General Assembly should also be read in this way. This report – particularly the introduction – has developed from a simple accounting duty into a special instrument of the Secretary-General's political leadership (see the next section of Hammarskjöld's reports).

Art. 98 and the process of the transfer of powers highlight the relevance of the interplay of the UN organs. The example of the 'policy of *extended responsibilities*' (Barudio 1989: 124) sketched above can be understood only against the background of a twofold functional shift within the organization of the UN system as resulting from the paralysis of Cold War antagonism (Delbrück

1964; Bailey 1962a: 24). As the Security Council blocked itself, which prevented it from properly fulfilling its task of maintaining peace, the General Assembly assumed a reserve mandate for peacekeeping, paradigmatically expressed in the 1950 'Uniting for Peace' resolution. Under this, the General Assembly can recommend action to solve threats to peace when the Security Council is not in a position to do so. The General Assembly, however, is a collective actor and thus able to execute and implement its decisions only up to a point. Hence, in a second shift of functions, the General Assembly transferred mandates to the Secretary-General, the remaining unit in the UN system capable of acting (Elaraby 1987: 179; Stein 1962: 22–5). Whenever the Security Council reached an impasse and could not agree on a course of action and the General Assembly did not want to become active, the Secretary-General was brought into play through Art. 98: 'Such impasses are the Secretary-General's open door' (Franck 1987: 5.11). For this reason, Bailey sees Art. 98 as even more crucial to the Secretary-General's political role than Art. 99 (1962a: 37). In this way, diplomatic innovations replaced standard procedures of the world organization that had proved to be ineffective (see also Franck 1987: 5.16).

The Secretary-General's actual role is thus a consequence of interpreting and implementing the vague provisions of the Charter in the light of the respective political constellations. In such a situation it is inevitable that the Secretary-General exposes himself to political controversies (Bourloyannis 1990: 645, fn 14), for he is expected to act when others cannot or will not. This shifts the focus to the support and trust that the other UN organs and, ultimately, the individual states place in the Secretary-General; the wording of Art. 98 and its use of the verb 'entrust' is symptomatic in this context.

Thus, the possibility and extent of discharging political functions depends on an operating mechanism that one could term a *spiral of trust* (Fröhlich 1997b). A Secretary-General whose initial actions earn the confidence of the member states will find further opportunities to shape a progressively independent role, which he can use to deepen members' trust, thereby building 'trust upon trust' (Gordenker 1967a: 21).[14] In principle, he has the opportunity to make use of an 'open-ended authority' (Nelan 1995: 70). On the other hand, a Secretary-General whose first efforts on the stage of international organizations and diplomacy are problematic or in vain may never have the opportunity to demonstrate his qualities of political leadership and build further confidence. Standing is lost at least as quickly as it is won (Gordenker 1967a: 129). In such a case, the Secretary-General's most important 'unofficial' function will increasingly become the focus of attention: that of the scapegoat for the failure of the individual states or the international community as a whole, something U Thant even called 'an important part of the Secretary-General's role' (1971: 598).

Accordingly, each Secretary-General must earn his own scope of action. This occurs particularly by proving his competence as a negotiator and by establishing international confidence in his person. The starting point for this is an understanding of the Charter that treats its legal provisions as the basis of an evolutionary process; as a type of constitution that can be adjusted to take account of changed political realities. Against this backdrop, Szasz maintains that it is futile to ask how the Secretary-General's respective political functions and their legitimacy can be defined:

> The fact is that the Secretary-General can in the political field do what he can get away with, i.e. in a given situation what the competent representative organs will encourage or at least tolerate, and preferably what is acceptable to any specially concerned states or other entities.
>
> (1991: 191)

At the same time, the qualifications mentioned by Szasz point to further determinants of the office, which will be summarized in an overview in the following section.

Determinants of the office

Skjelsbaek (1991: 104–9) distinguishes between five pillars on which the position of the Secretary-General rests:

1   moral standing/impartiality;
2   support of member states;
3   organizational position with the UN system;
4   personal abilities of the Secretary-General and his staff; and
5   his position within the diplomatic network.

Authors attach varying importance to these points. Oscar Schachter, a legal advisor to different Secretaries-General over many years, summarizes his experiences by saying 'that the strength of the Office depended much on the initiative and activism of the person in it' (quoted in Bettauer 1972: 88). Baehr and Gordenker, on the other hand, remind readers that the Secretary-General's actions are conditional on the confidence of and consultation with the member states, in particular the permanent members of the Security Council. An on-going dispute with even just one Council member can undermine his scope for action (1994: 31). Kanninen, by contrast, points to a further determinant: '[O]nly a major global crisis may provide the Secretary-General with an opportunity to move the UN to the forefront in economic and related fields, to act as '"a center for harmonizing the actions of nations" as envisaged in the UN Charter' (1995: 251). Starting with the overall international situation, he develops a situational profile of the leadership qualities required of a Secretary-General,[15] according to which he must fulfil at least the following conditions:

> – the Secretary-General has innovative ideas in terms of substance, form and organization (requiring for instance, an immediate creation of an informal group of top-notch advisors);

– the Secretary-General asserts himself or herself firmly in a new position of influence by launching coordinating initiatives with major players on the world scene (requiring, for instance, that the Secretary-General's informal advisors are also major figures in the world, able to make packages with all the major outside parties involved);
– the Secretary-General moves ahead under his or her own terms and not within the framework defined by parochial interests (e.g. as represented by the major powers or agency heads);
– the Secretary-General has maintained the perception of being an individual of the highest integrity, enjoying the trust and confidence of major and minor players in the world scene.

(Kanninen 1995: 235)

Although this ideal profile of the leadership qualities required of a Secretary-General was drawn up against the backdrop of Pérez de Cuéllar's efforts to resolve the UN's financial crisis, it is a sophisticated description of the fundamental determinants of the office – particularly as it links the role of personality with the overall international situation, the support of the member states and each individual conflict constellation. However, the Secretary-General can influence the last three conditions only indirectly because, as James points out, he cannot independently create situations that are 'suitable for his intervention' (1985: 41). Hence, the question of the Secretary-General's autonomy requires an extremely differentiated answer.[16] Nevertheless, Kanninen's list highlights the importance of the incumbent's personality in interaction with other conditions. For their part, the authors of the Charter were also aware of the special significance of the Secretary-General's personality. The report of the Preparatory Commission reads:

[T]he Secretary-General, more than anyone else, will stand for the United Nations as a whole. In the eyes of the world, no less than in the eyes of his own staff, he must embody the principles and ideals of the Charter. ... [He] has been given a quite special right which goes beyond any power previously accorded to the head of an international organization ... It is impossible to foresee how this article will be applied; but the responsibilities it confers upon the Secretary-General will require the exercise of the highest qualities of political judgment, tact and integrity.

(1945: 87, Chapter VIII, Sect. 2, Para. 16)

The fact that the Preparatory Commission draws up such a profile of the qualities required of the Secretary-General again demonstrates the experimental nature of the office. These requirements were set down – though scarcely more precisely defined – in the provisions of Art. 100 of the UN Charter:

1. In the performance of their duties the Secretary-General and the staff shall not seek or receive instructions from any government or from any other authority external to the Organization. They shall refrain from any action

which might reflect on their position as international officials responsible only to the Organization.

2. Each Member of the United Nations undertakes to respect the exclusively international character of the responsibilities of the Secretary-General and the staff and not to seek to influence them in the discharge of their responsibilities.

Art. 100 clearly states that the representative of the world organization must be in a position '... to detach himself even from his regional culture and perceptions to the extent that he is able to tackle the problems with which he is confronted as SG, without preference for his own culture and inherent philosophy' (Fiedler 1994: 1032). Once more the vagueness of the provisions for such international loyalty points to political practice. The incumbent's personality, his interpretation of the Charter's provisions, his political actions in cooperation with the other principal organs of the United Nations and his reactions to the overall international situation determine the reality of the 'quite special right' of the UN Secretary-General. Against this background, all UN Secretaries-General have developed and put into practice their personal conception of the office (see 'The Hammarskjöld tradition and its adoption by his successors' in Chapter 5). The following section offers a first look at Dag Hammarskjöld's views, as expressed in his annual reports.

Dag Hammarskjöld's conception of the UN, the Charter and his office

The Secretary-General's annual reports are an important medium for conveying the personal view of his office. No Secretary-General used the annual report simply as a bookkeeping exercise or a chronology of events; each has put his stamp on it and used it, some more passionately than others, to express his 'philosophy' of the world organization. Indeed, the annual reports have evolved into a sort of 'State of the World'[17] address. When a reporter labelled Hammarskjöld's report a 'State of the UN Message', Hammarskjöld let him know he thought the term appropriate (Lash 1962: 547).

The following analysis of Dag Hammarskjöld's reports between 1953 and 1961 serves as an introduction to his understanding of the Charter, his office and the UN as a whole.[18] Hammarskjöld's reports set a standard: '[T]he careful preparation of the annual reports and the tradition associated with them since Dag Hammarskjöld have given their words solemnity and moral weight generally considered to be of great consequence, and with the resultant widespread publicity' (Rovine 1970: 447). He deliberately gave them a political connotation as 'a body of doctrine built around his work and initiatives in the office of the Secretary-General' (Gordenker 1967a: 127; see also Dworkis 1955: 175–6; Jones 1994: 1048).

Function and significance of the Secretary-General's annual report

The duty to present an annual report to the General Assembly is laid down in Art. 98 of the Charter. The Covenant of the League of Nations contained a similar provision. Over the years, its tone has changed from one of restraint and consistent subordination to the will of the member states to that of Secretaries-General acting like 'stern schoolmasters lecturing a disappointing class' (Franck 1985: 133), even if the criticism was often delivered 'in the necessary walking-on-eggshells way' (James 1993: 29). Again, it was the practical implementation that turned an administrative provision of the Charter into a political instrument of the Secretary-General. This shift in importance is reflected in the very format of the text. Originally, the annual report consisted of two sections, one largely technical in which the Secretary-General fulfilled his duty to report, and a more personal introduction. In the course of time, the technical part of the report increasingly faded into the background as attention focused on the political statements in the introduction. In 1956 Hammarskjöld published the introduction on its own for the first time. Since 1978 the annual report has also formally consisted of one part, namely the former introduction (though it contains reporting elements) (Fiedler 1994: 1043). In the following, 'annual report' refers to this introductory section.

The political interpretation of the duty to report goes back to Trygve Lie. Pérez de Cuéllar sums up: 'This is not meant to be, and should never become, a mere rapporteur's job … Its submission is one of the ways in which the Secretary-General can act as initiator and can galvanize the efforts of the other parts of the UN' (1995: 129). At the same time, it reinforces the moral quality of the Secretary-General's role when he, 'embodying the higher aspirations of the Organization and the world community', speaks as 'the conscience of the earth' (Tinker 1992: 311). The annual report becomes a 'moyen d'affirmer l'autorité politique et morale du Secrétaire-Général' (Smouts 1991: 1325). Thus, Dolf Sternberger's dictum that words are deeds holds true for the Secretary-General's annual reports (1979: 54; see also Austin 1962). The unique position of the Secretary-General as personification of the organization as a whole thus finds its echo in the particular form and function of the annual reports (Dicke 1994: 127).

In this way, the annual reports provide the Secretary-General a platform for numerous activities, e.g.:

1   to articulate his ideas;
2   to criticize the behaviour of member states and remind them of their duties under the Charter;
3   to provide structural guidance for the annual debate in the General Assembly;
4   to appeal for solidarity while constituting a global public awareness;
5   to highlight global political trends and their consequences for the future of the UN and weigh up different alternatives for the development of the organization;

6   to update the missions defined in the Charter by presenting examples of specific challenges; and

7   to present concrete proposals and initiatives or espouse points on the agenda of the General Assembly.[19]

Given these points, a few remarks about the writing of these reports seem to be in order.

EXCURSION: THE WRITING OF HAMMARSKJÖLD'S ANNUAL REPORTS

The numerous drafts and rewritings of speech manuscripts in Hammarskjöld's private archive testify that, to an unusual degree, his public statements flowed from his pen; there are hardly any written comments by others. As a rule, additional remarks are limited to surprisingly few stylistic suggestions from Wilder Foote, the press spokesman, whom Hammarskjöld regularly consulted, particularly at the beginning of his term of office (Urquhart 1972: 66). Occasionally he submitted speeches intended for an American public to Andrew Cordier, his executive assistant, with the request for special remarks about the audience. With time there were fewer requests for such assistance (ibid.: 31). Although Hammarskjöld also let heads of departments prepare speeches and minor statements before special organs (Humphrey 1984: 210–12), he reserved the right to final editing, which could involve substantial revision. For the annual reports there was an 'administrative procedure': first, the Executive Office asked the respective departments to deliver background material on their field of work. This material had to be submitted four weeks before publication of the report and was intended exclusively for the more technical 'Report', not for Hammarskjöld's 'Introduction'. These commentaries were coordinated in the Executive Office under Cordier or Narasimhan. Foote was responsible for specifying the respective requirements for the departments. Hammarskjöld sent advance copies to a number of staff with a request for comments; as a rule, these were very few and dealt with details of the staff members' own fields of work. The report was always discussed at a meeting of the Under/Assistant Secretaries-General and department heads – which seldom resulted in major changes.[20] Using the example of the 1954 Report, Humphrey writes that he only received the draft late in the evening of the day before the discussion. He had the impression that the Secretary-General did not wish for a serious discussion of such texts (1984: 191).

Hammarskjöld wrote his major speeches, in particular the annual reports, himself and worked on them in up to four different and intensively edited drafts. The most specific record we have is Urquhart's estimate that Hammarskjöld dictated the 1961 Annual Report on a Sunday afternoon 'without break or stop' (1972: 31; Interview 1997) – a performance possible thanks to preliminary drafts. Schachter claims that he wrote drafts for the annual reports (including the last) (Interview 1985: 24) while Per Lind reports that Hammarskjöld set such high standards for his speeches that he did not want to leave this task to anybody else (Interview 1998). Occasionally he discussed the texts in greater depth with friends and acquaintances than he did with the 'responsible' staff members (Beskow 1969: 92; Urquhart 1972: 14). One cannot overrate the importance that Hammarskjöld attached to the annual reports, given that he declared his last report to be his political testament (Beskow 1969: 92; Urquhart 1972: 14). In this section Hammarskjöld's reports will be analyzed with the aim to gain a more detailed picture of his view on the organization, the UN Charter and his office.[21]

Analysis of Hammarskjöld's reports

1953: The potential of the United Nations.

The Introduction to Hammarskjöld's first annual report in 1953 (Introduction to the Eighth Annual Report, 15 July 1953, in CF II: 67–77; hereinafter AR 1953) contains a notable statement: 'In the chapters that follow, the governments of Member States will find a comprehensive review of their efforts ... to make progress through the United Nations, towards constructive solutions of problems of common concern to them all' (AR 1953: 67). This unmistakable emphasis on the will of member states as the ultimate driving force behind the activities of the United Nations reflects a demonstrative low-key view of his office. In the section on the 'Role of the UN' Hammarskjöld emphasizes the nature of the work of the United Nations as a process and notes two fundamental social trends: 'One of the trends is directed towards wider social justice and equality for individuals. The other is directed towards equality and justice between nations, politically but also in the economic and social sense' (ibid.: 68). These trends form the background for the work of the United Nations:

> The United Nations is a positive response by the world community to the fundamental needs of our time. ... Its efforts are significant in so far as they show the growing maturity of the Organization as an instrument by means of which the nations can solve conflicts threatening the natural evolution of the world community.
>
> (ibid.)

Several elements in this first definition of the UN deserve closer examination. Hammarskjöld stresses first the instrumental nature of the United Nations in conjunction with the reference to the will of the member states. At the same time, he sees the United Nations maturing parallel to the evolution of the world community. Thus, while Hammarskjöld takes a cautious view of the stage of development of the UN, he is at the same time extremely optimistic about the evolution of the world community, which he terms natural. In this framework, the work of the United Nations needs to be based on fundamental principles, of which he emphasizes two: '... a respect for international law and an acceptance of the obligations which that law imposes' as well as '... a truly international civil service free from all national pressures and influences ...' (ibid.: 68–9). In both respects Hammarskjöld notes serious shortcomings on the part of member states (lack of acceptance of the decisions of the International Court of Justice, etc.). All the same, the United Nations represent the most ambitious attempt to regulate international politics in a constructive manner. Hammarskjöld mentions three intrinsic elements of world organization whose acceptance by member states distinguished the UN from its predecessors:

> It is recognized that an international instrument for peace and justice must seek to work out a system of mediation, conciliation and collective security. There is the further general recognition of the vital importance, for sound development of the world community, of orderly progress of the nations towards a state of full economic development, self-government and independence. And finally, international cooperation is recognized as an essential instrument for a guided development towards greater social justice within the nations.
>
> (ibid.: 70)

Hammarskjöld saw these generally recognized principles as a type of 'magic triangle' of the goals of the UN. Collective security, economic development and international cooperation interact with and complement one another. This also means that none of these goals can be pursued in isolation. He emphasizes in particular the third component, international cooperation. By promoting a common international interest that goes beyond individual national claims, the United Nations can provide a basis for peace that is as fundamental as economic development and the concept of collective security. Hammarskjöld sums up the 'magic triangle' of UN objectives under the leitmotif of 'reconciliation':

> The United Nations as an instrument for preventing aggression will gain strength in proportion to its achievements as an instrument for reconciliation. Its authority in these respects will depend also on the solution of the underlying economic and social pressures leading to international conflicts.
>
> (AR 1953: 71)

This description of the UN's tasks illustrates a complex understanding of peace as something that will not materialize immediately and cannot be striven for directly – a peace that is the result of regular efforts to balance simultaneously collective security, economic development and international cooperation. The clear reference to international law puts Hammarskjöld's peace concept in the vicinity of the formula 'peace through justice' and 'rule of law'. Hammarskjöld believes that the potential of the world organization in all of these fields is 'only partly explored' (ibid.). All the same, he acknowledges that progress in these fields is very slow and many setbacks can be expected. Yet he does not believe that efforts for peace are futile:

> The present divisions of our world often appear unbridgeable and the obstacles to ultimate agreement insurmountable. But the landscape of international

affairs is not immutable. It is constantly shifting and moving, subject to all the influences at work in our world, in which new opportunities develop and the hope for ultimate solutions can never be abandoned.

(ibid.: 73)

He regards the work of the United Nations as one of these influences, e.g. as the only forum for public international debates. However, according to Hammarskjöld, the work of the UN must not be limited to meetings, committees and speeches: '… I believe that we have only begun to explore the full potentialities of the United Nations in these respects, especially the most fruitful combination of public discussion on the one hand and private negotiation on the other. But the opportunities are here, to be tested and used' (ibid.).

1954: Impartiality, not neutrality

The 1954 Annual Report (Introduction to the Ninth Annual Report, 12 July 1954, in CF II: 324–37; hereinafter AR 1954) returns to the instrumental nature of the United Nations, describing the organization as 'a tool created by the Governments of Members to serve them in their efforts to establish and maintain peace' and by no means 'an end in itself' (AR 1954: 327). After this qualifying statement, Hammarskjöld goes on to defend the UN as the pre-eminent instrument of peace in accordance with its Charter against the growing tendency to resolve security issues outside the framework of the UN, with the concomitant focus on regional organizations. Referring to the negotiations on Korea, Hammarskjöld characteristically defines the UN position:

> [T]he United Nations must oppose any policy in conflict with the principles of the Charter and must support a policy in accordance with those principles, not in a spirit of partiality, but as an expression of loyalty to the Charter. The attitude proper to the United Nations is thus not one of neutrality but one of active effort to further its most fundamental purposes.
>
> (ibid.: 328)

This definition of the role of the United Nations is significant in so far as it stresses the distinction between neutrality and impartiality. Hammarskjöld's remarks reveal that he views the content of the Charter as imposing a normative obligation that enables the world organization to take a stand – beyond pure procedural involvement. In so doing, the UN is not only a device for the community of states, but, via the normative expressions in its Charter, can take its own (detached) position even, and particularly, in disputes between different national interests. This accords it the role of a referee who in disputes may not be guided by the particular vested interests of a specific nation. Nevertheless, the organization is considerably hampered by the formation of blocs among its member states. Typical of Hammarskjöld's method of argumentation, the admission of shortcomings is followed by the optimistic response:

> But this is, in itself, an additional and compelling reason for doing everything possible to strengthen the United Nations. The increasing danger of destruction will sooner or later force us out of a system of balance of power into a system of true and universal international co-operation.
>
> (ibid.)

As in the previous year, Hammarskjöld points out that the potential of the UN had not been fully exploited. He rejects amending the Charter (ibid.: 334) on the occasion of the organization's tenth anniversary. It was far more important to exploit the organization's potential under the existing provisions and use it.

1955: New techniques of reconciliation

In the 1955 Annual Report (Introduction to the Tenth Annual Report, 8 July 1955, in CF II: 542–57; hereinafter AR 1955), Hammarskjöld emphasizes first the reduction in international tension, symbolized by the summit meeting between the great powers, the four-power agreement on Austria and the Bandung Conference (AR 1955: 544). He hopes that this new climate can enhance the diplomatic and political importance of the United Nations. Expanding on his thoughts in his first annual report he demands:

> The Organization should be more than an instrument of what may be described as conference diplomacy. ... Conference diplomacy may usefully be supplemented by more quiet diplomacy within the United Nations, whether directly between representatives of Member Governments or in contacts between the Secretary-General and Member Governments.
>
> (ibid.: 545)

In the context of a new significance for the United Nations Hammarskjöld brings himself into play via the concept of quiet diplomacy. He fleshes out his appeals of the preceding years: 'It is my hope that solid progress can be made in the coming years in developing new forms of contact, new methods of deliberation and new techniques of reconciliation' (ibid.: 546). As an example of the untapped potential of the Charter he mentions the introduction of regular meetings of the Security Council. The rather short passage on the position of the Secretary-General in the development of innovative efforts in negotiation and mediation is effectively underscored by the following report on Hammarskjöld's mission to free the American pilots in China (see Chapter 4). Hammarskjöld stresses further positive developments: 'The beginnings of a "common law" of the United Nations, based on the Charter, are now apparent; its steady growth will contribute to stability and orderliness' (ibid.: 548). As sources of this common law he identifies the advisory opinions of the International Court of Justice that are relevant for the UN and the work of the International Law Commission.

1956: New members and new tasks

The 1956 Annual Report (Introduction to the Eleventh Annual Report, 4 October 1956, in CF III: 267–88; hereinafter AR 1956) opens with an acknowledgment that with its growing membership, the United Nations is within reach of its goal of universality (a topic also of the previous reports). Hammarskjöld sums up:

> Because its Charter is a world Charter, the United Nations is a unifying force in a divided world. Because its institutions are world institutions, they are fitted to determine the common interest and enlarge the area of common grounds. This applies in full measure, I believe, to three great challenges of our times. These are: first, the relationship of the peoples of Asia and Africa with the peoples of the western traditions; second economic development for the majority of mankind which has so far shared so little in the fruits of the industrial age; third, the unresolved conflict between the ideologies that divide the world.'
>
> (AR 1956: 268)

This outline highlights the growing importance of the newly independent states of Asia and Africa in Hammarskjöld's annual reports. He shows himself primarily interested not in the economic aspects ('developing countries' vs. 'industrialized countries'), but in a more far-reaching perspective. For Hammarskjöld fulfilling the right of self-determination means 'that democratic ideals, which have carried many peoples to new heights, are given a world-wide application' (ibid.: 269). In his view, this corresponds with the philosophy of the Charter, though with a very specific emphasis:

> It is important to remember that the Charter endorses self-determination as a basis for friendly relations among nations. Both unrealistic impatience in the movement toward self-determination and wasteful resistance to it would contradict this philosophy of the Charter by leading to conflicts which might threaten peace.
>
> (ibid.: 270)

This statement exemplifies what Hammarskjöld understands by impartiality, not neutrality, of the United Nations. His statement is a reminder to the former colonial powers as well as the newly independent states. He again calls for the UN to intensify its activities as an 'instrument for negotiations of settlements, as distinct from the mere debate of issues' (ibid.). In a section on changes in the internal administration, Hammarskjöld explains his reform of the executive level of the Secretariat. He argues that the growing transfer of political functions demonstrates the 'desirability of a system sufficiently flexible to enable the Secretary-General to devote a major part of his time to specific political problems' (ibid.: 285). This he underlines with a reference to his mandate:

[The] executive head [of the Secretariat] under the Charter is the only elected officer and, for that reason, can delegate his responsibilities only to a limited extent ... So far I do not consider that the responsibilities of the Secretary-General have been such as to overburden him personally or to restrict his possibilities of fulfilling his various functions.

(ibid.: 285–6)

Again Hammarskjöld emphasizes the role of an independent international civil service that can serve as a unifying force precisely because it is not tied to national or ideological instructions. Typically, Hammarskjöld presents the enhanced political responsibilities of the Secretary-General and his staff in the context of a 'general trend in foreign service from what might be called political diplomacy to diplomatic administration of a policy-making type' (ibid.: 288).

1957: Acting under the conditions of the East–West conflict

After opening the 1957 Annual Report (Introduction to the Twelfth Annual Report, 22 August 1957, in CF III: 629–47; hereinafter AR 1957) with a fairly extensive report on the Suez and Hungarian Crises, Hammarskjöld once again turns to the role of the UN:

The Charter, read as a whole, does not endow the United Nations with any of the attributes of a super-state or of a body active outside the framework of decisions of Member Governments. The United Nations is, rather, an instrument for negotiation among, and to some extent for, Governments.

(AR 1957: 634–5)

Hammarskjöld obviously finds it necessary at this point to underline the instrumental nature of the United Nations once again, something he had done all too clearly in his first annual report. In 1957, however, he does so against the background of the Secretariat's unprecedented activities in organizing UNEF. Besides the UN's greater role as a result of the first peacekeeping force, there was also the Hungarian Crisis, in which the UN could do virtually nothing. Hammarskjöld emphasizes that this was not a fault of the UN as such or of the provisions of the Charter. The limits on the actions of the world organization 'result from facts of international life in our age which are not likely to be bypassed by a different approach or surmounted by attempts at merely constitutional reform' (ibid.: 635). Hammarskjöld again identifies the East–West conflict as a crucial impediment to the activity of the United Nations. Nevertheless, the organization can still do a great deal as 'an admittedly imperfect but indispensable instrument of nations in working for a peaceful evolution toward a more just and secure world order' (ibid.: 635). This is only possible 'by processes of organic growth in the system of custom and law prevailing in the society of nations' (ibid.: 635). Against the background of success in Suez and failure in Hungary, Hammarskjöld stresses that the world organization has to progress step by step, and must also reckon with setbacks. Hammarskjöld interprets the limitations imposed by East–West confrontation not as an argument against, but as an argument in favour of strengthening the role of the United Nations. Thanks to its claim to universality, it is better suited than regional alliances as an instrument of reconciliation: 'All the varied interests and aspirations of the world meet in its precincts upon the common ground of the Charter' (ibid.: 636). Hammarskjöld ends with the observation that in the previous two years the possibilities of multilateral diplomacy within the framework of the United Nations have been considerably strengthened and hopes that greater use will be made of this potential (ibid.: 637–8).

1958: Reducing the area of conflict

The 1958 Annual Report (Introduction to the Thirteenth Annual Report, 25 August 1958, in CF IV: 178–91; hereinafter AR 1958) opens with the familiar definition of the United Nations: 'As an instrument for reconciliation and for world-wide co-operation, the United Nations represents a necessary addition to the traditional methods of diplomacy as exercised on a bilateral or regional basis' (AR 1958: 178). Hammarskjöld speaks of setbacks in the year under review, mentioning as an example the adjournment of the disarmament talks. At the same time, he emphasizes the success of the Geneva meeting of disarmament experts and in the section on security policy presents the purely technical agreement on desirable standards as an important progress: '… by isolating certain non-political, scientific elements from the politically controversial elements in the total problem of disarmament, the area of conflict has been somewhat reduced' (ibid.: 179). His report on the Geneva conference on the peaceful use of atomic energy is in the same vein.

1959: The vacuum theory

The 1959 Annual Report (Introduction to the Fourteenth Annual Report, 20 August 1959, in CF IV: 445–69; hereinafter AR 1959) is more positive in tone and can point to a number of summit meetings between various statesmen. Yet here, too, Hammarskjöld warns against undermining the United Nations as the central forum with primary responsibility in certain fields of politics through contacts outside the organization. Members must avail themselves of the United Nations constantly so as not to lose touch with the relevant political challenges. Building on the concept of organic growth, Hammarskjöld expresses the concern that one day the organization will not be up to its challenges, if for a period it ceases to be the forum for political change in the world. If the growth of the United Nations is inhibited, it may not have the necessary strength and maturity that it needs to deal with the on-going development of challenges. Even if at the moment it appears that the United Nations is not needed to settle certain conflicts, excluding the organization will create a burden for the future: 'The work of today within and for the United Nations is a work through which the basis may be laid for increasingly satisfactory forms of international co-operation and for a future international system of law and order, for which the world is not yet ripe' (ibid.: 447).

Never before had Hammarskjöld expressed his pessimism about the willingness of the international community to establish a cooperative global order so clearly; but never before, either, had he so clearly turned this pessimistic assessment into an appeal for greater use of the organization. Starting from the necessity of international organization and cooperation 'which has emerged from bitter experiences and should now be considered as firmly established' (ibid.: 448), Hammarskjöld calls for evolutionary rather than revolutionary change in the work of the UN. At this point he clearly goes well beyond his original call for better use of the provisions of the Charter:

> The statement of objectives in the Charter is binding and so are the rules concerning the various organs and their competence, but it is not necessary to regard the working methods indicated in the Charter as limitative in purpose. Thus, they may be supplemented by others under the pressure of circumstances and in the light of experience if these additional procedures are not in conflict with what is prescribed. ... In this respect, the United Nations, as a living organism, has the necessary scope for continuous adaptation of its constitutional life to the needs.
>
> (ibid.: 448–9)

The experience gained since 1956 in using new techniques convinces Hammarskjöld that exploiting the full potential and methods indicated in the Charter is not enough; he declares legitimate other methods that are not explicitly named in the Charter, but do not conflict with its objectives. This is a significant moment in the conception of his office and his interpretation of the Charter. Hammarskjöld ascertains that the diversity of the functions transferred to him represent an evolution in procedural patterns 'for which no explicit basis is to be found in the Charter – although it may be said to fall within the scope of the intentions reflected in Article 99' (ibid.: 451). In other words, Hammarskjöld is thoroughly conscious of the new, activist role of his office – so conscious that he immediately qualifies these innovative developments:

> These decisions should not, of course, be considered as setting precedents changing the constitutional balance among the various organs of the United Nations. However, they have pointed to the possibility of developing new methods of approach of great political significance, which, after the thorough testing needed, may become part of a common law of organized international cooperation.
>
> (ibid.)

As much as Hammarskjöld welcomes these new developments, he is at pains not to show too much assertiveness concerning the office of the Secretary-General – particularly *vis-à-vis* the powers of the Security Council. He is, however, self-confident in his presentation of the concrete example of sending personal representatives to certain conflicts as part of his 'good offices': 'Such actions by the Secretary-General fall within the competence of his office and are, in my view, in other respects also in strict accordance with the Charter, when they serve its purpose' (ibid.: 452). Once again, Hammarskjöld bows to the precedence of the Security Council – but there is a remarkable shift in emphasis. Hammarskjöld no longer asks for the Security Council's permission each time for such activities, but points out instead that the Security Council may either accept such missions or resolve to tackle the issue at hand with an effort of its own, thereby inducing the Secretary-General to step aside. Here, too, Hammarskjöld denies the creation of precedents and instead stresses the concept of experience: '… what has been tried may provide experiences on which, later, stable and agreed practices may usefully be developed' (ibid.). Despite Hammarskjöld's carefully packed statements, his new self-confidence and the fundamental change in the office of the Secretary-General is all too obvious. Hammarskjöld's justification for the new developments is characterized by the same pragmatism he used to deduce effective negotiating methods from the general mission of the UN:

> The main significance of the evolution of the Office of the Secretary-General in the manner referred to above lies in the fact that it has provided means for smooth and fast action, which might otherwise not have been open to the Organization. This is of special value in situations in which prior public debate on a proposed course of action might increase the difficulties that such an action would encounter, or in which a vacuum might be feared because Members may prove hesitant, without fuller knowledge of the facts or for other reasons, to give explicit prior support in detail to an action, which, however, they approve in general terms or are willing should be tried without formal commitment.
>
> (ibid.)

What Hammarskjöld is presenting here in his typically roundabout way is a vacuum theory that by any measure goes well beyond the conventional understanding of the office. Based on the success of his various missions and the insight into the drawbacks of the routine procedures of the organization he calls for broad latitude and scope for the Secretary-General. No wonder that Hammarskjöld senses the need to qualify this development and stress that it is only 'an intensification and broadening' (ibid.) of the interaction between the different organs of the United Nations.

1960: Effective executive

In the 1960 Annual Report (Introduction to the Fifteenth Annual Report, 31 August 1960, in CF V: 122–41; hereinafter AR 1960), Hammarskjöld picks up the thread of the previous report by depicting the newly acquired importance of his office in a wider development of the transfer of responsibility from the gridlocked

Security Council to the General Assembly, which, as a collective organ, showed itself incapable of executive action. With the Congo Crisis, Hammarskjöld sees greater activity on the part of the Security Council. Yet despite this new shift (from the General Assembly back to the Security Council), there is no change in the procedure under which the Secretary-General acts for the Security Council 'as its main executive agent' (AR 1960: 128). This intensive employment of all resources of the world organization may well have been what Hammarskjöld imagined when he wrote his first annual report. Fully cognizant of the bloc confrontation, Hammarskjöld stresses that there were substantial areas in which ideological differences still play no role and in which, consequently, the United Nations could operate with notable success. 'Agreement may be achieved because of mutual interest among the big Powers to avoid having a regional or local conflict drawn into the sphere of bloc politics' (ibid.: 131). And this, Hammarskjöld feels, offers a perspective for UN action. As much as it had to become involved in these fields, it had to act with equally great restraint in view of the fundamental differences in bloc politics: '... [I]t is in such cases also practically impossible for the Secretary-General to operate effectively with the means put at his disposal, short of risking seriously to impair the usefulness of his office for the Organization in all the other cases for which the services of the United Nations are needed' (ibid.). In cases in which the conflicts develop on the margins of or even within the bloc confrontation, the goal must be 'to bring such conflicts out of this sphere through solutions aiming, in the first instance, at their strict localization' (ibid.). And here he comes back to his vacuum theory. Hammarskjöld uses the image of a vacuum attracting the things around it to describe the danger of local conflicts leading to bloc confrontation. Preventive diplomacy – a concept that will be analysed in greater detail below – is his response to this risk (see 'Summary' in Chapter 4). According to Hammarskjöld, the more intensive use of the United Nations, the innovation in methods and the successful practice of executive actions can be seen as a 'turning-point' (ibid.: 138) in the history of the UN. This is also clearly expressed in the 1960 definition of the world organization as an 'effective executive organ for joint action' (ibid.: 139). With this, the position of the organization has achieved a new quality in the international system:

> Thus, an increasing number of nations have come to look to the United Nations for leadership and support in ways somewhat different from those natural in the light of traditional international diplomacy. They look to the Organization as a spokesman and as an agent for principles which give them strength in an international concert in which other voices can mobilize all the weight of armed force, wealth, and historical role and that influence which is on the other side of a special responsibility for peace and security.
>
> (ibid.: 140)

Here Hammarskjöld presents himself (and the UN) as champion of the non-aligned countries and the small and medium-sized states that do not want to be drawn into bloc politics. As this group consists primarily of the newly independent countries of Africa and Asia, Hammarskjöld comes to the following dialectical identification of the role of the United Nations:

> The United Nations is an organic creation of the political situation facing our generation. At the same time, however, the international community has, so to say, come to political self-consciousness in the Organization and, therefore, can use it in a meaningful way in order to influence those very circumstances of which the Organization is a creation. … This concept of the role and of the future of the United Nations may go beyond the conventional thinking which sees in the Organization only, or mainly, a machinery for negotiation, but I am convinced of its realism …
>
> (ibid.: 140–1)

In this perspective the 1960 report is virtually a harbinger for Hammarskjöld's last report in 1961, in which all the issues of his previous reports come together in a general overview.

1961: Conflicting concepts of the world organization

Hammarskjöld starts the 1961 Annual Report (Introduction to the Sixteenth Annual Report, 17 August 1961, in CF V: 542–62; hereinafter AR 1961) with a description of two competing concepts about the character, authority and structure of the United Nations that have evolved particularly in the year under review:

> On the one side, it has in various ways become clear that certain Members conceive of the Organization as a static conference machinery for resolving conflicts of interests and ideologies with a view to peaceful co-existence, within the Charter, to be served by a Secretariat which is to be regarded not as fully internationalized but as representing within its ranks those very interests and ideologies.
>
> Other Members have made it clear that they conceive of the Organization primarily as a dynamic instrument of Governments through which they, jointly and for the same purpose, should seek such reconciliation but through which they should also try to develop forms of executive action, undertaken on behalf of all Members, and aiming at forestalling conflicts and resolving them, once they have arisen, by appropriate diplomatic or political means, in a spirit of objectivity and in implementation of the principles and purposes of the Charter.
>
> (AR 1961: 542)

Typical of Hammarskjöld, the next paragraph traces the conceptual roots of the two concepts. The conference concept is anchored in the venerable tradition of sovereign nation-states, in which the most one can strive for is peaceful coexistence between competing states. The second concept, by contrast, seeks 'possibilities of inter-governmental action overriding such a philosophy' (ibid.: 543). Beyond coexistence, this concept is concerned with cooperation. Ultimately, it is up to the member states to decide which concept the United Nations follows – however, Hammarskjöld clearly favours the second model. After these remarks, he turns to the Charter:

> The purposes and principles of the Charter are set out in its Preamble and further developed in a series of articles, including some which may seem to be primarily of a procedural or administrative nature. Together, these parts of the Charter lay down some basic rules of international ethics by which all Member States have committed themselves to be guided. To a large extent, the rules reflect standards accepted as binding for life within States. Thus, they appear, in the main, as a projection into the international arena and the international community of purposes and principles already accepted as being of national validity. In this sense, the Charter takes a first step in the direction of an organized international community, and this independently of the organs set up for international co-operation.
>
> (ibid.: 543–4)

Two points are notable in this paragraph: first, a clear avowal of the common purposes and principles to which all states in their own constitutions – different in form, but similar in content – have committed themselves, and consequently also accept in the Charter as binding for international interaction. Second, Hammarskjöld gives precedence to the principles of the Charter over the institutional structure of the United Nations. By again valuing content more highly than form, he reveals his exceedingly strong belief in the validity and enforceability of international norms, which he calls 'basic rules of international ethics' and which express themselves in various ways: the democratic principle is expressed in the equal weighting of votes in the General Assembly, whereas the principle of equal economic opportunity is incorporated in the UN Technical Aid Programme. The general principles of the Charter, therefore, provide legitimacy for an active organizational concept. At this point it becomes clear that Hammarskjöld's call for an active role for the world organization is not only a necessity resulting from the dangers and threats of a nuclear war, but is a consistent consequence of his specific concept of peace and 'reconciliation'. In this sense, development aid and technical aid are not just two separate tasks of the United Nations, but an essential part of its work for peace – justified by the claims of the Charter. In the same vein, the principles of the rule of law and of justice pervade the Charter:

> The principle of justice can be regarded as flowing naturally from the principles of equal political rights and equal economic opportunities, but it has an independent life and carries, of itself, the world community as far in the direction of an organized international system as the two first-mentioned principles. It has deep roots in the history of the efforts of man to eliminate from international life the anarchy which he had already much earlier overcome on the national level, deeper indeed than the political and economic

principles, which, as is well known, were much later to get full acceptance also in national life.

(ibid.: 546)

For Hammarskjöld, therefore, the conference concept of the United Nations falls short of the principles of the Charter. Moreover, the 'quasi-parliamentary-character' (ibid.: 549) of the General Assembly confers a political component on the United Nations that goes beyond the static conference model. The same applies to the authority of the Security Council. Hammarskjöld devotes particular attention to the right of veto and observes: '[W]ith the present arrangements, requiring a majority of seven and the concurring votes of the permanent members, a bridge between the traditional conference approach and a parliamentary approach is provided …' (ibid.: 550). Taking this as his basis, he defends the right of veto or the need for unanimity among the big powers, as otherwise the other member states could, through compliance or non-compliance with Security Council resolutions, be unintentionally drawn into the big-power conflicts.

Still, the organization is bound by the will of the member states; therefore, it is their function to make the Charter a 'living reality in practical political action' (ibid.: 552). Hammarskjöld concludes this section by renewing his appeal: 'The effort through the Organization to find a way by which the world community might, step by step, grow into organized international co-operation within the Charter, must either progress or recede' (ibid.). There is no third way. Hammarskjöld now turns to the Secretariat and brings together his aforementioned lines of thought. He first observes the Charter's silence on executive action, and then continues:

This does not mean that the Charter in any way closes the door to such arrangements or to executive action, but only that, at the stage of international thinking crystallized in the Charter, the conference approach still was predominant, and that the needs for executive action, if the new Organization was to live up to the expectations and to its obligations under the Charter, had not yet attracted the attention they were to receive in response to later developments.

(ibid.: 552–3)

Notwithstanding the diversity of the different forms of action adopted by the United Nations, Hammarskjöld sees certain common features in the appointment of sub-committees, observer groups and peacekeeping missions such as UNEF. All of them require centralized administrative structures to work effectively. As this can hardly be provided by the Security Council or the General Assembly, the Secretary-General has increasingly been entrusted with these tasks and more personal mandates. Hammarskjöld elucidates the position of the Secretary-General by considering the abovementioned provisions of Chapter XV of the Charter:

This has been done under Article 98 … and has represented a development in practice of the duties of the Secretary-General under Article 97. The character of the mandates has, in many cases, been such that in carrying out his functions the Secretary-General has found himself forced also to interpret the decisions in the light of the Charter, United Nations precedents and the aims and intentions expressed by the Members. When that has been the case, the Secretary-General has been under the obligation to seek guidance, to all possible extent, from the main organs; but when such guidance has not been forthcoming, developments have sometimes led to situations in which he has had to shoulder responsibility for certain limited political functions, which may be considered to be in line with the spirit of Article 99 but which legally have been based on decisions of the main organs themselves, under Article 98, and thus the exclusive responsibility of Member States acting through these organs. Naturally, in carrying out such functions the Secretariat has remained fully subject to the decisions of the political bodies.

(ibid.: 554)

He continues that this development has led the Secretary-General into the arena of political controversy – a development that Hammarskjöld calls unavoidable. According to Hammarskjöld, the arguments about his work run along the watershed between the different concepts of the United Nations he elucidated earlier. The office of the Secretary-General is an exact reflection of the conflict over the world organization as a whole – even more: the person of the Secretary-General turns the rather abstract debate into a tangible conflict. At this point, Hammarskjöld introduces the provisions of Art. 100 of the UN Charter as the only protection against the allegation of partiality. His remarks must be seen against the background of the Soviet Union's 1960 Troika Proposal to abolish the post of a single Secretary-General (see 'The instrument of "private diplomacy"' in Chapter 4). By embedding this proposal in the context of the antagonistic concepts of the world organization, he presents the conflict not as an attack on the person of the Secretary-General, but rather as an attack on the fundamental idea of international organization as such. Accordingly, he rejects the provision of the Troika Proposal to appoint an executive committee on the basis of the political power blocs (instead of a single Secretary-General) and defends loyalty to the international character of the organization in accordance with Art. 100 as the only protection against the allegation of partiality:

While it may be said that no man is neutral in the sense that he is without opinions or ideals, it is just as true that, in spite of this, a neutral Secretariat is possible. Anyone of integrity, not subjected to undue pressure, can, regardless of his own views, readily act in an 'exclusively international' spirit and can be guided in his actions on behalf of the Organization solely by its interests and principles, and by the instructions of its organs.

(ibid.: 556)

Significantly, the analysis of Dag Hammarskjöld's Annual Reports and the examination of the office in the preceding section both end with descriptions of the personal qualities required of the person of the officeholder. Before continuing, it is useful to briefly summarize some of Hammarskjöld's basic views.

The actions of the United Nations *Organization* reflect the intentions of its member states, who are using it as an instrument to fulfil the purposes and principles of the Charter. These purposes of the Charter are characterized as a 'magic triangle' made up of collective security, economic development and the promotion of international cooperation. However, the member states are divided along many lines – ideological, economic and cultural. As a result, the UN serves as a 'unifying force in a divided world'. Its work in the sense of an ambitious concept of peace is defined by the motto of 'reconciliation'. In this context, Hammarskjöld objects to a static concept of the world organization concerned solely with preserving peaceful coexistence. Such an approach is too limited: it needs to be complemented by a dynamic view of the United Nations in which the organization can evolve from a forum of debate into an institution with the potential for executive action – also, and particularly, in the interests of smaller states.

In Hammarskjöld's view, the *Charter* contains some fundamental rules of international ethics. Its provisions are rooted in three sources: first, the bitter experience of the world wars, second, intuitive convictions and an analogy with domestic principles and, third, the possibility and promise of shared views beyond economic, ideological and cultural differences, which were present in the agreement of member states when they founded the UN. Hammarskjöld seeks to give life to the Charter and make it reflect reality. But this does not mean the creation of a super-state; the expression of the intentions of member states remains a constitutive and indispensable element of the work of the world organization. On this basis, and parallel to the aforementioned three purposes of the United Nations (collective security, economic development and international cooperation), Hammarskjöld identifies in the Charter three fundamental principles, a basic accord, so to speak, of international organization: equal political rights, equal economic opportunities and the rule of law. According to Hammarskjöld, these principles, like the definition of the tasks of the United Nations, are interdependent. This pattern of purposes and principles pervades the individual provisions of the Charter; in cases of doubt, Hammarskjöld uses it to interpret the 'spirit' of the Charter. Understood in this way, the Charter does more than regulate procedural questions; it establishes a normative claim for the organization of international relations. In this sense, the world organization cannot be 'neutral', but it must always act impartially. As the first manifestation of the emerging awareness of an international community, the Charter should, in this sense, not be interpreted in a restrictive but in a dynamic, open and pragmatic way.

The *Secretary-General* is bound by the intentions of member states. Against this backdrop, he is able to assume only limited political functions. However, in the course of Hammarskjöld's term of office, the tone of this subordination changed from complete recognition of the primacy of member states to a barely concealed self-confidence. Yet Hammarskjöld does not view the expansion of his powers as a unilateral grab for power; rather, he justifies it as a pragmatic consequence of his 'vacuum theory'. According to this, the Secretary-General has an obligation to act even independently of direct instructions if this is necessary to fulfil the mission of the world organization, e.g. if decision-making in the Security Council is gridlocked and particularly if there is a possibility that the confrontation between the blocs will be drawn into the vacuum. Precisely in cases in which a conflict has not yet been brought to the attention of the other two UN bodies, the Secretary-General has the obligation to intervene at an early stage and without the harmful influence of excessive public attention. In such cases, the only grounds for action, sources of legitimacy and support for the work of the Secretary-General are strict observance of the requirements of international service. His political functions would be inconceivable without this sine qua non. As a person, he stands on the cutting edge of the organic growth of the world organization; he bears a particular responsibility for implementing the principle of international ethics in the Charter.

It is noticeable in the analysis of Hammarskjöld's annual reports that he often uses terms of organic growth to express his views on the office, organization and Charter (Jones 1994: 1047). This use of process-oriented and evolutionary concepts reflects the philosophy of Henri Bergson.[22] In addition to the contents of Hammarskjöld's library, there is other evidence that he was acquainted with Bergson's philosophy. In 1927, Bergson won the Nobel Prize for Literature for his principal work on creative development, a year in which Hammarskjöld's father was a member of the Nobel Committee. Hammarskjöld also repeatedly touched on the work of the French philosopher in his correspondence with Alexis Leger, a poet and diplomat (Leger 1993: 103). These references open up a further perspective on Hammarskjöld's remarks about office, Charter and organization.

Hammarskjöld made particularly clear references to Bergson in three speeches he delivered at the Universities of California and Chicago in 1954, 1955 and 1960.[23] Asked about the last of these in a press conference, Hammarskjöld responded: 'If you want to use such preposterous and "highfalutin" words as "creed" or "confession of faith", you might apply them to that speech, because I made an attempt there to set out my philosophy regarding the United Nations and the work we are all of us pursuing …' (CF IV: 594). At the same press conference he remarked:

> [T]he whole speech … was one regarding evolution, sociological evolution, and its expressions in higher and higher forms of society. Of course, we are working on the brink of the unknown because we have no idea as to what the international society of tomorrow will be. We can only do what we can now to find solutions, in a pragmatic sense, to the problems as they arise, trying to keep the sense of direction, and then we will see later on what comes out of it.
>
> I do not know if you are in any sense versed in philosophy. If you are, you may find a further clue to your question in the final words, where I happen to use the Bergsonian term 'creative evolution'.
>
> (CF IV: 599)

According to Bergson, experience is a crucial force for the organic growth of social institutions, and has to be employed and used creatively. Hammarskjöld expresses this thought in almost the same terms: 'The growth of social institutions is always one where, step by step, the form which adequately meets the need is shaped through selection, or out of experience' (Address on Human Rights and the Work for Peace at the Fiftieth Anniversary Dinner of the American Jewish Committee, 10 April 1957, in CF III: 556). He already stressed this principle, which he felt also applied to the arts, in a speech at the Museum of Modern Art in 1954: 'True art does not depend on the reality about which it tells. Its message lies in the new reality which it creates by the way in which it reflects experience' (CF II: 374). As Schachter emphasizes, this organic understanding also shaped Hammarskjöld's approach to law:

> Although Hammarskjöld often stressed the imperative quality of legal norms, this did not mean that he regarded law as an autonomous force which develops and is applied independently of political and social factors. He preferred to view law not as a 'construction of legal patterns', but in an 'organic sense'. As an institution which grows in response to felt necessities and within the limits set by historical conditions and human attitudes.
>
> (1983: 51)

In Hammarskjöld's comparison of the contrasting concepts of the static and dynamic models of the United Nations in particular one can recognize a reference to analogous thought of the French philosopher (Bergson 1954 distinguishes between static and dynamic religion), who used similar terms to characterize an object's potential and the lines of development inherent in it.

The connection to Bergson's thought also points to Maurice Hauriou's theory of institutions,[24] which is based on Bergson's ideas and can be fruitfully combined with Hammarskjöld's basic assumptions about the UN. Without going into detail, it should be noted that Hauriou's principle of the vitality of social institutions is rooted in the corresponding notions of Bergson (Hauriou 1965: 66). In the case of the United Nations, this idea, which must be distinguished from the function and purpose of the institution, would be that of the world organization or, in Hammarskjöld's specific case, 'reconciliation'. According to Hauriou, the specific nature of the central idea is that it still contains 'an element of indeterminable efficacy' (1965: 37), that must be realized through political leadership. By stating several times in his annual reports that the work of the United Nations is not bound by the institutional form of the UN and is not subsumed by it, he adopts Hauriou's understanding of the objective existence of social ideas.[25] In this context, an entry in Hammarskjöld's diary for 30 August 1956 reads almost as a paraphrase:

> … It is an *idea* you are serving – an idea which must be victorious if a mankind worth the name is to survive.
>
> It is an idea that demands your blood – not the weak form that it assumed in this historical phase. It is an idea you must help with all your strength – not

the work of human hands which just now gives you responsibility and the responsibility-creating chance to further it …

(*Markings* 1956: 39, 138)

Hammarskjöld's repeated reference to the still unexplored potential of the United Nations, his constant appeal to the Charter as 'basic rules of international ethics' and a manifestation of world community, his efforts for a concrete, experience-based realization of the central idea of the world organization, the concept of 'reconciliation' or the recurring emphasis on the Secretary-General's integrity and loyalty all fit well into the conceptual framework of Bergson's and Hauriou's theories. The relevance of political leadership and ethics in the Secretary-General's work and in the organic growth of the institution he serves emerges as a crucial factor. Up to now, however, it has not been systematically integrated into the overall international legal and political determinants of the office. The attempt shall be made in the following section.

Summary: political ethics as a power resource of the Secretary-General

The analysis of the determinants and rationale of the office of the Secretary-General raised the question of the importance of the officeholder's fundamental convictions and values as well as his interpretation of the objectives and principles of the UN Charter. This question becomes pressing when the Secretary-General acts within the framework of Hammarskjöld's 'vacuum theory' without the support of precedence or clear guidelines, but at the same time is inevitably drawn 'into the arena of political conflict' (Thant 1971: 593). According to insights of the theory of knowledge, people confronted with uncertainty or new challenges rely particularly strongly on their basic convictions as criteria of action (Kanninen 1995: 263; Goldstein and Keohane 1993b: 16). This general diagnosis also holds true for the Secretary-General's task. In situations of uncertainty the basic moral question becomes a political challenge for the officeholder: What shall I do?

Integration of political ethics into the determinants of the office

When political circumstances offer the Secretary-General a field of action, or when he has created one for himself, the next question is what direction he will take in this unknown territory. The Charter, as an overall legal and, in Hammarskjöld's definition, ethical construction, offers specific leitmotifs, but no definite legal or political guidelines. Moreover, the Secretary-General may not be guided by directives from states or by national interests. In contrast to national politicians, he does not receive any guidance from party manifestos or opinion polls. All he has at his disposal – as a 'compass' (Thant 1971: 590) as it were – is the 'spirit' of the Charter, in his interpretation. This role of 'guardian' (Morr 1991: 1137) and interpreter of the objectives of the Charter inevitably takes on a very personal note. In that context the Preparatory Commission spoke of the 'highest qualities of political judgement, tact and integrity' (Preparatory Commission of the United Nations 1945: 1044–5). Similarly, Art. 100 of the Charter calls for personal integrity, political judgement and international loyalty (or impartiality) as the paramount qualities required of the Secretary-General. These three abstract principles can be extended to include other – necessarily personally defined – moral principles. So here is the place of political ethics in the office of the Secretary-General with relevance for the organization as a whole.

From this location of political ethics, statements that, for instance, the Secretary-General can cope with his office 'only by virtue of his moral authority' (Schlüter 1978: 9–10) gain political substance. The Secretary-General's authority arises from formulating and applying political ethics, which form the necessary foundation for the indispensable confidence of the member states. Consequently, the office of the Secretary-General, more than almost any other political office, implies the need to formulate maxims of political ethics, communicate them convincingly in the political process and translate them into practicable programmes and activities. To this extent, the question of the Secretary-General's political ethics is definitely not one of political moralism. Brian Urquhart argues:

> Of all important public positions he [the Secretary-General] is perhaps the one in which spiritual strength, integrity, and courage are most essential to effective performance, for without them the office, lacking the normal trappings and supports of power, is an empty shell of high-sounding principles and good but unfulfilled intentions.
>
> (1964: 239)

For this reason, questions about whether the Secretary-General's actions are ethically grounded are not questions confined to the ivory-tower of philosophical speculation but questions going to the heart of international organization: the persuasiveness of the Secretary-General's ethical maxims is his immediate political capital (see also Birnbaum 1997: 299). And yet, is it possible for him to show political leadership in an office defined in this way? In this context, Gordenker speaks of 'intellectual leadership':

> Intellectual leadership compromises the production of new ideas for handling existing problems which continue into the future, making penetrating suggestions for coping with issues, or developing insights into a political agenda. ... Thus, intellectual leadership is characterized by departure from the routine and the willingness to break through taboos and to reorganize experience to give it new significance.
>
> (1993a: 635; 1967a)

Gordenker points out that 'bright ideas alone' are not enough. The political context, and hence the question of the extent to which the Secretary-General can act independently, remain decisive. Which brings us back to the question of the

Secretary-General's 'power' posed at the outset. This will be examined using Hannah Arendt's concept of power.

The 'power' of the Secretary-General according to Hannah Arendt's concept of power

Obviously, 'classic' definitions of political power cannot come to grips with the position of the Secretary-General. He does not have a clearly defined right of initiative or conventional 'instruments of power' (economic, financial or military resources, etc.). Instead, he always depends on support, has to permanently justify himself and to create trust and confidence. On the other hand, the fact that the Secretary-General's actions have obvious political consequences raises the question of how to describe this particular type of political power. In this connection, Hannah Arendt's concept of power is particularly revealing. In her comparison of concepts such as power, force and strength, Arendt arrives at the following definition:

> Power corresponds to the human ability not just to act but to act in concert. Power is never the property of an individual; it belongs to a group and remains in existence only so long as the group keeps together. When we say of somebody that he is 'in power' we actually refer to his being empowered by a certain number of people to act in their name.
>
> (1969: 44)

Applied to the Secretary-General's role, the need for the support and confidence of the member states does not contradict the existence of 'power' in this sense, but is its constitutive prerequisite: 'Power is always, as we would say, a power potential and not an unchangeable, measurable, and reliable entity like force or strength ...; nobody actually possesses [power], power springs up between men when they act together and vanishes the moment they disperse' (Arendt 1958: 252). The significance of public speech and the power of persuasion for this 'communicative concept of power' (Becker 1998: 169) should not be underestimated. Like so many of Hannah Arendt's concepts, this concept of power is not necessarily identical with and all-inclusive of conventional associations with this word.[26] However, she provides applicable categories for political situations that break open or revolt conventional routines and traditional structures (Arendt 1994). It is precisely in this regard that her definition can serve to better circumscribe analytically the unconventional, sensitive and unstable 'power' of the Secretary-General. Although Arendt herself emphasizes the ideal content of such definitions, which 'hardly ever correspond to watertight compartments in the real world, from which nevertheless they are drawn' (1969: 46), some structural parallels between Arendt's theoretical concept of power and actual examples taken from the office of the UN Secretary-General can be observed:

- According to Arendt, power needs legitimacy, which, given the inevitable plurality of a group's members and their conflicting interests, refers back to the origin of power, the past and the constitutive founding moment of the group – in the last analysis, to the social contract (ibid.: 53; Canovan 1983: 110–12). This point of view can be applied directly to the Secretary-General: his mission is to actualize the normative consensus of the founders of the United Nations and its objectives as laid down in the Charter. At the same time, this is the framework in which he has to act and prove himself. Up to now, all Secretaries-General have, when explaining their various missions in their reports and speeches, repeatedly referred to their original mandate so as to link their further actions to this initial consensus. In keeping with Hammarskjöld's understanding of the UN, this can be formulated as 'manifestations of commonality' in the terms of Hauriou.
- If Arendt sees the clearest occurrence of power in revolutionary situations, in which power, literally, 'is in the street' (1969: 49), Hammarskjöld's 'vacuum theory' may serve as a situational equivalent of Arendt's point of view. The need for action and the potential to act also exists in the political vacuum of institutions blocked and blocking themselves. This power potential is not in the street, but in the Secretary-General's office, once the Security Council and the General Assembly have failed to avail themselves of it. Precisely in this situation, it falls to the Secretary-General to take the lead by realizing the power entrusted to him under the Charter.
- According to Arendt, power can consolidate in 'authority' vested in persons or in offices. 'Its hallmark is unquestioning recognition by those who are asked to obey; neither coercion nor persuasion is needed' (1969: 45). Here, too, Dag Hammarskjöld provides an analogy. Owing to his active role in dealing with new challenges and blockades of the General Assembly and the Security Council, a somewhat offhand phrase gained currency among delegates and politicians: 'Leave it to Dag!'[27] This was, of course, no aboulic transfer of rights and functions; rather, by signing this blank cheque the member states involved were each following their explicit self-interest. The above-mentioned tacit application of Art. 99 depends to a certain degree on such expressions of personal authority.
- Finally, Arendt's qualification that power suddenly vanishes when its support structures disappear also applies. A parallel phenomenon is discernible in the possible downwards development in the spiral of trust as introduced above. Besides positive experiences, all Secretaries-General have also witnessed the sometimes drastic and rapid denial of opportunities to act after losing the trust of the member states or even just one Security Council member.

By way of conclusion, Gordenker describes this ambivalent position of the office as 'leadership without power'. In light of the above terminology, one can agree with this with regard to classical resources of power, yet at the same time speak of leadership with power as defined by Hannah Arendt. In this context, the Secretary-General has the task of performing several balancing acts simultaneously:[28] the balancing act between his administrative and political functions, the balancing act between independence and retaining the trust of the member states and the balancing act between ethical obligations and their pragmatic implementation. All of these are 'the elements of an insoluble equation, which nonetheless the Secretary-General must continually, and in all sorts of situations, attempt to solve' (Thant 1971: 591). In doing so he has to work with extremely fragile 'power' that he distils from the formulation and application of maxims of political ethics. This special task implies the opportunity – or even the duty – to become the 'source of leadership in advancing the maintenance of peace' (Gordenker 1993b: 634). To stay with the metaphor, the international circumstances determine when and at what height the Secretary-General must perform a balancing act, whereas the Charter and the trust of the member states are the wire on which he moves and, at the same time, from which he cannot deviate. Finally, his political ethics can be compared to the balancing pole that helps him to stay in equilibrium. Kofi Annan in fact used a similar image the first time he explained his understanding of his office (1998c). In this sense, the analysis has more precisely located political ethics and their significance among the determinants and operational context of the office. This serves as the basis for the reconstruction of the form and content of Hammarskjöld's political ethics to which we turn in the next chapter.

3 Principal elements of Dag Hammarskjöld's political ethics

The attempt to posthumously reconstruct the political ethics of a person is loaded with difficulties. As a rule, one has to fall back on probabilities and plausibility. Dag Hammarskjöld, however, was sometimes very articulate about the sources of his thoughts and actions. In this respect, the central document is his 1953 interview for the radio programme 'This I believe', in which he explicitly elaborated on the foundations of his ethical thinking. The key words and contexts provide guidelines for our analysis. The text is not exhaustive, and one must take into account that he wrote it soon after assuming office. Accordingly, our investigation goes beyond the influences named in the interview to include other as well as later factors. Nevertheless, the document is a solid basis for the following analysis. Hammarskjöld took great care in producing the text; some of his colleagues at the UN were presented with several drafts for comment. Because of the unique significance of this interview, the text is reproduced here in its entirety:

> The world in which I grew up was dominated by principles and ideals of a time far from ours and, as it may seem, far removed from the problems facing a man of the middle of the twentieth century. However, my way has not meant a departure from those ideals. On the contrary, I have been led to an understanding of their validity also for our world today. Thus, a never abandoned effort frankly and squarely to build up a personal belief in the light of experience and honest thinking has led me in a circle; I now recognize and endorse, unreservedly, those very beliefs which were once handed down to me.
>
> From generations of soldiers and government officials on my father's side I inherited a belief that no life was more satisfactory than one of selfless service to your country – or humanity. This service required a sacrifice to all personal interests, but likewise the courage to stand up unflinchingly for your convictions.
>
> From scholars and clergymen on my mother's side I inherited a belief that, in the very radical sense of the Gospels, all men were equals as children of God, and should be met and treated by us as our masters in God.
>
> Faith is a state of mind and the soul. In this sense we can understand the words of the Spanish mystic, St. John of the Cross: 'Faith is the union of God

with the soul.' The language of religion is a set of formulas which register a basic spiritual experience. It must not be regarded as describing, in terms to be defined by philosophy, the reality which is accessible to our senses and which we can analyse with the tools of logic. I was late in understanding what this meant. When I finally reached the point, the beliefs in which I was once brought up and which, in fact, had given my life direction even while my intellect still challenged their validity, were recognized by me as mine in their own right and by my free choice. I feel that I can endorse those convictions without any compromise with the demands of that intellectual honesty which is the very key to maturity of mind.

The two ideals which dominated my childhood world met me fully harmonized and adjusted to the demands of our world of today in the ethics of Albert Schweitzer, where the ideal of service is supported by and supports the basic attitude to man set forth in the Gospels. In his work I also found a key for modern man to the world of Gospels.

But the explanation of how man should live a life of active social service in full harmony with himself as a member of the community of the spirit, I found in the writings of those great medieval mystics for whom 'self-surrender' had been the way to self-realization, and who in 'singleness of mind' and 'inwardness' had found strength to say *yes* to every demand which the needs of their neighbours made them face, and to say *yes* also to every fate life had in store for them when they followed the call of duty, as they understood it. Love – that much misused and misinterpreted word – for them meant simply an overflowing of the strength with which they felt themselves filled when living in true self-oblivion. And this love found natural expressions in an unhesitant fulfilment of duty and in an unreserved acceptance of life, whatever it brought them personally of toil, suffering – or happiness. I know that their discoveries about the laws of inner life and of action have not lost their significance.

('Old Creeds in a New World', written for Edward R. Murrow's
programme 'This I believe', in CF II: 194–6)

A text that professes beliefs and expressly mentions influences ranging from Albert Schweitzer to the medieval mystic St John of the Cross is a remarkable document for an active politician in the twentieth century. Yet in 1953 it attracted little attention. It is the thesis of this study that this text was not a facile attempt at self-aggrandisement or a sanctimonious enumeration of self-imposed ethical obligations; rather, Hammarskjöld meant each sentence seriously – as his actions as Secretary-General demonstrate. In a letter to his friend Bo Beskow dated 24 November 1954 he explains the importance of the text:

The pages of 'This I believe', that you happened to see are not polite statements but deeply engaged ones, partly in self-criticism. They were written sometime last autumn but the last part says what I would say today: the counterpoint to this enormously exposed and published life is Eckhart and Jan van

Ruysbroeck. They really give me balance and – a more and more necessary – sense of humour. My salvation is to 'take the job damned seriously but never the incumbent' – but it has its difficulties. The roads to a basic conviction that in the deepest sense is religious can be most unexpected.

(quoted in Beskow 1969: 32)

Here Hammarskjöld refers to the interdependence between the quoted influences and his political activities, which will be investigated in greater detail in Chapter 4. He did not have a ready-made set of ethical values that he simply put into practice, but his experience in office moulded key concepts of his political ethics. In this chapter we shall first explicate and develop one by one the influences Hammarskjöld mentions. The interview text makes clear that these are not easily separable units of his political ethics. Rather, Hammarskjöld emphasizes the importance of the overall picture and the mutual influence, support, confirmation and qualification of these components.

Biographical influences: the Swedish tradition of an impartial civil service

Dag Hammarskjöld was born in Jönköping, in Central Sweden, on 29 July 1905. The Hammarskjölds were a noble family with a long tradition of government service. A forefather, Peder Michilsson, was raised to the nobility by King Charles IX for military services (the family name is composed of 'hammer' and 'shield'). Since then the family has continuously served the state in some capacity or other. Hammarskjöld's assistant, Sture Linnér (Interview 1998), outlines this family tradition as follows: 'In this context a noble man served the state without much personal benefit but with pride in his own honesty and integrity.' In the 1880s, the Hammarskjölds lost much of their wealth – including the family seat in Vaderum – through speculation in timber and the bankruptcy of a railway company in which they held an interest. As a result of this turn, Dag Hammarskjöld's father, Hjalmar, had to earn his leading position in the state through hard work, which he did through outstanding university results (after studies beset by financial difficulties), his expertise and his reputation as a lawyer (Lash 1961: 26–7). Already in these early professional positions, it was clear that Hjalmar Hammarskjöld would continue and advance the family tradition in the service of the state. One of the most important functions conferred on him was the governorship, which prompted the family, along with the two-year-old Dag, to move into the castle above the city in 1907. In Uppsala Hammarskjöld was influenced by the family tradition in all sorts of ways.

The family tradition: domestic politics, international law and literature

Almost all biographies of Hammarskjöld stress the formative influences of his childhood and youth (Thelin 1998, 2001). Söderberg (1962: 22) writes: 'In his family tradition there is an example of just about everything that Hammarskjöld did in later life; almost every one of his talents can be traced back over generations.' The strongest influence in this context was surely his father (Stolpe 1964a: 7–18), whose public life was dominated by three topics: Swedish politics, international law and literature.

Hjalmar Hammarskjöld's activities in Swedish politics are impressive: in 1907 he became governor of the province of Uppland and subsequently entered national politics as minister of education and religion under Prime Minister Christian Landenberg (Hershey 1961: 27), before being appointed prime minister of Sweden and minister of defence by royal decree on 17 February 1914. Hjalmar Hammarskjöld was an ardent defender of the Swedish neutrality in World War I. His policy of neutrality was rooted in international law, as he argued in a lecture on the subject to the Academy for International Law in 1923 (Hammarskjöld 1923: 53–141). He coined a much-quoted definition of neutrality: 'Being neutral is not a question of saying yes to both sides, but of saying no to both sides' (cited in Levine 1962: 61). During the war, however, this stance made him a lot of enemies. He was criticized for introducing food rationing in 1916, which made him extremely unpopular and coined the nickname 'Hunger-skjöld' (Söderberg 1962: 23). At school Dag was teased because of his father's unpopularity (Simon 1967: 30).[1] Eventually, in 1917, he resigned as prime minister. However, for all his pugnacious political activities, Hjalmar Hammarskjöld steered clear of party politics. He, like his sons after him, never joined a political party; instead, they were generally viewed as 'conservative independents' (Söderberg 1962: 26), who also worked under social-democratic prime ministers. Dag's eldest brother Bo followed most closely in the footsteps of his father, first as governor of the province of Södermanland and, from 1926 to 1934, as minister of state in the ministry of social affairs.

Besides – and sometimes alongside – his domestic political activities, Hjalmar Hammarskjöld was building a reputation in the field of foreign policy and international law. He was the Swedish delegate at many international conferences, for instance on copyright law and international private law (Berendsohn 1964: 1–2). He was his country's ambassador in Copenhagen (1905) and mediated in numerous international conflicts. The most outstanding example of this involvement is his crucial role in the negotiations on the dissolution of the union between Norway and Sweden in 1905 (owing to the negotiations he could not be at home for the birth of his son Dag). The high points of his activities in international law were his appointment as a member of the Permanent Court of Arbitration (1904–6) and his participation as a delegate to the Second Peace Conference at The Hague in 1907. Other commissions included participation in numerous courts of arbitration (Söderberg 1962: 25).

He also represented his country in leading positions at the League of Nations: in 1924 he was appointed chairman of the Committee on the Codification of International Law, and in 1932 he was the Swedish delegate at the Conference on Disarmament and the League of Nations. This involvement did not leave his children untouched (Barudio 1989: 100). The family interest in international law continued first with Dag's brother Åke, who, at the age of 29, was appointed Swedish delegate to The Hague, subsequently became Secretary-General of the Permanent International Court of Justice from 1924 to 1937 and a member of a series of arbitration commissions (Söderberg 1962: 26). Before that, in 1920–1, he was one of the first members of the international service in the Secretariat of the League of Nations. Because of his objectivity in opinions and argumentation, Åke was held in great esteem in international law circles and was appointed a judge at the Court of Justice in 1936 (see Hammarskjöld 1930, 1938). His career came to an abrupt end the following year, when he died of rheumatic fever.

Apart from his foreign and domestic political activities, Hjalmar Hammarskjöld also found the time to pursue a number of other interests. On completing his studies he had held a professorship in law at Uppsala. In time he returned to these academic interests. In 1918, he was elected a member of the Swedish Academy, the body that awards the Nobel Prize for literature. In this function, Hjalmar Hammarskjöld dealt with a huge number of literary works, to the benefit of his sons, who made intensive use of the home library. His literary interest was also shown in his translations of Spanish, Portuguese and Latin American folk songs. In 1928 he was appointed chairman of the board of directors of the Nobel Foundation. His son Sten followed most closely in the father's literary footsteps. After studying at the Columbia University School of Journalism, he wrote novels and short stories and worked as a journalist (for the *New York Times* among others; Levine 1962: 27).

Although Hjalmar Hammarskjöld paved the way for his sons in many fields, his domineering manner was undoubtedly also a negative influence. Some of Hammarskjöld's biographers make much of this influence – sometimes in ex-post psychological interpretations that are difficult to follow. Barudio (1989: 101) talks about the influence of the family tradition on Dag as a 'humiliating experience of mental "Sippenhaft"' and an 'existential neurosis of needing constant affirmation': 'Not even the appearance of mediocrity was allowed'. Barudio interprets this as an early crisis of identity that was manifested in a 'neurotic drive for high performance' and the tendency 'to gain trust by overworking and to confirm it by special achievements' (ibid.). We do know that Hammarskjöld often told the story that his father received his outstanding school-leaving results with the words: 'Åke did better' (ibid.: 107). In a letter to his friend Bo Beskow Dag Hammarskjöld speaks of a 'perpetual conflict with a dominating father image (in many ways unlike me) whose pressure I hated and whose weaknesses I consequently saw very clearly' (quoted in Beskow 1969: 33). Hjalmar Hammarskjöld was undoubtedly an extremely demanding person rooted in 'a type of strict Old Lutheran Christianity with a particular emphasis on doing one's duty' (Stolpe 1964a: 14), who at the same time kept his distance from the family. He spent the larger part of his annual leave without the family (Thelin 1998: 5). Disliking social occasions and celebrations, he stressed the need for quiet and seclusion to be able to work. On the other hand, he frequently complained in family correspondence that his wife and children did not write often enough – although they did so very regularly.

Hammarskjöld's judgement of his father

One of Dag Hammarskjöld's speeches provides some information on how he – in retrospect – perceived his father. Hjalmar Hammarskjöld died just a few weeks after his son was appointed Secretary-General. After his death, for the first time in the history of the Swedish Academy a son was offered his father's seat. One of the customs of the Swedish Academy is that a new member is obligated to introduce himself with a speech about his predecessor. Dag Hammarskjöld's appreciation of Hjalmar Hammarskjöld on 20 December 1954 was a gripping portrait that between the lines about family traditions and his father said as much about the speaker as the subject.[2] According to his executive assistant Andrew Cordier, Hammarskjöld spent more time preparing this speech than any political speech in his time at the UN (Dusen 1965: 14).

In his eulogy (CF II: 399–414) the Secretary-General expressly stresses that his picture of his father is very personal. The dominant impression of a strict man is clear from the sentence: 'A man of firm convictions does not ask, and does not receive, understanding from those with whom he comes into conflict' (ibid.: 400). A little later: 'A mature man is his own judge' (ibid.: 412). Here, Hammarskjöld is playing on the use of 'Hungerskjöld' as a term of abuse and at the same time underscoring the fact that political actions and the resultant responsibilities reflect the officeholder's personal convictions.

Hjalmar Hammarskjöld's conservative outlook went hand in hand with a 'strong sense of independence of public administration and with his feelings about the duties accompanying the responsibilities of officials' (ibid.: 408). Sweden's policy of neutrality during World War I tested this attitude to the utmost. In this connection, Hammarskjöld points out that the Scandinavian countries wrote a joint diplomatic note to the warring parties in August 1914 to remind them that the policy of neutrality protected some of the principles that they, too, had subscribed to until recently. Hammarskjöld attributed this initiative to his father (ibid.: 411). In keeping with this sentiment, Hjalmar Hammarskjöld himself preferred to work in the background. Hammarskjöld quotes his father from a debate in the Swedish parliament in 1925: 'Who takes the initiative, who exerts influence, is so utterly indifferent compared to the one great question: to make our country secure for the future.' Hammarskjöld sums up: 'To the nineteen-year-old listener in the gallery, these words epitomized a life of faith in justice and of self-effacing service under a responsibility which unites us all' (ibid.: 414). This is a relatively accurate description of the formative influence of his family and in particular his father. Hammarskjöld's characterization of his father's legal thinking is also informative:

> [T]he idea seems to be that society is welded together by that higher 'reason', common to us all, which is the bearer of justice. Against this background we can understand his faith in a 'supranational' justice, through which may be created an international *Civitas Legum*. In attempting to interpret the internationalism represented by Hjalmar Hammarskjöld, this seems to me to

be the key. *Civitas Dei* was a thing of the past. The present-day attempts to form an international organization with common executive organs had not yet been begun. Instead, there is a glimpse here of a world society, where national states live under the protection of an internationalism which gains its strength from the very logic of justice itself, not from dictates of power, and in which, therefore, the only international organs needed are of a judicial nature.

(ibid.: 405)

Hammarskjöld will return to this thought, partly verbatim, in his 1961 Annual Report (AR 1961: 546). In the eulogy, the idea of an international community based on law has a specifically 'Swedish' component, because Hjalmar Hammarskjöld had underlined the importance of international law for small countries in particular: '[F]or a small country, international law, in the final analysis, is the only remaining argument, and ... its defence is therefore worth sacrifices even in the egoistical interest of the country itself' (ibid.: 411). Dag's own approach, however, goes beyond that of his father when he speaks of the 'present-day attempts to form an international organization with common executive organs'. At the time, he, as Secretary-General of the United Nations, was in the middle of these 'present-day attempts'. His perspective, however, shows itself to be heavily influenced by his father.[3]

Hammarskjöld's journey through life along the family tradition

In his choice of career, Hjalmar Hammarskjöld's youngest son followed in his father's footsteps in Swedish politics and literature. He left school with his university entrance examination in 1923 and enrolled in economics, philosophy and French at the University of Uppsala. An excellent student, he took his first examination at 19. However, he was dissatisfied with his choice of subjects, as a complaint to Anna Söderblom makes clear: 'I had thought that I was going to learn about ideas and their travels through the ages and not waste my time on the love affairs of the authors' (quoted in Söderberg 1962: 35–6). After the first examination he switched to economics and law. As part of his law examinations he spent a year (1929–30) doing research in Cambridge and attended lectures by, among others, John Maynard Keynes (Dusen 1965: 54).

When his parents moved into the Stockholm house of the Nobel Foundation, Dag changed university. In Stockholm he got to know a number of important scholars, among them Gunnar Myrdal, Eli F. Heckscher and Gustav Cassel. Alf Johansson and Erik Lundberg were close fellow students of Hammarskjöld (Lash 1961: 37–8). In his studies he was influenced by the so-called Stockholm School of Knut Wicksell, whose theories of economic policy borrowed from John Maynard Keynes (ibid.: 37). Axel Hägerström, Hammarskjöld's philosophy professor, was a leading mind in this movement. Even before Hammarskjöld completed his doctoral thesis he was engaged in activities outside of the university. He also followed in his father's cultural and literary footsteps: as a student he wrote a play that was published with a small print run, but did not sell well (Hershey

1961: 46). At the age of 22 he was one of the student organizers for the University of Uppsala's 450th anniversary celebrations (ibid.: 49). Later, in 1940 he was elected to the board of directors of the Swedish Tourist Association (becoming deputy-president in 1950) and was chairman of the Swedish Mountaineering Club from 1945–6. In this capacity, he edited a series of publications, including anthologies with descriptions of nature and poems (Hammarskjöld *et al.* 1943; Hammarskjöld 1962; Berendsohn 1964: 7).

Hammarskjöld initially started off on an economic career – it seemed that he would continue the family tradition in Swedish politics. In 1930, shortly after receiving his Bachelor of Law degree, he was appointed to a government Commission on Unemployment, on which he sat until 1934. It is not clear whether he was proposed by Gösta Bagge, a Conservative, or Ernst Wigforss, a Social Democrat (Söderberg 1962: 40–1). In any case, Hammarskjöld quickly gained a reputation as an important advisor on economic policy. At the time, Dag's brother Bo was minister of state in the Ministry of Social Affairs. Berendsohn considers the cooperation between the Hammarskjöld brothers as a significant factor in the creation of the Swedish welfare state. Indeed, the two drafted a number of important bills together (Lash 1961: 43). The Stockholm School of Dag's university years had relocated more or less seamlessly to the levers of political power (ibid.: 39). Hammarskjöld's doctoral thesis in economics, which he completed in 1933, was written against this background. Titled 'The spread of business cycles', it formed part of the final report of the Unemployment Commission (Thelin 1998: 8; Söderberg 1962: 42), and reflects Hammarskjöld's profound thoughts, as well as his laborious way of expressing them. Large sections were also devoted to the international conditions and consequences of monetary policy. Hammarskjöld himself added a typically ambiguous touch by quoting the duchess in *Alice in Wonderland* in his foreword: 'That's nothing to what I could say if I chose' (quoted in Hershey 1961: 51). He was awarded a doctorate 'cum laude', a disappointing mark by Hammarskjöld's standards. Myrdal, against whom Hammarskjöld had to defend his thesis before the faculty, thought that Hammarskjöld had written the work negligently (Lindegren 1971: 9). Some felt that this 'disappointing result' discouraged him from pursuing an academic career. Although he was occasionally asked to lecture in economics at the University of Stockholm, he never took up university teaching systematically.

Instead, the Social Democrat Ernst Wigforss, one of Sweden's leading proponents of a planned economy, and the Conservative Gösta Bagge came to his assistance: at Bagge's suggestion, Hammarskjöld was appointed secretary of the Swedish National Bank. A year later Wigforss, finance minister since 1932, appointed him minister of state in his ministry, where Hammarskjöld worked until 1945 and was responsible for the budget under the exceptional conditions of the world war. He also accepted other responsibilities (Berendsohn 1964: 3): in 1937 he was appointed to the committee that oversaw the Swedish Economic Institute (and remained a member until 1948); in 1940 he was elected to the board of the Foreign Exchange Office; and in 1941 he became chairman of the supervisory board of the Swedish National Bank.

Per Lind, one of his closest colleagues and acquaintances, reports that by the end of the 1940s Hammarskjöld had a reputation throughout the Swedish civil service as 'some kind of wonder boy' (Interview Lind 1998; Hershey 1961: 54; Hoek 1953: 13). He had earned this reputation partly because he was indefatigable. To the astonishment of his colleagues, even on very little sleep his concentration and the demands he made of himself hardly slipped (Berendsohn 1964: 5). Nevertheless, by holding positions in the finance ministry and the Swedish National Bank, he was in a situation that he had earlier judged to be a threat to the political independence of the central bank (Barudio 1989: 110). It was possible for Hammarskjöld to justify and master both positions simultaneously only because he understood his position as that of a strictly non-partisan employee; he saw the undoubtedly political dimension of his work as 'a continuation of the activity of the objective civil servant' (Hammarskjöld 1951a: 391–6; Söderberg 1962: 7). Some, however, found him arrogant and overly self-confident (Interview Birnbaum 1998).

Entering international politics

After World War II, Hammarskjöld's field of activity shifted increasingly in the direction of international politics. Even before then, he had been responsible for international affairs at the finance ministry. During the war he had worked on economic and financial support for neighbouring Norway and worked with the Norwegian government-in-exile. At the same time, Sweden's policy of neutrality meant that he had to take care not to provoke the German occupying force. For his commitment, he later received Norway's only decoration, the Grand Cross of the Order of St Olaf (Lash 1961: 36–7). After the war, economic policies focused on rebuilding economic relations, modalities of credit payments, reparations and economic reconstruction. In all these questions Hammarskjöld was the central figure in Sweden. In 1945 the government appointed him as a permanent advisor in international financial and economic affairs. And then he moved to the Ministry of Foreign Affairs under Foreign Minister Östen Undén. His doctoral thesis had already foreshadowed this transition from economic expertise to international policy, and his writings from this time underscore the shift (Hammarskjöld 1945a: Suppl. A, 1–24; 1945b: Suppl. B, 1–24).

This applies equally to two other early texts of Hammarskjöld's published in *Tiden* as 'The Civil Servant and Society' and 'Politics and Ideology' in 1951 and 1952 (Hammarskjöld 1951a, 1952; Stolpe 1964a: 55–7; Kelen 1966: 44–6; Zacher 1970: 10–15). In the short article on civil servants he justifies his role as an impartial official with political responsibility in a social-democratic government. The *Tiden* articles caused a stir in Sweden (Interview Birnbaum 1998). Hammarskjöld explicitly deals with the question of political ethics and accentuates certain fundamental points that we shall return to later. For instance, he defends the concept of the British civil service and emphasizes that a position in the civil service is incompatible with the pursuit of party allegiance or other particularist interests; the only proper orientation for a civil servant is the interest of the state in its entirety, which he complies with by distinguishing between his official duties and his private preferences: 'The fundamental and obvious rule of a civil servant's ethics is to serve society, not a group or party or any special interests' (quoted in Kranz 1973b: 19). In Hammarskjöld's view the impartial expert's influence on the political process should be limited to giving advice in internal meetings to those with political responsibility – but in doing so he can have substantial influence. Hammarskjöld refers to Albert Schweitzer (see also 'Christian mysticism' below) whose obligation of a universal legal ethic for him justified this concept of service to society: '"respect for the individual" and his "dignity" is the only acceptable standard for state action' (Barudio 1989: 113). He returns to this question in the article on 'Politics and Ideology' and indicates that there is a relationship between a country's domestic political structure and its peacefulness towards other countries (Barudio 1989: 138).

Hammarskjöld's international interest soon turned to other tasks. In 1947–8 he was the Swedish delegate to the Paris negotiations for the Marshall Plan and Organization for European Economic Cooperation (1948–53) (Hammarskjöld 1951b). The Swedish 'wonder boy' turned out to be also impressive on the international stage. The head of the Norwegian delegation to the OEEC, for instance summed up: 'I never heard of anybody who worked with Hammarskjöld in these years and was not impressed with his capacity to see things in a realistic way and remain neutral when seeking a solution that would take all interests into account' (quoted in Lash 1961: 52). In 1950, he was appointed chairman of the Swedish delegation at UNISCAN, an organization to promote economic cooperation between Great Britain and Scandinavia. In 1951, Prime Minister Tage Erlander named him his permanent advisor; soon after he joined the government as deputy foreign minister, which completed his move to the international sphere. Hammarskjöld was soon tested by crises, such as when the Soviet Union shot down a Swedish airplane over the Baltic Sea in 1951 (Simon 1967: 61–2). As Foreign Minister Undén was on holiday, Hammarskjöld coordinated the Swedish response to this incident. Contrary to the hopes of some NATO countries that Sweden would abandon its policy of neutrality, Hammarskjöld succeeded in settling the crisis without giving ground on Sweden's basic policy. Despite his success and his rapid advance, he made it clear that he had no intention of joining a political party (Berendsohn 1964: 6). This circumstance signalled the limits of his national career – higher political office is associated with election and a mandate from which he would be barred without party affiliation. For a short time his work had also taken him to the United Nations: Hammarskjöld was deputy head of the Swedish delegation during the Sixth Session of the UN General Assembly in 1951–2 and head of delegation during the following session.

Against this background, Hammarskjöld's appointment as Secretary-General of the United Nations, while a surprise, was not quite as extraordinary as it seemed at first glance. According to a report from Bo Beskow, a few days before Hammarskjöld's nomination, he and Hammarskjöld had talked about the successor question in New York during a sitting for a portrait. Beskow spontaneously asked Hammarskjöld if he could imagine being among the candidates, and he had answered: 'Nobody is crazy enough to propose me – and I would be crazy to accept.' (quoted in Beskow 1969: 12). At this point the negotiations in New York had reached an impasse. A number of names – Carlos P. Romulo (the Philippines), Lester Pearson (Canada), V. L. Pandit (India), Prince Wan Waithayakon (Thailand), Nasrollah Entezam (Iran), Charles Malik (Lebanon), Padilla Nervo (Mexico) and Ahmed Bokhari (Pakistan) (Urquhart 1972: 11–13; 1993a: 243; Lash 1961: 15–23) – had unofficially been tested and rejected, usually because of Soviet objections (Gross 1964: 2–10).

To resolve this situation, the French representative Henri Hoppenot (1961) presented four names as a procedural measure that he thought the USA would support. The Soviet Union could then react to this list. Apart from Nasrollah Entezam, Padilla Nervo and the Dutchman Dirk U. Stikker, the list also included Dag Hammarskjöld, with whom Hoppenot had worked at the OEEC (Montgomery 1975: 12). The British representative, Sir Gladwyn Jebb (Kelen 1966: 26), had also got to know Hammarskjöld while working on the Marshall Plan and in the General Assembly. He confirmed that Hammarskjöld – who had also caught the attention of Anthony Eden – was suitable for the job.[4] The name also meant something to Ernest Gross, an American diplomat who attended the meeting with Henry Cabot Lodge. He had met Hammarskjöld at a reception at the Norwegian embassy in autumn 1952, where the two had a long conversation as they were working on similar questions in connection with the Marshall Plan. In this context, Gross regards Hammarskjöld as 'one of the unsung architects of the idea of the European Community' (1964: 1). When the name Hammarskjöld was mentioned, Gross immediately whispered to Lodge that Hammarskjöld was an excellent man whom he could personally recommend. Valerian Zorin, the Soviet representative, kept his opinion to himself and said he needed to consult Moscow first. At the next meeting a few days later he made known that Hammarskjöld was acceptable (the Chinese delegation was not present at this private meeting on account of Russia's stand on Taiwan). Hammarskjöld had struck up numerous acquaintanceships at international conferences and obviously left a good impression as the responses from the respective foreign ministries were all positive. Gross sums up: '[H]e was extremely well known, to a professional group' (1964: 35; Urquhart 1972: 14). The agreement was officially announced on 31 March.

Hammarskjöld had not been informed about the deliberations in New York and thus was surprised by the nomination. Sven Dahlman, the Swedish ambassador in Cairo, who visited Hammarskjöld on the evening he heard the news, reports that Hammarskjöld thought the first calls from newspapers were April-fool jokes – until after the third call he accepted that the news was true (recounted in Åhman 1963: 5). Naturally, his nationality stood him in good stead: he was regarded as a neutral candidate after several earlier proposals had suffered shipwreck on the East–West divide. 'In other ways, too, the Hammerskjold who came to the UN in 1953 was very much a product of Sweden's approach to foreign affairs' (Lash 1961: 55–6). Two notable consequences of this approach were his efforts to remain neutral and his emphasis on international law – points of which his father was a living example. On being offered the job, Hammarskjöld sought his father's advice, who – probably with reference to family tradition – advised him without reservation to accept the office.

The appointment offered Hammarskjöld 'the possibility of leaving the professional blind alley in the Swedish government' (Barudio 1989: 114). This is underscored in a subsequent letter to Ernst Wigforss, in which Hammarskjöld openly admits: 'In this international work I have lost the sense of inner cleavage that I felt at home in Sweden' (quoted in Söderberg 1962: 17). The representatives in the Security Council associated with the name Hammarskjöld Sweden's neutrality, the technocratic image of an expert in economic matters and, above all, a fairly non-political personality, something they were looking for after their experience with Lie.[5]

'The only true profile': Hammarskjöld's spiritual diary

Among the personal effects that Hammarskjöld packed for his last trip to Africa and left next to his bed in his room in Leopoldville was a small book published in 1689: a French edition of *The Imitation of Christ* by Thomas à Kempis (Thomas à Kempis 1952; Erling 1987: 356). Given Hammarskjöld's interest in antiquarian books for his private library, this fine edition was not unusual. Eyebrows were raised, however, when Hammarskjöld's assistant Sture Linnér found a leaf in this book – a page mark, as it were – on which Hammarskjöld had neatly typed his oath of office (Simon 1967: 184–5).[6] Was this coincidence, or did Hammarskjöld see a connection between the obligations of his office and the thoughts of a medieval mystic? This speculation became certainty with the finding of a second paper. Per Lind (Interview 1990: 11), whom Hammarskjöld had asked to take charge of his private papers if anything should happen to him, found a 160-page manuscript on the bedside table in Hammarskjöld's New York apartment with an undated, personal letter addressed to Leif Belfrage, Hammarskjöld's former colleague at the Swedish foreign ministry:

> Dear Leif:
>
> Perhaps you may remember I once told you that, in spite of everything, I kept a diary which I wanted you to take charge of someday. Here it is.
>
> It was begun without a thought of anybody else reading it. But, with my later history and all that has been said and written about me, the situation has changed. These entries provide the only true 'profile' that can be drawn. That is why, during recent years, I have reckoned with the possibility of publication, though I have continued to write for myself, not for the public.
>
> If you find them worth publishing, you have my permission to do so – as a sort of *white book* concerning my negotiations with myself – and with *God*.
>
> Dag

(Markings: v)

The diary was published and immediately became a bestseller. It went through several editions and was translated into a number of languages (Auden 1964; Hammarskjöld 1966a, 1966b and 1967).[7] Yet, many readers and even friends and colleagues greeted the posthumous publication of Hammarskjöld's diary with astonishment and surprise (Ascoli 1965: 37–40). The popularity of the book is probably explained by expectations of anecdotes, remarks about personalities of his time and previously unpublished information about behind-the-scenes politicking. Such expectations were let down completely. Not one politician is mentioned, or, directly, any political activities – an 'anti-memoir' (Urquhart 1964: 232). Instead, the pages contain rather cryptic impressions of nature, prayers and poems, many in the form of Japanese haikus. And yet – covertly articulated – there are references to Hammarskjöld's public life: 'In *Markings* we read nothing of the issues and dilemmas which make the United Nations a place of such a great significance, but the sound of the world's storms is clearly to be heard in, with, and under the meditations' (Aulén 1969: 152). The diary is not a political autobiography, but an intellectual work that quickly became a 'spiritual classic of our century' (Lipsey 1996: 12). Hammarskjöld reveals himself as a twentieth-century mystic.[8] This side of such a rational public figure jarred with people's image of him (Sundstrom 1962; Sobosan 1974: 11).

Hammarskjöld's mention of mysticism in the Murrow interview early in his Secretary-Generalship should have tempered surprise. This trait of Hammarskjöld also came through now and then in the presence of his colleagues. Sture Linnér (Interview 1998), for instance, reports that before the departure from Ndola, he and Hammarskjöld talked about the concept of love in medieval mysticism. There were also other occasional indications of this interest of Hammarskjöld. Still, the fact that Christian mysticism should interest the UN Secretary-General, let alone influence his political ethics and his actions struck people as strange. That said, Hammarskjöld's comment about the 'only true profile that can be drawn' places on every biographer an obligation to attach particular weight to these notes.[9]

In order to deal with this topic, it is essential to briefly look at basic concepts in the history and tradition of Christian mysticism and the relevance of this spiritual diary in this tradition. Large parts of Hammarskjöld's notes are incomprehensible without some knowledge of this special religious background with its own language and images (Knyphausen 1965: 8). As it is, there have been many misunderstandings, even open accusations of blasphemy, schizophrenia and identification with Christ (examples in Dusen 1969: 173–4; Clausen 1964).

The tradition of spiritual diaries and mysticism

The concept of mysticism embraces a number of different spiritual experiences; in everyday use there is also an undertone of otherworldliness, bizarreness and ecstasy. Yet mysticism is a constant component of the history of European thought and the world's major religions; its roots go back to antiquity, early Christianity and Islam.[10] The word 'mystic' (from the Greek 'myein': to close the eyes, ears, mouth) means a fundamental religious phenomenon based on the experience of an immediate, intuitive contact with the Absolute, the Unconditional, 'God' (Wehr 1995a: 9; Beyschlag 1980b; Sudbrack 1990). For Borchert (1997: 11) mysticism means: 'knowing from experience that everything is somehow connected, that everything is originally one'. Waldenfels (1990: 383). defines mysticism as 'living on the existentially perceived and experienced, verbally inexpressible life-determining basis of human existence'.

Knowledge of this mystic experience is drawn mainly from the writing of people who report such experiences. They have their own, mystic language and often describe their experiences as a path that gradually or suddenly opens up and, accompanied by many positive and negative spiritual stages, brings them to meet God. The goal of this journey is the 'unio mystica', the union with God; there is a vast body of accounts of this in varying intensity and forms of experience. An analogous path in the Christian tradition, though not necessarily mystic, is the imitation of Christ, which as the 'prototype of all Christian mysticism' (Wehr 1995a: 54) is and was the point of reference for many mystics. The literary form of this path is the mystical progress report – often in the form of a diary following the example of the *Confessions of Saint Augustine*. The basic elements of mystic language in this account (Borchert 1997: 29–60) include an enormous variety of metaphors and sensory perceptions drawn from nature, music and eroticism, which influence in particular the so-called bride mysticism (of, among others, Mechthild of Magdeburg). As the chosen images are only an approximation of what is essentially indescribable experience, 'to express something that is almost inexpressible' (ibid.: 27; Haas 1996), mystic images often seem full of contradictions and paradoxes reminiscent of dreamlike visions. The distinction between Self and Other blurs, the mood can swing abruptly between euphoria and dejection.

One of the conventional images of mysticism is that of the individual who turns his back on the world and as a hermit seeks this special proximity to God in asceticism and spiritualization as an end in itself. There is a strong tradition of solitude in mysticism. However, there is also an outward-looking form of mysticism with a strong ethical element driven by not only spiritual desire, but also the need to articulate itself in worldly activities: 'It is an inwardness that seeks the outside world to perfect itself' (Werner 1990: 203). The work of the Apostle Paul is frequently referred to in this connection (Wehr 1995a: 35–6). But over and above this there is a series of important 'worldly' mystics such as Augustine, Bernhard of Clairvaux, Ignatius of Loyola and Vincent de Paul. Pierre Teilhard de Chardin and Edith Stein, too, emphasize the mystical experience realized in action (ibid.: 167–9).[11] In this way, mystic experience often taps into an extraordinary capacity for work (ibid.: 121).

The attraction of medieval mysticism for a UN Secretary-General in the atomic age nonetheless needs to be explained more closely. A first parallel could probably be discussed in the respective historical background. Medieval mysticism and one of its most important phases, the 'devotio moderna', were characteristic of the 13th and 14th centuries (Janowski 1978). This was a time in which plague, death and chaos were part of everyday life (on this context, Riehle 1984: 172–3).

In this situation some priests deliberately chose not to put their faith in human deeds, actions, and plans as their daily confrontation with death underlined the futility of these ways. Instead, they turned to God and put their fate in his hands without reservation. This commitment calls for complete trust in fate, calling and God's will. And this constellation contains analogies to the situation of the UN Secretary-General. He had a responsible position that called for him to act in a world that the superpowers could turn into a nuclear inferno at any time, even if by accident or for an insignificant reason. Thus, the twentieth-century scenario of global threat and the atmosphere of calamity in the thirteenth and fourteenth centuries may be regarded as analogous constellations. How did Hammarskjöld's mystical bent express itself in this constellation?

The structure of the diary and its importance for Hammarskjöld

Just casually paging through the diary reveals the complexity of the notes.[12] Hammarskjöld did not make entries continually or regularly, and there is no consistency in the length of entries. There is a gap from 1931, when he moved from Uppsala to Stockholm, to 1941. On 7 April 1953 – the day of his election as Secretary-General and the evening before his departure for New York – Hammarskjöld starts to date individual entries. In addition, from the entry 'Easter 1960' onwards, religious feast days are explicitly noted. But even before then there were entries that corresponded to specific feast days. The dating alone is indicative of the diversity of the diary. Prose, from short, fragmented remarks to longer paragraphs, dominates until mid-1958. From 1953 onwards, quotes from different sources (often in the original language) and self-composed prayers appear with increasing frequency. From 1958 on, poems can cover several pages ('From Uppsala', 'Summer', 'Far Away', 'Hudson Valley', etc.). Finally, between October 1958 and the end of 1960 we find more than 100 three-line haikus (Maurina 1965). The frequency of entries varies considerably over time – it was not a diary kept with any regularity.

The diary was undoubtedly 'edited' (Sundén 1967: 15–16; Ruhbach 1987: 310), which can be easily deduced from the motto on the first page: 'Only the hand that erases can write the true thing' (*Markings*: 3), which Hammarskjöld borrowed from the Swedish poet Bertil Malmberg.[13] Hammarskjöld probably typed up notes that he had collected as loose sheets and pieces of paper in 1956–7.[14] Some sheets have yellowed far more than others (Dusen 1965: 34) and the imprint of the typewriter varies considerably – without any chronological pattern. This impression also strengthens the suspicion that Hammarskjöld edited the diary.[15] A remarkable number of dated entries were written on weekends, which Hammarskjöld often spent at his country residence in Brewster.

Markings is unquestionably mystical in tone: the title alone refers to a topos in the mystic tradition (concerning searching and maturing). Over and above this, the tone and issues of *Markings* contain typical ingredients of classic reports of mystic experience (Mohr 1998: 42). Symptomatically, not all of the entries are written in the first person; subject and personal pronouns change (Progoff

1965: 228–9). Knowledge of this background, i.e. the mystic tradition in which Hammarskjöld was at home, serves to refute many of the rumours about him as a person, such as ostensible over-confidence and blasphemy. Hammarskjöld did not have an exaggerated opinion about himself or mania about being close to God; he kept largely to the conventions of other, earlier typically mystic diaries and their search for the 'unio mystica' – but in his own way. His diction as well as his choice of works and images is reminiscent not only of earlier mystics, but also of contemporary writers, such as Djuna Barnes and Saint-John Perse, both of whom he translated into Swedish (Perse 1960, 1989; Barnes 1985; see also 'Summary' to this chapter). Hammarskjöld shows himself also influenced by Swedish authors such as Vilhelm Ekelund, Karin Boye, Hjalmar Gullberg, Bertil Ekman and Gunnar Ekelöf, some of whom are quoted in the diary.[16]

As Hammarskjöld writes in the letter to Leif Belfrage, when he began keeping the diary he had no intention of publishing it. The first mention of publication appears in an entry in 1952:

> How ridiculous, this need of yours to communicate! Why should it mean so much to you that at least *one* person has seen the inside of your life? Why should you write down all this, for yourself, to be sure – *perhaps*, though, for others as well?
>
> (*Markings* 1952: 23, 87)

The pivotal role of 1956 (see Chapter 'UN presence and blue helmets', Chapter 4) with its interweaving of external activity and inner reflection is underscored at the end of the year when Hammarskjöld returns to the question of the diary's meaning for him and of the possibility of publication.

> You ask yourself if these notes are not, after all, false to the very Way they are intended to mark. These notes? – They were signposts you began to set up after you had reached a point where you needed them, a fixed point that was on no account to be lost sight of. And so they have remained. But your life has changed, and now you reckon with possible readers, even, perhaps, hope for them. Still, perhaps it may be of interest to somebody to learn about the path about which the traveller who was committed to it did not wish to speak while he was alive. Perhaps – but only if what you write has an honesty with no trace of vanity or self-regard.
>
> (*Markings* 1956: 61, 144)

These quotations highlight a characteristic of the diary, the tension between humility and self-criticism on the one hand and vanity and self-regard on the other (see also *Markings* 1956: 60, 144). Such tensions determine the structure and leitmotifs of the diary. At first sight, it is difficult to reconcile this picture of Hammarskjöld with the life and career of the 'wonder boy' described above.

Leitmotifs of the diary entries

The first entry, dated 1925 to 1930 under the heading 'Thus it was', is already indicative of what will follow. These lines address many of the basic topics and give a first impression of Hammarskjöld's language and images:

> I am being driven forward
> Into an unknown land.
> The pass grows steeper,
> The air colder and sharper.
> A wind from my unknown goal
> Stirs the strings,
> Of expectation.
>
> Still in the question:
> Shall I ever get there?
> There where life resounds,
> A clear pure note
> In the silence.
>
> Smiling, sincere, incorruptible –
> His body disciplined and limber.
> A man who had become what he could,
> And was what he was –
> Ready at any moment to gather everything
> Into one simple sacrifice.
>
> (*Markings* 1925–30: 1/2, 5–6)

Besides the thought of sacrifice, which will return often (Specker 1999), these lines are a powerful reflection of Hammarskjöld's seeking, questioning nature. There are three central questions or leitmotifs in *Markings*: the journey inwards, the frontier experience encountering the unheard-of and the challenge of self-realization through self-surrender; these may also be read as stations on Hammarskjöld's way.

The journey inwards

An entry in 1950 broadens this basic tenor of self-criticism to include the aspect of loneliness, and can be viewed as programmatic for the diary:

> The longest journey
> Is the journey inwards.
> Of him who has chosen his destiny,
> Who has started upon the quest
> For the source of his being
> (Is there a source?) –

He is still with you,
But without Relation,
Isolated in your feeling
Like one condemned to death
Or one whom imminent farewell
Prematurely dedicates
To the loneliness which is the final lot of all.

(Markings 1950: 4, 58)

Hammarskjöld's notes record this journey inwards. The questioning, doubting tone indicates that this is no easy journey, but an extremely arduous, lonely search for the self. The obviously negative undertones point to the fact that already in the early entries Hammarskjöld was fighting against self-doubt and disorientation. Thoughts of death are not rare (King 1982; Progoff 1965), like the following from the second half of the 1920s: 'Tomorrow we shall meet, / Death and I. / And he shall thrust his sword / Into one who is wide awake' *(Markings* 1925–30: 3, 6). This topic continues until the beginning of the 1940s. While at first glance the following entry appears depressing and fatalistic, it contains the germ of a solution that would become crucial for Hammarskjöld:

There is only one path out of the steamy jungle where the battle is fought over glory and power and advantage – one escapes for the snares and obstacles you yourself have set up. And that is – to accept death.

(Markings 1941–2: 9, 13)

In the second half of the 1940s the death topic grows even more dominant. He has visions of a person drowning *(Markings* 1945–9: 4, 36), a woman who wants to kill herself in water *(Markings* 1945–9: 6, 38) and a man who shoots himself *(Markings* 1945–9: 7, 38–9).[17] Parallel to this, Hammarskjöld paints a picture of a confused life; resignation gains the upper hand, various symbols and images express an experience of crisis and decay in which 'it seems so much more difficult to live than to die' *(Markings* 1945–9: 10, 32). Owing to alternating subjects (he, I, we, etc.), it is difficult to identify the subject. There are also clear references to his working life, even reflections on injustices towards colleagues. These diary entries reveal an almost hopeless depression behind the brilliant façade of an inexorable career. In 1950, Hammarskjöld's despair is shown in the description of a creeping death in the face of which he feels helpless day in and day out:

In a whirling fire of annihilation,
In the storm of destruction,
And deadly cold of the fact of sacrifice,
You would welcome death.
But when it slowly grows within you,
Day by day,
You suffer anguish,

Anguish under the unspoken judgement which hangs over your life,
While leaves fall in the fool's paradise.

(Markings 1950: 2, 37)

Self-doubt leads to unsparing self-criticism: 'At least he knew this much about himself – I know what man is – his vulgarity, lust, pride, envy and longing. / Longing – among other things, for the cross' (*Markings* 1950: 44, 55). What is meant by this 'cross' is still unclear at this point; what is clear is a predominantly negative view of things. The essence of human existence, the meaning of life and the inadequacy of his own personality – these are Hammarskjöld's topics in these years. In addition, statements about the superficiality of human contact and physical love are veritable cries of loneliness and disappointed or rejected friendship (*Markings* 1950: 28, 45). He often discusses the superficiality of interpersonal dialogue (*Markings* 1950: 8, 39). These expressions of resignation come together in an extremely graphic image in 1950:

> Your ego-love doesn't bloom unless it is sheltered. The rules are simple: don't commit yourself to any one and, therefore, don't allow anyone to come close to you. Simple – and fateful. Its efforts to shelter its love create a ring of cold around the Ego which slowly eats its way inwards towards the core.
>
> (Markings 1950: 22, 43)

These words, at the latest, make it clear that Hammarskjöld was in the middle of a crisis about meaning, life and identity. The question of the meaning and purpose of his gifts, his 'talents' was also asked repeatedly; his career was not enough: 'Time goes by: reputation increases, ability declines' (*Markings* 1950: 17, 41). He accuses himself of ambitiousness (*Markings* 1951: 37, 69) – proof that Hammarskjöld, despite whatever narcissism may come through in these lines, was his own most critical observer.[18] The indefatigability and endless capacity for work that his colleagues so admired at this time take on a very different significance when he tersely writes: 'Work as anaesthetic against loneliness, books as a substitute for people –!' (*Markings* 1952: 4, 82). Above all, he lacks a perspective in life:

> Never let the success hide its emptiness from you, achievement is nothingness, toil its desolation. And so keep alive the incentive to push on further, the pain in the soul which drives us beyond ourselves. Whither? That I don't know. That I don't ask to know.
>
> (Markings 1950: 47, 55)

The idea of sacrifice reappears (*Markings* 1950: 46, 56). Yet Hammarskjöld has no answer to the question for what and to which purpose he should sacrifice himself. Fatalism gains the upper hand: 'Committed to the future – / Even if that only means "*se préparer à bien mourir*"' (*Markings* 1951: 17, 65). In 1952, there is another reference to death: 'The hardest thing – to die *rightly*. – An exam nobody is spared – and how many pass it? And you? You pray for strength to meet the test – but also for leniency on the part of the examiner' (*Markings* 1952: 5, 82). In the same year Hammarskjöld considers the option of suicide, but rejects it:

> Fatigue dulls the pain, but awakes enticing thoughts of death. So! That is the way in which you are tempted to overcome your loneliness – by making the ultimate escape from life. – No! It may be that death is to be your ultimate gift from life: it must not be an act of treachery against it.
>
> (*Markings* 1952: 19, 81)

At the frontier of the unheard-of

In the following entries, the vocabulary of mysticism will increasingly colour the language. The despairing scrutiny of society and his environment that pervaded entries prior to the 1950s turned more and more, and eventually almost exclusively, inwards, but did not yet offer a change in his life's prospects. Hammarskjöld increasingly articulates his self-doubt, the dominating sense of loneliness and the unanswered question of the meaning of his life and the proper use of his talents. Only slowly does a sense of change and of a perspective grow. At the same time, Hammarskjöld has a growing – vaguely formulated – feeling that his situation requires a decision of him: 'There is a point at which everything becomes simple and there is no longer any question of choice, because all you have staked will be lost if you look back. Life's point of no return' (*Markings* 1952: 22, 66). And shortly after this entry one reads:

> Dare he, for whom circumstances make it possible to realize his true destiny, refuse it simply because he is not prepared to give up everything else?
>
> The man who is unwilling to accept the axiom that he who chooses one path is denied the others must try to persuade himself, I suppose, that the logical thing to do is to remain at the crossroads. – But do not blame the man who does not take a path – nor commend him, either.
>
> (*Markings* 1951: 27, 67)

Renewed mention of the crossroads here is accompanied by the thought of the calling, which gradually gains ground in the notes. But for the time being, the nature of this calling, its goal and how it should be realized are left open. It is highly significant, however, that this reflection is followed by the first lengthy passage in which Hammarskjöld grapples with Jesus' fate and the latent thought of sacrifice associated with it. In other words, here is a – diffuse – perspective of imitation or succession (Sundén 1967: 71), at this point surrounded by considerable doubt. Hammarskjöld's search is still encumbered with a number of open questions. He seeks answers in contemplation, expressed in powerful descriptions of nature. Another year passes before, in 1951, there is an indication that his search is moving in the right direction and the crisis is being resolved:

Now. When I have overcome my fears – of the others, of myself, of the underlying darkness:
At the frontier of the unheard-of.
Here ends the known. But, from the source beyond it, something fills my being with its possibilities.
Here desire is purified and made lucid: each action is a preparation for, each choice an assent to the unknown.

(*Markings* 1951: 47, 76)

This assent is still a silver lining on the horizon, but 'Yes' will henceforth play a crucial role in the diary. Hammarskjöld is still at the frontier. The notion of mystic experience intensifies in an almost paradigmatic series of pantheistic experiences with erotic overtones:

So rests the sky against the earth. The dark still tarn in the lap of the forest. As a husband embraces his wife's body in faithful tenderness, so the bare ground and trees are embraced by the still, high, light of the morning. I feel an ache of longing to share in this embrace, to be united and absorbed. A longing like carnal desire, but directed towards earth, water, skies, and returned by the whispers of the trees, the fragrance of the soil, the caresses of the wind, the embrace of the water and light. Content? No, no, no – but refreshed, rested – while waiting.

(*Markings* 1951: 50, 77)

Hammarskjöld ends this year, 1951, with an attempt to define the aforementioned frontier of the unheard-of:

At the frontier of the unheard-of –' The unheard of – perhaps this simply refers to Lord Jim's last meeting with Doramin, when he has attained absolute courage and humility in an absolute loyalty towards himself. Conscious of the guilt, but at the same time conscious of having atoned, so far as atonement is possible in his life – by what he has done for those who are now asking for his life. Untroubled and happy. Like someone wandering by himself along a lonely seashore.

(*Markings* 1951: 62, 80; also Specker 1999: 120–1)

At the beginning of 1952, Hammarskjöld, using these concepts of courage, humility and loyalty towards oneself, talks about a way that has opened up and to which he is now being led. Significantly, in this context he devotes a lengthy section to reflecting on the words: 'Thy will be done –' (see *Markings* 1952: 3, 81). His doubts[19] have lost the shrill urgency and hopelessness of crisis and appear in a much gentler light:

… An intellectual hesitation which demands proofs and logical demonstration prevents me from 'believing' in this, too. Prevents me from expressing and interpreting this reality in intellectual terms. Yet through me there flashes this vision of magnetic field in the soul, created in a timeless present by unknown multitudes, living in holy obedience, whose words and actions are a timeless prayer.

– 'The Communion of Saints' and – within it – an eternal life.

(*Markings* 1952: 14, 84)

It is obvious that many of Hammarskjöld's open questions have been cleared up, without his having found direct answers to them. The growing frequency of inexpressible, unheard-of and indescribable states of mind keeps to the classic path of mystic literature. Hammarskjöld has received the call; however, he still seeks final confirmation in the form of an immediate concern: 'Pray that your loneliness may spur you into finding something to live for, great enough to die for.' And again: 'Give me something to die for – !' (*Markings* 1952: 18/16, 85). Hammarskjöld has found a context and a path for his search, which now focuses single-mindedly on finding a concrete purpose, a mission to which he can commit himself and in so doing realize his true existence. He has arrived at a classic station in mystic thinking: self-realization (to use a modern term) through self-surrender.

The challenge of self-realization through self-surrender

Regardless of whether the reader may follow all of Hammarskjöld's mystic experiences or not, the fact remains that Hammarskjöld's appointment as Secretary-General of the United Nations was an answer to his desire for a mission, was the concrete expression of his call (Progoff 1965: 230–1). Hammarskjöld himself saw the inquiry from New York in this light, as the confirmation of his call and what this actually entailed for him. For him, his term of office as Secretary-General begins under an unequivocal mystic omen. The year 1953 appears to have answered and resolved the crisis in Hammarskjöld's life. As external sign of this breakthrough, the hymn 'Night is drawing night' used as a leitmotif in recent years no longer indicates resignation but heralds a positive attitude:

– Night is drawing night –'
For all that has been – Thanks!
To all that shall be – Yes!

(*Markings* 1953: 1, 89)

Nothing could signal the turnaround in Hammarskjöld's inner life more clearly than these short lines. The feeling of being called and of security in a spiritual context is also expressed in the punctuation; not Hammarskjöld, but God is the author of the change in his life. He feels that his prayer has been heard and he has been called in equal measure:

When in decisive moments – as now – God acts, it is with a stern purposefulness, a Sophoclean irony. When the hour strikes, He takes what is His. What have *you* to say? – Your prayer has been answered, as you know. God has a use for you, even though what He asks doesn't happen to suit you at the moment. God, who abases him whom he raises up.

(*Markings* 1953: 4, 89)

Here for the first time the seeming paradox of self-realization through self-surrender is forcefully acknowledged; henceforth, this paradox runs through the entire diary (*Markings* 1956: 21, 114–15). Equally symptomatic is the joy articulated about and inner acceptance of this seeming paradox (*Markings* 1953: 5, 90).[20] Hammarskjöld will solve this paradox on his birthday in 1959, using the concept of humility:

Humility is just as much the opposite of self-abasement as it is of self-exaltation. To be humble is *not to make comparisons*. Secure in its reality, the self is neither better nor worse, bigger nor smaller, than anything else in the universe. It *is* – is nothing, yet at the same time one with everything. It is in this sense that humility is absolute self-effacement.

To be nothing in the self-effacement of humility, yet, for the sake of the task, to embody its whole weight and importance in your bearing, as the one who has been called to undertake it. To give to people, work, poetry, art, what the self can contribute, and to take, simply and freely, what belongs to it by reason of its identity. Praise and blame, the winds of success and adversity, blow over such a life without leaving a trace or upsetting its balance. Towards this, so help me God –

(*Markings* 1959: 4, 174)

The mystic phrase: 'Not I, but God in me' (*Markings* 1953: 6, 90), embodies the new perspective of 1953. This phrase has led a number of critics to suspect Hammarskjöld of blasphemy. But to repeat: a comparison with the style and content of mystic texts puts this statement in its correct light. The same holds for the following entries:

I am the vessel. The draught is God's. And God is the thirsty one.

He who has surrendered himself to it knows that the Way ends on the Cross – even when it is leading him through the jubilation of Gennesaret or the triumphal entry into Jerusalem.

To be free, to be able to stand up and leave everything behind – without looking back.

To say *Yes* –

(*Markings* 1953: 9/11/12, 91)

Here mention of the Cross refers directly to Jesus' example – the perspective of imitation is openly admitted. The passion and intensity of these statements should be seen against the background of his appointment, which, Hammarskjöld senses, resolves the external crisis of meaning in his life as well. 'Yes' without reservation is Hammarskjöld's answer to his self-doubt: 'To say Yes to life is at one and the same time to say Yes to oneself. / Yes – even to that element in which one is most unwilling to let itself be transformed from a temptation into a strength' (*Markings* 1953: 14, 92). Later, the connection between mystic experience and personal life experience reappears: '… From this perspective, to "believe in God" is to believe in yourself, as self-evident, as "illogical", and as impossible to explain: if I can be, then God *is*' (*Markings* 1956: 13, 127). This new attitude goes hand in hand with thoughts on the concept of maturity, the subject of three entries in 1953.

Although the resolution of Hammarskjöld's inner quest predates his appointment as Secretary-General, this event intensifies it. The basically positive tenor of 1953, building on the trailblazing 1952, continues in 1954, when after quoting the hymn line he adds: 'Let me finish what I have been permitted to begin. / Let me give all without any assurance of increase' (*Markings* 1954: 1, 95). Looking back, Hammarskjöld compares his seeking to blindman's bluff. He also considers, in typically mystic language, that at another level of perception finding and successfully searching are easy and self-evident (*Markings* 1955: 19, 107). Increasingly, he finds answers to the questions that surfaced during the crisis of meaning in the preceding years:

> Then I saw that the wall has never been there, that the 'unheard-of' is here and this, not something and somewhere else, that the 'offering' is here and now, always and everywhere – that the 'surrendered' is what, in me, God gives of Himself to Himself.
>
> (*Markings* 1954: 5, 96)

The unmistakable mystic mood of these passages is underscored by a quotation from St John of the Cross. The unheard-of has become reality for Hammarskjöld, as two successive passages show:

> The 'unheard-of' – to be in the hands of God. – Once again a reminder that this is all that remains for you to live for – and once more the feeling of disappointment which shows how slow you are to learn.
> So long as you abide in the Unheard-of, you are beyond and above – to hold fast to this must be the First Commandment in your spiritual discipline.
>
> (*Markings* 1954: 20/25, 100–1)

The once dominant question of death also appears in another light. A 1955 entry reads:

> In the old days, Death was always one of the party. Now he sits next to me at the dinner table: I have to make friends with him.

In this intuitive 'anamnesis' which has become my Ariadne's thread through life – step by step, day by day – the end is now as real to me as tomorrow morning's foreseen tasks.

(*Markings* 1955: 18, 106–7)

The mystic experience cannot be accurately described; however, death losing its frightening connotations is a typical sign of mystic experience (Borchert 1997: 21). Hammarskjöld's perception of a new emotional and spiritual state is always precarious. Yet it gives him a basic security, as an entry about a dream expresses in late 1955:

In a dream I walked with God through the deep places of creation; past walls that receded and gates that opened, through hall after hall of silence, darkness and refreshment – the dwelling place of souls acquainted with light and warmth – until, around me, was an infinity into which we all flowed together and lived anew, like the rings made by raindrops falling upon wide expanses of calm dark waters.

(*Markings* 1955: 55, 118)

Given the stress, disappointments, crises and challenges of his office, this equanimity does not persist unscathed. Particularly after his re-appointment, death is again the subject of a number of entries: 'Do not seek death. Death will find you. But seek the road which makes death a fulfilment' (*Markings* 1957: 42, 159). However, in classic mystic manner, the mystic perspective provides a basis for his unflagging commitment.[21] Interestingly, the entries for 1961 contain verses that Hammarskjöld started writing on 7 July 1960 and continued until early 1961: visions of death and sacrifice that have led to speculation about premonitions of the crash in Ndola (*Markings* 1961: 6, 206–7). Their tenor also coloured the entries in June and July:

Standing naked
Where they have placed me,
Nailed to the target
By their first arrows.

Again a bow is drawn,
Again an arrow flies,
– and misses.
Are they pretending?
Did a hand shake,
Or was it the wind?

What have I to fear?
If their arrows hit,
If their arrows kill,

What is there in that
To cry about?

Others have gone before,
Others will follow.

(Markings 1961: 9, 210)

Tired
And lonely.
So tired
The heart aches.
Meltwater trickles
Down the rocks.
The fingers are numb,
The knees tremble.
It is now,
Now, that you must not give in.

On the path of the others
Are resting places,
Places in the sun
Where they can meet.
But this
Is your path,
And it is now,
Now, that you must not fail.
Weep
If you can,
Weep,
But do not complain.
The way chose you –
And you must be thankful.

(Markings 1961: 12, 213; dated 6 July 1961)

Van Dusen disputes the view that here Hammarskjöld is voicing premonitions or even anticipations of his later plane crash. He remarks that fresh sheets of paper lay next to the dairy, and *Markings* does not create the impression that it had been completed (Dusen 1965: 35). In any case, the tone of the final entry in the diary dated 24 August 1961 is unmistakably positive. The challenge of loneliness is not overcome with his new position, but in contrast to the helpless entries in the early years, the predominant tone is conciliatory and optimistic:

Is this a new country
In another world of reality
Than Day's?
Or did I live there

Before day was?

I awoke
To an ordinary morning with grey light
Reflected from the street,
But still remembered
The dark-blue night
Above the tree line,
The open moor in moonlight,
The crest in shadow.
Remembered other dreams
Of the same mountain country:
Twice I stood on its summits,
I stayed by its remotest lake,
And followed the river
Toward its source.
The seasons have changed
And the light
And the weather
And the hour.
But it is the same land
And I begin to know the map
And to get my bearings.

(*Markings* 1961: 19, 222)[22]

This short excursion through the entries does not touch on, let alone illuminate, all the facets of the diary. Serious scientific analysis of personal expressions, professions and confessions has fairly narrow limits if it is not to drift into dubious, ex-post depth analyses of Hammarskjöld's personality. Nevertheless, it should be clear that any examination of his personality that excludes this aspect will be seriously flawed. The next step is to study the consequences of Hammarskjöld's mystic experience and reading of classic mystic texts for his political ethics.

Christian mysticism: serving in the imitation of Christ

In this section we shall analyse references to Hammarskjöld's favourite mystic thinkers and their ideas with a view to establishing their influence on the ethics expressed in the diary. The 'classic' authors in question are Meister Eckhart, Thomas à Kempis, and St John of the Cross. How did Hammarskjöld become acquainted with these texts? Some will have been recommended by Sven Stolpe, a boyhood friend (Simon 1967: 42). In time, Hammarskjöld himself developed a deep, abiding interest in the mystics – already in his youth he often mentions Christian devotional literature in letters to friends (Birnbaum 2000). Several quotations in the diary underline Hammarskjöld's on-going interest in these texts (Hughes 1995). Which thoughts and arguments did Hammarskjöld borrow from the medieval mystics, how did he process them and integrate them into his thinking?

Meister Eckhart: 'habitual will'

The sheer number of quotations from Meister Eckhart indicates the importance Hammarskjöld must have attached to this leading figure in German mysticism (1260–1327).[23] Hammarskjöld quotes from a 1934 edition that he probably acquired shortly after it appeared (Meister Eckhart 1934).[24] The book lay right next to his writing desk; an official telegram from April 1956 served as a bookmark at a place quoted in the diary at the time (Sundén 1967: 52). Once again, a triviality points to the close connection between Hammarskjöld's outer and inner life. To analyse this connection more closely, we first need to elaborate on some of the principal characteristics of Meister Eckhart's mysticism. Borchert gives a brief list of Eckhart's specific contributions to mysticism. He is said to be the first mystic to formulate the following:

> – That we must come to self-realization through self-knowledge: through the knowledge that we ourselves are nothing, yet at the same time noble, because we are from God.
> – That the highest form of mysticism leads to deeds.
> – That the last measure of our actions lies in ourselves: in the 'cause' from which God wants to be born in us, from our conscience.
> – That in the face of God we must become ourselves: 'Leave God for God's sake'. Bid farewell to him to the extent that he is the object of our having and desiring.
> – That rejecting external things, asceticism, goes hand in hand with openness towards everybody and everything in daily life.
> – That mysticism is a dual process: the more we concentrate everything in us on the 'cause', to this extent will God come into us.
>
> (1997: 238)

Some of these points are obvious leitmotifs in Hammarskjöld's diary. However, Eckhart's version of an active outward-looking mysticism deserves special attention. His sermon on Mary and Martha formulates this view virtually as a manifesto (Meister Eckhart 1979b: 280–9; Aulén 1969: 116). In Hammarskjöld's edition of the Sermons it is heavily underlined in pencil. According to Wehr (1994: 90; Sundén 1967: 74–5), the text is important because, among other things, Eckhart wanted to stimulate an 'active imitation of Christ among his listeners' and 'transform inner experiences into the practical deeds of charity' (Wehr 1995a: 198).

Eckhart's emphasis on the active in his interpretation of the story of Mary and Martha goes, exegetically speaking, 'against the literal meaning' (Werner 1990: 201; on the background Eckert 1981: 109–10; Leppin 1997). More crucial for this study than the question of exegetic orthodoxy, however, is the fact that Hammarskjöld's many references to Eckhart's interpretation places him in this tradition of outward-looking mysticism. For him ethics and mysticism are constitutively linked, as the following diary entry on his birthday in 1958 makes clear:

> ... Still a few years more, and then? The only value of a life is its content – for others. Apart from any value it may have for others, my life is worse than death. Therefore, in my great loneliness, serve others. Therefore: how incredibly great is what I have been given, and how meaningless what I have to 'sacrifice'.
>
> (*Markings* 1958: 9, 166)

But Eckhart means incomparably more to Hammarskjöld than just a witness to active mysticism. A closer look at the quotations reveals Hammarskjöld's particular interest in three interlinked concepts of Eckhart's: detachment, the birth of God in the soul and habitual will.

Eckhart's concept of detachment has many parallels with the quest that Hammarskjöld describes in the earlier passages in his diary. In Eckhart's view, the drift and the criticism of the craving for recognition expressed there are obstacles in the path of mystic experience: 'Man's own will leads to unrest and the loss of inner unity. Only detachment, the everlasting letting go of own will, makes possible creative deeds in inner union with God' (Brandt 1995: 229). Thus, Eckhart does not view detachment as rejecting the world, but as detachment from the egoistic striving and the purposeless hectic of many activities.[25] In this sense, the concept was important for Hammarskjöld. A comparable instance of this record appears in the sermon to Mary and Martha, which Hammarskjöld underlined in pencil in his edition:

> Three points are particularly important in what we do, namely that one acts in accordance with order, reason and consciousness. By 'in accordance with order' I mean that whatever the situation one is ready for the next demand; 'in accordance with reason' that at that time one does not know of a better way of acting; and 'in accordance with consciousness' that through hard work one is constantly aware of the life-giving truth with its sweet now.
>
> (Meister Eckhart 1979b: 285)

The point is not the fundamental renunciation of the world's concerns, challenges and risks, but the dissociation from alleged but ultimately wrong scales (Meister Eckhart 1991: 141). Eckhart (ibid.: 146) uses the image of a slate covered in writing that must first be wiped clean so that God can write on it. In an entry on the night before his fifty-second birthday Hammarskjöld uses the image of a lens – it is difficult to overlook the parallels to Eckhart:

> You are not the oil, you are not the air – merely the point of combustion, the flash-point where the light is born. You are merely the lens in the beam. You can only receive, give and possess the light as a lens does.

If you seek yourself, 'your rights', you prevent the oil and air from meeting in the flame, you rob the lens of its transparency. Sanctity – either to the Light or to be self-effaced in the Light, so that it may be born, self-effaced so that it may be focused or spread wider.

You will know Life and be acknowledged by it according to your degree of transparency, your capacity, that is, to vanish as an *end*, and remain purely as a *means*.

(*Markings* 1957: 28/29, 155–6)

In his quest for the unheard-of, Hammarskjöld goes through a cleansing process – a classic phase in mystic thought and experience also described by Eckhart. Eckhart gives this personal demand for maturity (which, incidentally, reverses the Kantian principle often quoted by Hammarskjöld that man should not be treated only as a means but as an end in himself) greater significance by linking it with another concept, that of the habitual will (Brandt 1995: 220–31). This concept is noted in Hammarskjöld's diary for the first time in a direct quotation from Eckhart on 8 April 1956:

'There is a contingent and non-essential will: and there is, providential and creative, an habitual will. God has never given Himself, and never will, to a will alien to His own: where He finds His will, He gives Himself' (Meister Eckhart).

(*Markings* 1956: 11, 126)

This is a key concept for Hammarskjöld, underscored by the fact that he soon returns to this topic:

Semina motuum. In us the creative instinct became will. In order to grow beautifully like a tree, we have to attain a peaceful self-unity in which creative will is transformed into instinct. – Eckhart's 'habitual will'.

(*Markings* 1956: 31, 135)

Eckhart's concept of habitual will is a term for the mystic relationship between God and the person who trusts in God. Accordingly, man must discover his inner, 'divine' core that allows him to be receptive to the will of God. If this condition is fulfilled, the divine will and the individual will become one. The direction and intensity of God's will becomes instinctive, which is not experienced as a limitation of personal will, but as the highest form of freedom, as being heard and as a calling.[26] Hammarskjöld grappled with this topic particularly intensively in 1956, during the tension and strain of the Suez Crisis (see 'UN presence and blue helmets' in Chapter 4). Reviewing the successful crisis management in an entry on Christmas Eve 1956, he quotes Eckhart on God '[I]t is He, indeed, who does what we do ...' (*Markings* 1956: 57, 143). The important point of this habitual will is that it does not go hand in hand with a supposed loss of freedom: 'Hammarskjöld sees "Yes to fate" not as fatalism, but as the undertaking to do God's will' (Brandt

1995: 225). On Christmas Day 1956 he comes back to this thought – inspired by the feast day of Christ's Birth – and reflects on Eckhart's word about God's birth in the soul (which goes back to Origines) (Haas 1984: 162–3; Winkler 1997: 81–107):

> 'Of the Eternal Birth'– to me, this now says everything there is to be said about what I have learned and have still to learn.
> 'The soul that would experience this birth must detach herself from outward things: within herself completely at one with herself. You must have an exalted mind and a *burning* heart in which, nevertheless, reign *silence* and stillness' (Meister Eckhart).
>
> *(Markings* 1956: 58, 143)

The paradox that silence is the source of greatest activity runs parallel to the motif of self-realization through self-surrender and suffering (Jaspert 1992b), as Hammarskjöld, following similar thoughts of Eckhart, describes in 1958:

> That piece of pagan anthropomorphism: the belief that, in order to educate us, God wishes us to suffer. How far from this is the assent to suffering, when it strikes us because we have obeyed what we have seen to be God's will.
>
> *(Markings* 1958: 5, 164)

Self-realization through self-surrender is not just a matter of actions and works, but, especially, of outlook, as Hammarskjöld underlines with another Eckhart quotation on 16 February 1958:

> 'Believe me: this, too, belongs to perfection, that a man so undertakes works, that all his work fuse into one work. This must be done "in the Kingdom of God". For I tell you the truth: all works which man does outside of the Kingdom of God are dead, but those he does in the Kingdom of God are alive ... just as God is not distracted or changed by any of his words, nor, too, is the soul so long as it works according to the law of God's Kingdom. Such men, therefore, may do works or do them not, but remain all the while undisturbed. *For works neither gives them anything, nor takes anything from them*' (Meister Eckhart).
> 'In the Kingdom of God –; – all works are equal there, my smallest is as my greatest, my greatest as my smallest. – About works in themselves there is something divisive which causes a division in the souls of men, and brings them to the brink of disquiet' (Meister Eckhart).
>
> *(Markings* 1958: 2/3, 163–4)

This takes up the aforementioned idea of security and inner stability through mystic experience, an aspect dealt with in great detail in an entry on 4 August 1959, shortly after Hammarskjöld's fifty-fourth birthday:

To have humility is to experience reality, not in relation to ourselves, but in his sacred independence. It is to see, judge and act from the point of rest in ourselves. Then, how much disappears, and all that remains falls into place.

In the point of the rest at the center of our being, we encounter a world where all things are at rest the same way. Then a tree becomes a mystery, a cloud a revelation, each man a cosmos of whose riches we can only catch glimpses. This life of simplicity is simple, but it opens to us a book in which we never get beyond the first syllable.

(Markings 1959: 4, 174)

With this we have established basic principles of Hammarskjöld's mysticism, and shall now broaden their compass by reference to St John of the Cross and Thomas à Kempis.

St John of the Cross: 'The Dark Night of the Soul'

St John of the Cross (1542–91) is the only mystic mentioned by name in the Murrow interview, which, like the references in the diary, underscores his significance for Hammarskjöld.[27] Whereas Eckhart's mysticism has a pronounced activist tenor, that of John of the Cross is more contemplative. At the same time, he was extremely dedicated to various concerns; but his enormous influence in social and religious matters was rooted in his deep contemplation. His principal work, 'The Dark Night of the Soul' (St John of the Cross 1995; Aulén 1969: 60) captivates by its 'lyricism glowing with mystic fervour' (Wehr 1995a: 159).[28] Once again, a few references are enough to establish a relationship with the diary. Associating the hymn of approaching night, one of Hammarskjöld's leitmotifs particularly in the years of crisis and quest (Meadow 1984), with the mysticism of John of the Cross considerably expands its reach and depth.[29] John uses the image of the dark night to describe necessary stages in preparation and purification that eventually culminate in the 'unio mystica'. It is not difficult to imagine that in John's powerful description of the mystic quest Hammarskjöld sees a means of expression for his own mystic experience. In the Murrow interview, Hammarskjöld cited John's definition of faith as the union of God with the soul – a thought reminiscent of Eckhart's birth of God in the soul and present in many mystic writings. Huls points out that, strictly speaking, John does not use the definition of faith that Hammarskjöld formulates (Huls 1991).[30] Rather, he talks repeatedly of faith as a 'means' of uniting the soul with God. Notwithstanding this, there are a number of passages in the writings of John of the Cross and in Hammarskjöld's diary that are similar to and support the meaning of the Murrow interview. Hammarskjöld writes in 1954, probably in connection with his radio interview, which was published the same year:

'Faith is the marriage of God and the Soul' (St John of the Cross).

Faith *is*: It cannot, therefore, be comprehended, far less identified with the formulae in which we paraphrase what is.

– '*en una noche oscura*'. The dark night of the Soul – so dark that we may not even look for faith. The night in Gethsemane when the last friends left you have fallen asleep, all the others are seeking the downfall and God is silent, as the marriage is consummated.

(*Markings* 1954: 7, 97)

Here Hammarskjöld undoubtedly quotes John of the Cross to express a personal, similar experience. To describe this relationship more precisely, we need to re-examine John's definition of the union of God and the soul. In 'The Ascent of Mount Carmel' he writes (without referring directly to the concept of 'faith'):

And so, when we speak of union of the soul with God, we speak not of this substantial union which is continually being wrought, but of the union and transformation of the soul with God, which is not being wrought continually, but only when there is produced that likeness that comes from love …. The former is natural, the latter supernatural. And the latter comes to pass when the two wills – namely that of the soul and that of God – are conformed together in one, and there is naught in the one that is repugnant to the other. And thus, when the soul rids itself totally of that which is repugnant to the Divine will and conforms not with it, it is transformed in God through love.[31]

In an entry on 10 April 1958, Hammarskjöld illustrates the underlying attitude, the fundamental relationship between God and the believer:

In the faith which is 'God's marriage with the soul', you are one in God and, God is wholly in you
Just as for you, He is wholly in all you meet.
With this faith, in prayer you descend into yourself, to meet the Other,
in the steadfastness and light of the union,
see that all things stand, like yourself, alone before God.
And that each of you acts in an act of creation, conscious, because you are a human being with human responsibilities, but governed, nevertheless, by the power beyond human consciousness which has created man.
You are liberated from things, but you encounter in them an experience which has purity and clarity of revelation.
In the faith which is 'God's marriage with the soul', everything, therefore has a meaning,
So live, then, that you may use what has been put into your hand …

(*Markings* 1958: 7, 165)

This elucidates another aspect of Hammarskjöld's mysticism: besides Eckhart's ethic imperative of active mysticism, we have here the fundamental motivation that ensues from the divine relationship and makes all things possible: 'To have faith – not to hesitate. Also: not to doubt. "Faith is the marriage of God and the Soul." In that case, certainty of God's omnipotence *through* the soul: With God, all things are possible, *because* faith can move mountains' (*Markings* 1956: 25, 132). The demand to act as God requires is combined with trust and hope in the meaning and the success of such acts (as measured by divine, not human criteria). Ultimately, this leads back to the tension between self-realization and self-surrender, as another reference to God's marriage to the soul in a 1957 entry makes clear:

> Courage and love: equivalent and related expressions for your bargain with Life. You are willing to 'pay' what your heart commands you to give. Two associated reflexes to the sacrificial act, conditioned by a self-chosen effacement of the personality in One. One result of 'God's marriage to the Soul' is a union with other people which does not draw back before the ultimate self-surrender.
>
> (*Markings* 1957: 47, 160)

Thus, Hammarskjöld's reflections on St John of the Cross are very close to similar concepts of Eckhart (in particular his concepts of detachment and habitual will). There are also close parallels in his use of images to describe the way to union. According to John, too, various conditions must be fulfilled to achieve God's marriage with the soul: fundamental is the grace of God's love, and then the receptivity of the soul, which John describes using the following image:

> A ray of sunlight is striking a window. If the window is in any way stained or misty, the sun's ray will be unable to illumine it and transform it into its own light, totally, as it would if it were clean of all these things, and pure …[32]

The parallels between this and Meister Eckhart's image of the slate wiped clean and Hammarskjöld's transparent lens are unmistakable. Moreover, there is an obvious similarity between this passage and an entry from the early 1940s:

> You cannot play with the animal in you without becoming wholly animal, play with falsehood without forfeiting your right to truth, play with cruelty without losing your sensitivity of mind. He who wants to keep his garden tidy doesn't reserve a plot for weeds.
>
> (*Markings* 1941–2: 18, 15)

In addition, John refers to love – the word that Hammarskjöld particularly emphasized in the Murrow interview. This word gives John's mystic statement an ethical aspect. Hammarskjöld explained:

> 'Love' – that much misused and misinterpreted word – for them [the mystics] meant simply an overflowing of the strength with which they felt themselves filled when living in true self-oblivion. And this love found natural expressions in an unhesitant fulfillment of duty and in an unreserved acceptance of life, whatever it brought them personally of toil, suffering – or happiness.
>
> (CF II: 196)

John has his own understanding of love: 'For him love means: entering into a relationship, responding to affection, opening up to the counterpart in every situation, to every he–she–it as to a Thou' (Dobhan and Körner 1995: 14). The basic prerequisite for this attitude is again humility and the withdrawal of oneself, for 'connecting-with and self-reference or tying-everything-to-oneself are opposites' (ibid.). Hence, in the texts of John of the Cross Hammarskjöld finds many similarities with the convictions that he had already found in Eckhart. Over and above this, John's concept of love helps Hammarskjöld far more than Eckhart to describe the intensity of his mystic experience and his associated, often desperate quest. John's statements of prerequisites for the mystic experience influence Hammarskjöld decisively through the key concepts of humility and withdrawal of the self. In addition, John emphasizes the concrete connecting with other people that must stand at the beginning of mystically motivated activity. To complete the profile of Hammarskjöld's mysticism we must now look at the contribution of Thomas à Kempis.

Thomas à Kempis: 'The Imitation of Christ'

'The Imitation of Christ' is attributed to Thomas à Kempis (1379–1471), making him one of the great mystic writers. The history of the reception and influence of the book is considerable (e.g. in the work of Maximilian Kolbe, Dietrich Bonhoeffer and Edith Stein; Wehr 1995a: 212). Thomas himself described the central themes of his text as follows: 'Whoever desires to understand and take delight in the words of Christ must strive to conform his whole life in Him' (1952: 9). The particular significance of Thomas à Kempis's book for Hammarskjöld is illustrated by a quotation from it in his diary the day before his departure for New York:[33]

> Their lives grounded in and sustained by God, they are incapable of any kind of pride; because they give back to God all the benefits He has bestowed on them; they do not glorify each other, but do all things to the Glory of God alone.
>
> (*Markings* 1953: 8, 91)

Here we find the ideas of subordination to God, humility and modesty that Thomas regards as essential for imitating Christ. These ideas are also present in Eckhart and John, albeit differently formulated and emphasized.[34] However, the similarity between the ideas of Eckhart, John of the Cross and Thomas goes even further thanks to their stress on active mysticism: 'This spirituality centres not on ecstatic intensity in union with Christ, but on the life in imitation of the historical Son of God' (Janowski 1978: 28). The idea of linking absolute devotion, high demands on oneself and constant self-criticism (Lipsey 1997) appears in the second direct quotation from Thomas. Hammarskjöld noted Thomas's typical admonition in a diary entry in 1955 – about the time of his visit to China (see 'The instrument of "private diplomacy"' in Chapter 4):

The purer the eye of her attention, the more power the soul finds within herself. But it is very rare to find a soul who is entirely free, whose purity is not soiled by the stain of some secret desire of her own. Strive, then, constantly to purify the eye of your attention until it becomes utterly simple and direct.

(*Markings* 1955: 3, 103)

This absolute devotion and obligation attained by imitating Christ is also the subject of the third passage Hammarskjöld takes from Thomas. On his fiftieth birthday he notes: 'Why do seek rest? You were only created to labour' (*Markings* 1955: 21, 107). However, Hammarskjöld's commitment and intensive efforts at imitation do not lead him to identify with Christ, as the following quotation of 25 December 1955 underscores:

But when in this way they taste God, be it in Himself or in His works, they recognise at the same time that there is a distance between the creature and the Creator, time and eternity. … Enlighten my soul that she may find her life and joy in Thee, until, transported out of herself by the excess of happiness, she binds herself to Thee with all her powers and in all her motions.

(*Markings* 1955: 53, 118.)

Apart from the unbridgeable distance to God, imitation of Christ for Thomas means a union of the will, not of the being (Hughes 1995: 177). According to Sundén (1967: 64), it is not a question of identifying with Christ, 'but of an interpretation of Christ: Hammarskjöld seeks to understand Jesus from his own situation in life'. In this sense, Thomas à Kempis' book is a constant appeal and guide to 'Christian' life. Its uncompromising approach is reflected in the quotation in Hammarskjöld's final entry in 1955: 'Il faut donner tout pour tout' (*Markings* 1955: 66, 122). As in the cases of Eckhart and St John of the Cross, Hammarskjöld does not accept all of Thomas à Kempis's ideas (Erling 1987: 353). This is underscored by the fact that Hammarskjöld only rarely attributes any of his fundamental ideas to a single author. For instance, on 30 March 1956, Good Friday, Hammarskjöld quotes Blaise Pascal in his reflections on the Imitation:

The third hour. And the ninth. – They are here. And now. They are now.
'Jesus will be in agony even to the end of the world. We must not sleep during that time' (Pascal).
We must not – And for the watcher is the far-off present also present in his contact with mankind among whom, at every moment, Jesus dies in someone who has followed the trail marks of the inner road to the end:
love and patience
righteousness and humility,
faith and courage,
stillness.

(*Markings* 1956: 10, 126)

Hammarskjöld also cites biblical passages in which he recognizes the call to imitate Christ in the manner described above (Sundén 1967: 58–60):

> '... But when they shall deliver you up, take no thought how or what ye shall speak: for it shall be given you in that same hour what ye shall speak. For it is not ye that speaks, but the Spirit of your Father which speaketh in you' (*Markings* 1956: 29, 134).
> '... O Caesarea Phillippi: To accept condemnation of the way as its fulfillment, its definition, to accept this both when it is chosen and when it is realized' (*Markings* 1945–9: 13, 36).

It should not be forgotten that for Hammarskjöld imitation is 'not identity but discipleship' (Aulén 1969: 4). It was more important for him to grasp the principle of Jesus than to exalt himself. In this context, imitation is above all a personal challenge inseparably bound to ethical concerns: 'Therefore, before all else, attend diligently to your own affairs; then you may properly be concerned for your neighbour also' (Thomas à Kempis 1952: 71). Hammarskjöld's social commitment is singular in that it starts with an unsparing look at himself; in the context of Thomas à Kempis's *Imitation of Christ* this has a political implication: 'Firstly, be peaceful yourself, and you will be able to bring peace to others' (ibid.: 70). Against this backdrop we shall sum up the above with a profile of Hammarskjöld's ethical mysticism as revealed in his diary entries.

A profile of Hammarskjöld's mysticism: reason, ethics, universality

Hammarskjöld's own summary of his mystic experience in an entry on Whit Sunday 1961 illustrates the impossibility of adequately expressing it in words, or defining it more precisely. Given the concentrated array of topics from previous years, the entry reads as a review after paging through the entries:

> I don't know Who – or what – put the question, I don't know when it was put. I don't even remember answering. But at some moment I did answer Yes to Someone – or Something – and from that hour I was certain that existence is meaningful and that, therefore, my life, in self-surrender, had a goal.
> From that moment I have known what it means 'not to look back' and 'to take no thought for the morrow.'
> Led by the Ariadne's thread of my answer through the labyrinth of Life, I came to the place where I realized that the Way leads to a triumph which is a catastrophe, and to a catastrophe which is a triumph, that the price for committing one's life would be reproach, and that the only elevation possible to man lies in the depth of humiliation. After that, the word 'courage' lost its meaning, since nothing could be taken from me.
> As I continued along the Way, I learned, step by step, word by word, that behind every saying in the Gospels stands one man and one man's experience.

Also behind the prayer that the cup might pass from him and his promise to drink it. Also behind each of the words from the Cross.

(Markings 1961: 5, 205)

This touches on several points including the predominant idea of the Imitation in which life acquires a meaning that gives certainty and insight, and therefore constant peace and inner equilibrium. With this in mind, Hammarskjöld described mysticism to his friend Bo Beskow as a 'counterpoint to this enormously exposed and public life' (quoted in Beskow 1969: 32). This inner strength makes it possible for him to accept the paradox of self-realization through self-surrender. The person of Jesus Christ is the crucial point of orientation; his 'human' side is the guarantee that imitation is a viable option despite man's faults. Hammarskjöld's colleagues and staff were aware of the resultant peace and stability: in his review of the diary, Urquhart (1964: 239) writes of a 'continuing effort to preserve the still center of contemplation and mystical experience which makes it possible for the outer world of action to be faced from an impregnable position of spiritual calm and strength'. As shown above, Meister Eckhart, St John of the Cross and Thomas à Kempis are the primary sources for Hammarskjöld's mystic profile with its emphasis on active mysticism, habitual will, outer activity through inner experience, self-realization through self-surrender, humility and the undertaking to imitate Christ. Other factors that shaped Hammarskjöld's strongly ethical mysticism include the relationship between mysticism and reason, the ethical consequence of mystic experience and the universality of mystic experience.

The relationship between mysticism and reason

The first point to note is that Hammarskjöld's mystic thought did not contradict the highly rational manner of the Secretary-General's public image. For Hammarskjöld, reason and mysticism are not opposites; indeed, they can be mutually conditional. In Hammarskjöld's view, reason can be the starting point of a way of thinking that leads to mysticism, and vice versa: the everyday consequences of mystic thinking can be highly rational. In this context, the still aimless description of a mystical longing in 1950 that grew out of the reflection on a Kantian maxim reads as a personal programme (Aulén 1969: 24):

'Treat others as ends, never as means.' And myself as an end only in my capacity as a means: to shift the dividing line in my being between subject and object to a position where the subject, even if it is in me, is outside and above me – so that my *whole* being may become an instrument for that which is greater than I.

(Markings 1950: 52, 57)

This passage in the edition of Kant's *Metaphysics of Morals* in Hammarskjöld's private library is heavily underlined.[35] Hammarskjöld adopts Kant's view as a guideline for his relations with others – but, for mystic reasons, not for his personal life. Later, in connection with the above-mentioned parable of the lens, he returns to this idea and demands of himself '... according to your degree of transparency, your capacity, that is, to vanish as an end, and remain purely as a means' (*Markings* 1957: 29, 156). According to Hammarskjöld, only through personal humility can people realize the Kantian maxim. Here, reason and elements of mysticism merge seamlessly and this mutual complementarity is a much discussed reference point in the literature on mystic experience. In 1955, Hammarskjöld writes a lengthy passage on the constitutive connection between reason and mysticism that, typically, sets a high standard for himself:

> How would a moral sense of Reason – and of Society – have evolved without the martyrs to the faith? Indeed, how could this moral sense have escaped withering away, had it not constantly be watered by the feeder-stream of power that issues from those who have forgotten themselves in God? The rope over the abyss is held taut by those who, faithful to faith, which is the perpetual ultimate sacrifice, give it anchorage in Heaven.
>
> 'Those whose souls are married to God have been declared the salt of the earth – woe betide them, if the salt should lose its savour.'
>
> (*Markings* 1955: 9, 105)

At this point at the latest it is necessary to mention another influence in Hammarskjöld's mysticism. As mentioned above when discussing Hammarskjöld's annual reports, Henri Bergson was a crucial influence on Hammarskjöld who owned a copy of Bergson's book on the two sources of morality and religion, published in 1932 (Bergson 1992). Some of Bergson's formulations on the nature of 'dynamic religion', which in his view is driven by the example and witness of mystic experiences of individuals, are surprisingly similar to statements by Hammarskjöld. A comparison between Hammarskjöld's quotation of the 'moral sense of reason' and a passage in Bergson reveals unmistakable similarities:

> Would the philosophers themselves have so confidently laid down the principle, so little in keeping with everyday experience, that all men participate equally in a higher being, if there had not been mystics to embrace all humanity in one simple indivisible love?
>
> (ibid.: 182)

The idea of imitation, the principle of love, the potential of unbounded energy and the union of divine and human will – Bergson has fitted all of these into the categories of his life view: 'In our eyes, the ultimate end of mysticism is the establishment of a contact, and thus of a partial unity with the creative effort revealed by life' (ibid.: 172). For Bergson (like Hammarskjöld), this type of mysticism, which he finds primarily among Christian mystics, necessarily goes hand in hand with action.

The ethical consequence of mystical experience

Hammarskjöld has a very special understanding of mysticism, rooted in self-realization through self-surrender, yet compatible with or open to reason. This understanding includes the ethical consequence of mystic experience, as expressed in the following entry that contrasts sharply with an internalized concept of mysticism:

> ... – a contact with reality light and intense like the touch of a loved hand: a union in self-surrender without self-destruction where his heart was lucid and his mind loving. In sun and wind, how near and how remote –. How different from what the knowing ones call Mysticism.
>
> (*Markings* 1955: 31, 110)

The hermit's mysticism does not interest Hammarskjöld. 'Knowing ones' is Hammarskjöld's ironic opinion of an intellectual view of mysticism in contradistinction to his active approach to mysticism: '[F]or Hammarskjöld, mystics are real flesh and blood persons who have chosen to risk a lifetime in service' (Hardy 1978: 271). Hammarskjöld himself notes succinctly at the end of 1955:

> The 'mystical experience.' Always here and now – in that freedom which is one distance, in that stillness which is born of silence. But – this is a freedom in the midst of other human beings, the silence a silence among people. The mystery is a constant reality to him, who, in this world, is free from self-concern, a reality that grows peaceful and mature before the receptive attention of assent.
>
> In our time the way to salvation is necessarily through action.
>
> (*Markings* 1955: 65, 122)[36]

This provides the justification for the union or symbiosis that Auden emphasized between (what he called) *via activa* and *contemplativa*: to stand among other human beings and yet free from 'worldly' egoism; 'detached' in Meister Eckhart's sense. The bridge between the two is Hammarskjöld's demands on himself that run as leitmotif through a series of entries (*Markings* 1925–30: 9, 8; 1925–30: 11, 8; 1956: 34, 136; 1957: 11, 150; 1957: 19, 153 and 1957: 25, 154, 9, 150).

The universality of mystic traditions

In the introduction to this chapter we emphasized that mysticism is a basic spiritual phenomenon shared, in various forms, by all world religions.[37] According to one of his colleagues, in his last years Hammarskjöld's spirituality increasingly aspired to a universal claim that transcended an exclusively Christian view (reference in Dusen 1965: 175). Aulén comments: 'Hammarskjöld has searched – we might say, eagerly searched – for statements that can transcend the barriers between different religions' (1969: 45; see also Hartman 1966: 114). Interestingly, the idea of a universal experience had already been considered by Bergson (Wehr 1994: 125; Bergson 1992).[38] In this context, the following entry is symptomatic; Hammarskjöld ends it with the note that the author is the Chinese philosopher Tzu Ssu, and points out the similarity between his thoughts and those of Eckhart:

> The ultimate experience is the same for all:
> 'Only the most absolute sincerity under heaven can bring the inborn talent to the full and empty the chalice of the nature. He who can totally sweep clean the chalice of himself can carry the inborn nature of others to its fulfilment … this clarifying activity has no limit, it neither stops nor stays … it stands in the emptiness above with the sun, seeing and judging, interminable in space and time, searching, enduring … unseen it causes harmony; unmoving it transforms; unmoved it perfects' (Tzu Ssu, not Eckhart).
>
> (*Markings* 1956: 30, 134)

This literary trick underlines Hammarskjöld's intention 'to view Eckhart's "habital will" as a specific form of a universal experience, an experience expressed by other thinkers and in other religions' (Brandt 1995: 230). But there are further parallels, as Hammarskjöld exemplifies in the draft of a unity of Christian and Confucian trinity (Aulén 1969: 48):

> – looking straight into one's heart –
> (as we can do in the mirror-image of the Father)
> – watching with affection the way people grow –
> (as in imitation of the Son)
> – coming to rest in perfect equity.
> (as in the fellowship of the Holy Ghost)
> Like the ultimate experience, our ethical experience is the same for all. Even the Way of the Confucian world is a 'Trinity'
> With the love of Him who knows all,
> With the patience of Him whose now is eternal,
> With the righteousness of Him who has never failed,
> With the humility of Him who has suffered all the possibilities of betrayal.
>
> (*Markings* 1956: 32/33, 135)

Hence, for Hammarskjöld the basic accord of love, patience, righteousness and humility in ethical mysticism is also universally applicable. Apart from these Confucian parallels,[39] it is interesting to observe that in one place Hammarskjöld also quotes the poet Rumi, who practised Sufism, the Islamic form of mysticism (see also Erling 1987: 348). This knowledge of potential common interests was important for Hammarskjöld in his 'worldwide service as Secretary-General of the United Nations' (Aulén 1969: 50). The search of an acceptable ethical foundation for his work was always at the back of his mind: 'His duties made it even more imperative for him to re-enact in his inner conscience his public actions and weigh them according to ethical criteria' (Ascoli 1965: 39). Particularly in the course of his second term with its daily stresses and strains, the affirming, orienting signposts are again accompanied by tones of resignation. However, from the framework of orientation provided by the classic texts that Hammarskjöld uses it is not difficult to recognize his attempt to reflect his work and that of the United Nations in his diary, as exemplified in the entry of 30 August 1956 on his understanding of the UN:

> ... It is this idea which you must help towards victory with all your strength – not the work of human hands, which just now gives you responsibility and the responsibility-creating chance to further it.
>
> Knowing this, it should be easy for you to smile at criticism of decisions misunderstood, ridicule of expressions misinterpreted as 'idealism', declarations of war to the death upon that to which, for all outward appearances, you are devoting your life.
>
> But is it so easy? No – for the pettiness you show in your reactions to other people about whose motives you know nothing, renders you – very justly – vulnerable to the pettiness you encounter in interpretations of your own efforts.
>
> Only on one level are you what you can be. Only in one direction are you free. Only at one point are you outside time. The good fortune of 'Sunday's child' is simply this: that he meets his destiny at that point, in that direction, on that level.
>
> (*Markings* 1956: 39, 138)

Here at the latest is a clear connection with the office of the Secretary-General. His remark about the idea and its passing form in this historical situation is a direct reflection of a crucial idea about the nature of the United Nations that Hammarskjöld expresses in his annual reports. The diary and the ethical mysticism that Hammarskjöld develops in its pages are an indispensable source for a deeper understanding of Hammarskjöld's political work: it opens up his personal perspective of his political activity. In Chapter 4 we shall look at direct points of contact. Before that, we need to consider other influences. One that is as indispensable as ethical mysticism is Albert Schweitzer, whom we turn to now.

Albert Schweitzer: a new ideology of co-existence

In his *Tiden* article of 1951, Hammarskjöld made it clear that he found Schweitzer's ethics a valuable aid in coping with political problems and his public responsibilities. The concept of the impartial civil servant has several consequences:

> The first consequence is respect for the results of the efforts and attempts of early generations to find solutions to problems, in other words a thoroughly conservative trait. Another consequence is the influence of respect for the individual on political decision-making. This gives rise to two demands: for the greatest possible freedom for each person to plan his own life, on the one hand, and for social justice in the form of equal rights and equal opportunities for all on the other. These two demands are a mixture of liberal and radical social elements. Finally, as a matter of course, Schweitzer's ethics subordinates the interests of the individual to those of the whole; there is a moral duty of loyalty towards, first, the state in the form of the nation and, second, a wider solidarity as found in internationalism.
>
> (Hammarskjöld 1951a, in Stolpe 1964a: 56–7)

Thus, Schweitzer's ethics point to solidarity rooted in the reverence for life that transcends national and political boundaries and must nourish the activity of civil servants and their service to the state. In the Murrow interview, Hammarskjöld's reference to Schweitzer centred on this ideal of service – admittedly more as an active expression of charity:

> The two ideals which dominated my childhood world met me fully harmonized and adjusted to the demands of our world of today in the ethics of Albert Schweitzer, where the ideal of service is supported by and supports the basic attitude to man set forth in the Gospels.
>
> (CF II: 195)

Hammarskjöld studied Schweitzer intensely (Aulén 1969: 32–7). It is plausible that his interest was aroused by the Olaus Petri Lectures that Schweitzer held in Uppsala at the invitation of archbishop Nathan Söderblom. It is very probable that the 15-year-old Hammarskjöld attended these lectures (Simon 1967: 34); as son of the governor, he may have been introduced to Schweitzer at the archbishop's house, where the Alsatian guest and his wife stayed while in Uppsala. It must be emphasized that the Olaus Petri Lectures were anything but a routine series of lectures for Schweitzer: in them he presented the core ideas of his philosophy of culture for the first time. In addition, they were a decisive biographical stage in his development, a return to his scientific research after the disruption of war. Not least, he took Söderblom's advice and organized other talks and organ concerts to raise funds to enable him to return to Africa. In Uppsala, Schweitzer articulated for the first time his doctrine of reverence for life embedded in his philosophy of culture (Schweitzer 1987). Hammarskjöld's private library contains most of Schweitzer's works.[40] To understand Hammarskjöld's appreciation of Schweitzer, we need to briefly consider the main points of Schweitzer's ethics and philosophy.

Focal points of Schweitzer's philosophy and ethics

A comprehensive discussion of Schweitzer's work or points of criticism – e.g. the question of the theological 'correctness' of Schweitzer's views – exceeds the scope of this work (see Clark 1962; Günzler 1996: 154–66). The focus of the following discussion is on those aspects of Schweitzer's work that Hammarskjöld adopted and how this affected his political ethics. Initially, Hammarskjöld appears to have been interested particularly in the *Quest for the Historical Jesus*. Friends whom Hammarskjöld joined for a tour in northern Sweden in 1948 reported that he took the original German edition with him and read it intensively, often lost in thought. He was so enthusiastic about the book that he recommended it to his friends (Dusen 1965: 96).

Quest for the historical Jesus

One of the principal ideas of the book is Schweitzer's interpretation of the *Imitation of Christ*; more than almost anybody before him, he interprets it as a call to action in real life. Building on a research report on the historical Jesus, he develops the thesis that the *Imitation of Christ* is not an abstract, religious mental exercise, but a call to act here and now. The closing paragraph of the book is in effect an appeal:

> He [Jesus] says the same word, 'Follow me!', and sets us to those tasks which he must fulfil in our time. He commands. And to those who hearken to him, whether wise or unwise, he will reveal himself in the peace, the labours and the sufferings that they may experience in his fellowship, and as an ineffable mystery they will learn who he is….
>
> (Schweitzer 2001: 487)

Imitation is no longer a theological formula, but a demand to tackle the problems of the age. An essential element in Schweitzer's concept of imitation is his emphasis on the 'consistent eschatology' of Jesus: Schweitzer took the (heavily criticized) view that Jesus acted in expectation of the imminent end of the world and the realization of the kingdom of God (1998b: 13; Beyschlag 1980a: 326). From the eschatological point of view, Schweitzer categorizes Jesus' ethics as 'interim ethics' (1984: 628). This concept has been misinterpreted in some quarters; Schweitzer did not intend at all to describe these ethics as provisional or relative (Gräßer 1997b: 55). The expectation of the coming of the kingdom of God in no way diminishes Jesus' ethics; rather it is the source of their extraordinary power: 'Without eschatology the ethics of Jesus would lack the enthusiasm, the "immediacy" and "enormity" that wants to and can determine our "way of thinking"' (ibid.: 59). By placing Jesus in his historical context, Schweitzer resists efforts to transplant the son of God into the present. Simply receiving the ideas and deeds of Jesus by copying him into the present in a time machine, as it were, does not do justice to the historical Jesus. Rather, each age in the history of Christianity must discover for itself the spirit of the absoluteness of Jesus' ethical demands (Schweitzer 1998b: 55–6).

This argument gave Schweitzer the change of perspective needed to bring the example of Jesus to life. The expectation of the end of the world gives Jesus' ethics their particular quality: 'An ethic of enthusiasm, seemingly focused upon an optimistic world-view, forms part of a pessimistic world-view! That is the magnificent paradox in the teaching of Jesus' (Schweitzer 1987: 146). Schweitzer develops this thought in his biographical notes: 'The essence of Christianity is an affirmation of the world that has passed through a negation of the world' (1998b: 57; see also Schweitzer 1923). He views the example of Jesus as an approach to liberating the ethical force of Christianity: 'This activist ethic is what is wanted to provide the cardinal point of an evolution from a Christian-pessimistic to a Christian-optimistic philosophy' (1987: 145). Here Schweitzer formulates a problem that is also important in mysticism: what is the motivation and importance of ethical actions in a world characterized precisely by the lack of ethical behaviour? Some mystics reacted by withdrawing from the world into an inner life. Schweitzer was quite the opposite: 'To the question, how man can be in the world and in God at one and the same time, we find the answer in the Gospel of Jesus: "By living and working in this world as one who is not of the world"' (1923: 73–4). This thought is closely tied up with Schweitzer's concepts of world-view and life-view ('Weltanschauung' and 'Lebensanschauung'), in context of which he developed his formula of reverence for life.

Reverence for life

Schweitzer developed his philosophy of culture in Africa against the background of the catastrophe of World War I. The motivation for the book is the desire to respond to the complete breakdown of ethical standards and protective walls in the course of the war (Körtner 1988: 331). Not surprisingly, his cultural philosophy is pessimistic. Schweitzer (1987: 3) believed that 'philosophy's renunciation of her duty' was a crucial factor in the outbreak of the war. His main accusation, supported by numerous examples from the history of philosophy, is that philosophy increasingly sidelined the 'fundamental' questions of human existence. This abstinence left it impotent against the spreading rationality of 'Realpolitik' – which Schweitzer sees as only ostensibly oriented to reality: '[P]ractical politics were, therefore, in truth impracticable politics, because they allowed popular passion to come in, and thereby made the simplest questions insoluble' (ibid.: 31).

Schweitzer regarded the catastrophic development in the philosophical and intellectual fields that preceded the world war as cultural decline, as for him there is a constitutive bond between culture and ethics: 'Civilization is the product of an optimistic-ethical conception of the world' (ibid.: 91). According to Schweitzer, political communities whose culture is in decline are not in the position to develop and establish strong ethical principles. Instead, the tendency is to treat values as relative, which leads to growing pessimism. At this point we need to explain Schweitzer's use of the concepts of world-view and life-view and their interaction.

For Schweitzer world-view is 'the content of the thoughts of society and the individuals which compose it about the nature and object of the world in which they live, and the position and the destiny of mankind and of individual men within it' (ibid.: 49). This is where Schweitzer locates the origin of the decline of culture and ethics, whose witness he became with the outbreak of World War I at the latest. The consequence: 'The reconstruction of our age, then, can begin only with a reconstruction of its theory of the universe' (ibid.: 52). But where can one find the positive and powerful elements of a world-view that will provide the foundation on which culture and ethics can flourish? In Schweitzer's opinion, man cannot develop any coherent world-view by observing reality or nature: '[Nature] is a wonderfully creative force, and at the same time senselessly destructive force. We face her absolutely perplexed. What is full of meaning within the meaningless, the meaningless in what is full of meaning: that is the essential nature of the universe' (ibid.: 273–4). Schweitzer goes even further:

> I believe I am the first among Western thinkers who has ventured to recognize the crushing result of knowledge, and the first to be absolutely sceptical about our knowledge of the world without at the same time renouncing belief in world – and life – affirmation and ethics.
>
> (ibid.: 76)

Schweitzer's recognition that reality is a cause for pessimism does not lead him to resignation. On the contrary: if the contradictions in reality set limits to cognition, Schweitzer's response is to replace the focus on the outer reality with a focus on the simple fact of inner life. According to Schweitzer, the lack of a meaningful context in the outer world does not imply a lack of meaning in the lives of individuals. For him, the interaction between world-view and life-view is just the opposite: 'World-view is a product of life-view, not vice versa' (ibid.: 78).

This immediately raises the question of how to fill life-view with meaning. Schweitzer emphasizes that knowledge here must take a very specific form, for which he uses the word 'mysticism'. By this he means something a little different from what the medieval mystics meant, though his concept also contains elements of the latter (Gräßer 1997c: 91–4; Schweitzer 1998a): 'The ultimate knowledge, in which man recognizes his own being as a part of the All, belongs, they say, to the realm of mysticism, by which is meant that he does not reach it by the method of ordinary reflection, but somehow or other lives himself into it' (Schweitzer 1987: 55). Schweitzer treats mysticism as a complementary form of knowledge: 'Thus reflection, when pursued to the end, leads somewhere and somehow to a living mysticism, which is for all men everywhere a necessary element of thought' (ibid.: 56). In the words of his autobiography: 'Rational thinking, if it goes deep, ends of necessity in the irrational realm of mysticism. It has, of course, to deal with life and the world, both of which are nonrational entities' (ibid.: 237). Schweitzer draws the consequence: 'Every world- and life-view which is to satisfy thought is mysticism. It must seek to give to the existence of man such a meaning as will prevent him from being satisfied with being a part of the infinite existence in merely natural fashion, but will make him determined to belong to it in soul and spirit also, through an act of consciousness' (Schweitzer 1987: 301). For Schweitzer, this conscious act is the acknowledgement of life by one's own will: 'The way to true mysticism leads up through rational thought to deep experience of the world and of our will-to-live' (ibid.: 81; 1998b: 155). Schweitzer's formula of reverence for life is based on this will to live:

> With Descartes, philosophy starts from the dogma: 'I think, therefore I exist'. With this paltry, arbitrarily chosen beginning, it is landed irretrievably on the road to the abstract. It never finds the right approach to ethics, and remains entangled in a dead world- and life-view. True philosophy must start from the most immediate and comprehensive fact of consciousness, which says: 'I am life which wills to live, in the midst of life which wills to live'.
>
> (1987: 309)

This formula has immediate ethical consequences: 'The basic principle of ethics, that principle which is a necessity of thought, which has a definite content, which is engaged in constant, living, and practical dispute with reality, is: Devotion to life resulting from reverence for life' (ibid.: 306). The change in Schweitzer's perspective 'from the individual to the collective, ethical act' (Steffahn 1996: 125) lies in the recognition of individual consciousness and the simultaneous realization of the ethical consequence. In this context he talks in a very special sense of love that underlies this principle; pity is not the sole source of ethics: 'Love means more, since it includes fellowship in suffering, in joy, and in effort, but it shows the ethical only in a simile, although in a simile that is natural and profound' (Schweitzer 1987: 311). In other words, reverence for life does not produce only a passive attitude (e.g. of 'let live'), but also contains an active attitude of devotion and service. At this point the similarities with Hammarskjöld become clear. Their correspondence provides further details about these similarities and their political relevance.

The Hammarskjöld–Schweitzer correspondence

Besides occasional references to Schweitzer in the diary and in his speeches,[41] the main source of information about the relationship between Hammarskjöld and Schweitzer is their correspondence. It opens with a letter from Schweitzer dated 19 December 1953 noting Hammarskjöld's avowal of his ethics:

> Quand vous avez été élu Secrétaire-Général de l'UNO [sic] j'ai appris par une Revue Anglaise, que vous aviez des sympathies pour mes idées et que votre devise était Servir. Je voulais alors vous écrire, non pour vous féliciter

de votre élection, car il ne faut pas vous féliciter de devoir remplir un poste des plus difficiles mais pour vous envoyer mes bons voeus.

(KB DHS: Albert Schweitzer, Letter to Dag Hammarskjöld of 19 December 1953)[42]

Schweitzer mentions that he often visits Sweden and may visit the USA, in which case it might be possible to arrange a meeting. Hammarskjöld replies on 13 January 1954, thanking Schweitzer for his best wishes and the encouragement that he drew from Schweitzer's letter. He encloses the text of the Murrow interview 'qui montre bien quelles sources d'inspiration ont été pour moi votre vie et votre pensée' (KB DHS: Dag Hammarskjöld, Letter to Albert Schweitzer, 13 January 1954). Regarding the meeting with Schweitzer, Hammarskjöld proposes several options:

> Il y a tant de choses dont j'aimerais m'entretenir avec vous, tant sur le plan de la pensée pure que sur le plan des services que les Nations Unies peuvent rendre aux peuples indigènes qui font depuis si longtemps l'objet de vos préoccupations.
> Je ne voudrais pas terminer cette lettre sans faire allusion au Prix Nobel de la Paix qui vous a récemment été décerné. L'Institut Nobel a agi là avec une très grande sagacité: aucun parmi les hommes d'aujourd'hui n'a contribué autant que vous-même au développement des conditions spirituelles que présupposent la fraternité mondiale et une paix durable.

Here Hammarskjöld himself talks about the connection between spiritual foundations, theoretical reflection and the practical work of the United Nations, which he sees realized in exemplary fashion in Schweitzer's life and work. At the same time, he provides the context in which he understands Schweitzer's views: for him they are the basis of a 'fraternité mondiale' and a 'paix durable'. In other words, Hammarskjöld understands Schweitzer's thinking in a political context.

After the initial exchange of letters and expressions of mutual appreciation, the correspondence stops, until Hammarskjöld writes to Schweitzer again in July 1955. He announces that his assistant Benjamin Cohen wants to visit Schweitzer during a forthcoming trip to Africa so as to tap his experience of Africa for the benefit of the Secretariat. Over and above this, Hammarskjöld tells of his plan to invite Schweitzer to speak at the celebrations on the tenth anniversary of the United Nations – an idea that did not come to fruition mainly because of Schweitzer's travel difficulties. But Hammarskjöld's letter also includes an appeal:

> Pourtant, vous savez comme moi que le monde entier a absolument besoin d'une idéologie propre à conférer un sens valable aux efforts de tous les peuples et à donner des bases nouvelles et saines au principe de la 'co-existence'. Or, je suis persuadé que, même dans le domaine strictement politique dont s'occupe l'Organisation des Nations Unies, il vous appartient de lancer un

message capital au monde. J'ai déjà eu l'occasion de vous dire qu'à mon avis, il serait possible de animer la vie internationale d'un esprit nouveau en faisant mieux connaître l'attitude même que vous avez essayé d'expliquer aux hommes de notre génération. C'est précisément la raison pour laquelle nous autres, aux Nations Unies, avons contracté une dette de gratitude à votre égard pour ce que vous avez fait et pour ce que vous symbolisez; mais c'est aussi pourquoi nous espérons – avec témérité excessive, peut-être – que vous accepterez d'ajouter votre voix puissante aux appels qui sont faits en faveur du respect mutuel des peuples, au sens même où nous entendons cette expression à l'Organisation des Nations Unies.

(KB DHS: Dag Hammarskjöld, Letter to Albert Schweitzer of
21 July 1955)

Hammarskjöld regards Schweitzer as a source of ideas and the representative of an 'idéologie propre' that offers fresh arguments for the principle of coexistence. He hopes that this 'ideology' will act as a stimulus in international politics. Here and elsewhere Hammarskjöld uses the concept of 'ideology' in the philosophical rather than the political sense.

In his writings, Schweitzer was not consistent in how he applied his ideas to international politics. The consequences of the 'reverence for life' for international politics are mostly kept fairly general (Schweitzer 1991c: 31). For instance, he determines that opportunism has failed as the basis of public actions. The failure of unethical 'Realpolitik' leads him to call for a new approach:

[T]rue power for the state as for the individual is to be found in spirituality and ethical conduct. The state lives by the confidence of those who belong to it; it lives by the confidence felt in other states. Opportunist policy may have temporary successes to record, but in the long run it assuredly ends in failure.

Thus ethical world- and life-affirmation demands of the modern state that it shall aspire to making itself an ethical and spiritual personality.

(Schweitzer 1987: 342–3)

This is the basis for Schweitzer's view that a reorientation of public life, too, is indispensable, and most likely the motivation for his concluding reference to Kant's essay 'Perpetual Peace':

Kant published, with the title *Towards Perpetual Peace*, a work containing rules which were to be observed with a view to lasting peace whenever treaties of peace were concluded. It was a mistake. Rules for treaties of peace, however well intentioned and however ably drawn up, can accomplish nothing. Only such thinking as establishes the sway of the mental attitude of reverence for life can bring to mankind perpetual peace.

(1987: 344)

This passage illustrates how Schweitzer's claim to absoluteness for his ethics leads him – in contrast to Hammarskjöld – to disregard the importance of other categories, such as the rule of law, to which Hammarskjöld very much pays tribute. This demand for peace-oriented thinking, which in his view was essential if international organizations were to carry out their tasks, is also the basic message of his Nobel Peace Prize speech in 1954 (Schweitzer 1991d). By adopting these considerations, Hammarskjöld expanded the application of the strategic concept of 'coexistence' beyond the level of bilateral relations between states (Krushchev 1959) and gave it an unexpected ethical interpretation over and above its routine political meaning. Hammarskjöld felt the concept was ambiguous, and responded to a journalist's request for a definition with: 'I could write a whole essay on that' (PC 14 January 1954, in CF II: 453). There is, however, a link between Schweitzer's formula of 'life which wills to live, in the midst of life which wills to live' and international coexistence based on the fact that states and peoples will to live amidst states and peoples which will to live. In any case, Schweitzer becomes a point of reference and an intellectual resource for Hammarskjöld, a point he wants to convey in his work:

> J'ajoute que, pour ma part, je vous dois beaucoup à titre personnel, mais aussi dans l'exercise de mes fonctions, car dans les multiples allocutions que j'ai eu l'occasion de prononcer et dans les nombreux débats auxquels j'ai participé, j'ai toujours essayé de faire partager les idées auxquelles vous avez su donner une expression tellement admirable, tant dans votre oeuvre écrite que dans le travail que vous accomplissez jour après jour.

Moreover, certain passages in Schweitzer's teachings dealt directly with questions Hammarskjöld himself was grappling with in his diary.[43] However, Hammarskjöld's and Schweitzer's views do not always coincide, as other passages from this correspondence illustrate.

Years pass before a telegram from the Secretary-General re-establishes contact in January 1960. Hammarskjöld, flying past Lambarene on the way to Brazzaville, wishes Schweitzer Happy New Year. Around July, Schweitzer writes a letter to Hammarskjöld in Leopoldville, once again suggesting a meeting and proposing possible routes and pick-up points. He ends with the words: 'Let me briefly say how I admire what you are doing in the case of the former Belgian Congo. It is a great feat of the United Nations' (KB DHS: Albert Schweitzer, Letter to Dag Hammarskjöld, n.d.). Hammarskjöld replies with a short letter in which he expresses his regret that his busy schedule does not allow him to spend even a few hours with Schweitzer. At the beginning of March 1961 Schweitzer writes another letter in which some remarks differ from his previous statements:

> Since things in the Congo have taken such a turn for the worse I think of you every day and even sometimes at night, everything you have to bear and struggle with. I cannot believe the ingratitude and the smear campaign against you. But those people will not get the better of you.

As an old African I believe that letting the Africans fight out their feuds will cause fewer deaths than intervening. The presence of Indian troops is a dangerous development. Who guarantees that the Indian troops will really act as UN troops and be seen and recognized as such? It would be different if the UN had its own troop instead of hiring, as it were, foreign troops. I fear that Africans will never see Indian troops as UN troops. They will never get that into their skulls. That is too complicated for them.

Hopefully everything will end better when the Africans reach agreement among themselves on breaking up the Belgian Congo into 5 or 6 national states. The Belgian Congo was something artificial that could exist only as a colony, but not as a free African state.

(KB DHS: Albert Schweitzer, Letter to Dag Hammarskjöld,
7 March 1961)

Here, the 'old African' suddenly views the previously praised 'great feat' of the UN as pointless and even obstructive. Hammarskjöld disapproves of these words, which were probably meant as friendly, as evidence of an utterly different reading of the conflict. He expresses his view in a very businesslike letter of 17 March:

I can image what dark feelings you as an experienced African must have following developments in the Congo. However, it is my duty to implement the decisions of the United Nations and in this connection I have to look at the situation in the world as a whole. Hence, the impression that events seen in isolation make no sense is probably unavoidable. But I am firmly convinced that the Congo affair will gradually improve.

(KB DHS: Dag Hammarskjöld, Letter to Albert Schweitzer,
17 March 1961)

Urquhart (Interview 1997) reports that Hammarskjöld was extremely irritated by Schweitzer's letter and that he fell markedly in his esteem. Linnér (Interview 1998), by contrast, doubts that even this last correspondence will have had a lasting effect on Hammarskjöld's great respect for Schweitzer. Ralph Bunche had a similar experience with Schweitzer in 1955 when he visited him in his home town and afterwards noted: 'We differed, but in most friendly ways, on Africa. He clearly fears nationalism and takes a paternalistic view. The politically-minded African is not at all understood by him' (private note, quoted in Urquhart 1993a: 260–1).

The meeting that Schweitzer again raised in his letter ('I am 86 years old; one may not postpone our meeting too long.') does not take place, even though Hammarskjöld is as eager as Schweitzer. When he flies to Leopoldville on 13 September 1961, he still plans to make the long-promised visit to Schweitzer in Lambarene (Simon 1967: 174). Hammarskjöld adds: '– but in my present life the unexpected occurs all too often.' In the end it is the death of the younger correspondent in the tragic plane crash in Ndola that ends the correspondence with the old man concerned about his lifespan. But what was Schweitzer's influence on Hammarskjöld?

Schweitzer's influence on Hammarskjöld

Schweitzer's influence on Hammarskjöld can be summed up in the call for a concrete Imitation of Christ in the here and now, the relationship between mysticism and ethics, the ethics of service and the new ideology of coexistence in the age of the atomic bomb.

Concrete imitation in the here and now

Schweitzer's thoughts on this topic are repeated in Hammarskjöld's writings, even down to similar wording. In this light, the aforementioned sentence 'In our era, the road to salvation necessarily passes through the world of action' (*Markings* 1955: 65, 122) in Hammarskjöld's diary seems less strange; rather, it reads like an accurate interpretation of certain basic insights of Schweitzer. Once again, the question of ethical action is focused on the person of Jesus and the demand to imitate him. To this extent, Schweitzer's analysis fits in with Hammarskjöld's interest in the medieval mystics. Schweitzer, however, goes beyond the ethical ideas of mystical thinking, already present in Eckhart, through his very concrete image of Christ: 'Christ was a real person; "the hero of the Gospels" is not some or other mystical figure' (Sundén 1967: 88). Instead, this Jesus symbolizes an *attitude*, for '... the spirit of Jesus does not renounce the world, but aims at transforming it' (Schweitzer 1987: 143). This transformation takes place in helping others. For Schweitzer, Jesus is the example 'that the ethical is the individual's active self-devotion to others' (ibid.: 144). This insight sets the tone of an entry in 1951, in which Hammarskjöld meditates on Jesus, describing him as 'a young man, adamant in his committed life'.[44]

The relationship between mysticism and ethics

Hammarskjöld and Schweitzer both made the experience that rationality alone could not give them satisfactory answers to the meaning of life and the world. However, the discovery of the mystic experience did not imply the opposite or fundamentally call this rationality into question. Rather, the two forms of cognition belong together. Schweitzer and Hammarskjöld had virtually identical views on the relationship between mysticism and ethics. For both, mysticism was not an otherworldly activity through which the individual attains perfection; it may never become an end in itself. Instead, it must always be practice-oriented (Schweitzer 1987: 304). Both combine this insight with an emphasis on the universality of mystical experience as found in all major religions of the world. Schweitzer's studies in this respect primarily illustrate his – at the time unconventional – interest in genuine dialogue with non-European cultural circles (Schweitzer 1957: ix–x ; Günzler 1996: 21–5).

However, it must be added that Schweitzer's concept of mysticism is not simply an expansion of what Hammarskjöld had already found in the Christian mystics. Certainly, Schweitzer reformulated many thoughts of the medieval mystics for the contemporary world (Dusen 1965: 49). Yet Hammarskjöld and Schweitzer held very different views about the mystic classics. Hammarskjöld understood them far less internalized than Schweitzer does (Hughes 1995: 178; Aulén 1969: 39), who questions whether the mysticism of, say, Meister Eckhart has any ethical relevance (Schweitzer 1957: 210). It is possible that Hammarskjöld grasped that Schweitzer was closer to the medieval mystics than Schweitzer himself (with his categorical judgement of them) could realize (Werner 1990).

The ethics of service

Hammarskjöld thought Schweitzer's views exemplary inasmuch as he not only formulated conclusions, but lived by them in his work in Lambarene (Steffahn 1996: 16). The ethics of service in the here and now is a combination of a life in Imitation of Christ and the fundamental reverence for life. This is closely related to Schweitzer's concept of the community of will with Jesus. For Schweitzer, like Hammarskjöld, mysticism is an understanding between wills (Schweitzer 2001: 486). Ethics is thus 'a devotion to life inspired by reverence for life' (Schweitzer 1987: 311). The life-view of reverence for life can, according to Schweitzer, give rise to an optimistic and ethical world-view – and therefore produce culture. Accordingly, the formula of reverence for life is the key to the spiritual reconstruction of the foundations of human coexistence. Against this background, the principle of reverence for life reunites 'the traditional paths of the ethics of self-perfection and the ethics of self-surrender' (Günzler 1996: 80). Hartman (1966: 106) argues: '[T]he sacrifice of one's individual for the universal life is one form of reverence for life. … [T]he individual existence is always meaningful if it remains devoted to the service of universal Life.' The effect of these thoughts on Hammarskjöld is shown not least in a diary entry (see also Aulén 1969: 33–4) of 1942 that reflects the immediacy of Schweitzer's influence in that it virtually paraphrases the principle of reverence for life:

> Our secret creative will divines its counterpart in others, experiencing its own universality, and this institution builds a road towards knowledge of the power which is itself a spark within us.
>
> (*Markings* 1941–2: 25, 17)

Both Schweitzer and Hammarskjöld construe from this primarily an ethics of service. Over and above this, both agree that any social ethics is, in the final analysis, rooted in the ethics of the individual (Günzler 1996: 81–2). Starting with Jesus' sermon, Blessed are the Peaceful, the problem of peacelessness has been a crucial challenge for politics (see Schweitzer 1952). Politics must change the mentality of people if it wants to build protective barriers against new threats. Hence, Schweitzer and Hammarskjöld see the peacelessness of man, in contradistinction to political discord, as the actual problem.[45]

A new 'ideology' of coexistence in the age of the atomic bomb

This shared basis of individual ethics and ethics of service leads Schweitzer and Hammarskjöld to similar evaluations of political questions. Thus, Schweitzer emphasizes the importance of mutual trustworthiness, without which all efforts to achieve peace in international relations are doomed to failure. For this reason Schweitzer felt that the atomic bomb only increased the urgency for international understanding, whereas the real problem lay in the way people and peoples thought about each other (Schweitzer 1951c). In his Nobel Peace Prize speech Schweitzer emphasized that the work of international organizations, such as the United Nations, depended also and particularly on this context: 'The institutions created to preserve peace can do what is demanded and hoped of them only to the extent that the spirit generates among nations a new way of thinking about peace' (Schweitzer 1991d: 127). Public opinion plays a major role in this development, but for effective mediation it is necessary to turn to international leaders (Spear 1978: 34–5). In Schweitzer's opinion, the huge challenges of the time demand utopian steps with unprecedented urgency:

> Only to the extent that they [the peoples] think in terms of a reverence for life will they be completely trustworthy for each other.
>   A utopia? If we do not realize this utopia, we will be helpless in the face of atomic weapons and the disaster they portend. Only by thinking in terms of true humanity can the atomic weapons be removed from the world and peace can enter into force.
>
> (1962: 176)

Given so much agreement, it is not surprising that Schweitzer studied Hammarskjöld's diary intensively (Linnér 1989: 129) and described his relationship with the Secretary-General as 'a close kinship of mind especially in questions of ethics' (Dusen 1965: 181). Moreover, a kindred spirit links the work on the thirty-eighth floor of the UN headquarters in New York and the work in the hospital in Lambarene, even if the circumstances of the respective decisions and everyday life were very different. In addition to that, neither has any illusions about the human condition. Both clearly articulate their recognition of the pessimistic undertone of their times. But they do not leave it at that. Driven by the same sense of urgency to act in order to improve relations between people and states, they advocate and support this with new ethical convictions. This sense of urgency in view of the enormity of the problems to be solved also brought Hammarskjöld into contact with Martin Buber.

Martin Buber: genuine dialogue as a precondition of peace

Hammarskjöld established contact with Buber relatively late in life although Stolpe reports discussing Buber with Hammarskjöld in 1930 (Stolpe 1964a: 40).[46] At any rate, the German-Jewish philosopher is not mentioned in the Murrow interview.[47] On 16 April 1958 Hammarskjöld sent a letter to Jerusalem in which he introduced himself ('You do not know me personally, but I am afraid you have not been able to escape knowing about me') (KB DHS: Dag Hammarskjöld, Letter to Martin Buber, 16 April 1958). As reason for his letter, Hammarskjöld writes '[t]hat I just read the newly published American edition of your collection of essays, "Pointing the way".' He goes on to try to explain what he particularly liked about this collection of essays:

> I wish to tell you how strongly I have responded to what you write about our age of distrust and to the background of your observations which I find in your general philosophy of unity created 'out of the manifold'. Certainly, for me, this is a case of 'parallel ways'.

Hammarskjöld could not have used clearer words in a letter establishing contact than 'parallel ways' to describe his relationship with Buber's philosophy. At the same time, the formula of the age of distrust provides a first indication of the political significance he attaches to Buber's work. Just how highly Hammarskjöld thought of this book and how closely he applies its message to the work of the United Nations can be deduced from the fact that he presented a copy of the book to Andrew Cordier, his executive assistant with the following dedication: 'Andy, These perceptive comments on basic UN problems' (quoted in CF IV: 69). To establish this connection, we must take a closer look at the contents and message of this collection of essays and of other texts of Buber that were relevant for Hammarskjöld.

Focal points of Buber's political philosophy

Once again, a comprehensive presentation and critical appreciation of Buber's philosophy goes beyond the scope of this study. The object of the following remarks is to enhance the understanding of the correspondence. The selection of Buber texts has been guided by Hammarskjöld's own information on his reading of Buber.

Political essays: 'Pointing the Way'

In the collection of essays (Buber 1963a) mentioned in Hammarskjöld's first letter, the editor Maurice S. Friedman classified the contributions by topic; in particular the last section, titled 'Politics, Community, and Peace' contains a number of writings, that – taken together – constitute Buber's political philosophy

(Weltsch 1963). This philosophy is based on some basic considerations that can be described as follows:

Buber – influenced, like Schweitzer, by the experience of World Wars I and II – assumes a 'crisis of the human race' (Buber 1963b: 191). This crisis is of a fundamental nature and concerns the very foundations of personal and social life: 'In the human crisis which we are experiencing to-day these two have become questionable – the person and the truth' (Buber 1936:105). Largely due to the efforts of totalitarian systems, people are collectivized, i.e. deprived of their responsibility and their being as persons. Truth, on the other hand, has been politicized, i.e. rendered unsuitable for genuine dialogue. Starting with this observation, Buber identifies a point of departure for overcoming the resultant crisis:

> But in order that man may not be lost there is need of persons who are not collectivized, and of truth which is not politicized. ... There is need of the person as the ground which cannot be relinquished, from which alone the entry of the finite into conversation with the infinite became possible and is possible. There is need of man's faith in the truth as that which is independent of him, which he cannot acquire for himself, but with which he can enter into a real relation of his very life ....
>
> (ibid.: 107–8)

In his inaugural lecture in Jerusalem, Buber links this diagnosis with a classic topic in sociology: 'New institutions could not bring salvation if a new spiritual attitude were not prepared beforehand to prevent the degeneration and perversion of the institutions' (ibid.: 177). Buber then formulates this prerequisite even more radically:

> Man must change himself in the same measure as the institutions are changed in order that these changes may have their expected effect. If the new house that man hopes to erect is not to become his burial chamber, the essence of living together must undergo a change at the same time as the organization of living.
>
> (ibid.: 179)

The solution to the crisis of the human race has to begin with the individual. Consequently, Buber (1963c: 217) advocates 'a genuine personal ethos' moulded by service and participation in the common good as the basic requisite of functioning social organizations. To this end, he developed maxims describing what is required of individuals. The core of these maxims goes back to a basic demand of his: 'You shall not withhold yourself' (Buber 1963d: 109). Mankind will regain its personality through the commitment of the individual in the technical and collectivized world. Buber holds the anonymity, passivity and powerlessness of modern mass society responsible for many undesirable political trends. Alongside and simultaneous with the collectivized person is the problem of politicized truth, which renders human understanding almost impossible in crucial questions, for '[i]t is simply trust that is increasingly lost to men of our time' (Buber 1963e: 237):

> During the First World War it became clear to me that a process was going on which before then I had only surmised. This was the growing difficulty of genuine dialogue, and most especially of genuine dialogue between men of different kinds and convictions. Direct, frank dialogue is becoming ever more difficult and more rare; the abysses between man and man threaten ever more pitilessly to become unbridgeable. ... [T]his is the central question for the fate of mankind. Since then I have continually pointed out that the future of man as man depends upon a rebirth of dialogue.
>
> (Buber 1963f: 222)

Peace means far more for Buber than the absence of war (Susser 1984: 58). It is necessary that people enter into a genuine dialogue so that the 'vox humana' (Buber 1963e: 234) will be heard: 'War has always had an adversary who hardly ever comes forward as such but does his work in stillness. This adversary is speech, fulfilled speech, the speech of genuine conversation in which men understand one another and come to a mutual understanding' (ibid.: 236).

Regaining man's personality and the rebirth of dialogue are the two mutually supporting therapies called for in view of the 'pathology of our time' (ibid.: 238). The question of how to implement these solutions initially produces a sobering result. Precisely the political representatives of states that perform a certain function as role models are too caught up in propaganda and mutual distrust that they could open up new paths: '[T]he diplomats do not address one another but the faceless public' (ibid.: 237). Thus, they perpetuate and deepen the state of distrust. Buber therefore calls for new representatives of the people: 'Coming together out of hostile camps, those who stand in the authority of the spirit will dare to think with one another in terms of the whole planet' (Buber 1963f: 228). The goal of this new, conciliatory thinking over the barriers between the camps is to grapple with a reality that 'must be freed from its encrustation of catchwords' (Buber 1963g: 230). '[T]hey who have in common the language of "human truth" must form a "crossfront" away from the well-trodden political fronts' (Buber 1963c: 219). Buber regards the organization of social life on the basis of political groupings as sensible and inevitable – but the decision to join a specific group does not release people from their personal responsibility and their conscience before God. The 'inner front' within the political groups distinguishes itself in that it always recognizes that which is monopolizing, tactical and blinding in the own group and through this recognition can join the internal front in the other groups. These reflections of Buber referred particularly to the situation of the Cold War, as a quotation from his speech on receiving the Peace Prize of the German Book Trade illustrates:

> The preparation for the final battle of homo humanus against homo contrahumanus has begun in the depths. But the front is split into as many

individual fronts as there are peoples, and those who stand on one of the individual fronts know little or nothing of the other fronts. ... The so-called cold war between two gigantic groups of states with all its accompaniments still obscures the true obligation and solidarity of combat, whose line cuts right through all states and peoples, however they may name their regime. The recognition of the deeper reality, of the true need and the true danger, is growing.

(Buber 1963e: 233–4)

Against the backdrop of the award of the Peace Prize of the German Book Trade to a 'surviving arch-Jew', Buber (ibid.: 234) speaks of the special obligation that the experience of National Socialism places on him, too: 'The survivor who is the object of such honours is taken up into the high duty of solidarity that extends across the fronts: the solidarity of all separate groups in the flaming battle for the rise of a true humanity. There is no higher duty on earth at the present hour.' Buber puts great hope in the concept of the 'crossfront': 'This can be more important for the future of our world than all fronts that are drawn to-day between groups and between associations of groups; for this front, if it is everywhere upright and strong, may run as a secret unity across all groups' (Buber 1936: 94). In other words, this may well have been a point of contact for that which Hammarskjöld referred to as 'unity created out of the manifold' in his first letter. According to Buber, the formation of crossfronts is the only way in which humanity can tackle its great task: overcoming the 'universal mistrust of our age' (1963f: 222).

The urgency with which Buber (1963e: 237) formulates these thoughts does not underestimate the difficulties in implementing them – quite the opposite: 'It is just the depth of the crisis that empowers us to hope.' Buber calls this combination of urgency and the recognition of facts of '... that great realism that surveys all the definable realities of public life ... but is also aware of what is most real of all, albeit moving secretly in the depths – the latent healing and salvation in the face of impending ruin' (ibid.). Nor does Buber have any illusions about the magnitude of change when he states: 'Only so can conflict certainly not be eliminated from the world, but be humanely arbitrated and led towards its overcoming' (ibid.: 238). These considerations must be seen in the context of Buber's general philosophy of dialogue. Strictly speaking, Buber's political texts grew out of his philosophy of dialogue. A 1961 letter shows that at the time of writing Hammarskjöld had read only the more general writings on the principle of dialogue (KB DHS: Dag Hammarskjöld, Letter to Martin Buber, 17 August 1961). The fact that Hammarskjöld had become acquainted with Buber's practice-oriented thinking before reading the theoretical foundations is testimony of how closely these two fields are related. Buber's philosophy of dialogue inevitably has political implications (Susser 1984). Therefore we shall briefly consider these texts too.

The principle of dialogue

In the second volume, to which Hammarskjöld refers in their correspondence, Buber collected a series of texts that present the essential pillars of his philosophy of dialogue. The most important reference text is 'I and Thou', published in 1923 (Marcel 1963). On the first page of this text Buber formulates a number of sentences which he subsequently explains individually:

> To man the world is twofold, in accordance with his twofold attitude.
> The attitude of man is twofold, in accordance with the twofold nature of the primary words which he speaks.
> The primary words are not isolated words, but combined words.
> The one primary word is the combination I–Thou.
> The other primary word is the combination I–It; wherein, without a change in the primary word, one of the words He and She can replace It.
> Hence the I of man is also twofold.
> For the I of the primary word I–Thou is a different I from that of the primary word I–It. …
> The primary word I–Thou can only be spoken with the whole being.
> The primary word I–It can never be spoken with the whole being.
> There is no I taken in itself, but only the I of the primary word I–Thou and the I of the primary word I–It.'
>
> (Buber 1966: 3–4)

And further: 'As experience, the world belongs to the primary word I–It. The primary word I–Thou establishes the world of relation' (ibid.: 6). This world of relation arises in three spheres: life with nature, life with men and 'life with spiritual beings' (ibid.). Crucial for Buber is the fact that: 'In every sphere in its own way, through each process of becoming that is present to us we look out toward the fringe of the eternal Thou; in each we are aware of a breath from the eternal Thou; in each Thou we address the eternal Thou' (ibid.). For Buber this reference to the presence of God is extremely significant and in a certain way forms a connection between Buber's mystic and dialogue phases (Schiller 1990: 282–306), as some passages prove: 'The aim of relation is relation's own being, that is, contact with the Thou. For through contact with every Thou we are stirred with a breath of the Thou, that is, of eternal life' (Buber 1966: 63). The wholly practical philosophy of dialogue becomes a connecting bridge in the sphere of faith: 'The extended lines of relations meet in the eternal Thou' (ibid.: 75). In Hasidism, the form of Jewish religiousness with a strong focus on the omnipresence of God as well as the relationship between God and man, Buber did not see negating, passive mysticism, but active and thus ethical mysticism. The main idea in Hasidism is the call to serve God in every possible action, also and especially in everyday life, with the 'active sense-spirit of the loving man' (Buber 1963i: 28; Buber 1918). This emphasis on reciprocity and man's capacity for relationship is for Buber the foundation of human existence:

The primary word I–Thou can be spoken only with the whole being. Concentration and fusion into the whole being can never take place through my agency, nor can it ever take place without me. I become through my relation to the Thou; as I become I, I say Thou.

All real living is meeting.

(Buber 1966: 11)

Presence and 'reality' only become established in the act of meeting. In connection with Buber's notion of 'between' (Buber 1929: 56) he also uses the concept of love, which as a self-engendered momentary occurrence symbolizes the fleetingness and intensity of genuine encounter that he describes, even though dialogue and love do not coincide for him (ibid.: 39). However, the circumstances of the age are very different. Dialogue between people increasingly consists of addressing a respective 'it' or thing. The similarity to Kant's demand not to see people only as a means, but also always as an end in themselves, which Hammarskjöld also absorbed, is not accidental.[48] This is the point at which the philosophy of dialogue establishes its political connection; for it is precisely at the political level that Buber feels the practice has taken root of viewing people as a calculation of utility, instead of paying attention to the overall context of society, which is only possible through justice and genuine encounter: '[I]n times of sickness it comes about that the world of It, no longer penetrated and fructified by the inflowing world of Thou as by living streams but separated and stagnant, a gigantic ghost of the fens, overpowers man' (Buber 1966: 53–4).

Thus, Buber objects to both excessive individualism (which gets lost in the monologue with itself) and collectivism: 'Community is where community happens. Collectivity is based on an organized atrophy of personal existence, community on its increase and confirmation in life lived towards one another' (Buber 1929: 51). This insight is at the same time the central message of his study of the problem of man, in which he states: 'Individualism sees man only in relation to himself, but collectivism does not see man at all, it sees only "society"' (Buber 1938: 241). In contrast to these two false alternatives, Buber refers to 'the realm of between' (ibid.: 246), which corresponds to the fundamental fact of the expression of life in meeting in genuine dialogue. Thus, the central object of anthropological questioning is 'neither the individual nor the collective, but man with man' (ibid.). By becoming organized in political camps and groups, man has been deprived of the possibility of actively pursuing his personal responsibility in the public sphere: 'The group has relieved you of your political responsibility. You feel yourself answered for in the group; you are permitted to feel it' (Buber 1936: 91). Besides the above-mentioned political consequence, the philosophy of dialogue also contains a religious, ethical prerequisite that Buber describes as follows:

I say, therefore, that the Single One, that is, the man living in responsibility, can make even his political decisions properly only from that ground of his being at which he is aware of the event as divine speech to him; and if he lets the awareness of this ground be strangled by his group he is refusing to give God an actual reply. ... I consider the human person to be the irremovable central place of struggle between the world's movement away from God and its movement towards God.

(ibid.: 93–4)

As in the case of Schweitzer, the correspondence between Hammarskjöld and Buber is testimony to the effect of Buber's mixture of philosophy of dialogue, religion and demands on the person.

The Hammarskjöld–Buber Correspondence

Hammarskjöld ends his letter mentioned at the beginning of this section with the hope that he will meet Buber on one of his trips to Israel. Just two days later, however, he sends another letter to Buber – at Princeton University. Hammarskjöld had learnt from the newspaper that Buber was about to give some guest lectures there. The Secretary-General would be 'happy and proud' if Buber could come to New York during his stay in Princeton 'to visit us at the United Nations' (KB DHS: Dag Hammarskjöld, Letter to Martin Buber, 18 April 1958).

Buber, by now in America, replied with a few short lines on 22 April, in which he nevertheless emphasized: 'What you tell me in your letter to Jerusalem is very important to me' (KB DHS: Martin Buber, Letter to Dag Hammarskjöld, 22 April 1958). Just how important is shown in the resoluteness with which he proposes a meeting of the two in New York on the afternoon of 1 May, which eventually takes place. Buber describes the atmosphere in an obituary for Hammarskjöld for the Swedish radio:

When we met in New York in the house of the rather oddly so-called United Nations, it became apparent that we were indeed both interested in the same thing; he, who in the most forward position of international responsibility, and me in the solitude of an ivory tower, which is in truth a guard tower from which one has to espy all the distances and depths of the planet's crisis. As I say, we were interested in the same thing. We were tormented in the same way by the illusion of language that was pervaded by a fundamental mutual distrust between representatives of states and groups of states, who in an unchanging routine talked out of the window at cross purposes. Both of us hoped, both of us believed that in time before the catastrophe, loyal representatives of the people, loyal to their true mission, would enter into a genuine dialogue, into genuine negotiations with one another, in which it would become apparent that the interests that bind peoples are still stronger than those that separate them. Genuine negotiations in which it would become apparent that cooperation – I do not say 'coexistence', that is not enough, I say and mean, despite all the enormous difficulties: cooperation is preferable to destruction together. For there is no third alternative, only one of the two: common realization of the huge common interests or the end to all that people on the one side and people on the other side care to call human civilization.

(1962: 33–4)

Hammarskjöld reflected upon Buber's visit in a letter to Erik Lindegren, with whom he was working on the translation of Saint-John Perse:

> I saw the other day old Martin Buber – he really is a great man – who said that he felt that we had come to a stage where the individual life had been completely gobbled up by political life and that political life now represents a world without any exit and without any entry. He talked about our dehumanised existence where language has ceased to have its normal function of communication in order to establish a living contact between human beings. I think he is basically right, and I think that is one reason why the poets should add a new dimension to their task as guardians of straight human communication where the respect for the word is still maintained.
>
> (KB DHS: Dag Hammarskjöld, Letter to Erik Lindegren,
> 3 May 1958)

Hence, the dangers that Buber saw in the collectivized person and the politicized truth immediately became a subject of discussion between him and the Secretary-General. During his two trips to Israel in September 1958 and January 1959 Hammarskjöld takes the time for two lengthy meetings with Buber at his home in Jerusalem (CF IV: 94–5). Buber's account gives a brief insight into the meeting in January 1959:

> At the centre of our discussion was the problem that has repeatedly preoccupied me in the course of my life: intellectuals' failure in their historical undertakings. I illustrated this with one of the best examples we have: Plato's failure to found his just state in Sicily. I felt, and Hammarskjöld, I was certain, felt it as I did: we too were recipients of that letter in which Plato told about his failure and how he overcame this failure.
>
> (1962: 35)

Shortly after this second meeting, Hammarskjöld announces at a press conference on 5 February that he is thinking about translating three or four essays from 'Pointing the Way' into Swedish and that he and Buber have reached agreement on it: 'On very many points I see eye to eye with him; on other points, naturally, there must be nuances. But as to the basic reaction, I think that he has made a major contribution and I would like to make that more broadly known' (CF IV: 326). Moreover, in June 1959 he draws up a memorandum for the Swedish Academy in which he discusses the possibility of awarding Buber the Nobel Prize for Literature. Interestingly, he comes to the conclusion that Buber should rather be awarded the Nobel Peace Prize (quoted in Hodes 1971: 145–6). This proposal was also discussed in the Norwegian Academy, but dropped on account of continuous controversies over Buber's political views.

The correspondence is renewed only on 17 August 1961 with a letter from Hammarskjöld. Once again, the reason is his reading of Buber:

> The last few days I have been reading some studies of yours which I had not seen before. They are the five papers which have been published in English under the collective Title 'Between Man and Man', and I think especially of 'Zwiesprache', 'Die Frage an den Einzelnen', and parts of 'Was ist der Mensch'.
>
> After having finished reading these studies, I feel the need to send you again a greeting – after far too long a time of silence, understandably only in the light of the pressure of circumstances. In what you say about 'signs', about the 'questions' and the response and about the Single One and his responsibility, with reference also to the political sphere, you have formulated shared experiences in ways which made your studies very much what you would call a 'sign' for me.
>
> (KB DHS: Dag Hammarskjöld, Letter to Martin Buber,
> 17 August 1961)

As before, Hammarskjöld finds fascinating parallels between Buber's comments and his own views. To underscore this agreement he writes: 'It is strange – over a gulf of time and a gulf of differences as to background and outer experience – to find a bridge built which, in one move, eliminates the distance.' Hammarskjöld ends by saying that he is still thinking about translating something by Buber into Swedish:

> I still keep in mind the idea of translating you so as to bring you closer to my country men, but it becomes increasingly difficult to choose and of course I can not envisage any more extensive work. Also, the more I sense the nuances in your German, the more shy I become at the thought of a translation which, at best, could render only a modest part of its overtones.
>
> (ibid.)

Five days later, Buber writes from Jerusalem, thanking Hammarskjöld for the letter: 'It is for one, even more than what you said in our first talk, a token of true integral understanding, – rather a rare gift in this world of ours' (KB DHS: Martin Buber, Letter to Dag Hammarskjöld, 23 August 1961). Then he comments on Hammarskjöld's translation plans: 'Were I asked, which of my books a Swede should read first, I should answer: "The most 'difficult' of them all, but the most apt to introduce the reader into the realm of dialogue," I mean: "I and Thou".' To underline this suggestion, he encloses a new edition of the book with his epilogue and a lecture on language held the previous year. Hammarskjöld replies three days later, thanking Buber for the book and continuing:

I am certain that I am reading you correctly if I see reflected in your reply a silent 'Aufruf' that I try a translation of this keywork, as decisive in its message as supremely beautiful in its form.

This decides the issue and, if I have your permission, I shall do it even if it may take some time.

(KB DHS: Dag Hammarskjöld, Letter to Martin Buber, 26 August 1961)

The final reference to the question of time must be stressed, as in his enquiry Hammarskjöld had pointed out that he could not undertake an extensive work. Yet Buber did not choose any of the essays that Hammarskjöld had explicitly mentioned and praised, but his most ambitious work, in which those peculiarities of Buber's German that Hammarskjöld had described as difficult are particularly pronounced. Nevertheless, he accepts the task with enthusiasm. On the same day he contacts the Swedish publishers Bonnier asking them to regulate the formal questions with Buber. Hammarskjöld ends his letter to Buber with the sentence: 'If this all works out, may I tell you how much it would mean to me also by providing me with a justification for a broadened and intensified contact with you personally.'

This letter is followed by another on 5 September 1961, in which Hammarskjöld tells Buber that his friend John Steinbeck will be visiting Jerusalem and suggests that they meet: 'He [John Steinbeck] is, as you will know, one of those observers of life in our generation, who feel that its survival will depend on our ability to know ourselves and to stick to basic human values with the will to pay what it may cost' (KB DHS: Dag Hammarskjöld, Letter to Martin Buber, 5 September 1961). Given the focus on Hammarskjöld's political ethics, this assessment is a programmatic formulation. Hammarskjöld regards the ethical endeavours that he has also noted in Buber as the concern of a generation in which, through the use of the word 'our', he includes Buber.

Hammarskjöld's last letter to Buber dealt with technical publication matters between Bonnier und Buber (KB DHS: Dag Hammarskjöld, Letter to Martin Buber, 12 September 1961). Hammarskjöld did not get very far with his translation of 'I and Thou'. Among his personal papers left in Sture Linnér's lodgings were twelve typed pages covering the opening pages of the book (KB DHS: Dag Hammarskjöld, typed manuscript (Swedish)). Hammarskjöld had asked Linnér to look at them. He was well aware of the linguistic difficulties of translating into Swedish, as he had previously tried to translate Buber's 'Legend of Baalshem' (Urquhart 1972: 41). The work on Buber's text was as demanding for him as the writing of his diary; at any rate, he regarded the translation as a 'personal declaration' (KB DHS: Dag Hammarskjöld, Letter to Georg Svensson, 12 September 1961), and after he started translating on 26 August 1961 he made no further entries in his diary (Urquhart 1972: 41). Another seven handwritten pages of translation were found at the site of the plane crash in Ndola (KB DHS: Dag Hammarskjöld, handwritten manuscript: 7–14). It is possible that he was continuing his work on the translation during the flight to Ndola. The fact that Hammarskjöld was thinking about Buber in his last hours is underscored by the incident reported by

Linnér, in which Hammarskjöld talked to him about the similarities between the concept of love as used by Buber and the medieval mystics.

Buber's influence on Hammarskjöld

In contrast to the medieval mystics and Schweitzer, the diary and the Murrow interview do not provide clear evidence for Buber's influence on Hammarskjöld. But Hammarskjöld's public utterances vividly indicate the inspiration that he drew from Buber's writings for his political work. The occasion of the first reference to Buber is a dispute in the Security Council in April 1958 – a few days after Hammarskjöld's first letter to Jerusalem. In a debate the Soviet Union accuses the United States of deliberately disregarding Soviet security interests in the Arctic by flying nuclear armed bombers over it (CF IV: 3–4). The Unites States responds to this accusation by proposing the creation of a zone of inspection over the Arctic that would protect both sides against surprise attack. The Soviet Union reacts to this proposal with scepticism and mistrust. Its reaction is the mirror image of a behavioural pattern evident a few days earlier when the Soviet Union's unilateral declaration (that it would stop testing atomic weapons) was similarly received with deep scepticism in the West.

Hammarskjöld speaks in the Security Council on 29 April and refers to these two examples of mutual mistrust. He expressly mentions that this is an unusual procedure, but it is the duty of the Secretary-General to act to promote the goals of the organization:

> [H]e [the Secretary-General] can not assume for himself any kind of right to, so to say, 'speak for man' but he must subordinate himself to his duty to express the significance of the aspirations of man, as set out in the Charter, for problems before this Council or the General Assembly.
>
> (CF IV: 70)

Referring to his previous support for the Soviet proposal to stop atomic tests, Hammarskjöld declares that he must support the American proposal for the same reasons. The behaviour of both sides in not accepting the extremely reasonable proposals of the respective other side, prompts Hammarskjöld to note that '[t]he stalemate in the field of disarmament has been permitted to last far too long' (ibid.). There are a number of reasons for this, such as waiting for the other side to take the first step. But this is not the heart of the problem, which Hammarskjöld presents as follows:

> Still another reason, and of course the basic one, is the crisis of trust from which all mankind is suffering at the present juncture and which is reflected in an unwillingness to take any moves in a positive direction at their face value and a tendency to hold back a positive response because of a fear of being misled.
>
> Such initiatives as those to which I have referred … might have a major impact if treated in good faith which is, of course, not the same as to let down

one's guard. And they could, if followed through, provide a first frail basis for the development of some kind of trust.

(ibid.)

The similarity in thinking is unmistakable. How closely he compares Buber's thoughts with his own is also shown by the fact that he sends this statement to his friend Bo Beskow in Sweden with the remark that it was a risky step, but made clear how he saw the present global situation (Beskow 1969: 137). Thus, according to Hammarskjöld, the main problem in disarmament talks lies in the lack of mutual trust. National representatives had apparently not yet realized that the people in their respective countries were desperately waiting for their leaders to get them 'out of the present nightmare' (Statement, 29 April 1958, in CF IV: 71). Here the Secretary-General adopts central ideas of Buber and transfers them almost unchanged into the political reality of a UN Security Council meeting.

Just how seriously he takes the problems discussed in the meeting is underlined by his remarks at subsequent press conferences, in which he returned to this topic. In a press conference on 1 May – on the morning of his meeting with Buber – Hammarskjöld yet again explains his motivation and, referring to the question of disarmament, states:

... I have the feeling that we have missed the bus. And we should not be too sure that the road will remain open for buses in all the future. That sense of urgency, that sense of responsibility, in the face of every new opening, from wherever it comes and whatever its immediate limited substance, was what prompted me, what made me feel that it was one of the occasions where public statements by the Secretary-General are very much part of his duty and a very adequate supplement to private diplomacy.

(CF IV: 74; see also Urquhart 1972: 315–22)

The spiritual understanding between Hammarskjöld and Buber had thus produced initial results in the form of Hammarskjöld's initiative. For the time being, it would remain unsuccessful (see CF IV: 80). On 2 May, the Soviet Union vetoed the proposal of an Arctic zone of inspection, and the Soviet ambassador to the UN, Arkady Sobolov, expressly criticized Hammarskjöld for 'taking sides', which he saw detrimental to the authority of the Secretary-General. Against the aforementioned background, however, precisely this rejection confirms the urgency of Hammarskjöld's and Buber's concern.

The Secretary-General not only refused to drop the topic, but gave it even greater priority in his activities. On 5 June 1958, Hammarskjöld received an honorary doctorate from the University of Cambridge and held a lecture titled 'The Walls of Distrust' in which he returns to Buber's ideas, according them the particular political significance of being quoted verbatim in a speech of the Secretary-General (CF IV: 90–4). After introductory remarks about the occasion, he turns to the question of 'spiritual leadership' needed in a time of growing conflict and violence. He introduces the conflict situation as being essentially determined by a division between West and East on the importance of the individual, his place in society and the forms of social organization. Hammarskjöld wants to move away from seeing this division solely in terms of East–West and comments:

> The dividing line goes within ourselves, within our own peoples, and also within other nations. It does not coincide with any political or geographical boundaries. The ultimate fight is between the human and the subhuman. We are on dangerous ground if we believe that any individual, any nation, or any ideology has a monopoly on rightness, liberty, and human dignity.
>
> When we fully recognize this and translate our insight into words and action, we may also be able to reestablish full human contact and communications across geographical and political boundaries, and get out of a public debate which often seems to be inspired more by a wish to impress rather than by a will to understand and to be understood.
>
> (ibid.: 91–2)

This passage is nothing more than a paraphrase of Buber's concept of the 'crossfront' presented above. After making such similar remarks, it is only consistent of Hammarskjöld to explicitly note his closeness to Buber, by mentioning him as 'one of the influential thinkers of our time, whose personal history and national experience have given him a vantage point of significance' (ibid.: 93). He goes on to quote exceptionally long excerpts from a speech Buber gave in Carnegie Hall in 1952 titled 'Hope in this Hour' (also reprinted in 'Pointing the Way' (1963f: 223–4) dealing with the erosion of trust and decay of communication through the predominance of suspicion and ideology). Hammarskjöld apologizes for quoting Buber extensively; however, 'out of the depth of his feelings Martin Buber has found expressions which it would be vain for me to improve' (CF IV: 93). The extent to which this statement reflects Hammarskjöld's very own perceptions is made clear by Saint-John Perse's remarks in a letter to the Secretary-General in the course of their intensive exchange on the nature of modern poetry and politics that Hammarskjöld's Cambridge speech is a manifesto of a 'supranational ethics':

> Votre allocution à Cambridge apporte un élément nouveau à ce que vous pouvez évoquer, personellement, de vos convictions, de vos appréhensions et de vos espérances, avec toute la philosophie qui s'en dégage, pour un avenir de la communauté internationale. On perçoit bien, avec vous, toute la délicatesse d'une conclusion morale qui doit d'abord faire fond sur l'évolution des esprits de la sauvegarde humaine de toutes ressources 'spirituelles'. Depuis que l'U.N.O. a trouvé sa fin en elle-même, dans l'universalité, il faut bien se dire, avec quelque réalisme, qu'elle ne relève plus en fait du pragmatisme immédiat des hommes d'État, mais d'une éthique sur-nationale en [voie] cours d'élucidation et d'imposition éventuelle.
>
> (Letter from Leger to Hammarskjöld, 15 June 1958, quoted in Leger 1993: 136)

Whether one shares the urgency in this assessment or not, the closeness to Buber is clear. This note completes the analysis of the individual elements in Dag Hammarskjöld's political ethics. The following summary will put some of the leitmotifs in their context.

Summary: personal ethics and international responsibility

The various basic elements in Dag Hammarskjöld's political ethics resemble a jazz piece in which the different soloists return again and again to the basic melody each in accordance with his instrument and temperament, interpreting it from his own perspective. In keeping with this image, the above-mentioned influences are not only compatible with Hammarskjöld's views and determine them, but the influences themselves are bound up with each other. Dealing with Hammarskjöld offers a key to a form of 'generational discourse', whose concerns and questions, notwithstanding the diversity of the participants, are interrelated (Fröhlich 2001a: 28–32).

A strong common element in the above-mentioned basic elements of Hammarskjöld's political ethics is his life-affirming interpretation of the medieval mystics, who also interested Söderblom and Bergson (Interview Linnér 1998; Aulén 1969: 14–16 and Plug 1985: 313) as well as Schweitzer and Buber. Buber and Schweitzer were somewhat more critical of the classics, which they read in a different way from Hammarskjöld. Buber, in particular, refused to be called a mystic after he had developed his philosophy of dialogue (Wehr 1996: 11). Nevertheless, he continued to think highly of Hasidism as an outward-looking form of mysticism (Dusen 1965: 188) and praised Hammarskjöld's knowledge of the works of Meister Eckhart (Hodes 1971: 143). The call for personal dialogue between prominent international politicians and the necessity of ethically motivated leaders was a cause that both Schweitzer and Buber supported (Spear 1978: 36). Both strove to establish a 'teaching of being human among humans' (ibid.: 58). Hence, it is not surprising that Schweitzer and Buber knew and held each other in high esteem.

Uppsala's archbishop, Nathan Söderblom, is a sort of personified link to other basic elements of Hammarskjöld's political ethics; not only did he bring Schweitzer to Uppsala, but he also wrote theological works on the concept of 'vocation' (Söderblom 1914) and corresponded with Bergson (Plug 1985: 301). In turn, there is also a link between his philosophy of life and Schweitzer's (Stolpe 1965; Beyschlag 1980a: 320; Lash 1961: 233–4). Over and above these connections between the respective elements, Hammarskjöld also had his own interpretations:

> What he 'discovered' in his contact with the medieval mystics acted as a corrective to an intellectualistic conception of faith. Even more, it operated as a corrective to a one-sided ethical conception of the Christian life. We must not forget Hammarskjöld's *but*, when, in his radio address of 1953, he turned from Albert Schweitzer to the medieval mystics., it seems that he

interpreted Schweitzer as one who more or less identified the stream of love which appears in human life with God or the divine element. In the mystics' explanation of the 'inner Life', however, God was in his own being purely the center, the all-dominating power. ... This did not mean a reduced accent on ethics and action, but it meant that life received a new center – and *Markings* bears consistent witness to that fact.

(Aulén 1969: 117)

Hartman (1966: 108) interprets Schweitzer and the mystics as stations in the development of Hammarskjöld's views: '... Hammarskjöld's religious development proceeded from scepticism to a belief in the Reverence for Life principle; and from that to the mystical conception of faith as the union of God and the soul.' Once writing about Buber, Hammarskjöld himself formulated in his characteristic way how the plurality of the paths and patterns of influence produced his ideas. In his proposal to the Nobel Committee, Hammarskjöld wrote:

Without examining the logical validity of Buber's formula and all its implications, one can accept it as the expression of an extremely fertile philosophy of life and can understand how influential it has become. It has touches of a mystical pantheism, while it still retains the depth and drama of the dualistic relationship with the divine. At the same time, in its relationship with man it is a translation of Kant's thesis of man as an object in itself, in terms which gave this thesis a new human warmth and richness.

(quoted in Hodes 1971: 145–6)

Bearing in mind such distinctions and contrasting complementaries, the following paragraphs seek to present the overarching arguments of the basic elements of Hammarskjöld's political ethics. In these, we can expect to find what Hammarskjöld called the 'formula and task of our generation'. The following points may be components of this formula.

Service: calling, imitation and reverence for life

The concept of service is one of the dominant themes running through Hammarskjöld's political ethics. The central importance of the concept is underscored by the fact that it is present in all the basic elements Hammarskjöld analysed: in the family tradition of government service, in the mystics' call for imitating Christ, as practical consequence of reverence for life, and in the philosophy of Buber, who explained: 'Man can do justice to the relation to God in which he has come to share only if he realises God anew in the world according to his strength and to the measure of each day' (Buber 1966: 114). However, the challenge of service is only possible if the calling goes hand in hand with integrity of action.

Integrity: inner examination and outer activity

The diary illustrates a development in thought similar to that undergone of the mystics, Schweitzer and Buber: through self-reflection man finds himself, on the basis of which he is able to recognize his calling, which in turn leads him to accept responsibility for others. Finding oneself is an inner dialogue that serves to protect personal integrity in the outside world and discuss 'personal prerequisites for peacefulness' (Graevenitz 1967; see also Henkel 1999). In a speech at Johns Hopkins University in 1995 on the occasion of the tenth anniversary of the United Nations, Hammarskjöld had already formulated the close connection between personal ethics and international ethics (CF II: 502–7). At the end of his address he apologized: 'You may be surprised by an approach to international service and to the problems raised by present-day developments in international life which, like mine today, is concerned mainly with problems of personal ethics' (ibid.: 507). But once the separate elements of Hammarskjöld's political ethics are reconstructed, the connection is less strange. One must agree with Zacher that '... Hammarskjöld saw the normative bases of the United Nations as an extension of his own philosophical principles into international affairs.' (1970: 10–15). Max Ascoli termed these views of Hammarskjöld's 'Christian ethics at its best' (1965: 40). This raises the question of the relevance of these ethical ideas in a global context.

Universality: unity and solidarity of mankind

Hammarskjöld's political ethics do not draw from Christian roots alone. It must be stressed once more that through his interest in European, Jewish, Muslim and Asian mysticism Hammarskjöld found a 'universal element in the experience of mysticism' (Barudio 1989: 105). Buber and Schweitzer were also interested in non-European cultures and their thinking (Buber 1909; Schweitzer 1957). Hammarskjöld's personal conception and careful design of the meditation room in the UN headquarters is a notable manifestation of the intercultural foundations of his thinking (see Beskow 1969: 77–107; Barudio 1989: 149; Riedmaier 1966). In an explanatory text for visitors, Hammarskjöld wrote about the block of iron ore standing in the middle of the room illuminated by a thin ray of light from above: 'We may see it as an altar, empty not because there is no God, not because it is an altar to an unknown God, but because it is dedicated to the God whom man worships under many names and in many forms' (CF II: 711). In this sense, he saw the United Nations as 'inspired by what unites and not by what divides the great religions of the world' (Address World Council of Churches, 20 August 1954, in CF II: 352). But this approach did not compel uniformity, as he pointed out, quoting Schweitzer: 'It is not the function of education to compel uniformity. Nor is it the function of the United Nations to produce one world in that sense. For good reasons, Albert Schweitzer has called it a betrayal of the very idea of civilization to claim priority and predominance for any special national variety of civilization' (Address at the Annual Meeting of the Association of American

Colleges, 13 January 1954, in CF II: 253–4). An address at the University of Lund in 1959 contains the clearest expression of his thoughts on this topic (CF IV: 380–7). He started by examining one particular consequence of World War I: 'The whole closed European cultural circle was broken up in a reappraisal of all values' (ibid.: 382). He continued: 'Many of us have had contact with the European world of the fading nineteenth century – the typical attitudes of which have, of course, reached far into our own – and then experienced the breakdown of the European circle of culture, spiritually, politically, and geographically, finally seeing at last the beginning of a new synthesis on a universal basis' (ibid.). Prerequisite for this synthesis is solidarity and mutual respect on the part of all when dealing with different cultures. 'I used the word solidarity. It is a key word in this connection, and to me it is the answer to the irritable questions and reactions which are still sometimes forthcoming from those who have entrenched themselves in the past and view almost as a traitor any European who does not weep over the receding power of Europe' (ibid.: 383.) The UN is founded on precisely this concept of solidarity:

> In these circumstances, it appears evident that no nation or group of nations can base its future on a claim of supremacy. It is in its own interest that the other groups have opportunities equal to those it has had itself. To contribute to this is an act of solidarity which is not only good for the whole but, in the long run, rebounds to the advantage even of those who take the action. It means that leadership is substituted for power – leadership both in giving other peoples their chances and in assisting them, without issuing commands, to find the best way to develop their spiritual and material resources.
>
> (ibid.: 384)

Here, Hammarskjöld's understanding of the potential of the United Nations and his office are in direct agreement with the objectives of his political ethics. However, for him intercultural thinking is bound up with shared fundamental experiences.

Cooperation: imperative against the backdrop of the global threat

In their works, Schweitzer and Buber clearly articulate the motivation for their search for a new, viable basis of human coexistence through reference to the catastrophic world wars. In his annual reports, Hammarskjöld referred to this (in Buber's words), 'experience of the Vesuvian hour' (Buber 1994c: 304; Wehr 1996: 152) to urge international cooperation. It is not least this similarity of views that led the younger Hammarskjöld to identify Buber and Schweitzer in his letters as members of his generation.[49] Against this background, the technical possibility of nuclear war is an echo of this experience that cannot be ignored. Hammarskjöld and Schweitzer are closest to each other in their assessment of the danger of atomic warfare. Buber, by contrast, broadens the programme of coexistence in Schweitzer's philosophy to include the duty of cooperation. When in this context

Buber laments the loss of the ideal of fraternity (understood as openness to understanding) as the basis of cooperation and agreement between the competing ideals of liberty and equality (1952: 314–15), he catches in a nutshell a subsurface structure in their contemporary thinking that is reflected in the simple words of Art. 1 of the Universal Declaration of Human Rights of 1948, according to which all people born free and equal ... should 'act towards one another in a spirit of brotherhood'. Neither Schweitzer nor Buber nor Hammarskjöld understood this call as a naïve postulate or just as a renaissance of the French Revolution.

Fighting optimism: the attitude of 'quand-même'

Common to all three is the awareness of the difficulties in implementing these concepts. At the same time, they resist being identified with an ostensible 'realism' that lacks the power to change circumstances: 'To the question of whether I am a pessimist or an optimist, I answer that my knowledge is pessimistic, but my willing and hoping are optimistic' (Schweitzer 1998b: 242). This is the basis on which Schweitzer criticized the 'Realpolitik' of World War I. Buber claims for himself: 'What I mean is not a vague idealism, but a more comprehending, more penetrating realism, a greater realism, the realism of a greater reality' (Buber 1963f: 323). Hammarskjöld, too, supports this form of 'optimism', as he explained to UN correspondents at the beginning of his second term:

> It is not the facile faith of generations before us, who thought that everything was arranged for the best in the best of worlds or that physical and psychological development necessarily worked out toward something they called progress. It is in a sense a much harder belief – the belief that the future will be all right because there will always be enough people to fight for a decent future. ... It is in a sense a switch from the atmosphere of pre-1914 to what I believe is the atmosphere of our generation in this time – a switch from the, so to say, mechanical optimism of previous generations to what I might call the fighting optimism of this present generation. We have learned it the hard way, and we will certainly have to learn it again and again and again.
>
> (CF IV: 64)

Hammarskjöld demonstrated this fighting optimism on various occasions. For instance, the Secretary-General writes in a letter to Ben Gurion on 18 August 1956 after several requests to the Israelis to observe the ceasefire: 'As a matter of course I shall not relax in my efforts, but if we were not to register any progress beyond where we now stand, it will have to be in a spirit of "quand-même"' (KB DHS: Dag Hammarskjöld, Letter to David Ben Gurion, 18 August 1956). The concept of *quand-même* recalls the writings of Albert Camus. Hammarskjöld referred to existentialist thinking a number of times (Henderson 1969: 16–17). Hughes (1995: 171) points to the existentialist nature of Hammarskjöld's interest in questions of loneliness, finiteness and death. However, the attitude of '*quand-*

même' also appears in Schweitzer's thesis of world affirmation through world negation in his research for his 'Quest for the Historical Jesus'.

The emphasis on '*quand-même*' eventually leads back to the medieval mystics: 'The inner freedom that puts aside all concern for esteem, honour and prosperity for oneself makes possible the political independence with which Dag Hammarskjöld filled his office. It gave him an inner immunity against the massive attacks he had to face. … This inner force is manifested in Hammarskjöld's inexhaustible optimism' (Schäfer 1970: 374–5). Max Weber identified this attitude as one of the prerequisites for a political career: 'Only whoever is sure that he will not be shattered when the world, seen from his point of view, is too stupid or too base for what he will offer it, and in spite of all that, is still capable of saying: "all the same", he alone has the vocation for politics' (1989: 64).

At first glance, the combination of the basic elements of Hammarskjöld's political ethics expressed in the above-mentioned concepts may seem eclectic. Nevertheless, the integration of different approaches in an overarching perspective seems to be characteristic of Hammarskjöld's thinking. The 1951 article on the civil servant defends a similar procedure in determining guidelines for civil servants: 'To the superficial observer it may seem that the mix of conservative, liberal, social-radical and internationalist elements is really eclectic. But he overlooks the fact that the individual elements all come from the same basic outlook …' (quoted in Stolpe 1964a: 57). Ultimately, the apparently contradictory polyphony of deep faith, existential pessimism, mystic experience, the classical legacy of the Enlightenment, a scientific awareness of the dangers of atomic war, political realism and the plain experience of the horrors of war came together in astonishing harmony in a 'new way of thinking'.[50]

Art, literature, politics: Global standards

Hammarskjöld's integrative way of thinking goes hand in hand with the application of the same principles in various fields: 'Dag often compared the problems in art and science with those he encountered in his own field of work – a moral and philosophical comparison' (Beskow 1969: 72). This perspective shows Hammarskjöld's multifarious interests in art and literature in a different light, as they, like his political concerns, are closely tied up with his ethical views. The photographer (Hammarskjöld 1987: 17–32) of Mount Everest, whose pictures and accompanying text appeared in the *National Geographic* magazine in 1961 (CF V: 298–304), was looking for the universality of spiritual experience and the experience of the inner self in the interplay with outer natural experience. The translator of Saint-John Perse's 'Chronique' (Leger 1993; Perse 1989 and Sauvage 1960) traced humanity's journey of exploration through the evolution of history in those verses. Djuna Barnes' (Grace 1987) play *The Antiphon*, for him, confirmed both the translator's wrestling for genuine dialogue and the diagnosis of his own and society's inability to communicate. Hammarskjöld's preoccupation with literature, for which he kept an hour or two free every day, was 'un complément indispensable' (Sauvage 1960: 1) to diplomacy: 'N'oubliez pas non plus le genre de monde où nous vivons ici. Le problème de traduire, de transposer, d'exprimer les choses dans des langues différentes ne nous quitte jamais. Traduire, transposer, mais c'est notre existence quotidienne, permanente. J'en ai souvent discuté avec Léger' (ibid.: 6).

This application of the same principles, norms and standards to different fields is most explicit in Hammarskjöld's approach to the work of Barbara Hepworth (Fröhlich 2001a). They agreed very closely on basic assumptions about artistic and public life. Hepworth, for instance, wrote that Hammarskjöld's work at the United Nations was a 'constant inspiration' for her work (KB DHS: Barbara Hepworth, Letter to Dag Hammarskjöld, 22 May 1958). She explained: 'You have the fully integrated "vision" which demonstrates the naturalness & beauty of the spirit of man which all of us, in varying degrees, are striving to obtain by the unity of mind & imagination'(KB DHS: Barbara Hepworth, Letter to Dag Hammarskjöld, 16 October 1959). Hammarskjöld reciprocated in kind, when he commented on a sculpture that Hepworth sent him in July 1961:

> I have now had it before me a couple of weeks, living with it in all shades of light, both physically and mentally, and this is the report: it is a strong and exacting companion, but at the same time one of quiet and timeless perspective in inner space. You may react at the word exacting. But a work of great art sets its own standard of integrity and remains a continuous reminder of what should be achieved in everything.
>
> So you hear that your gift gives me great joy of a kind which ultimately is of great help, whatever our specific task may be.
>
> (KB DHS: Dag Hammarskjöld, Letter to Barbara Hepworth, 11 August 1961)

On the occasion of the unveiling of her sculpture 'Single Form' in memory of Hammarskjöld in front of the UN headquarters, Hepworth elaborated: 'Dag Hammarskjöld had a pure and exact perception of aesthetic principles, as exact as it was over ethical and moral principles. I believe they were, to him, one and the same thing, and he asked of each one of us the best we could give' (UN Press Release HQ 212, 11 June 1964). Conor Cruise O'Brien's assessment was similar: 'Mr. Hammarskjöld thought and felt as much about literature as he did about politics. He believed, with an almost mystical intensity of conviction, that the two fields were really one and required the same qualities' (1961: 17). And Urquhart (1964: 234) went as far as to say: 'As part of a general and continuous process of self-realization, he developed standards of behaviour and religious feeling with great care and persistence. These religious and ethical standards were applied to everything he did, both private and public, so that there was an impressive consistency in his approach to all aspects of his life.' Hammarskjöld himself often highlighted these parallels:

> In modern international politics – aiming toward that world of order which now more than ever seems to be the only alternative to disruption and disaster – we have to approach our task in the spirit which animates the modern artist. We have to tackle our problems without the armour of inherited convictions

or set formulas, but only with our bare hands and all the honesty we can muster. And we have to do so with an unbreakable will to master the inert matter of patterns created by history and sociological conditions.

(Address at the Inauguration of the Twenty-fifth Anniversary of the Museum of Modern Art, 19 October 1954, in CF II: 375)

Hammarskjöld's mediation between different aspects of life was a constitutive part of his view of integrity: 'Integrity in the sense not only of purity and honor but also of seeing life as a consistent whole, subject in all its parts to the same rules of conduct and standards of performance' (Urquhart 1972:18). At Johns Hopkins University he explained in1955:

> What is true in a life of action, like that of a politician or a diplomat, is true also in intellectual activities. Even a genius never achieves a lasting result in science without patience and hard work, just as in politics the results of the work of the most brilliant mind will ultimately find their value determined by character. Those who are called to be teachers or leaders may profit from intelligence but can only justify their position by integrity.
>
> (CF II: 507)

This raises the question of whether this kind of articulation and application of ethical principles does justice to the properties of the political sphere. In other words, what is the relationship between Hammarskjöld's ethics and the classic conflict between politics and morality? Regarding political practice, this question will be dealt with in Chapter 4. Concerning theory, the specific nature of Hammarskjöld's political ethics enables us to establish certain orientations here. The writings of Buber that Hammarskjöld mentions give useful indications, although Buber speaks primarily of religion rather than ethics. In his discussion of Gandhi, Buber asks the question: 'Does religion allow itself to be introduced into politics in such a way that a political success can be obtained?' (1963h: 128). He starts by distinguishing the inherent rationale of each field: 'Religion means goal and way, politics implies end and means' (ibid.). Although Buber's concept of politics is largely negative, he recognizes that the political sphere is necessary to regulate mankind's coexistence. Taking the political actions of Ghandi as an admittedly special example he concludes (ibid.: 129): 'He cannot wrestle uninter-ruptedly with the serpent; he must at times get along with it because he is directed to work in the kingdom of the serpent that he set out to destroy.' In his view, there is no simple way of combining religion and politics: 'Only in the polis of God will religion and politics be blended into a life of world community, in an eternity wherein neither religion nor politics will any longer exist' (ibid.). Besides this insight Buber develops a bridge between ethical duty and political reality in the measure of *'quantum satis'*:

> As much as one can at the time; *'quantum satis'* means in the language of lived truth not 'either–or', but 'as-much-as-one-can'. If the political

organization of existence does not infringe on my wholeness and immediacy, it may demand of me that I do justice to it at any particular time as far as, in a given inner conflict, I believe I am able to answer for. At any particular time; for here there is no once-and-for-all: in each situation that demands decision the demarcation line between service and service must be drawn anew – not necessarily with fear, but necessarily with that trembling of the soul that precedes every genuine decision.

(1963c: 217)

Many entries in Hammarskjöld's diary testify to the repeated, tense search for the '*quantum satis*' rather than the attempt to transfer ethical convictions with a claim to absoluteness. Hammarskjöld's ethics are not least for this reason 'political ethics': they allow for the flexibility needed to recognize the intrinsic order of the political sphere. Former presidential candidate and US ambassador to the United Nations, Adlai E. Stevenson, observes:

Hammarskjöld also understood that the machinery not only needs lofty goals and high principles but it has to work in practice – that it has limited, not unlimited functions; that it has finite, not infinite, capabilities under given circumstances at a given time. He saw that the effectiveness of the Organization is measured by the best consensus that can be reached by the relevant majority of the relevant organ and that reaching it is a highly pragmatic exercise.

(1965: 53)

This leads us to the next chapter and to the analysis of concrete political action in Hammarskjöld's term of office.[51]

4 Connections between ethical thought and political action

'You don't fill a political vacuum with ethics alone' (Interview Urquhart 1997). Urquhart's words draw attention to the fact that Hammarskjöld's political actions were more than just ethical reflections; they had to be transformed into and applied as political instruments. It is this transformability and application that defines the quality of political ethics. In this context, Nayar lists three instruments of Hammarskjöld: 'quiet' or 'private diplomacy', with the goal of preparing an acceptable compromise behind the scenes; 'preventive diplomacy' aiming at the limitation of local conflicts and preventing them from snowballing into a confrontation between the superpowers; and UN presences, i.e. the active involvement of the United Nations on the spot. Nayar finally sees Hammarskjöld as 'the originator and formulator of these basic concepts' (1974: 54). Gordenker reaches a similar conclusion: 'He [Hammarskjöld] left a record of innovation, represented by the 'Peking formula', 'preventive diplomacy', and the United Nations 'presence', and of a magisterial hand in dividing complex problems into smaller, more tractable ones' (1967a: 326).

Once again, these concepts cannot easily be separated from each other. Preventive diplomacy was, so to speak, the overarching concept behind all of Hammarskjöld's actions. At the same time, the concept of the 'international civil servant' is the basis for these new forms of action, and will therefore be discussed together with the instruments of 'private diplomacy' and 'the UN presence'. Each case study will be treated in three stages: a detailed reconstruction of the conflict, Hammarskjöld's reaction, and an attempt to link the instrument applied with basic elements of Hammarskjöld's political ethics. In this way Kanninen's question of what remains after analysing the legal, political, historical and military aspects of a decision will be taken up once more: 'But what about the content of basic moral values, and motivations stemming from … deeply-held-beliefs? Does the adherence to certain fundamental values affect decisions taken?' (1995: 261). While it is not possible to examine all of the conflicts, crises and efforts at mediation in which Hammarskjöld was involved, the three case studies will enable us to meaningfully structure his period in office. Hammarskjöld was not the sole architect and administrator of the concepts and instruments presented in this chapter. Besides the crucial interaction with member states, he was surrounded by a remarkable team which we shall briefly sketch before turning to the individual case studies.[1]

Work routines in the UN Secretariat: Hammarskjöld's team

A glance at the organizational chart shows the pre-eminence of the Executive Office in the Secretariat (see Figures 4.1 and 4.2). According to Gordenker, during Hammarskjöld's period in office it was the real 'center for all important work on political matters' (1967a: 118) headed by Andrew Cordier, an American, who was Hammarskjöld's Executive Assistant for almost his entire incumbency. He is unequivocal about his relationship with Hammarskjöld: 'Everything that concerned the Secretary-General concerned me' (1964: 5). By retaining Cordier, who was already an established and experienced official under Lie, Hammarskjöld had a fixed point of reference in the Secretariat. Cordier explained the procedural routine to the new man and to this extent acquainted him with the administration. It was also Cordier who suggested that Hammarskjöld personally greet all staff members at the headquarters. Following this advice, in his first days in office Hammarskjöld shook the hands of all of the approximately 3,500 employees in New York and repeated this procedure after his re-election in 1958 (1967: 15). This symbolic act had a motivating and positive effect at UN headquarters.

The offices of Cordier and the Secretary-General were separated by the offices of two secretaries. Hammarskjöld and he met spontaneously several times a day, apart from appointments such as the weekly meeting of the executive offices on Friday morning. They also often ate lunch and dinner together, an opportunity to talk that both valued. Hammarskjöld discussed just about every matter with Cordier, from technical details to the interpretation of Security Council resolutions. Cordier's duties included shielding Hammarskjöld from the outside world. His letters to Hammarskjöld show that he functioned as a type of information filter for the Secretary-General and as a conduit for the various heads of national delegations and permanent representatives who wished to present their concerns to the Secretary-General. They saw in Cordier a sounding-board on which they could test the thrust of their argument and the chances of success. Over and above this, Cordier played an important role in proposing and selecting management personnel for the Secretariat. As a rule he attended all of the very varied *ad hoc* working groups in the Secretariat. Apart from Cordier's 'internal' functions, Hammarskjöld also sent him on several mediation missions and information trips, for example, to the Middle East and the Congo. In 1961, Cordier resigned from the Executive Office to make life easier for Hammarskjöld, who was increasingly accused of favouring the West in the top echelons of the UN. His successor was C.V. Narasimhan, an Indian.

The Executive Office therefore can be described as heart of the Secretariat. One of its tasks, discussed above in connection with the annual reports, is preparing speeches for the Secretary-General. On taking office, Hammarskjöld appointed a former colleague in the Swedish Foreign Ministry to the Executive Office. Per Lind had previously worked in the embassy in Washington (Lash 1961: 22). According to the organizational chart, he was Chief of the General Assembly Section until 1956. In fact, he had very little to do with the General Assembly at all. He was a sort of personal assistant to Hammarskjöld. Lind's discreet conception of his

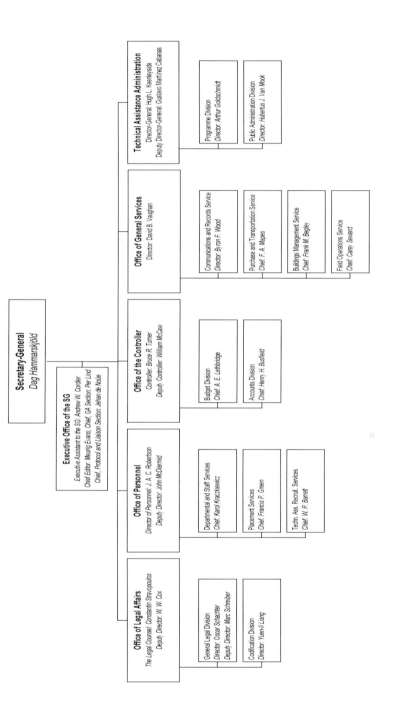

Secretary-General
Dag Hammarskjöld

Executive Office of the SG
Executive Assistant to the SG: Andrew W. Cordier
Chief Editor: Meuning Evans; Chief, GA Section: Per Lind
Chief, Protocol and Liaison Section: Jehan de Noüe

Office of Legal Affairs
The Legal Counsel: Constantin Stravopoulos
Deputy Director: W. W. Cox

General Legal Division
Director: Oscar Schachter
Deputy Director: Marc Schreiber

Codification Division
Director: Yuen-li Liang

Office of Personnel
Director of Personnel: J. A. C. Robertson
Deputy Director: John McDiarmid

Departmental and Staff Services
Chief: Karol Kraczkiewicz

Placement Services
Chief: Francis P. Green

Techn. Ass. Recruit. Services
Chief: W. P. Barrett

Office of the Controller
Controller: Bruce R. Turner
Deputy Controller: William McCaw

Budget Division
Chief: A. E. Lethbridge

Accounts Division
Chief: Henn. H. Busfield

Office of General Services
Director: David B. Vaughan

Communications and Records Service
Director: Byron F. Wood

Purchase and Transportation Service
Chief: F. A. Mapes

Buildings Management Service
Chief: Frank M. Begley

Field Operations Service
Chief: Carey Seward

Technical Assistance Administration
Director-General: Hugh L. Keenleyside
Deputy Director-General: Gustavo Martínez Cabañas

Programme Division
Director: Arthur Goldschmidt

Public Administration Division
Director: Hubertus J. Van Mook

Figure 4.1 Structure of the Secretariat, 1955 (Office level) (Compiled from *UN Yearbooks* 1952–62)

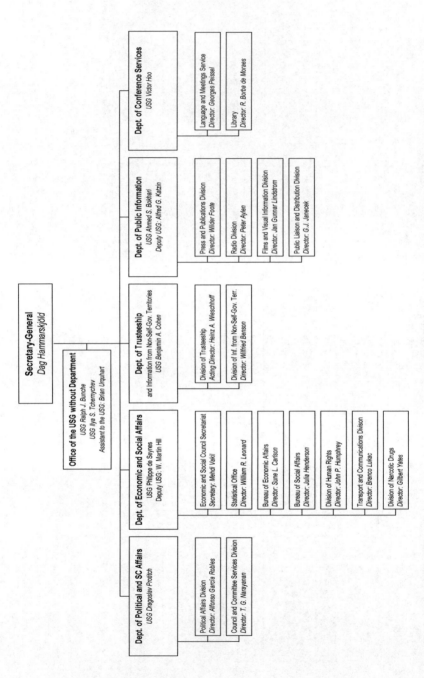

Secretary-General
Dag Hammarskjöld

Office of the USG without Department
USG Ralph J. Bunche
USG Ilya S. Tchernychev
Assistant to the USG: Brian Urquhart

Dept. of Political and SC Affairs
USG Dragoslav Protitch

Political Affairs Division
Director: Alfonso Garcia Robles

Council and Committee Services Division
Director: T. G. Narayanan

Dept. of Economic and Social Affairs
USG Philippe de Seynes
Deputy USG: W. Martin Hill

Economic and Social Council Secretariat
Secretary: Mehdi Vakil

Statistical Office
Director: William R. Leonard

Bureau of Economic Affairs
Director: Sume L. Carlson

Bureau of Social Affairs
Director: Julia Henderson

Division of Human Rights
Director: John P. Humphrey

Transport and Communications Division
Director: Branco Lukac

Division of Narcotic Drugs
Director: Gilbert Yates

Dept. of Trusteeship
and Information from Non-Self-Gov. Territories
USG Benjamin A. Cohen

Division of Trusteeship
Acting Director: Heinz A. Wieschhoff

Division of Inf. from Non-Self-Gov. Terr.
Director: Wilfried Benson

Dept. of Public Information
USG Ahmed S. Bokhari
Deputy USG: Alfred G. Katzin

Press and Publications Division
Director: Wilder Foote

Radio Division
Director: Peter Aylen

Films and Visual Information Division
Director: Jan Gunnar Lindstrom

Public Liaison and Distribution Division
Director: G.J. Janecek

Dept. of Conference Services
USG Victor Hoo

Language and Meetings Service
Director: Georges Peissel

Library
Director: R. Borba de Moraes

Figure 4.2 Structure of the Secretariat, 1955 (Department Level) (Compiled from *UN Yearbooks* 1952–62)

office is best illustrated by his statement that his job was to carry Hammarskjöld's briefcase. The significance of this lies in the daily contact with Hammarskjöld. Lind's importance for Hammarskjöld in the initial years is demonstrated by his inclusion in the small negotiating delegation that Hammarskjöld took to Peking.[2] Besides this function as a type of personal assistant for whatever Hammarskjöld wanted him to do, Lind also looked after Hammarskjöld's connections to his homeland, which, as a neutral country, was an important ally among the member states. Finally, he was also entrusted with a number of very practical tasks and took care of the technical details of many of Hammarskjöld's public appearances and addresses (Interview Lind 1990). The crucial element in the relationship was their mutual personal trust: Hammarskjöld and Lind had known each other for years and Lind and his wife were among the select few that Hammarskjöld regularly invited to his weekend retreat near Brewster.

Towards the end of Hammarskjöld's incumbency, he accorded another Swede this 'honour'. Hammarskjöld appointed Sture Linnér, an acquaintance from his university days in Uppsala and an expert on economics as well as on Africa, as head of the civil operation in the Congo. The appointment of Linnér underlines just how much Hammarskjöld valued personal trust and hierarchy-independent management. When offered the job, Linnér asked the Secretary-General why he had not picked someone from within the UN administration, who would be better acquainted with the internal rules and regulations, Hammarskjöld replied:

> … I would like you to come because you don't know the rules and regulations and I would not like you to become acquainted with them because I need someone I trust who speaks the same language, in more than the literal sense, and who understands where I would be driving and who would not feel hampered by the usual civil servant caution, looking things up in the textbook all the time, but, would go ahead and create rules breaking the old ones in the process if necessary.
>
> (Interview Linnér 1990: 6)

In contrast to this and despite its impressive title, the Department of Political and Security Council Affairs played a secondary role in the Secretariat during Hammarskjöld's term in office. This was partly because it was traditionally headed by a Soviet diplomat. Under Hammarskjöld – and all of his successors for that matter – Soviet staff were never part of the Secretary-General's immediate advisors; they were held to be 'generally untrustworthy because of their close links to the Soviet Mission' (Sutterlin 1991: xii). This disregard was not one-sided; the Soviet Union appointed its Under Secretary-General (USG) explicitly as its national representative with little regard for his status as a servant with international loyalties. This practice of treating the Soviet USG as a national appointee with a political duty to report back affected the Soviet position in the organizational structure. Sometimes the Soviets were completely cut out of the information flow; moreover, their office was not on the thirty-eighth floor (Interview Linnér 1998; Franck 1985: 104–10). Hammarskjöld exhibited some degree of resistance to the appointment of Soviet USGs and stressed his authority in the selection of personnel and the principle of international allegiance of all UN employees, as defined in the Charter. He rejected several Soviet proposals for positions. That said, political affairs were conducted elsewhere: '[P]olitical affairs came to be regarded by many officials as the closely-held speciality of a small group, chosen personally by the Secretary-General without regard to organizational niceties' (Gordenker 1967a: 103).

A decisive figure in this small group was Ralph Bunche, an American (see Urquhart 1993a and Bunche 1995). He was one of the two new USGs without portfolio appointed by Hammarskjöld. In contrast to the position of the Department of Political and Security Council Affairs, here a fairly insignificant title conceals real political relevance, as the USG was used for special missions of the Secretary-General. Bunche had already carried out special missions and tasks of this nature under Trygve Lie, when he was formally responsible for the Trusteeship Council. In 1950, he received the Nobel Peace Prize for negotiating a ceasefire in the Middle East following the death of his then superior, Count Folke Bernadotte (Touval 1982: 54–75; Italiaander 1967: 62–6). At an early stage Hammarskjöld decided to employ Bunche in a top position in the Secretariat. Already in 1953 he told the Indian president of the General Assembly, Vijaya Lakeshmi Pandit, Nehru's sister, that he intended to make Bunche his Number Two at the UN (Urquhart 1993a; 245–6). Initially, there were some misunderstandings between the two: the first time Hammarskjöld discussed his plans with Bunche, his language was so complicated that Bunche wondered afterwards whether the conversation was an indication that the Secretary-General had no use for him. However, these initial irritations were soon forgotten in a harmonious division of labour in which each treated the other with the greatest respect and trust (Hall 1969: 49–59). Bunche worked for the Secretary-General partly on an *ad hoc* basis as 'trouble-shooter' (Trachtenberg 1983: 160) in different negotiations and permanently on questions of atomic energy and decolonization. His role during the initial UN peacekeeping operations was further evidence of his status (see also 'UN presence and Blue Helmets' later in this chapter). Per Lind believes that in Hammarskjöld's final years Bunche was even more important than Cordier (Interview 1998). Urquhart calls him Hammarskjöld's 'personal assistant in active political work and peacekeeping' (1972: 77). When, owing partly to the geographic considerations at the executive level and for reasons of age, Bunche tendered his resignation in June 1961, Hammarskjöld urged him not to do that to him (Urquhart 1993a: 340). Bunche stayed on, which is all the more remarkable in the light of his poor health. Bunche summed up his relationship with Hammarskjöld in the following words: 'Dag Hammarskjöld was the most remarkable man I have ever seen or worked with. ... [He] was the most dedicated person I have ever seen. He gave every minute of his time to his work. I learned more from him than from any other man. ... He was brought in as an administrator, but volcanic as Dag was, he was also an astute political man. He had a combination of political sense and perfect timing' (quoted in Hall 1969: 54). After this appreciation, it should not be surprising that in 1961

Bunche made use of his right as a Nobel Peace Prize winner, to submit a name to the Norwegian Committee (Urquhart 1993a: 346).

Bunche's department included a number of other experts whom Hammarskjöld valued. Brian Urquhart, a Briton, was Bunche's right-hand man and to this extent active in the background on most politically sensitive missions.[3] Another who in time gained Hammarskjöld's confidence was Heinz A. Wieschhoff, a German-born Africa expert initially employed in the Trusteeship Council. Just as Wieschhoff and Bunche advised the Secretary-General in African affairs, Ahmed S. Bokhari, the Pakistani USG for Public Information, advised the Secretary-General in Asian matters, in addition to his normal duties (Simon 1967: 76). For political reasons, the second USG without portfolio was filled with a Soviet candidate. Here, too, the comments above about the USG for Political and Security Council Affairs apply: over the years Hammarskjöld rejected several lists and Soviet proposals, before approving, for instance, Ilya S. Chernychev, whom he knew as former ambassador to Sweden (Interview Lind 1998; Urquhart 1972: 53). But even he could not attain a position of permanent influence, because, as a rule, Soviet USGs were recalled after two years.

Apart from the USGs without portfolio the Office of Legal Affairs has to be mentioned (Dicke 1998: 83). As noted above in the case of Cordier, the legal counsel's work for the Secretary-General was not limited to internal functions. He was unofficially used by the national delegations to test the practicability and soundness of proposals in international law. Besides requests from other UN bodies, the Office of Legal Affairs was frequently approached by individual delegations for assistance in drafting texts relating to pending resolutions (Interview Schachter 1985: 8). Hammarskjöld's legal counsel, Constantin Stravopoulos, a Greek, did play a significant role and drew up some crucial legal opinions for the Secretary-General. Hammarskjöld had even closer personal contact with the director of the General Legal Division, Oscar Schachter, an American, whose role has already been mentioned in the context of Hammarskjöld's speeches. According to Cordier, Hammarskjöld thought Schachter 'rather more useful than his chief' (Cordier 1964: 305). This may be due to the fact that the two had very similar conceptions of international law. Schachter was well aware of the Secretary-General's dynamic concept of his office and the legal consequences of that approach. Speaking in general terms about various controversial issues he concluded: '[A] legal opinion of the Secretary-General made the law on [the] subject' (Interview Schachter 1985: 7; Schachter 1948). Schachter stresses Hammarskjöld's interest and appreciation of international law underlining the influence of his father, Hjalmar (Interview Schachter 1985: 11). With Cordier, Bunche and, to a slightly lesser degree, Schachter we have mentioned the cornerstones of Hammarskjöld's working environment. Hammarskjöld used this small group, with a few additions, to constitute a series of fairly informal task forces. The most important of these was probably the so-called Congo Club, consisting of Bunche, Cordier and Wieschhoff, which was responsible for the Organisation des Nations Unies au Congo (ONUC) (Rovine 1970). This focus on just a few people was particularly important for crisis management. Cordier reports that one of Hammarskjöld's frequent sayings in this connection was 'It is not wise to have too many men on deck during a storm' (quoted in Zacher 1970: 44). The first such storm came up in 1955.

The instrument of 'private diplomacy'

Quiet or private diplomacy has always been a constitutive element of international negotiation. Yet Hammarskjöld's use is unique since he gave it a special justification and grounded it in an overall philosophical and political context. '"Quiet diplomacy" has in truth become the phrase which is most closely associated with Hammarskjöld, and he seems to sum up in his person the virtues of this sort of activity; here is the quiet diplomat *par excellence*' (James 1959: 627). The position of the Secretary-General is particularly convenient for quiet diplomacy, as one of his main tasks is 'to act as a channel for communication and for consultation between delegations' (Nayar 1974: 62). On the other hand, this quiet diplomacy did not always meet with approval, especially in the early years of the UN. It was hoped that the creation of the world organization would promote openness in international negotiations. A new type of diplomatic activity appeared to be taking root, the so-called parliamentary diplomacy (Thompson 1965; Jessup 1956). Lie was serious about implementing this principle (Hamilton 1950; Barros 1989). Hammarskjöld took a different tack (Nayar 1974: 54). He viewed private and public diplomacy not as competitive, but as complementary, each suited to different phases of conflicts as required.

The Peking Mission, analysed below, was Hammarskjöld's first major political challenge and basically established his reputation as Secretary-General.[4] The international political background to this question of imprisoned American airmen could not have been more dramatic – both China and the USA threatened to resort to arms; for a while the latter did not exclude the use of atomic weapons. Hammarskjöld developed the 'Peking Formula', which created a crucial precedent for the political authority of the Secretary-General. No other event in Hammarskjöld's incumbency lends itself so well to an analysis of quiet diplomacy;[5] indeed, in keeping with his character, it would, as shall be seen below, be better described as 'private' or 'confidential' diplomacy.

Conflict situation: imprisonment of American pilots in China

The immediate cause for Hammarskjöld's negotiations was a consequence of the Korean War. After the cessation of hostilities, one of the main points at the Geneva peace talks was the return of soldiers on both sides. In addition to the routine exchange of prisoners of war, there was the question of soldiers whose whereabouts were unknown. These included 15 American airmen, of whom there was no sign. In response to enquiries, the People's Republic declared that they were being held on suspicion of violating Chinese airspace and espionage. Eventually, on 23 November 1954, Radio Peking announced that 13 of the Americans had been charged by a military court and received prison sentences of between four years and life. The men were the crew of two aircraft shot down in 1953. The USA vehemently denied the charge of spying and pointed out that at the time the aircraft were under the command of the United Nations. Moreover, they had not operated in Chinese airspace, but had been shot down while distributing leaflets behind enemy lines in North Korea. In other words, the crew members were prisoners of war who had to be returned to the USA under the terms of the armistice agreement.

The airmen's fate quickly became a domestic political issue in the USA, provoking angry public reactions. In the Senate, the Republican leader, William F. Knowland, demanded a sea blockade of China and possibly the use of additional force. The Eisenhower administration did not want the conflict to escalate into a military confrontation and initially attempted to work through unofficial diplomatic channels via friendly states, but without any success. Finally, on 4 December, the president and his foreign policy advisors decided to refer the question to the United Nations. On the morning of 6 December, the US ambassador to the UN, Henry Cabot Lodge, informed Hammarskjöld that Washington was considering requesting the Secretary-General to intervene personally in the China question. This request was unusual in that in similar cases the mandate for negotiations was normally extended first to the president of the General Assembly. However, the current session of the General Assembly was about to close and the current president, the Dutchman Eelco von Kleffens, was, from a diplomatic point of view, compromised in that Dutch soldiers fought in Korea. To get around this, the USA and 14 other western states submitted a two-part resolution to the General Assembly. In the first part, China was accused in the strongest terms of disregarding the Korean Armistice Agreement: the General Assembly 'condemns, as contrary to the Korean Armistice Agreement, the trial and conviction of prisoners of war illegally detained after 25 September 1953' (GA Res. 906 (IX), 7 December 1954, quoted in CF II: 417). This condemnatory section was followed by instructions to the Secretary-General to intervene in this matter:

> The General Assembly, …
> 3. Requests the Secretary-General, in the name of the United Nations, to seek the release, in accordance with the Korean Armistice Agreement, of these eleven United Nations Command personnel, and all other captured personnel of the United Nations still detained;
> 4. Requests the Secretary-General to make, by the means most appropriate in his judgment, continuing and unremitting efforts to this end and to report progress to all Members on or before 31 December 1954.[6]
>
> (CF II: 417)

The Secretary-General was requested in unmistakable terms to act, and the General Assembly granted him considerable scope for personal action. On the other hand, the strong condemnation of China made any concessions of the Chinese leadership unlikely. The situation was further complicated by the fact that the People's Republic had no representation at the United Nations and had frequently disputed the legitimacy of resolutions passed by the General Assembly. Hence, from the start the question of the People's Republic's representation, i.e. its replacing Taiwan at the United Nations, was at least indirectly on the agenda of the Secretary-General's negotiating initiative. The situation was further complicated by the military escalation between the People's Republic and Taiwan: many observers viewed China's bombing of the islands of Quemoy and Matsu in autumn 1954 as the first step towards an invasion of Formosa and violent 'reunification'. This option in turn affected the strategic interests of the USA, which served as protector of the National Chinese government (Eisenhower 1964: 501–28). Thus, the question of the treatment of US citizens and prisoners of war abroad and American concerns about possible communist expansion in the Pacific (see a letter from Eisenhower to Churchill in February 1955, quoted in Eisenhower 1964: 513) formed an explosive mixture, and Taiwan received far-reaching defence guarantees from the USA. The People's Republic did not lack in threatening gestures either: the statement is attributed to Chou En-Lai, the Chinese foreign minister, that in the event of war between the US and China, China could lose a 100 million people – but there would still be another 450 million Chinese left (Eisenhower 1964: 524).

The question of the airmen's release, which other diplomatic channels had failed to resolve, was difficult enough. But the tangle of other international political problems made Hammarskjöld's mission extremely sensitive. Lodge later declared that Hammarskjöld had put 'his life's reputation as a diplomat on the chopping block' (quoted in Urquhart 1972: 102). The fact that the General Assembly resolution had granted him great personal freedom to manoeuvre ('by the means most appropriate in his judgment') was not a coincidence; the Secretary-General had asked some co-sponsors of the resolution to include such a phrase in their draft. In a statement to the General Assembly after it passed the resolution on 10 December Hammarskjöld again emphasized precisely this personal scope. How would he use this leeway?

Hammarskjöld's response: the Peking mission

Immediately after the end of the General Assembly session, Hammarskjöld sent a telegram to Chou En-Lai in which he referred to the instructions of the General Assembly – but without the text of the resolution. He continued:

> Taking into consideration all facts and circumstances the Secretary-General must, in this case, take on himself a special responsibility. In the light of the concern I feel about the issue, I would appreciate an opportunity to take this matter up with you personally. For that reason I would ask you whether you could receive me in Peking.
>
> (CF II: 422)

On 17 December Chou En-Lai replied in a cable that did not in any way qualify China's position as regards the 'condemned' spies, but reacted positively to the personal mission mentioned by Hammarskjöld: 'In the interest of peace and relaxation of international tension, I am prepared to receive you in our capital, Peking, to discuss with you pertinent questions. We welcome you to China' (CF II: 423). With the formulation 'pertinent questions', Chou En-Lai succeeded in maintaining the Chinese position by not officially announcing that the government of China would discuss the question of the American airmen with the Secretary-General. Hammarskjöld accepted the invitation the same day (ibid.).

A few days before his departure, Hammarskjöld invited his external legal counsel, Ernest Gross, and Philip Jessup, at the time professor for international law at Columbia University, to dinner in order to discuss the legal implications of the mission. Until the early hours of the morning the three went through Hammarskjöld's possible strategies and answers to any questions that Chou En-Lai might raise, using role-playing to work through each (Gross 1964: 45–9; Urquhart 1972: 99). Constantin Stravopoulos, the UN legal counsel, also prepared memoranda for Hammarskjöld on the legal foundation of the Peking mission (KB DHS: C. A. Stravopoulos, Interoffice Memorandum: Definition of the Secretary-General's Mandate of 21 December 1954). Preparations also included thorough research of possible relevant information. Hammarskjöld's briefcase contained a comprehensive documentation of relevant speeches as well as international treaties and agreements (UNA DAG–1/5.1.3. Box 3). As far as the airmen were concerned, the Secretary-General had the full backing of the USA. The US Air Force provided all the relevant information on the airmen, aircraft and the mission in statutory declarations.

Prior to leaving for Peking on what Hammarskjöld described in a letter to Leif Belfrage shortly before his departure as 'one of the most extraordinary experiments in modern diplomacy' (KB DHS: Dag Hammarskjöld, Letter to Leif Belfrage, 29 December 1954), he sent identical letters to the foreign ministers of the UK, the USA and the USSR in which he formulated his approach once again. In these letters he made it clear that he could not refer directly to the UN resolution, as this was the only way to circumvent China's foreseeable negative attitude and retain 'a maximum chance for the UN "to crash the gate"' (KB DHS: Dag Hammarskjöld, Letter to Anthony Eden, 15 December 1954). Hammarskjöld also deliberately refrained from a 'sounding operation' to establish the Chinese position. A clear positive signal was not to be expected. And if the Chinese signalled a negative attitude in advance, it would be impossible to find common ground. Hammarskjöld stressed that he wanted to produce results 'without any moral commitments to Peking for the United Nations or the Secretary-General' (ibid.). In other words, he assured the governments concerned that he would not become involved in e.g. any substantive discussions about Chinese representation in the UN. In this connection, Trachtenberg (1982) talks of a '"tactic" of letter writing', because by informing the foreign ministers he took them into his confidence and gave them the chance to object to his plan. In the absence of such objections, Hammarskjöld could take this as a reinsurance in the form of express or tacit approval of his mission should it fail.

Hammarskjöld arranged the practical details of the trip through the Chinese ambassador in Stockholm, who had been selected for this purpose through India's diplomatic channels with Peking (Urquhart 1972: 101). Hammarskjöld had to go to Sweden anyway to deliver the eulogy to his father in the Swedish Academy. Uno Willers, Hammarskjöld's friend and director of the Royal Library, established contact with the Chinese ambassador in Stockholm, General Keng Piao. Willers invited Hammarskjöld and Piao to a private lunch at his home on 19 December, where they finalized the organizational details of the visit which would start on 5 January. On the way to Peking, Hammarskjöld called on the heads of government in London, Paris and New Delhi to learn about their experiences of Chinese foreign policy and the personality of the foreign minister. From the start, Hammarskjöld had stressed that his negotiations would be strictly confidential in order to avoid complications in the negotiations, a point he had reiterated in a press conference on 18 December (CF II: 426). Hammarskjöld justified this restriction with the object of his trip. Quoting Kierkegaard, he explained: 'To succeed means to realize the possible. The possible has to be realized. I should just hate to see any development which would reduce our chances of realizing what was possible' (ibid.: 429). The negotiations in Peking were shrouded in secrecy. Journalists worked under tight restrictions and could approach the Secretary-General only on the sightseeing tours.

For many years, the minutes of the meetings were kept secret in the United Nations Archives (UNA DAG–1/5.1.3–3 'Dag Hammarskjöld. Basic Documents visit to Peking 1954/55. Re: Korean Pow's UN Command Personnel'; Cited in the following as Peking [date]). The minutes are partly verbatim records and partly summaries of Hammarskjöld's or Chou En-Lai's statements, and allow a fairly detailed reconstruction of the negotiations. Hammarskjöld's delegation consisted of Ahmed S. Bokhari; Humphrey Waldock, a professor for international law at the University of Oxford; Per Lind, Hammarskjöld's personal assistant; Aase Alam, his secretary; William Ranallo, his bodyguard; and Gustav Nystrom, a Swede who acted as interpreter. By including Waldock, Hammarskjöld bypassed the Legal Office, a very unusual step. Oscar Schachter points out that Waldock was part of the group because Hammarskjöld learnt that he had supervised the doctoral thesis of Chou Chen, a close advisor of Chou En-Lai's (Interview 1989: 11–12).

The first meeting between Hammarskjöld and Chou En-Lai took place on the evening of 5 January, a short ceremony of welcome and general exchanges, of which no minutes were kept. The delegations met in the 'Hall of the Western Flowers' on the afternoons of 6, 7, 8, and 10 January (the 9th was a Sunday). Only the Secretary-General and Chou En-Lai spoke. The first session on 6 January began at 3 p.m. and lasted until 6.30 p.m.

Hammarskjöld opens the talks by reading a prepared statement in which he sketches the framework of his mission. This is followed by an appeal that this meeting might serve to ease some points of friction in world politics. He then refers to Chou En-Lai's offer in his cable to discuss 'pertinent questions' and soon raises the 'question of prisoners' (Peking 6 January 1955: 2). He proposes that they first deal with this concrete question, because the General Assembly has given him a special mandate only for this matter. As for more general political questions, he states: 'In other cases my participation in the discussion will have to be strictly limited to what follows from my general position which means that I can only take note of your observations and give you whatever general comments I may have to make in order to clarify the situation from my angle' (ibid.). With this restriction Hammarskjöld makes it clear that he does not have the intention to negotiate political questions of wider import – such as the anticipated discussion about China's representation at the UN.

Hammarskjöld then proceeds to define his legal position on the visit in detail. This definition is the 'origin' of what became known as the so-called Peking Formula; for this reason it is presented in full:

> Under the Charter of the United Nations the Secretary-General is entitled – and, being entitled, in my view obliged – to take whatever initiative he finds appropriate in order to get under control or reverse developments leading to serious tensions. His rights and obligations in this respect are not limited to Member Nations. They are of world-wide application and were given him when he was established in his post not only by a majority of the General Assembly but by the unanimous vote of the permanent members of the Security Council. When he acts for the purpose indicated, it is not, and can never be permitted to be, on behalf of any nation, group of nations or even majority of Member Nations as registered by a vote in the General Assembly. He acts under his constitutional responsibility for the general purposes set out in the Charter, which must be considered of common and equal significance to Members and Non-Members alike.
>
> The constitutional position of the Secretary-General as I now define it, is the basis on which I have approached you and on which I have come here. Thus, sitting here at this conference table I do so as Secretary-General, not as a representative of an Assembly majority or of any national or individual interests. From what I have said follows also that I cannot commit anybody or any nation, or the Organization, to anything. I can solely engage myself and that only within the limits set by the Charter.
>
> (ibid.)

In this statement Hammarskjöld explains his mission and, in particular, his responsibility, which is in principle not restricted to the members of the UN. He then argued that the Charter and not the condemnative resolution of the General Assembly is the 'legal basis for my action' (ibid.: 3). Hammarskjöld creates for himself an autonomous space for negotiation and also precludes the anticipated accusation that he is acting only in the interests of the large UN members, or even just the USA. But he does not contest that the charges of the General Assembly are justified, either. In any case he shows himself aware of the fact that China, as a non-member, would not feel itself bound by a resolution of the General Assembly. Hammarskjöld proceeds to emphasize that immediately after the General Assembly passed its resolution, he conducted his own, independent investigation into the question of the American airmen: 'For this study which has been based on all evidence that can be produced on the other side as well as on what you have given publicity, I claim impartiality' (ibid.). In other words, the Secretary-General stresses that his international obligations and his scope for action are ultimately tied to his impartial approach.

Hammarskjöld then presents the evidence that he had assemled in favour of the fliers and their UN mission and thus claims that the American airmen should be regarded as prisoners of war who must be treated in accordance with the provisions of the Korean Armistice Agreement. Of course, he detaches himself from intervening in the judicial decisions of the Chinese courts. However, his evidence could influence the 'final political evaluation of the case' on the part of the Chinese government and result in a 'possible decision to release the men – for example on the basis of their good behaviour during two years of imprisonment, in line with statements from your side in Geneva' (ibid.: 27). Hammarskjöld has not taken long to come to the point and even ventured to present a possible solution for the dispute. However, he then emphasizes:

> When the Secretary-General of the United Nations has engaged himself and his office, with all the weight it carries in world opinion, for the fate of the prisoners … it does not mean that I *appeal* to you or that I *ask you* for their release. It means that – inspired also by my faith in your wisdom and in your wish to promote peace – I have considered it my duty as forcefully as I can, and with deep conviction, to draw your attention to the vital importance of their fate to the cause of peace. I could have based my approach to you on the fact that the General Assembly has asked me to seek their release. I have not done so. I could have acted as spokesman of the Organization for which, and under the orders of which, the prisoners served. That – although justified – would have made me a representative of a party to the conflict. My position is stronger than that.
>
> (ibid.: 7–8)

Hammarskjöld links the fate of the prisoners with the cause of peace and the improvement or deterioration of international relations. He adopts the radical stance of not referring to the resolution of the General Assembly or to the United Nations Organization as such – he acts solely on his personal responsibility as Secretary-General. It is clear that the 'position … stronger than that' has a purely ethical basis. This ethical position is combined with a personal appeal:

> You may feel that I exaggerate: how can the fate of these men be of such significance? However, I know that I am not exaggerating. This case is one of those which history suddenly lifts up to key significance – as is evidenced by the sheer fact that, against all odds, it has brought me around the world in order to put before you, in great frankness and trusting that we see eye to eye on the desperate need to avoid adding to existing frictions, my deep concern both as Secretary-General and as a man.
>
> (ibid.: 8)

In his reply to Hammarskjöld, Chou En-Lai first recognizes Hammarskjöld's special position at the negotiations. He then proceeds to make clear the consequences that the Chinese draw from this position: as a non-member of the UN, China was not obligated to the Secretary-General in any way, nor could the People's Republic obligate Hammarskjöld in any way. Chou En-Lai then emphasizes clearly that the General Assembly resolution was utterly unacceptable. The 'spies' were an internal Chinese affair – the label 'prisoners of war' was wrong, and for this reason the rules of international law did not apply to this case. Hammarskjöld vehemently opposes this interpretation. A crucial difference of opinion has emerged. The provisional result of the first round of talks is negative on balance, as Chou En-Lai underscores in his summing up: 'There were a great number of differences – he and the Secretary-General were not even using the same language. For that reason Mr. Chou En-Lai did not believe that they would be able to find a solution or a common view without approaching the matter from the angle of general political questions' (ibid.: 10). Hammarskjöld counters by stressing the priority of the question of the prisoners. The negotiations were then adjourned.

The second session took place the next day from 3 p.m. to 6.45 p.m. This time Chou En-Lai opens the discussion by replying to Hammarskjöld's statement of the previous day, which he had gone over carefully. Notwithstanding their differences, he expresses the hope that 'through contacts and frank exchange of views it would be possible to reach some common point of view leading to continued contacts in the interest of peace' (Peking 7 January 1955: 11). In response to the results of Hammarskjöld's investigation, he presents five that substantially reiterate Peking's position, but also include more precise details about the alleged espionage of some of the airmen. He bases his presentation mainly on the cases of John J. Downey and Richard G. Fecteau – whom the USA had already dropped from their list – asserting that they at any rate were working for the CIA, and that between their cases and those of the other 11 detainees there were clear parallels. These cases were part of the continual and systematic attempt of the USA to spy onthe People's Republic of China under cover of the Korean War.

In contrast to China's policy, the USA, according to Chou En-Lai, had adopted a very restrictive attitude on, for example, exit permits for Chinese students. For Chou En-Lai, this problem is also part of the overall current situation. In this connection he also raises the question of China's representation at the UN:

> First of all, delegates representing the reactionary rule of Chiang Kai-Shek, a rule forsaken by the Chinese people, were still in the United Nations while a government representing six hundred million people was deprived of a seat at the United Nations in gravest violation of the Charter. A handful was recognized while a people representing 1/4 of the world was left out. This was a continued injustice.

> (ibid.: 17)

In addition, he criticizes the USA for its 'aggressive intentions' (ibid.: 19) towards the People's Republic displayed in the defence treaty with Taiwan. Peking is fully prepared to continue to develop its policy of peaceful coexistence, but the other side must do likewise, which the USA could prove by, for instance, withdrawing its troops from Taiwan. Hammarskjöld replies briefly to Chou En-Lai's statements and restricts himself essentially to the question of the detained Americans, on which he saw considerable differences in their points of view.

The third session on 8 January 1955 is the longest. The meeting again started at 3 p.m. and ended only at 8.10 p.m. It was Hammarskjöld's turn to open the meeting, which he does by replying to the statements made by the Chinese foreign minister the previous day. This time Hammarskjöld deals with the general political points by putting Chou En-Lai's remarks in the context of the Cold War. Then, with remarkable openness, he addresses one of the fundamental problems of this situation:

> Many of the words you used with such deep conviction in describing your fear of aggression I have heard used in other countries concerning you. You may seem to have substantial reasons for your fear, but so have others for theirs. … Ideologically you fear the development of 'American imperialism'. The others, in the same way, referring to Communist ideology, fear your urge for 'world revolution' or 'world domination'.
>
> Thus, we have run into what I would call a tragedy of errors, in a most serious form reflecting the situation in that little Peking opera which we saw yesterday night where two men were fighting each other in the dark, each of them believing that he had been threatened by the other man.
>
> The deadlock of this tragedy of errors must be broken. That is the very essence of the problem of international tensions. And in order to break it, somebody must begin, somewhere.
>
> (Peking 8 January 1955: 22)

After a more general political digression, Hammarskjöld focuses again on the concrete question of the detainees attempting to refute Peking's reading of their intentions. He then addresses Chou En-Lai's two concrete concerns in a more general context: China's representation at the United Nations and the question of the Chinese students in the USA. Hammarskjöld explains:

> As to the question of representation, you know from public statements what is my attitude. I have said publicly that I consider the Organization as based on the principle of universality and, it being so, I consider it a weakness and an anomaly that this people, one fourth of mankind, is not represented in our work. You said yourself, with some bitterness, that you believed that the problem could not be solved for some time yet. Let me only say, that I consider this appraisal of yours as realistic.
>
> (ibid.: 26)

Once again it is striking how little Hammarskjöld tries either in form or content to accommodate his counterpart or make even the vaguest promises – which he could perhaps have employed to nudge along the negotiations, particularly as he had already taken a clearer stand elsewhere on the question of representation.[7] Concerning the students, Hammarskjöld cites substantially lower figures than Chou En-Lai, but promises to look into the matter as some students have written to him, too. After these statements, Hammarskjöld makes two concrete proposals: first he asks whether it is not possible to speed up the legal procedures of the court case so that, in agreement with the principles that China had expressed in Geneva, 'the time of detention or uncertainty for all concerned' (Peking 8 January 1955: 27) could be shortened. With this proposal he takes up the option of a compromise on early release indicated in the first round of talks. Second, he proposes, also on humanitarian grounds, that he be given information on the detainees' condition that he can take to their families.

Chou En-Lai reacts first to Hammarskjöld's description of the general political situation. He again presents the Chinese view on Taiwan and implies that Hammarskjöld cannot be regarded as impartial after what he has said, but is on the side of the USA. Hammarskjöld interrupts Chou En-Lai at this point and roundly rejects this interpretation: 'The Secretary-General further wanted to make it clear that just as he did not represent any country, he did not speak against any country either. … Thus he neither could nor would engage with Mr. Chou En-Lai in a discussion of the policy of other governments' (ibid.: 30). Once again, Hammarskjöld's determination and steadfastness is remarkable, particularly in the light of how even a verbal indication of relative sympathy for some of the Chinese charges against the USA could perhaps have brought some movement into the negotiating log-jam. The Chinese foreign minister for his part goes even further by asserting that there is any number of examples to show 'that the United Nations has become a tool of US aggression' (ibid.). The Chinese government stands by its charge of spying.

Chou En-Lai continues by thanking Hammarskjöld for promising to look into the question of the Chinese students. Then he turns to the Secretary-General's concrete proposals. He starts by confirming China's position in Geneva, thereby alluding to the option of an early release of individual detainees. He also declares that he is prepared to give the Secretary-General information about the detainees and photographs for their families. He then goes on to propose that, if the detainees' families so wish, they may visit their relatives in China. The Chinese Red Cross could organize and take responsibility for these visits.

After Chou En-Lai's statement Hammarskjöld concludes: 'I guess you may be right in saying that we cannot here and now arrive at common conclusions as to the facts. However, I feel that in the course of these discussions we have built up a mutual respect which makes us trust that the other party will reach its *final* conclusion in a spirit of justice and fairness – before his own conscience!' (ibid.: 36). Chou En-Lai agrees with this and stresses that on no account should the discussions give rise to new tensions.

The last session on 10 January is also the shortest, lasting from 4 p.m. to 5.20 p.m. After a formal opening in which the two sides express their thanks for the visit and the hospitality, Chou En-Lai gives an extremely short but positive summary: 'We knew something before but now we know more' (Peking 10 January 1955: 37). As a request of the Secretary-General, he formulates the hope 'that you will be able, at times which you consider appropriate, to tell those countries concerned, although not friendly towards us, especially the United States, about China, our views and position' (ibid.). Terse though the statement is, it is a sign that the Chinese accept Hammarskjöld's position as a mediator. Reading between the lines, there has been a barely noticed change in the Chinese position: contrary to previous practice, the Chinese foreign minister speaks of the 'question of the convicted airmen' (ibid.) – not the 'spies'. This small change in tone is followed immediately by a warning to the USA: 'If the US Government should want to continue the uproar on this question without justification, the Chinese people will not be intimidated and take no step to change its position' (ibid.: 38). In diplomatic terms, this 'warning', however, includes the option that there might be a change in position if the US would refrain from further public pressure. Chou En-Lai underlies Peking's policy of peaceful coexistence and his offer to allow the families of the detainees to visit them. If the USA abandoned its hostile attitude to China, cooperation between the two states would be possible. This optimistic but restrained tone was followed by an appreciation of the Secretary-General:

> [W]e would like to express our admiration and respect for the expressions you have given to your intentions to fight for the purpose and principles of the United Nations as its Secretary-General. ... We understand very well that after you leave China you will face some difficulties, but we believe that with the spirit you have manifested and your prestige as an individual and as Secretary-General, you will promote peace.
>
> (ibid.)

Whatever the outcome, China wants to stay in contact with Hammarskjöld. In this respect, Hammarskjöld's strategy has been successful. His determination to remain impartial – despite the temptation of short-lived advantages in the negotiations – has left the desired impression. Reading between the lines, there are admittedly vague and intangible, but recognizably optimistic tones. Against this background, Hammarskjöld makes another attempt to more clearly define this underlying optimistic tone: 'On this point the Secretary-General wanted "bluntly" and "frankly" to point out to Mr. Chou En-Lai that what the Secretary-General might say about China on the basis of his widened knowledge obviously would carry very much more weight if the Chinese Government saw its way to meet him and accept his viewpoints in the Prisoner question ...' (ibid.). Again, Hammarskjöld mentions the option of early release from detention. Chou En-lai picks up this ball, even if his reply is oracular:

... Mr. Chou En-lai said that as regards the spy cases, the Chinese courts had reached their conclusions 'on the basis of legal considerations' exercising their sovereign right. The political relations between the United States and China were another matter. Mr. Chou En-Lai felt convinced that the Secretary-General, 'in an objective way' would find it possible to keep those two aspects of the matter apart.

(ibid.: 39)

Despite returning to the 'spy' label, Chou En-Lai indirectly adopts the distinction Hammarskjöld made at the first session between the legal and political aspects of the question and indicates at least the possibility of revising the court's conclusions for political reasons. The two parties then agree without any further discussion on the prepared text of the joint communiqué. It is remarkably vague:

As a result of the suggestion for a personal discussion made by the Secretary-General ... we had talks in Peking on January 6, 7, 8, and 10, 1955. In these talks reference was made at the same time to questions pertinent to the relaxation of world tension. We feel that these talks have been useful, and we hope to be able to continue the contact established in these meetings.
(Joint Communiqué by the Secretary-General of the United Nations and the Premier and Foreign Minister of the People's Republic of China, 10 January 1955, in CF II: 436)

No mention is made of the detained American airmen; the only indirect reference is to Hammarskjöld's cable that raised the topic. Otherwise, China's face-saving formula of 'pertinent questions' is used.

Informed by Cordier and Foote (Urquhart 1972: 113), Hammarskjöld was ready to react to initial charges that the joint communiqué indicated that the mission could only be judged a failure. On 13 January, Hammarskjöld declared on arrival at the airport: 'My visit to Peking was a first stage in my efforts to achieve the release of the eleven flyers and other United Nations Command personnel still detained. I feel that my talks with Mr. Chou En-Lai were definitely useful for this purpose. We hope to be able to continue our contact. The door that has been opened can be kept open, given restraint on all sides' (CF II: 441). He explained this approach in somewhat greater depth at his first press conference after the trip by presenting his understanding of 'quiet' diplomacy as a means to avoid 'the so-called full light of publicity ... at a stage where that might render the solution more difficult because it might tend to freeze positions' (CF II: 442). To spare the Chinese public pressure, Hammarskjöld could not publicize the implicitly optimistic tone from Peking. However, he immediately sought a personal meeting with American Foreign Minister Dulles to present the results of his talks in Peking and the importance of restraint on both sides for a solution of the case. The two met on 19 December 1954. Hammarskjöld mentioned Peking's offer to allow the detainees' families to visit and wanted to sound out Washington's views on the offer before announcing it publicly, but Dulles did not react. Two days later, however, the offer was announced on Radio Peking. The angry US reaction followed promptly, denouncing the Chinese proposal as a propaganda trick. At the same time, the exchanges over the Taiwan question grew harsher. This was a considerable setback for Hammarskjöld, who had hoped to mediate an internal understanding between the parties that would have removed the question of the prisoners of war from the public arena.

Besides Dulles, Hammarskjöld informed Eden about the Peking Mission in a lengthy letter in February 1955 and noted that the text of the communiqué was not that different from the possible formulation that he had discussed with Eden before the trip (KB DHS: Dag Hammarskjöld, Letter to Anthony Eden, 16 February 1955). In this letter Hammarskjöld mentioned the possibility, despite the initial American rejection, of raising the option of visits by the detainees' families again after some time had passed, because he felt such visits offered a framework and occasion for the eventual release of the airmen by China. On account of various distracting factors, the visit never did materialize. In particular the continued tension between Taiwan and the People's Republic prevented the USA from adopting a more reserved tone towards China (Urquhart 1972: 119–25). Hammarskjöld continued to exchange news with Peking through Keng Piao in Stockholm. He got the impression that the cautiously optimistic tone of the negotiations and Peking's need to release the airmen on its own conditions without any pressure – to save face – were unchanged. Instead of direct family visits, the families were allowed to write letters to the prisoners. In this connection, Hammarskjöld insisted that he needed some sign from China to credibly urge politicians in America to show restraint. On 30 May 1955 came the first indication that China had changed its position: Peking announced the immediate release of four of the detained airmen (Levine 1962: 114). In the meantime, however, further Indian and Swedish initiatives for negotiations had complicated the situation (Urquhart 1972: 123–4).

The final release of the American airmen came about against a very special background: in early July, Keng Piao asked Willers what present Hammarskjöld would like for his 50th birthday. Willers replied that the release of the airmen was the best he could think of (ibid.: 125). This conversation was followed by several enquiries by the Chinese on the exact date of the birthday. On 1 August, the following message from Chou En-Lai was conveyed to the Swedish ambassador in Peking:

> The Chinese Government has decided to release the imprisoned U.S. fliers. This release from serving their full term takes place in order to maintain friendship with Hammarskjöld and has no connection with the UN resolution. Chou En-Lai expresses the hope that Hammarskjöld will take note of this point. …
>
> The Chinese Government hopes to continue the contact established with Hammarskjöld. …
>
> Chou En-lai congratulates Hammarskjöld on his 50th birthday.
>
> (ibid.: 126)

Hammarskjöld heard the news while holidaying in the south of Sweden (Beskow 1969: 49–54) and was overjoyed with the successful conclusion of the Peking Mission. In his reply to Chou En-Lai, however, he stressed that it was important for him that Chou En-Lai did not leave the impression that he drew a distinction between Hammarskjöld the man and Hammarskjöld the Secretary-General. At the same time, he was aware that his birthday was not the only reason for the airmen's release; negotiations at embassy level in Geneva had brought a general rapprochement on the repatriation of prisoners of war between the People's Republic and the USA on 25 July (Urquhart 1972: 126–7).

Political ethics and private diplomacy

Several aspects of Hammarskjöld's approach in Peking reflect basic elements of his conception of his office and of his political ethics. These will be summarized in a few general points.

The 'tragedy of errors' and the 'walls of distrust'

There is an extraordinary similarity between Hammarskjöld's comments on the general 'psychological' aspect of the international situation and the thoughts of Buber, which he really discovered only later. What Hammarskjöld calls the 'tragedy of errors' in the Peking talks is in effect another formulation for the 'walls of distrust', a term he would adopt from Buber for his 1957 speech. The fact that the Peking trip and Hammarskjöld's statements preceded his intensive preoccupation with Buber underscores, first, how at home Hammarskjöld must have felt with Buber's concept and, second, that Hammarskjöld not only reproduced this and other concepts, but developed his own versions sometimes independently and sometimes analogously. In May 1958, after intervening in the Security Council to discuss the American proposal for the Arctic zone of inspection, Hammarskjöld used Buber's terminology to further elaborate his concept of quiet diplomacy and his analysis of reciprocal fear and distrust at a press conference:

> What the Secretary-General can do professionally … for the reduction of distrust – this is mostly far away from the public eye and from the public knowledge. He does, in diplomatic contacts, if he succeeds in maintaining the right kind of position, represent to a certain extent a kind of common denominator. He is in a position to interpret in an objective, and at least unemotional and detached sense, the stands of the various parties and can, for that reason, without assuming any kind of role of mediator, smooth out quite a few misunderstandings. … I am basically not a believer in public statements by the Secretary-General. It is a preaching in a way which I do not think belongs to the Secretary-General normally, and I think you would agree with me that the fact of soothing statements is nil …
>
> (CF IV: 84–5)

The connection of these thoughts to the Peking mission is rather obvious.

'Genuine dialogue' and the negotiations in the 'Hall of the Western Flowers'

In his analysis Buber also indicates the answer to the age of distrust. Buber advocated personal contact between heads of government, who should observe certain principles of mutual respect and dialogue. Hammarskjöld's practice reflects this demand to a recognizable degree. Wherever possible he preferred personal conversations away from the emotions of public debate. He always based his arguments on 'factual' and 'objective' reasons; he refused to indulge in ideological discussions and political sparring matches. In this way, Hammarskjöld – without perhaps knowing Buber's exact terminology – followed Buber's call to 'imagining the real' (Buber 1906: 286) or 'personal making present' (ibid.: 284) that for Buber was the prerequisite of genuine dialogue. He told journalists: 'I go to Peking because I believe in personal talks' (quoted in Beskow 1969: 35). And later he stated:

> I do believe, to use what has become a famous term, thanks to Camus and Buber and others – I do believe that development in human terms of what they call dialogue is badly needed. But dialogues require a few things: objectivity, a willingness to listen, and considerable restraint. Those are human qualities. No one of them is very remarkable, but they are called for, and if they lead to a 'dialogue', I think it is very reasonable to let that dialogue develop within the more or less traditional framework, that is to say, a little bit out of the glare of publicity, which robs you of a few headlines, but helps us all.
>
> (quoted in Kelen 1966: 132–3)

Moreover, if one looks at the negotiations themselves and Hammarskjöld's subsequent statements, the somewhat abstract vocabulary of personal 'humility' and 'integrity', on which Hammarskjöld reflects so much in his diary, acquire stangible meaning.

Humility and integrity as factors in the success of the mission

The minutes of the negotiations show that Hammarskjöld was resolutely impartial and objective, and extremely sensitive about his personal integrity. A 1955 diary entry contains a clear reference to the Peking mission: '"To the pure all things are pure." But if a man can only reach this state by making compromises, then this striving is itself an impurity. In such matters there are no differences of degree' (*Markings* 1955: 5, 104). Apart from this personal context, Schachter points to the significance Hammarskjöld attached to arguments with legal quality in his diplomacy: 'An examination of his conciliation efforts shows that he relied to a considerable extent on establishing a common ground of principles to which both sides could adhere. An essential element in this process was to suggest general standards which had a legal quality, whether as an accepted norm of international law or as a rule which was implied by or closely related to a principle of law' (Schachter 1983: 51).

This behaviour appears to have accounted for much of the impression he made on the Chinese. The place of 'humility' in such a situation is particularly obvious. On his return, Hammarskjöld faced enormous public expectations. He did in fact have positive news, but it was implicit and hedged with preconditions. To avoid damaging the result, he had to defend the anodyne text of the communiqué. Resisting the temptation to impress and the pressure of expectations required precisely the humility that Hammarskjöld demanded of himself again and again. Looking back at the Peking trip, Hammarskjöld wrote in a letter to Beskow: 'Such a situation relieves you of the last traces of an "I" which later does its utmost to push forward again' (quoted in Beskow 1969: 36). Years later, talking to Kay Rainey Gray, a journalist, he described his feelings on arriving back in New York: 'My feet hardly touched the ground. I had a good story to tell, but couldn't tell it!' (Gray 1987: 41).

The Peking mission thus finds its reflection in Hammarskjöld's diary. On the day the General Assembly authorized the visit and the exchange of telegrams with Chou En-Lai he copied the following Bible passage into his diary[8] (Dusen 1969: 131): 'God spake once, and twice I have also heard the same: that power belongeth unto God; / and that thou, Lord, art merciful: for thou rewardest every man according to his work' (*Markings* 1954: 26, 102). His diary also contains other entries that correspond with his political experiences made during the Peking Mission and have the thought of the imitation of Christ as their theme.[9]

The imperative of empathy and face-saving in managing negotiations

An entry at the end of 1955 deserves special mention. Read in connection with Hammarskjöld's negotiating experience, this passage is a guide to his concept of 'quiet diplomacy'. For that reason the entire entry is given here:

'Concerning men and their way to peace and concord –?'
The truth is so simple that it is considered pretentious banality. Yet it is continually denied by our behaviour. Every day furnishes new examples.
It is more important to be aware of the grounds for your own behaviour than to understand the motives of another.
The other's 'face' is more important than your own. If, while pleading another's cause, you are at the same time seeking something for yourself, you cannot hope to succeed.
You can only hope to find a lasting solution to a conflict if you have learned to see the other objectively, but, at the same time, to experience his difficulties subjectively.
The man who 'likes people' disposed once and for all of the man who despises them.
All first-hand experience is valuable, and he who has given up looking for it will one day find – that he lacks what he needs: a closed mind is a

weakness, and he who approaches persons or painting or poetry without the youthful ambition to learn new language and so gain access to someone else's perspective on life, let him beware.

A successful lie is doubly a lie, an error which has to be corrected is a heavier burden than truth: only an uncompromising 'honesty' can reach the bedrock of decency which you should always expect to find, even under deep layers of evil.

Diplomatic 'finesse' must never be another word for fear of being unpopular: that is to seek the appearance of influence at the cost of its reality.

(Markings 1955: 39, 114; see also Urquhart 1963: 140)

Once again, these rules of behaviour and standards of empathy can be linked to Buber's ideas. In other words, even before reading Buber, Hammarskjöld was aware of the necessity and requirements of genuine dialogue.[10] Another 1955 passage which deals with the vital 'respect for the word' can also be associated with Buber's approach and interpreted as a direct reflection of the negotiations in Peking (*Markings* 1955: 37, 112; see also Erling 1999: 39). Cordier later recalls that they had discussed Buber in the Secretariat in the context of private diplomacy (1967: 3). Hammarskjöld's private diplomacy – exercised personally or through a number of representatives – is, however, intrinsically linked to the concept of UN presence that will be treated in the following section.

UN presence and blue helmets

The Charter makes no reference to the instrument of the world organization that accounts for much of the contemporary perception and the activity of the UN: the 'blue helmets'. The first peacekeeping mission in the literal sense was a political innovation during Hammarskjöld's term of office and may be interpreted as a tangible expression of his concept of the UN presence (Gordenker 1967a: 235–319; Smouts 1971: 72–89; Urquhart 1993). This mission, the United Nations Emergency Force, emerged as a direct response to the political and military challenges of the Suez Crisis: an explosive mixture of long-simmering regional and international conflicts, economic interests and the prestige of individual states that threatened to involve the two superpowers.[11]

Hammarskjöld was thoroughly aware of the importance of the subsequent reconstruction of events and decisions. After the Suez Crisis Hammarskjöld had some of his staff put together a sort of annotated diary supplemented with documents that contained a day-by-day, and at times hour-by-hour, account of the details of events, even telephone calls with individual ambassadors. This material, labelled 'Suez Story' (KB DHS: 'Suez Story' as put together and marked by D. H. and kept in his safe in his office UN HQ, New York 1956–7), which was transferred from his safe to the Stockholm Archives also includes a document dating from August 1957: 'Notes on part of my personal participation in the developments 29 October–20 November 1956' (KB DHS: Dag Hammarskjöld, Notes, 2 August 1957).

Conflict situation: The Suez Crisis

On 26 July 1956 Gamal Abdel Nasser nationalized the Suez Canal Company. With this action at the latest, the Western countries perceived Nasser as a ruthless and unpredictable Arab leader who sought to extend his personal sphere of influence. Shortly before, with Egypt's recognition of the People's Republic of China and the agreement to buy Soviet weapons via Czechoslovakia, the USA had withdrawn the financial assistance promised for the construction of the Aswan Dam. Thus, from the start the crisis affected the relationship between the superpowers. After the nationalization of the Suez Canal Company, though, the reactions of the USA and the Soviet Union were fairly muted. By contrast, France and Great Britain, the countries directly affected by the nationalization and with strategic interests in the former mandate territory, began to consider the option of using military force against Egypt. In the course of August and September a series of secret meetings and consultations took place between France and the UK on the one hand and France and Israel on the other. At first, Paris kept the British in the dark about its cooperation with Israel, while sending the latter large undercover shipments of arms (CF III, Introduction: 8–25). Under the surface the conflict over the political order in the Middle East was taking on new forms.

Meanwhile, the United Nations was also dealing with the conflict. Immediately after the nationalization, Hammarskjöld had, as an exercise in private diplomacy, initiated a series of informal meetings with foreign ministers Selwyn Lloyd, Christian Pineau and Mahmoud Fawzi in his office in New York. They focused on the questions of the future use of the canal and a settlement of the different claims and interests. To general surprise, these talks produced acceptable results in a relatively short time. The heart of the agreement consisted of six principles on the use of the canal, which the Security Council officially endorsed on 13 October (CF III: 292–303). A diplomatic settlement appeared to be within reach, notwithstanding Soviet resistance to some of the Franco–British implementation plans.

The next day, the French prime minister, Guy Mollet unofficially proposed a coordinated military action with Israel code-named 'Operation Musketeer' to his British colleague Anthony Eden (Urquhart 1972: 159). The plan was for Israel to attack Egypt from Sinai, whereupon Britain and France would set the two parties an ultimatum to cease hostilities and withdraw. The plan assumed that the Egyptians would not agree, whereupon French and British units – as forces of law and order, as it were – would land in Egypt to occupy the Canal Zone, separate the combatants and secure the waterway. Moreover, re-establishing *de facto* Franco–British influence and inflicting a military defeat on Egypt could possibly precipitate the overthrow of Nasser, whom France, in addition, suspected of supporting the Algerian independence movement. Eden agreed to the plan and immediately withdrew his unsuspecting foreign minister from New York, where he was busy with the final negotiations of the Six-Point Plan.

The Israeli surprise attack on 29 October was followed a day later by the pre-conceived Franco–British ultimatum giving both parties 12 hours to cease hostilities. This news burst in on the Security Council meeting on the morning of

30 October. Hammarskjöld was shocked by the course of events – he felt that he had been deceived by Israel, Great Britain and France, especially as he had been working with these countries towards a constructive solution for the Middle East. In his report of August 1957 he writes: 'The situation seemed to me to be one where the whole position of the UN was at stake and where the very least I could do was to play my position in order to get freedom of action in relation to the two permanent Members, which appeared to have put the UN aside, both in substance and in form' (KB DHS: Hammarskjöld, Notes: 2). On the afternoon of 31 October he spoke at a meeting of the Security Council to establish the principles of his position as Secretary-General in the new circumstances:

> The principles of the Charter are, by far, greater than the Organization in which they are embodied, and the aims which they are to safeguard are holier than the policies of any single nation or people. As a servant of the Organization, the Secretary-General has the duty to maintain his usefulness by avoiding public stands on conflicts between Member Nations unless and until such an action might help to resolve the conflict. However, the discretion and impartiality thus imposed on the Secretary-General by the character of his immediate task, may not degenerate into a policy of expediency. He must also be a servant of the principles of the Charter, and its aims must ultimately determine what for him is right and wrong. For that he must stand. A Secretary-General cannot serve on any other assumption than that – within the necessary limits of human frailty and honest differences of opinion – all Member Nations honor their pledge to observe all articles of the Charter.
>
> (CF III: 309)

Reminiscent of a judo fighter, Hammarskjöld exploited the broad attack on the principles of the United Nations to counteract using the 'paradox of an attacker yielding power to the victim' (Murphy 1970: 172). He then went a step further, stating that if the member states did not share the Secretary-General's conception of his office they were, of course, free to act accordingly. Behind this stood nothing less than the implicit threat of either his resignation or the challenge of a vote of confidence. He never seriously considered the option of resigning – the declaration was a deliberately calculated political tool (Åhman 1963: 9). Hammarskjöld was taking a risk, but he calculated correctly: the national representatives in the Security Council vied with one another in offering messages of confidence and support. Louis de Guiringaud for France and Sir Pierson Dixon for Great Britain joined in the chorus. Like the American representative, both had received Hammarskjöld's text that morning. Just at the moment at which the United Nations appeared to be excluded, this move of Hammarskjöld's focused attention on the significance of his office; his speech to the Security Council is a classic example of 'moral force in action'.[12]

However, there was no chance of the Security Council finding a constructive solution to the crisis, as the UK and France used their vetoes to block any attempt and instead started bombing Egyptian positions in preparation for an invasion.

Thanks to 'Operation Musketeer', a lot of problems, including questions of economic relationships and oil supply, were suddenly out of control. France and Great Britain, 'old' colonial powers, opposed a young, independent country that belonged to the new group of non-aligned states. In addition, Nasser's ambitions of pan-Arabic leadership pitted him against Israel, with which he had had a series of bigger and smaller armed clashes. At the superpower level, by contrast, the crisis pitched the USA and the Soviet Union into a race for dominance in the Middle East. One aspect of this race concerned the respective appeal to the non-aligned states, whose actions would gain the support of this group. The Soviet Union did not hesitate long and offered Nasser arms as well as Soviet 'volunteers' for the Egyptian 'liberation struggle' (Maloney 1999: 264–6). The USA was in a difficult situation: it disapproved strongly of the action of the UK and France. At the same time, it had to take into account the danger that the British and French operation posed to the future of the Western alliance. London and Paris risked doing considerable harm to the traditionally good relations among NATO partners. The fact that the operation was launched just days before the US presidential elections on 6 November made the conflict all the more explosive. In addition, the Soviet invasion to quell the Hungarian uprising had lit the fuse of another powder keg in the East–West conflict. Moscow tried to use the Suez Crisis to distract attention from its actions in Budapest. Indeed, the Soviet Union threatened to use nuclear weapons against Britain and France and, well aware of Washington's position, urged Washington to take part in a joint military operation (CF III: 337). The USA desperately sought a diplomatic solution to this situation that would end the Franco–British venture while enabling them to save face.

In this situation the 'Uniting-for-Peace' resolution (Nolte 1995b; Delbrück 1964: 87–99) was applied for the first time, a peace-keeping option developed in the aftermath of the Korean War that allowed the General Assembly in an emergency meeting to take up a threat to world peace if the Security Council did not fulfil its obligations. The procedure originally devised by the USA to relativize a Soviet veto was now to be applied 'against' two Western allies. The General Assembly convened in emergency session on 1 November at the request of Yugoslavia (with the clear support of the USA) (Interview Frederick 1986). In view of the sensitive context, Washington put on a show of public reserve – while putting intense diplomatic and above all economic pressure on France and Britain behind the scenes. Instead, Canada intervened in the negotiations. Ottawa not only maintained special relations with the USA, but also with its 'mother countries' Great Britain and France. It also held a position in the Commonwealth that could prove useful for mediation between the newly independent countries and the colonial powers. When the session opened, Lester Pearson, the Canadian foreign minister, exploited his country's position to guide the debate towards a proposal that he had developed soon after the Korean War and now dusted off: the United Nations could deploy its own international peacekeeping troops (Pearson 1957a, 1973: 244–78).

Hammarskjöld's response: The United Nations Emergency Force

Pearson repeatedly raised this subject with Hammarskjöld, who was initially very sceptical. Nevertheless, in the General Assembly on the morning of 2 November the Canadian proposed establishing a 'truly international peace and police force' (GAOR, 1st Emergency Special Session, 562nd plenary meeting, 1 November 1956: 36; see also Urquhart 1993a: 265–90). Before the sitting the proposal had been presented to the Americans; under the agreement between Pearson and his colleague, John Foster Dulles, the latter rose to speak as soon as Pearson finished his speech and demanded that Canada submit a concrete proposal for such a force (Pearson 1973: 247). American pressure was having some effect and Great Britain cautiously signalled a change in position. The previous day Anthony Eden had expressed the view that the 'police action' by British and French troops could possibly be followed by an international presence (quoted in CF III: 316). In recognition of Canada's special position, London had transmitted an advance copy of Eden's speech to the Canadian delegation in New York (Pearson 1973: 246).

This opened up a possible solution, but the idea of an international peacekeeping force was still far from reality. Over lunch with Pearson on 2 November Hammarskjöld was still hesitant (CF III: 319–22) on account of the enormous risk involved for the United Nations. He writes in his recapitulation of the events: 'Not by way of opposition, but in order to see to it that the Canadian initiative would be taken on the basis of realistic assumptions, I spelled out some of the obvious difficulties into which we would run' (KB DHS: Hammarskjöld, Notes: 3). These questions included: Could the legal problems relating to such a force be solved? Was the UN actually in a position to organize such a force? Would Franco–British influence allow it to operate as an international force rather than as a belated legitimation of intervention?

Pearson's original proposal had run into problems precisely on the last point, as it had foreseen a UN force made up primarily of English and French soldiers (Rovine 1970: 288; Eden 1962: 611). That evening the Secretary-General had dinner with Pearson, Cordier and Bunche in Pearson's suite in the Drake Hotel and articulated his deep reservations about Pearson's plan (Cordier 1964: 424). However, the idea of an international force survived the discussion. Under the pressure of events and after receiving clarification about some of his concerns, Hammarskjöld finally declared himself convinced at lunch in his office on the thirty-eighth floor the next day, 3 November (Kelen 1966: 75). After the decision in principle, he got to work exceptionally quickly, meeting with several heads of delegation in the course of the day (Lash 1961: 97–111). First, the possible creation of a peacekeeping force in accordance with the 'Uniting-for-Peace' procedure needed to find broad support among member states in the General Assembly. Hammarskjöld and Pearson coordinated this with a small circle of UN delegations that took a positive view of the plan and represented their respective regional groupings in the General Assembly. Initial members of the group were Hans Engen (Norway), Arthur Lall (India) and Francisco Urrutia (Columbia) (CF III: 319). It was Lall who passed on to John Holmes, one of Pearson's staff, the crucial information that after being informed by Egyptian UN Ambassador Loutfi, Nasser agreed to the Canadian plan in principle (Pearson: 1973: 251). Building on the efforts to clarify, coordinate and convince various member states, that same evening Canada proposed a draft resolution that included, in addition to the efforts to reach a ceasefire, the following passage:

> The General Assembly, …
> Requests as a matter of priority, the Secretary-General to submit to it within forty-eight hours a plan for the setting up, with the consent of the nations concerned, of an emergency international United Nations force to secure and supervise the cessation of hostilities in accordance with all the terms of the aforementioned resolution.
> (GA Res. 998 (ES–I) 3 November 1956, quoted in CF III: 320)

The prior efforts to sound out and take account of the voting positions in the different groups paid off: Canada's resolution was passed by a vote of 57 to 0 with 19 abstentions.[13] A major factor in this success was tying the functions of the Emergency Force directly to the goal and monitoring of the ceasefire. Once the resolution was passed, the ball was in Hammarskjöld's court. His only concrete instruction was to present a plan within 48 hours, an almost impossible deadline. Yet, before it expired Hammarskjöld proposed to the General Assembly that a United Nations command be established for the future Emergency Force. As its head he recommended the chief of staff of the United Nations Truce Supervision Organization, General Burns, who was familiar with the problems of the region. In a telegram to Burns Hammarskjöld expressed doubts about the idea – but also the necessity of testing the only concrete option for a solution: 'My personal lack of optimism is of course no excuse for not exploring the field' (quoted in Urquhart 1972: 178).

In his interim report of 4 December, Hammarskjöld reported the formation of a UN command and other guidelines: '[A]s a matter of principle, troops should not be drawn from countries which are permanent members of the Security Council' (quoted in CF III: 335). Besides keeping out the rival superpowers, which were competing for influence in the region, the principle reflected the desire to exclude the participation of Britain and France, who could have used the UN cover to legitimize their intervention after the event. On 5 November Hammarskjöld dictated his report during breaks in the General Assembly sitting and between further meetings with Pearson, Cordier and Stravopoulos among others. He gave the first draft to Bunche for comments. The report was finally ready at 2 a.m. on 6 November – Pearson had sat polishing it with the Secretary-General until the very end. Time was as much of the essence as ever. British and French paratroopers had landed in Port Said the day before, starting the invasion of Egypt. Moscow became even more critical, and the number of angry voices in the Commonwealth was also growing. Hammarskjöld forwarded his report to Paris and London without delay. A favourable constellation was forming in Britain in particular: the government was under enormous domestic political pressure from the opposition, and the USA continued to apply strong economic and political pressure. According to Cordier and Foote, Hammarskjöld's report arrived at just the right time providing 'a line of retreat at a moment when the various pressures to halt the ill-started military adventure had built to overwhelming proportions' (CF III: 340).

In his second report on UNEF Hammarskjöld laid down the principles for the first United Nations peacekeeping mission (UN Doc. A/3302 6 November 1956, quoted in CF III: 344–51). The force would be under the international command of the United Nations. Hammarskjöld drew a clear distinction between this international command and authorizing individual states to act on behalf of the UN, as was the case in Korea. Partly for pragmatic reasons, the command was given to General Burns; thus the constitutional structure of the UNTSO became the model for UNEF. In Hammarskjöld's view this settled two other points, namely the independence of the Chief of Command in recruiting officers and the exclusion of personnel from permanent members of the Security Council (ibid.: 346). On the basis of this view Hammarskjöld rejected British, French and also Egyptian proposals that the parties involved should have a voice in the selection of the different national contingents.

Hammarskjöld also underlined the 'emergency' character of the force and thus from the start the temporary nature of its mandate, as established by the General Assembly resolution. Its function was 'to secure and supervise the cessation of hostilities'. He then expanded on this point: 'It follows from its terms of reference that there is no intent in the establishment of the Force to influence the military balance in the present conflict and, thereby, the political balance affecting efforts to settle the conflict' (ibid.: 347). Furthermore, Hammarskjöld pointed out that UNEF was acting on the basis of the 'Uniting-for-Peace' Resolution. Consequently, it could not resort to Security Council sanctions under Chapter VII and depended on the consensus of the parties involved – in particular as regards permission for the international force to enter the operational area. There were also strict limits on the functions of the force on the ground:

> The force obviously should have no rights other than those necessary for the execution of its functions, in cooperation with local authorities. It would be more than an observers' corps, but in no way a military force temporarily controlling the territory in which it is stationed; nor, moreover, should the force have military functions exceeding those necessary to secure peaceful conditions on the assumption that the parties to the conflict take all necessary steps for compliance with the recommendations of the General Assembly.
>
> (ibid.: 348)

These statements were followed by remarks on organizational, logistical and financial questions that will not be dealt with here (even though some, especially financial, aspects were very controversial). To summarize: the Secretary-General formulated five basic principles that would henceforth serve as a model for other UN peacekeeping missions:

1   The peacekeeping mission is in principle an emergency measure and limited in time.
2   The peacekeeping mission shall be carried out with complete impartiality. Its deployment may not in any way change or prejudice longer-term political or military power relationships. Force may only be used in self-defence.
3   The permanent members of the Security Council are excluded from supplying troops for peacekeeping missions.
4   The peacekeeping mission shall be under the unified command of a single UN officer.
5   The deployment of peacekeeping units depends on the consensus of the parties involved, in particular that of the respective host country.

Hammarskjöld emphasized the 'exploratory character' (ibid.: 350) of his report and pointed out that much would ensue as concrete steps were implemented. He suggested that an 'advisory committee to the Secretary-General for questions relating to the operations' be established and underlined: 'If the force is to come into being with all the speed indispensable to its success, a margin of confidence must be left to those who will carry the responsibility for putting the decisions into effect' (ibid.: 350–1).

In the end, Tunisia's representative, Mongi Slim, submitted a resolution that the Secretary-General be authorized to establish a peacekeeping force. He was very close to Hammarskjöld and had cleared the wording of the resolution with him in advance to ensure that it contained Hammarskjöld's main principles (GA Res. 1001 (ES–I) 7 November 1956; Franck 1984: 484). The resolution to establish UNEF was adopted after a debate by 64 votes to 0 with 12 abstentions. The USSR declared its doubts about whether UNEF was compatible with the Charter, but chose to abstain as Egypt had voted in favour. At the same time, an advisory committee was established with representatives from Brazil, Canada, Ceylon, Columbia, India, Norway and Pakistan (CF III: 355–7; Yugoslavia was added later). Thus the institution was founded on which the further development and implementation of UNEF would be incumbent. The meetings of this committee were strictly confidential, but written notes of its meetings are in the United Nations Archives (These 'verbatims' are kept mainly in UNA DAG–1 5.0.1.0. Box 1; quoted in the following as AC UNEF [date]). These notes make possible a more detailed account of the creation of UNEF, Hammarskjöld's personal influence and how he approached this problem.

Hammarskjöld himself viewed the advisory committee as an opportunity for a quick decision on unresolved questions that should actually be clarified by the General Assembly. In one of the meetings he states that the committee should be 'an ad hoc executive organ … which is entitled to function for the General Assembly and where, of course, matters can be clarified, understood and analyzed in an entirely different way and where it is not a matter for this or that kind of public scrutiny' (AC UNEF 20 November 1956: 1). Hammarskjöld repeatedly stressed the confidentiality of the meetings, for instance by stating 'that certainly at present no closed meetings are held at the United Nations which have more interesting political overtones than our discussions here' (AC UNEF 12 March 1957: 5). However, it was assumed that the participants informed their governments, and possibly other delegations, about the meetings. Cordier describes the sense of this instrument as follows: it lies in using a diplomatic partnership to keep the policies of the Secretary-General 'on the rails' (1960: 10) of the views of member states.

The committee met for the first time on the evening of 14 November. In accordance with the provisions of the resolution, the participants were the UN ambassadors from Brazil (Cyro de Freitas Valle), Canada (Lester Pearson), Ceylon (R.S.S. Gunewardene), Colombia (Francisco Urrutia), India (Arthur Lall), Norway (Hans Engen) and Pakistan (Muhammad Mir Khan) (CF III: 355–7). As a rule, the meetings were held in the conference room or in the Secretary-General's office and lasted between 60 and 90 minutes; sometimes the committee met twice a day. Only in exceptional cases were members represented by a deputy.

Hammarskjöld structured the discussion by regularly summarizing the state of the discussion and the different opinions. The introductory words 'I shall try to sum up' (for instance in AC UNEF 13 December 1956: 10) became virtually a trademark of his method of consensus- and result-oriented summarizing. Looking back, Hammarskjöld explains: 'Instead of a vote, the chairman sums up his conclusions from the debate, and any member of the committee is free to go on record with his objections to the summing up. Never in the course of these years has any such observation been put on record in the committee' (Address to a Meeting of Both Houses of Parliament under the Auspices of the British Group of the Inter-Parliamentary Union 2 April 1958, in CF IV: 50). The committee decided on the language of texts, which sometimes involved protracted discussion on the legal meaning and political consequence of individual words.

In the committee, it soon became apparent which members fulfilled which roles. Arthur Lall, who kept a very close eye on the interests and rights of Egypt, tended to ask the critical questions. Lester Pearson, as a rule, presented the view of the Western states. However, there was seldom any tension; indeed at times the atmosphere was quite cheerful. Hammarskjöld often asked his staff to supplement the political arguments with businesslike progress reports. Ralph Bunche played a crucial role in this respect. After the decision of the General Assembly, Hammarskjöld had turned to him and said: 'Now, Corporal, go get me a force' (Rovine 1970: 289). Bunche's role should not be underestimated, as in 1948 he had drawn up the principles governing UNTSO that Hammarskjöld directly referred to (Urquhart 1993a: 266). Urquhart calls UNEF 'a force he [Bunche] had virtually created' (ibid.: 285). And continues: 'It was Bunche's task to transform Hammarskjöld's 'metaphysical' subtleties into practical arrangements on the ground' (ibid.: 271). In a private note of April 1957 Bunche recorded on the occasion of a visit: 'Seeing UNEF in operation out here and its remarkable success, I do feel a sense of quiet pride in the knowledge, known only to a few out here, that I was primarily responsible for the organization of the force, the getting off the ground, and have been directing it from the beginning. It is, perhaps, my finest achievement, exceeding the armistice negotiations' (ibid.: 297). In the committee Bunche was responsible for organizational, technical and logistical questions. Among other things, he had to grapple with the question of how to give the force a common identification. In this context the idea emerged of painting the helmet of the soldier in the blue of the flag of the United Nations.[14] At the same time, Bunche coordinated the offers and queries of the member states related to providing troops. In mid-November he remarked: 'This is the most popular army in history – an army which everyone fights to get into' (AC UNEF, 14 November 1956: 29).

The actual dispatch of troops immediately ran into difficulties. In the first weeks telegrams flew back and forth between Hammarskjöld and General Burns and other representatives on the spot about the scope and meaning of Egypt's 'sovereign consent' to the deployment of UNEF. The force was not founded on Chapter VII of the Charter and therefore was unable to apply any sanctions against Egypt or any other country. This was not the only reason why the committee continually faced the question of the extent to which the actions of UNEF could be reconciled with the Charter. In connection with the different claims to the future of the Gaza Strip, ambassador Lall explained that this was to some extent a grey zone; thus the organization could not act there under Chapter VII of the Charter, but this did not mean that it necessarily had to refer to the alternative Chapter VI, which regulates the pacific settlement of disputes (AC UNEF, 14 March 1957: 14). Hammarskjöld commented on this grey zone with an almost roguish tone: 'It may be one of those famous vacua' (ibid.: 21). A short time later the Brazilian representative coined what became a classic formulation by remarking: '[I] think we are in Chapter six and a half' (ibid.: 25). Hammarskjöld picks up this thought and categorizes the Uniting-for-Peace resolution in this corner. However, he adds: '[T]he trouble is that it does not give us the rights of Chapter VII, although it presents us with some of the problems of Chapter VII' (ibid.). At the same time he emphasizes that the vagueness of the General Assembly resolutions, which as a rule is useful in terms of the flexibility of the UN's work, would be very problematic once the force would be challenged with substantial problems.

In this sense, Hammarskjöld felt prompted on 12 November to ask Fawzi in an *aide-mémoire* to define the point of 'sovereign consent' more closely. Hammarskjöld wrote:

> However, I want to put on record that the conditions which motivate the consent to entry and presence, are the very conditions to which the tasks established for the Force in the General Assembly resolution, 4 November, are directed. Therefore, I assume it to be recognized that as long as the task, thus prescribed, is not completed, the reasons for the consent of the Government remains valid, and that a withdrawal of this consent before completion of the task would run counter to the acceptance by Egypt of the decision by the General Assembly.
>
> (KB DHS: Dag Hammarskjöld, Aide-mémoire to Fawzi,
> 12 November 1956)

Thus, in Hammarskjöld's view, consent to the mission also entailed acceptance of the continued presence and activity of the force: the government undertook to accept the purpose and goal of the mission until its mandate was fulfilled. In the event of differences of opinion over the completion of the mission, the UN and Egypt could negotiate and the matter could be taken before the General Assembly. Hammarskjöld emphasized: 'You know that we are not coming, begging for permission, but offering assistance as friends' (ibid.). Fawzi immediately rejected this reading and threatened to cancel the whole undertaking if even the most minor restriction on Egypt's sovereign rights was open to debate. Hammarskjöld sought to address the lack of clarity with the so-called good faith agreement (D'Amato 1984: 107–9), which would establish the procedural modalities for a UNEF withdrawal and safeguard the position of the UN in the event of unilateral termination by Egypt, without affecting Egypt's sovereignty in sensitive areas. The good faith agreement was the result of numerous drafts and diplomatic formulations of compromise and was finally accepted as an annex to Hammarskjöld's UNEF report of 20 November. The crucial passage reads:

> The Government of Egypt declares that, when exercising its sovereign rights on any matter concerning the presence and functioning of UNEF, it will be guided, in good faith, by its acceptance of General Assembly resolution 1000 (ES-I) of November 5, 1956. … The United Nations takes note of this declaration of the Government of Egypt and declares that the activities of UNEF will be guided in good faith, by the task established for the Force in the aforementioned resolutions; in particular, the United Nations, understanding this to correspond to the wishes of the Government of Egypt, reaffirms its willingness to maintain UNEF until its task is completed.
>
> (CF III: 375–6)

Hammarskjöld recorded his interpretation of the text in several notes in the file on the 'Suez Story' (KB DHS: Drafts for *Aide-mémoire* n.d.) and added it to an authorized *aide-mémoire* of his version on 5 August 1957 (KB DHS: Dag Hammarskjöld, *Aide-mémoire*, 5 August 1957). He admits that there was an 'element of gambling' in the repeated queries and rejections or declarations of differences of opinion.

The question of 'sovereign consent' arose from Nasser's refusal to accept Norwegian, Danish or Canadian units in UNEF, as they represented NATO countries. Hammarskjöld referred once more to the principle underlying the General Assembly resolution that UNEF was a genuinely international emergency force and not just a collection of national units; but in recognition of Egypt's reservations, he included Yugoslav and Indonesian contingents to prevent a Western preponderance (CF III: 363). Hammarskjöld explicitly defended this procedure in the committee: 'I think that this combination of stand and principle which I consider necessary in view of the precedent which we will set for the future development of a police force is reasonable' (AC UNEF 14 November 1956: 1). This problem flared up once again when the Canadian defence ministry sought to deploy an infantry battalion with the name 'The Queen's Own Rifles' (CF III: 370–1) thus offering a problematic allusion to the British Forces. Although the battalion fulfilled all the technical prerequisites, great care had to be taken to avoid sending the wrong political signals. To this end, after the Egyptians lodged a complaint Hammarskjöld was even prepared to put up with the temporary annoyance of the Canadian government. However, he was able to obtain Egyptian agreement to the inclusion of other Canadian troops as part of UNEF's air transport.

'Sovereign consent' was, in several respects, the diplomatic hurdle holding up the stationing of UNEF. On 16 and 17 November Hammarskjöld negotiated with Nasser for seven hours, who finally made up his mind to accept the text after thrice threatening to call off the entire operation (KB DHS: Dag Hammarskjöld, *Aide-mémoire*, 5 August 1957: 7–8). Although a clearer formulation in terms of international law would have been desirable, it could not be realized. Hammarskjöld hoped that the good faith agreement would be more valuable in such situations than legal definitions of the contents:

> I feel myself that this is an operation where the exact legal text is much less important than the moral and political factors – that is, the good faith point – is more valuable. Because if Egypt – which I do not believe – would do something here, which certainly goes against what was the intention of the General Assembly, with this kind of registration on the stands, the attack would be less one for saying 'Well, this is against the letter of the law', than 'This is bad faith' and, for that reason, to be outlawed and condemned. Therefore, this is a stronger stand.
>
> (AC UNEF, 19 November 1956: 13)

To demonstrate his personal involvement and that of his office, Hammarskjöld accompanied the first UNEF units to Egypt on 16 November, which underscored the international character of the force (Gray 1987: 45). He explained this step in the committee: '[I]t would make it easier for them to understand that it was an international Force, if the Force followed, and might make them look at it in the right way' (AC UNEF 14 November 1956: 25).

But there was more to the incident than the improvised deployment of the force and the principles behind it. The Emergency Force had to struggle with manifold challenges and tests, many of them about its status. In these cases, Hammarskjöld had to defend pragmatically the principles he had formulated. For instance, there was a constant danger that the force's international character would be compromised by the perception that it legitimized the Franco–British invasion after the event. Hammarskjöld responded by taking an uncompromising stand on this matter – often under great difficulty – and assuming full responsibility for the possible failure of the venture. In answer to a journalist's question at a press conference on 12 November he remarked: 'We should not be losing our time concerning what may be my personal troubles or personal merits. I can tell you one thing, that if it would in any way help the United Nations for me to be a scapegoat, I would be quite happy to be one' (CF III: 369).

One of the first issues that could have hardened suspicions of a Franco–British connotation to UNEF was the offer of the two governments to clear the Suez Canal of ships deliberately sunk to block it. Sir Pierson Dixon had already raised this issue on 6 November in his declaration of consent to Hammarskjöld's UNEF plans (quoted in CF III: 341). Hammarskjöld had written to the British foreign minister the next day: 'I shall as soon as possible revert to your offer to assist in the technical work to be undertaken in order to reopen the Suez Canal. At present I am exploring the possibility of undertaking this task under United Nations auspices through agents from nations not engaged in the present conflict' (quoted ibid.: 359). Experts thought it virtually impossible to clear the canal without British and French assistance; that this was not the case is one of the great logistical successes of the UN (Urquhart 1972: 198–202).

Hammarskjöld also had to maintain the international character of the force in the practical question of transport for UNEF. Thus, he declined a US offer to transport the first UN contingents, even though this would have been the easiest and quickest solution. To avoid political complications, Hammarskjöld picked a UNEF meeting place near Naples. Most contingents were flown there in American aircraft, whence Hammarskjöld arranged for Swissair to fly them onto Egyptian territory (CF III: 362). Similarly, the Secretary-General declined to accept any technical equipment from the British and French troops, although this decision caused serious logistical problems and impediments. In addition, the financing of the operation was controversial from beginning to end, though not serious enough to prevent the force from being sent.

It is clear from this that the Secretary-General was still walking a tightrope: he carried responsibility for the entire operation. This covered the application, calculation and coordination of ethical forces and political powers. His principled stand was also motivated by his realization that UNEF was a precedent for future missions. Even at the start he spoke of the enormous difficulties of ensuring that UNEF 'get[s] the start it deserves and set[s] a precedent which the United Nations needs' (PC 12 November 1956, in CF III: 367). Later, following a report by his legal counsel, Constantin Stravopoulos, he unequivocally spoke of 'an extremely valuable precedent for the future' (AC UNEF 8 December 1956: 11) in a comment in the committee. This is all the more surprising because Hammarskjöld generally avoided any intimation that his actions could create precedents; precedent contradicted his view of organic growth (see 'Dag Hammarskjöld's conception of the UN, the Charter and his office' in Chapter 2) and could foster the image of a 'power-hungry' Secretary-General. This highlights his very public role in establishing UNEF: 'While the original conception of the emergency force was not his, Hammarskjöld clearly was the chief agent in its construction and the formulation of its basic principles, and was of course its primary administrative officer' (Rovine 1970: 291). Pearson himself in his Nobel Peace Prize speech confirmed that Hammarskjöld deserved most credit for the establishment of UNEF (1957b: 104). This new type of peacekeeping mission was made possible by the combination of Pearson's idea, Bunche's organizational ability and Hammarskjöld's principled stand and leadership. Here was a 'dream team' of international organization; coincidentally, all three were awarded the Nobel Peace Prize.

One reason for the success of this innovation was the favourable international constellation. The supportive role of the USA in particular should not be overlooked.

US president Eisenhower personally praised Hammarskjöld's 'leadership' (quoted in Simon 1967: 109) and expressed his total confidence in the Secretary-General. In a letter to the US president, Hammarskjöld, in turn, acknowledged the Americans' indispensable help (KB DHS: Dag Hammarskjöld, Letter to Dwight D. Eisenhower, 24 November 1956). The political constellation that had made it possible to contain the conflict within the framework of the United Nations also explains why it was not possible to find a similarly constructive solution for the simultaneous crisis in Hungary (Lash 1961: 111). Here, too, Hammarskjöld had tried to establish a role for the United Nations by offering to mediate and to visit Hungary. Consistent rejection by the Soviet Union and the puppet government in Hungary made further steps – even in the General Assembly – impossible:[15] there was no space and no will for 'good faith'. In 1956 UNEF managed to defuse the Suez Crisis with its diverse and unpredictable regional and international consequences and kept it under control for several years afterwards. However, the good faith agreement, the fragile, but only possible compromise, did not prevent Egypt's unilateral termination of the UN peacekeeping operation in 1967 and the withdrawal of the force (Tandon 1968; Morgenthau 1963).[16] UNEF's immediate success – a UN peacekeeping force as a theoretical and practical innovation – made the saying 'Leave it to Dag!' a slogan of international diplomacy. Hammarskjöld had succeeded, with the help of the General Assembly and the advisory committee, in 'structurally' (Barudio 1989: 142) entrenching his freedom of action and his 'power' – a power based on his moral authority in the sense of his 'devotion' to the principles of the UN. Again, Hammarskjöld's concept is rooted in his political ethics.

Political ethics and UN presence

The peacekeeping force is a good example of how a vacuum offers potential to exploit one's scope for action: Hammarskjöld 'turned out to be a genius of sorts, a leader who could turn vague instructions from the General Assembly and the Security Council into functioning peacekeeping armies in the Sinai and the Congo' (Nelan 1995: 70). He started with considerable doubt about Pearson's actual proposal and ended by establishing UNEF. According to Barudio, the creation of UNEF is a case in which one can observe how 'elementary positions in his [Hammarskjöld's] otherwise so private philosophy of life can be successfully applied in the realm of high politics' (1989: 142). In the context of discussing Hammarskjöld's political ethics, the concept of the peacekeeping force can be seen as a development of several lines of his thought. One particularly conspicuous point is the sheer physical endurance and his principled stand on political ethics. Hammarskjöld devoted a lot of space to both in his diary. The Suez Crisis was a time of particularly frequent entries, some of which dealt with the political events discussed above. They afford an insight into Hammarskjöld's personal views and his motivation at this time.

Devotion to principle and innovation based on religious reflection

In a section dated 1 to 7 November, Hammarskjöld first quotes from the Bible and then adds a passage that deals with 'love' as the source and motivation of personal achievements exercised in humility. The following entry can be read as a personal exhortation to humility and self-discipline: 'It was when Lucifer first congratulated himself upon his angelic behaviour that he became the tool of evil' (*Markings* 1956: 46, 140). At the same time, these entries could be interpreted as comments on the behaviour of Britain and France. In the midst of many reports and sometimes confusing ultimatums and consultations Hammarskjöld notes: 'Without our being aware of it, our fingers are so guided that a pattern is created when thread gets caught in the web' (*Markings* 1956: 47, 140). This characteristic conception of a comprehensive sense that can be manifested in personal actions is also obvious in the entry for 17 November 1956, in which he writes of the constant presence of divine will: 'My device – if any: / Numen semper adest. / In that case: if uneasy – why?' (*Markings* 1956: 48, 140). Though it may seem astonishing that at this hectic time Hammarskjöld was writing and reflecting on sentences like these, one is compelled to the conclusion that precisely this preoccupation is the key to the intensity of his work at this time. Another symptomatic entry in this context reads: '– Not I, but God in me!' (*Markings* 1957: 4, 148).

The Suez Crisis coincided with the design of the UN meditation room, which Hammarskjöld was personally overseeing (Åhman 1963: 7). Pauline Frederick reports that one day during the crisis he called together the staff that was present and – to their surprise – took them into the room to discuss certain questions of design. In an entry for 29 November, against the backdrop of his growing personal responsibility, he dwells on the question of fame and humility:

> … If only the goal can justify the sacrifice, how, then, can you attach a shadow of importance to the question whether or not the memory of your efforts will be associated with your name? If you do, is it not all too obvious that you are still being influenced in your actions by that vain dead dream about 'posterity'?
>
> (*Markings* 1956: 53, 141)

These reflections can go hand in hand with 'down-to-earth' descriptions and judgements, as a letter to Bo Beskow on 20 October 1956 illustrates: 'Suez was my third child. The parents arrived in great bewilderment and some fury. God knows how this will end – but the brat cries less now and perhaps, with good assistance, I can teach it to walk' (Beskow 1969: 62).

Meister Eckhart and the successful establishment of UNEF

On Christmas Day 1956 Hammarskjöld summarized his experience of the Suez Crisis – with clear reference to Meister Eckhart and Thomas à Kempis:

Your own efforts 'did not bring it to pass', only God – but rejoice if God found a use for efforts in His work.

Rejoice if you feel that what you did was 'necessary', but remember, even so, that you were simply the instrument by means which He added one tiny grain to the Universe He has created for his own purposes.

'It is in this abyss that you reveal me to myself – I am nothing and I did not know it.'

'If, without any side glances, we have only God in view, it is He, indeed, who does what we do. … Such a man does not seek rest, for he is not troubled by any unrest. … He must acquire an inner solitude, no matter where or with whom he may be. He must learn to pierce the veil of things and comprehend God within them' (Meister Eckhart).

(*Markings* 1956: 57, 143)

Faced with the challenge, uncertainty and political pressure of the Suez Crisis, Hammarskjöld finds strength and confirmation of his conduct in the conviction that his actions are part of an overarching 'meaning'. The close correlation between outer experience and inner reflection is underscored by the entry two days later of his thoughts on Meister Eckhart's concept of the eternal birth. At the end of 1956, in the middle of these thoughts, a passage appears in which for the first time Hammarskjöld thinks about the significance of his notes and possible readers. The word 'Markings' is also used. At the start of 1957 Hammarskjöld again notes that political negotiations, too, are a test of personal integrity and the ability to put aside personal judgements.

The most dangerous of all moral dilemmas: when we are obliged to conceal truth in order to help the truth to be victorious. If this should at any time become our duty in the role assigned us by fate, how strait must be our path at all the times if we are not to perish.

(*Markings* 1957: 2, 147)

Here, too, as in the Peking mission, Hammarskjöld's integrity is demonstrable – for instance, in rejecting British and French assistance.

UN peacekeepers as a moral force

In a speech to UNEF soldiers originally drafted by Bunche (Urquhart 1993a: 272), Hammarskjöld expressed the novel aspects of this peacekeeping instrument:

As members of the United Nations Emergency Force you are taking part in an experience that is new in history. You are soldiers of peace in the first international force of its kind. You have come from distant homelands, not to fight a war but to serve peace and justice and order under the authority of the United Nations.

Thus the opportunity for service which is yours is not to be measured by your numbers or your armor. You are the front line of a moral force which extends around the world, and you have behind you the support of millions everywhere.

(CF III: 405)

Hammarskjöld regarded UNEF as the realization of 'moral force', which had to be safeguarded by practical, at times even banal, decisions. For him, the peacekeeping force was a concrete application of the 'basic rules of international ethics' laid down in the Charter. Hammarskjöld himself functioned as concrete representation of the United Nations when, for instance, he accompanied the first units to Egypt as personification of the international character of the force. Urquhart reports another even more telling incident in 1955 when, after a series of violations of the line of demarcation between Israel and Egypt in Gaza, he rode in a jeep accompanied by just one driver along the demarcation line, although all his staff and advisors urgently warned him that in the tense situation he could very well come under fire. Hammarskjöld is said to have replied: 'I don't care, I'm going to do it. I just want to prove a point, that this is what this is: this is an armistice line' (Urquhart 1984: 42). UNEF's designation as the 'front line of a moral force' can easily be linked with Buber's concept of the crossfront. The experiences made with UNEF were one of the compelling reasons for giving Hammarskjöld another term thus endorsing his practice of international civil service, the third and final concept to which we now turn.

The 'international civil servant'

An analysis of Hammarskjöld's political ethics repeatedly ends in the personal requirements of international service. Hammarskjöld did not invent the principle of the international civil servant, but he certainly helped to define it;[17] it is also a particular expression of his political ethics. Hammarskjöld developed his doctrine of international service against the background of a bitter political clash with the Soviet Union and the political events in the Congo.[18] This clash became public in the General Assembly in 1960, producing some of the most turbulent sessions in the history of the United Nations.

Conflict constellation: the troika proposal

Nikita S. Khrushchev intended to make a dazzling appearance as communist leader at the 15th Session of the General Assembly of the United Nations, and, as tribune supported by the neutral and non-aligned states, instrumentalize the meeting as an attack on capitalism (Urquhart 1972: 457–93). In preparation for a particularly powerful articulation of Soviet policies on the Congo, the Soviet UN ambassador Vassily Kuznetsov had been replaced by the deputy foreign minister, Valerian Zorin (CF IV: 174). The developments in the Congo would be used as a platform to demand the end of all forms of colonialism. This put the role of the

Secretary-General on the agenda, as the Soviet Union had several times accused him of bias in favour of the 'colonial powers'. Moreover, Khrushchev personally disliked Hammarskjöld, whom he contemptuously referred to as 'cham' (lout) after Hammarskjöld criticized Soviet economic and military aid to the Congo (Grinevskij 1996: 475). Hammarskjöld's insistence that ONUC – in keeping with the principles formulated for UNEF – could not allow any actions that changed or prejudiced the balance of political and military power was a source of increasing annoyance to Khrushchev. Like Lumumba, he demanded that ONUC should actively intervene to end Katanga's secession. In his memoirs, Khrushchev's speechwriter records that as the situation became increasingly confusing – at times Lumumba, Kasavubu and Mobutu all claimed to be in charge – and the secession of Katanga persisted, the Soviet leader threw a tantrum: '"I don't give a damn about the UN!" he screamed in anger. "It isn't our organization. This useless lout sticks his nose into important matters that are none of his business. He claims power that he's got no right to. We'll give him hell ...."' (ibid.: 476). This outburst led to his subsequent proposal that the UN be led by a troika. According to his plan, the Secretary-General would be replaced by a collegial body made up of representatives of the Western, communist and neutral states (Bailey 1962b). These representatives would no longer try to act in the interests of the organization, whatever they might be, but to consciously pursue the interests of their bloc and their group of states. A similar concept of deputy Secretaries-General had been discussed in the UN preparatory commission and rejected on the grounds that the big powers would then dominate the Secretariat and weaken the authority of the Secretary-General (Nayar 1974: 41). Khrushchev, however, thought it was a favourable opportunity to revive the idea. He overrode the reservations of his foreign minister, Gromyko (Grinevskij 1996: 476) and decided to make this a highlight of his speech to the General Assembly on 23 September 1960 (GAOR, 15th session, 869th plenary meeting, 23 September 1960).

In his speech, Khrushchev, as planned, first attacks the Western states fiercely for their continuing colonial interests: 'It is necessary to put an end to colonialism once and for all, to throw it on the dust-heap of history' (ibid: para. 178). The Western states are pilloried in detail, and their position contrasted with that of the peaceloving and sensible Soviet Union. Khrushchev then turns to the Congo. In this context he mentions the Secretary-General: 'The colonialists tried to bring this [the installation of a puppet government] about by crude methods. As they always do. It is deplorable that they have been doing their dirty work in the Congo through the Secretary-General of the United Nations, and his staff' (ibid.: para. 142). A little later Khrushchev presents a proposal for complete disarmament. After a disarmament agreement has been reached, the armed forces of all countries should be placed under international control, something Western representatives had in principle repeatedly suggested. The United Nations would be able to use them in accordance with a Security Council resolution. Before it could accept such responsibility, the structure of the UN would have to be substantially altered. The example of the Congo and the alleged misuse of the Secretary-General's position brings Khrushchev to his troika proposal:

The Soviet Government has come to a definite conclusion on this matter and wishes to expound its point of view before the United Nations General Assembly. Conditions have clearly matured to the point where the post of Secretary-General, who alone directs the staff and alone interprets and executes the decisions of the Security Council and the sessions of the General Assembly, should be abolished. ... The executive organ of the United Nations should reflect the real situation that obtains in the world today. ... The point at issue is not the title of the organ but that this executive organ should represent the States belonging to the military block of the Western powers, the socialist States and the neutralist States. ... In brief, we consider it advisable to set up, in the place of a Secretary-General who is at present the interpreter and executor of the decisions of the General Assembly and the Security Council, a collective executive organ of the United Nations consisting of three persons each of whom would represent a certain group of States. That would provide a definite guarantee that the work of the United Nations executive organ would not be carried out on the detriment of any one of these groups of States.

(ibid.: para 282–5)

The basic assumption of this proposal is that the three representatives would have equal rights and could make decisions only by mutual agreement (Grinevskij: 1996: 480). Urquhart views the troika proposal as 'an attempt to extend the veto power to the working of the Secretariat' (1972: 460). During the following discussion, Khrushchev, who had already got worked up during his speech, could no longer control himself and shouted at several speakers, completely ignoring the calls to order of the president of the General Assembly, the Irishman Frederick Boland. The latter banged his gavel so hard that it eventually broke. In the end, the only thing to do was to switch off the loudspeakers. The topic and the style of the debate had been set; later, on another topic, Khrushchev would take his shoe and hammer himself into history.[19] Hammarskjöld did not let it be noticed how severely this attack affected him personally. His calm face could, however, not alter the impression of many contemporary observers who saw the basic structure of the United Nations and the very existence of the world organization threatened by the troika idea.

Hammarskjöld's response: defence of the international civil servant

Khrushchev had spoken on a Friday. Late that evening Hammarskjöld showed his response to Ernest Gross, his legal advisor, who approved of his defence of the international civil servant, in particular with respect to small and medium-sized states, which had become something like Hammarskjöld's 'constituency' (Gross 1964: 69). But Gross expressed reservations about whether this strategy did not release the big powers from their responsibilities. Hammarskjöld overruled this objection, pointing out that the big powers were able to look after themselves; it was the small states that needed the world organization (ibid.: 69). He also showed his response to Bunche. However, the final version was as he had dictated it (Urquhart 1993a: 337). The General Assembly convened again only on the following Monday, 26 September, and Hammarskjöld was the first speaker: '[T]he General Assembly is facing a question not of any specific action but of the principles guiding United Nations' activities. In those respects it is a question not of a man but of an institution' (CF V: 196).

Hammarskjöld explained that the criticism of him did not pertain to concrete actions, but was aimed at the principles underlying his methods. Replying to criticism of his refusal to allow ONUC to support one or another party in the Congo he commented: 'It is common experience that nothing, in the heat of emotion, is regarded as more partial by one who takes himself the position of a party than strict impartiality' (Reply to Khrushchev, 26 October 1960: 197). Therefore, at the centre of criticism are the principles that guide the Secretary-General in fulfilling his office:

> … I have said, this is a question not of a man but of an institution. Use whatever words you like, independence, impartiality, objectivity – they all describe essential aspects of what, without exception, must be the attitude of the Secretary-General. Such an attitude, which has found its clear and decisive expression in Article 100 of the Charter, may at any stage become an obstacle for those who work for certain political aims which would be better served or more easily achieved if the Secretary-General compromised with this attitude.'
>
> (ibid.)

After his general response to the Soviet attack, Hammarskjöld added his own succinct view:

> I would rather see that office break on strict adherence to the principle of independence, impartiality, and objectivity than drift on the basis of compromise. That is the choice daily facing the Secretary-General: It is also the choice now openly facing the General Assembly, both in substance and in form. I believe that all those whose interests are safeguarded by the United Nations will realize that the choice is not one of convenience of the moment but one which is decisive for the future, their future.
>
> (ibid.: 197–8)

Hammarskjöld reminded the General Assembly once more that the operation in the Congo was the operation of all member states of the UN and to that extent it was up to them to articulate alternative ideas about its objective. Up to now the Secretary-General had not received any instructions from the Security Council or the General Assembly that contradicted his actions. Therefore:

> [A]s I said, this is your operation, gentlemen. It is for you to indicate what you want to have done. As the agent of the Organization I am grateful for any

positive advice, but if no such positive advice is forthcoming … then I have no choice but to follow my own conviction, guided by the principles to which I have just referred.

(ibid.: 198)

As expected, Khrushchev did not like Hammarskjöld's reply, and drummed his fist angrily on the table (Urquhart 1972: 461). A few days later, in the session on 3 October 1960, he launched a stronger attack:

In order to prevent any misinterpretation, I should like to repeat: we do not, and cannot, place confidence in Mr. Hammarskjöld. If he himself cannot muster the courage to resign, in, let us say, a chivalrous way, we shall draw the inevitable conclusions from the situation. There is no room for a man who has violated the elementary principles of justice in such an important post as that of Secretary-General.

(GAOR, 15th session, 882nd plenary meeting, 3 October 1960, para. 30)

It was not enough that the current incumbent resign, the institution of the Secretary-General had to be abolished to prevent incidents such as had taken place under Hammarskjöld from occurring in the future. After this tirade against Hammarskjöld, Khrushchev grinned at the Secretary-General from the lectern. The president of the General Assembly, Boland, switched off his microphone, leaned across to Hammarskjöld and advised him not to respond immediately (Kelen 1966: 209; Urquhart 1972: 462–3). When he met Bunche and Cordier for lunch, he had already drafted his reply. He circulated the draft, asking only for comments on the style, not the content. The text was left unchanged.

On the afternoon of 3 October Hammarskjöld opened his response by recapitulating Khrushchev's attack (without mentioning him by name), adding that the General Assembly had the right to expect a reaction from the Secretary-General to such demands. In unusually plain words for him, Hammarskjöld spoke of the attempt to stand political realities on their heads by introducing false allegations (Second Statement of Reply, 3 October 1960, in CF V: 19).

He called on the members of the General Assembly to form their own picture: in particular the newly independent states had a voice and had expressly acknowledged the contribution of the United Nations. The Secretary-General then proceeded to describe the crucial situation in which he found himself. He repeated that in the final analysis it was a question not of his person but of the institution:

The man does not count; the institution does. A weak or nonexistent executive would mean that the United Nations would no longer be able to serve as an effective instrument for active protection of the interests of those many Members who need such protection. The man holding the responsibility as chief executive should leave if he weakens the executive. He should stay if this is necessary for its maintenance.

(ibid.: 200)

The attack of the Soviet Union meant that it felt it was no longer in a position to work with Hammarskjöld. This could be an important reason to resign. Yet, Hammarskjöld pointed out, for the Soviet Union it was not a question of finding a suitable successor to him, but of replacing the institution of the Secretary-General with a troika, a consequence for which he would not answer: 'By resigning I would, therefore, at the present difficult and dangerous juncture throw the Organization to the winds. I have no right to do so because I have a responsibility to all those Member states for which the Organization is of decisive importance – a responsibility that overrides all other considerations' (ibid.).

Hammarskjöld then unmistakably declared himself the advocate of the small and medium-sized states in the UN: 'It is not the Soviet Union or indeed any other Big Powers which need the United Nations for their protection. It is all the others. … I shall remain in my post in the interest of all those other nations as long as they wish me to do so' (ibid.: 201). Hammarskjöld's speech had been interrupted by applause several times; when he finished this sentence the General Assembly with few exceptions rose and gave him a standing ovation lasting several minutes, while Khrushchev continued to bang his fist on the table. Hammarskjöld, who had sought to interrupt the first wave of applause, was visibly embarrassed. Urquhart writes: 'For once in his life, Hammarskjöld had transgressed his own rule against the use of oratory, and as the ovation continued, he soon began to look acutely uncomfortable' (1972: 465). The Secretary-General ended his speech by underlining that, to return to Khrushchev's words about mustering the courage to resign, it was easier to resign than to resist. If it was the wish of the countries that regarded the UN as the best protection of their interests, he would continue to do so.

It was one of the most crucial and tense situations in Hammarskjöld's period in office. He was sure of some backing as a few days earlier his policy had received the support of an Emergency Special Session of the General Assembly. To his amazement, the next day he received an invitation to a reception given by the Soviet Union (Hammarskjöld's office enquired whether there was not a mistake). That evening Khrushchev was suddenly very friendly. In his farewell speech to the General Assembly on 13 October he said that he did not have a personal war with Hammarskjöld. Rather, he had a good personal relationship with him. He recalled Hammarskjöld's visit to Russia and that he was still in his debt as during their outing on the Black Sea together he had rowed, a favour Hammarskjöld had yet to return (CF V: 201; Levine 1962). Hammarskjöld then spontaneously rose and thanked Khrushchev – in a very subtle manner: he was happy to learn that Khrushchev had good memories of the Black Sea outing when he showed him the honour of rowing the boat they were in. He would like to return the favour and hoped that one day he would have the opportunity. He added: 'I am sure that he would discover that I know how to row – following only my own compass' (Third Statement of Reply, 13 October 1960, in CF V: 202). Hammarskjöld had every reason to believe that he had turned 'political ruination into a whacking diplomatic victory' (Kelen 1966: 213).

This superficial harmony, however, did not last. For one thing, the international climate had worsened since the failure of the Paris summit in May 1960 and the U-2 incident. The conflict with the Soviet Union came to a head with the murder of Patrice Lumumba. The Soviet Union openly accused Hammarskjöld of complicity and its representative in the Security Council, Zorin, announced in a letter of 13 February 1961 that henceforth it would not recognize Hammarskjöld as Secretary-General of the United Nations (Urquhart 1972: 506). The Soviet representative maintained this stand by, for instance, not writing to Hammarskjöld directly, but instead addressing communications to the Secretariat in general. The Soviet Union had also done this in the last weeks of Trygve Lie's incumbency. In a meeting of the Security Council on 15 February the Soviet representative again called for Hammarskjöld's dismissal – without asking for a vote. Hammarskjöld gave his view of the attack in two letters to Östen Undén. On 26 February he writes: 'Naturally, I am guided solely – and I really mean solely – by what is in the best interest of the UN, and the world community through the UN' (KB DHS: Dag Hammarskjöld, Letter to Östen Undén, 26 February 1961: 8). A few weeks later, after unabated pressure, he adds: 'I am afraid I am so much of an intellectual as to take a certain pleasure in the game when it is scaled down to these terms of an abstract problem concerning the right way to get or avoid "check mate in three moves"' (KB DHS: Dag Hammarskjöld, Letter to Östen Undén, 18 March 1961: 2).

In April 1961 Hammarskjöld thought that the 'third Russian assault seems to have been broken quite successfully' (KB DHS: Dag Hammarskjöld, Letter to Uno Willers, 9 April 1961). Nevertheless, he felt the necessity to clarify and justify the integrity of his position, which he did in a wide-ranging lecture at the University of Oxford on receiving an honorary doctorate (Hammarskjöld 1961).[20] In his Oxford lecture Hammarskjöld once more summarizes his view of the international civil service expressing his belief that the attack on his office and his person masked differences of political opinion about the concept of the international organization between the alternatives of mere conference machinery or a world organization with executive potential, a contrast that he had also presented in his annual report. Hammarskjöld emphasizes that acceptance of the Soviet attack on the conceptual foundations of an international civil service with international allegiance would be the equivalent of a 'Munich of international cooperation as conceived after the First World War and further developed under the impression of the tragedy of the Second World War' (ibid.: 489). He adds: 'To abandon or compromise with principles on which such cooperation is built may be no less dangerous than to compromise with principles regarding the rights of a nation. In both cases the price to be paid may be peace' (ibid). Indeed, even at that time the clash over the troika was discussed as a question that could decide the future existence of the organization (Morgenthau 1965: 32).

Political ethics and the international civil servant

Once again it is interesting to observe that Hammarskjöld's reflections have developed not in an ivory tower, but in the midst of utterly practical political challenges. Hammarskjöld shows himself guided by the basic elements of his political ethics, which are an integral part of his concept of the international civil servant. In this sense, the international civil servant is the nodal point of Hammarskjöld's political ethics. This is where personal ethics, institutional ethics and applied ethics meet to form a unique bond. The strands of this bond are as follows.

Service for the (international) community as a calling

Hammarskjöld's concept of the international civil servant was not just theoretical. Rather, he sought through his example to be the living prototype of the international civil servant. It is astonishing how well he succeeded in transferring the model of the national civil servant to the international level. Over and above this, there is a direct line between the concept of *vocatio*, in the Lutheran sense and Hammarskjöld. Barudio points out that in this sense there is a parallel between the opening of Hammarskjöld's reply to Khrushchev, 'I shall remain in my post', and Luther's reply at the Diet of Worms. Already in an address to the American Association for the United Nations in 1953 Hammarskjöld had underscored this understanding of public office. In that speech he had quoted from the Indian Bhagavadgita, the Chinese philosopher Lao-Tse, the Russian writer Fyodor M. Dostoevsky and, finally, US presidents Jefferson and Lincoln to explain his concept (Barudio 1989: 121). This picked up the thread from articles written years before in Sweden expressing a view of service to the community that he had learned from Albert Schweitzer. Finally, the concept of service finds further support in the medieval mystics' call to imitate Christ.

Another aspect of Hammarskjöld's personal background is particularly relevant to this call for service and devotion: Hammarskjöld's political socialization in a small, neutral country is nowhere more obvious than in his defence of the international civil servant. Just as his father held international law to be the only weapon and hope of small countries in international politics, Hammarskjöld attaches a similarly crucial importance to the UN as an organization and, combined with it, the international service.

Self-confident neutrality

The family tradition goes even further. Both Hammarskjöld's brother Åke and his father Hjalmar dealt with – and wrote articles on – the international civil servant. Åke Hammarskjöld's work at the International Court of Justice and in international service for the League of Nations as well as his academic reflections on an international civil service referred in strikingly similar ways to ideas that Dag Hammarskjöld updated and advanced (Hammarskjöld 1937). His interest in the role of a neutral civil service, and in service as an objective necessity in the tradition of the English or French civil service, pre-dates his appointment as UN Secretary-General (Barudio 1989: 112–13). Already in his statement after taking the oath of office he had underlined his experience in the Swedish civil service:

> My background is, as you know, the civil service of my country – a civil service strengthened by a long tradition and firmly founded on law. It is in the bodies by which the nations of Europe are trying to shape the future of that part of the world that I have gathered the experience I have of international cooperation. There I have learned the vital importance of loyalty, devotion and integrity in those engaged in the work.
>
> (CF II: 31)

Hammarskjöld's concept of 'self-confident neutrality' is not neutrality in the sense of tolerance for every value. Rather, it is neutrality in the sense of impartiality, of not showing preference, as he emphasized in his annual reports (Barudio 1989: 157). Regardless of how neutral Hammarskjöld had to be in his dealings with and between different states, he could not be neutral towards and indifferent to the principles, values and ethical guidelines of the Charter. These are the indivisible parameters and framework of his actions. An appropriate term for this during the Cold War was equidistance, an interpretation that Hammarskjöld took up in comparison with the Sputnik. Asked during his Moscow trip about his position in international politics, he replied: 'It's something like this: back in 1953 you and the other great powers and all the membership projected me into space like Sputnik and I've been keeping equal distance from all nations ever since' (quoted in Cordier 1964: 107).

A newspaper report early on in his term of office summed up: '[I]n practice and in speech he has been almost inhumanly impartial' (quoted in James 1959: 625). In Beigbeder's view, this qualifies Hammarskjöld as the 'archetype of the international civil servant' (Beigbeder 1988: 29–44) who had acquired an exceptional reputation and fulfilled an exemplary function for many employees in international service. In connection with his efforts to mediate between Israel and Jordan in 1954, Hammarskjöld himself emphasized that the Secretary-General must not only be impartial, but he must also always be seen to be impartial (PC 24 March 1954, in CF II: 244). He even hesitated about accepting the nomination for the Swedish Academy because of potential incompatibility with his status as an international civil servant (Lash 1959: 47).

Personal integrity based on self-reflection as a fundamental condition of political activity

The core of Hammarskjöld's concept of the international civil servant was the crucial notion of personal integrity. In this context, it had an immediate relevance for international politics. This concept of integrity operates at several levels. On the one hand, Hammarskjöld made it quite clear that integrity cannot be equated with neutrality, detachment or indifference towards the other determinants of political life. 'Integrity is a matter of personal ethics, without any necessary connection with national origin, religious conviction, or political viewpoint' (Bailey 1962a: 28). The decisive point is envisaging and revealing these other influences so as to assess and evaluate their effect on one's judgement and actions. Hammarskjöld's passage on the international civil servant's self-reflection could also be a motto for his diary, as meticulous self-reflection was his yardstick of personal integrity and humility. In the diary, the concept of integrity is a guiding principle and starting point for constant self-reflection. The later use of the concept in the Oxford lecture acquires a deeper dimension when read in conjunction with the corresponding entries in the diary, as footnotes, as it were. The most significant and meaningful entries were written shortly after one another, most probably in connection with the Peking Mission:

> On a really clean tablecloth, the smallest speck of dirt annoys the eye. At high altitudes, a moment's self-indulgence may mean death.
>
> *(Markings* 1955: 4, 103)

> Your position never gives you the right to command. It only imposes on you the duty of so living your life that others can receive your orders without being humiliated.
>
> *(Markings* 1955: 12, 105)

> A task becomes a duty from the moment you suspect it to be an essential part of the integrity which alone entitles you as a man to assume responsibility.
>
> *(Markings* 1955: 32, 111)

These sentences reveal the depth of Hammarskjöld's understanding of his office; they read almost as a paraphrase of Hannah Arendt's afore-mentioned view of power, as when he notes: 'Only he deserves power who every day justifies it' (*Markings* 1951: 18, 65).

The international civil servant as 'new man' in Buber's and Schweitzer's sense

Hammarskjöld's concept of the international civil servant is related in fundamental aspects to Buber's 'question to the single one' and the crossfront concept as well as to Schweitzer's call for leading personalities in international politics. Against this background, Hammarskjöld's international civil servant is neither simply an administrative necessity nor a compelling interpretation of the provisions of the Charter. It is above all an answer to the ethically motivated quest – by analogy to Buber and Schweitzer – for the model of a new humanism as the spiritual focus of the post-war era. Crucial to this is the call for the necessary maturity of mind, as Hammarskjöld defined it in an address at Johns Hopkins University (CF II: 503–4). Hammarskjöld's last annual report and his Oxford lecture may thus be read as a kind of treatise on statecraft for world organization in the twentieth century. The same ethical impulse that compelled Schweitzer, bolstered by his experience of World War I, to found a hospital in the jungle and Buber to experiment with living in the Arab quarter of Jerusalem, found expression in Hammarskjöld in his blueprint for the international civil servant. He stated his views on the place of public service almost as soon as he had assumed office:

> Of course, I – like all of you, like all engaged in diplomatic or political activity – have my views and ideas on the great international issues facing us. But those personal views of mine are not – or should not be – of any greater interest to you today than they were just a couple of weeks ago. Those views are mine as a private man. In my new official capacity the private man should disappear and the international public servant take his place. The public servant is there in order to assist, so to say from the inside, those who take the decisions which frame history. He should – as I see it – listen, analyze, and learn to understand fully the forces at work and the interests at stake, so that he will be able to give the right advice when the situation calls for it. Don't think that he – in following this line of personal policy – takes but a passive part in the development. It is a most active one. But he is active as an instrument, a catalyst, perhaps an inspirer – he serves.
>
> (Statement to the Press, 9 April 1953, in CF II: 29)

Hammarskjöld's call here for the private man to 'disappear' is a more radical formulation than he used elsewhere. The important point for him was that his international civil servant had nothing in common with naïve internationalism: '[M]y experience is that the best international civil servant is the one who, while being loyal and 100 percent loyal to the Organization, is not an internationalist in the sense that he has lost his roots in his own country' (PC 22 May 1953, in CF II: 45). As many examples testify, in fulfilling his office as Secretary-General Hammarskjöld the international civil servant never forgot his Swedish roots.

Summary: the ethical content of international cooperation and organization according to Hammarskjöld

To some degree, the concepts of quiet diplomacy, the UN presence and the international civil servant are based on traditional instruments of diplomacy. But as the respective references to his political ethics show, Hammarskjöld regarded each instrument as embedded in a wider political and ethical context. The reconstruction of their fundamental ethical structure is indispensable for a deeper understanding of these instruments.

Moreover these instruments are closely interconnected. Thus, Hammarskjöld used private diplomacy to establish UN presences, also through special representatives or groups of observers who in turn used quiet diplomacy and simultaneously – like the peacekeeping forces – were a variation of the underlying concept of the international civil servant. The central concept behind all this is the diplomacy of reconciliation, which Hammarskjöld regarded as the main mission of the United Nations. The concept points to the fact that in Hammarskjöld's perspective, concrete political actions and the idea of the world organization contain an ethical content that lays the foundations of the respective political conception. This shall now be summarized in a few points.

Diplomacy of reconciliation

Hammarskjöld spoke of diplomacy of reconciliation in his statement on taking office: 'It is for you to judge how I succeed, and it is for you to correct me if I fail. Ours is a work of reconciliation and realistic construction' (CF II: 31). The concept appears regularly in the annual reports, becoming a form of *leitmotif* of the work of the United Nations, to which he regularly returned. Looking back at these early announcements, Cordier sums up:

> Many listeners on that occasion took the word 'reconciliation' to mean a loose construction of the term 'conciliation' in the Charter. Little did they know at the time that he really meant exactly what he said and that the word contained, in his thinking and methods that he was later to apply, all that is involved in the full spiritual meaning of the term.
>
> (1967: 3)

Hammarskjöld himself frequently stressed that these were not pious words: 'A diplomacy of reconciliation – I use the term of the Charter – practiced under the Charter, must be guided toward the goal of justice, and it is not only a pious phrase' (Address to Both Houses, 2 April 1958, in CF IV: 47). Jones sees a particularly clear appeal to the *leitmotif* of reconciliation in the case of the Suez Crisis: 'In that case he [Hammarskjöld] was able to take a fundamentally religious goal – reconciliation – and make it part of the political process by which the crisis was resolved' (1994: 1047). Thus, 'diplomacy of reconciliation' can also mean a 'step-by-step process achieved through patient negotiation and skillful drafting of statements that could be agreed to by all the parties' (ibid: 1048; see also Schachter 1962: 6).

Given a definition of the United Nations as an instrument of compromise, mediation and reconciliation among the member states, it is clear that the work of the UN functions in its own way. The aspect of 'face-saving' is important for all parties. Reconciliation understood in this way has no place for exclusion and condemnation, as Cordier emphasizes: 'Well, of course, his faith in reconciliation was so great that it raised the provisions of the Charter, so to speak, in his own conduct of the office relating to conciliation, mediation and pacific settlement to a much higher level, both in philosophy and in methodology; so that in fact his whole approach was a different one than the one of condemnation' (1964: 371). This is in line with Hammarskjöld's definition of the UN as a 'unifying force in a divided world'. Asked in 1958 by a journalist whether 'moral condemnation of wrongdoers' would not give the United Nations greater influence in international politics (Lash 1959: 48), Hammarskjöld answered: 'I am perhaps not a moralist' (CF IV: 329). In April 1959 he repeated this quote in a speech in Mexico and added: 'Let me frankly admit that I consider it preposterous for anyone or any country or any group of countries, whether in a majority or not, to claim the right to be the final moral arbiter. Opinions reflected in the decisions of the United Nations organs are highly important without being presented with such a pretentious ambition' (CF IV: 348). Leaving moralistic claims aside, what gives the actions of the United Nations their significance?

The ethical stance of the United Nations

Just as Hammarskjöld dissociates himself from moralistic condemnation, so he is equally aware of the danger of a non-committal attitude that may result from the obligation of impartiality. As the analysis of the annual reports showed, Hammarskjöld's reading of the principles of the Charter obliges the UN to take a stand – and to act (Nayar 1974: 77). In the section on the international civil servant this was termed self-confident neutrality, which Hammarskjöld articulates clearly. Pechota summarizes: 'Independence and impartiality are perhaps the Secretary-General's strongest weapons. They should not, however, be confused with tolerance and neutrality. The Secretary-General cannot remain indifferent to or tolerate infringement of the Organization's purposes and principles' (Pechota 1972: 41).

According to Hammarskjöld, these principles and purposes of the organization are ethical – he calls the Charter, and not only in his annual reports, a collection of 'basic rules of international ethics'. In Schachter's words, Hammarskjöld believed 'that the law of the Charter embodied deeply held values of the great majority of the globe and therefore constituted imperatives of international life' (1983: 48). He made a point of expanding on the ethical tradition of the thoughts contained in the Charter in different places to audiences of different cultural and religious backgrounds, as for instance to a Jewish organization in 1957. In a 1956 talk to the Indian Council of World Affairs he referred to a sort of 'UN ideology':

> ... I feel that there is something that might be called a United Nations ideology ... There is in one of the Christian texts a statement which I think reflects ideas common to all philosophies and all great religions. I refer to the famous words of Saint Paul about the need for faith, hope, and charity, and I should like to try to define in those terms what I mean by United Nations ideology as I experience it in the Secretariat, in contact with representatives and, perhaps especially, in meeting the public wherever I go. I think it is proper to say that to the man deeply concerned about peace, about world affairs, in simple human terms the United Nations stand as a symbol of faith. It is also an instrument for action inspired by hope, and in many corners of the world it stands as a framework for acts of charity.
>
> (CF II: 659)

These points of reference determine the practical work of the United Nations: 'For the United Nations is not only a meeting place but a meeting place in which the instinct of mutual self-preservation is reinforced by the constant presence in the background of moral purpose' (Address at the Empire Club, 25 February 1954: 262; Interview Yorck 1997 also conveys this impression). This moral aspect should not be underestimated: 'The moral power exerted through the United Nations can become very great indeed. It has already influenced the course of history on some occasions – so far too few, alas. In the end such moral force can have the final word in deciding the issue of war or peace' (Address to the Advertising Council, 17 November 1954, in CF II: 387). At the concert on United Nations Day 1953, he characterized the world organization as 'a symbol of ideas, and ... an attempt to translate into action a faith – the faith which once inspired a Beethoven in the Ninth Symphony to his great profession of freedom, the brotherhood of man. And a world of harmony' (CF II: 107). Shortly afterwards he described the United Nations as 'faith and works': 'faith in the possibility of a world without fear and works to bring that faith closer to realization in the life of men' (Address at a public meeting organized by the United Nations Association at the Royal Albert Hall, 17 December 1953, in CF II: 201). In another address he compared the UN to a sort of secular church: '... I conceive the Secretariat and the Secretary-General in their relations with Governments as representatives of a secular "church" of ideals and principles in international affairs of which the United Nations is the expression' (Address at the dinner in his honour given by the American Association for the United Nations in cooperation with the New York University Institute for Review of United Nations Affairs, 14 September 1953, in CF II: 94). These descriptions may sound idealistic, but Hammarskjöld combined them with a pronounced realism based on the assumption that 'when trying to change our world we have to face it as it is' (Remarks at the luncheon of the United Nations Correspondents Association, 10 July 1953, in CF II: 58). And this includes the finding that the values and principles of the UN are far from becoming reality everywhere. The work of the United Nations thus comes under the heading of 'not yet accomplished'.

From coexistence to cooperation: paving the way for the future

Dorothy V. Jones has pointed out that Hammarskjöld's words and deeds were shaped by a very clear 'temporal perspective':

> He took action in the short-term world of international conflict and crisis, but his eye was always on the long-term effect. Would this or that action help or hinder the international community as it groped its way toward an uncertain future? From Hammarskjöld's perspective, it was necessary to do more than just contain a conflict or defuse a crisis. It was essential that the actions taken also encourage those habits of consultation and cooperation that could – some day – develop into reliable institutions for the achievement of international goals.

(1995: 136)

To this extent, Hammarskjöld combined his clear perspective and objectives with remarkable pragmatism in execution. Zacher puts it aptly as 'pragmatism in combination with a strong commitment to the ethical principles of the Organization' (1970: 13) and continues: 'Although Hammarskjöld was a pragmatic individual not prone to formulate ideal plans, he had a general vision of the political evolution of the world, and he wanted to set the world on the shortest and soundest path to its final goal' (ibid.: 248).

This path is marked by the poles of coexistence and cooperation discussed above. The principle of peaceful coexistence[21] is the starting point and medium-term goal of the UN, but here the focus must be on the relevant readings of Schweitzer's ideology of coexistence and Buber's necessity of cooperation discussed in our analysis of the principal elements of Hammarskjöld's political ethics. Hammarskjöld makes it clear that coexistence in the sense of a minimum demand for mutual tolerance cannot be the final goal of the United Nations:

> The very word 'coexistence' has very little of the elements of mutual understanding, confidence, and friendship. But it reflects one of the great needs of this moment in history – the need to 'buy time' while the constructive forces that work for world understanding and peaceful progress can gain strength and momentum.
>
> (From Message to New York Herald Tribune Forum on 'Patterns for Peaceful Change', 18 October 1953, in CF II: 99)

Coexistence is necessary, and often coexistence can be understood as the effort to keep the diplomatic process going – to keep the door open, as Hammarskjöld said after his Peking trip. The goal is clear; it is also clear that the world is still far from a system of sustainable cooperation: '[W]e are still far from being prepared for world community. It is because world community does not exist at a time when world interdependence has become a reality, that world organization has become a necessity as a bridge which may help us to pass safely over this period of transition' (Address to both Houses of Parliament, 2 April 1958, in CF IV: 46). Elsewhere he spoke of 'transition between institutional systems of international coexistence and constitutional systems of international cooperation' (Address at the University of Chicago, 1 May 1960, in CF IV: 583). However, he was careful to dissociate himself from any idea of a world state or a world government. In turn, he realistically expressed his view of a pragmatic and gradual approach in 1960:

> Those who advocate world government, and this or that special form of world federalism, often present challenging theories and ideas, but we, like our ancestors, can only press against the receding wall which hides the future. It is by such efforts, pursued to the best of our ability, more than by the construction of ideal patterns to be imposed upon society, that we lay the basis and pave the way for the society of the future.
>
> (ibid.: 585)

His concern was to act as consistently as possible in the interests of the long-term development of international cooperation and to safeguard the viability of the world organization (Wallensteen 1985: 162). In this sense, all the peacekeeping concepts he drew up with the perspective of the diplomacy of reconciliation had a preventive character, a fact he stressed in his 1960 annual report (Zacher 1970: 140). In the practice of 'active preventive diplomacy' (Address at Student's Association, 2 May 1959, in CF IV: 373), the ethical content of the idea of international cooperation and organization comes to a head in the office of the Secretary-General of the United Nations.

The Secretary-General as detached element

As seen above, Hammarskjöld, in keeping with his concept of the organic and dynamic growth of the United Nations, took the view that the Secretary-General should play a very active role. At times he consciously exceeded the original intention of the authors of the Charter in San Francisco. On the occasion of his re-appointment on 26 September 1957 he openly stated his understanding of the office, including the notion:

> that it is in keeping with the philosophy of the Charter that the Secretary-General should be expected to act also without ... guidance [from the other main organs or member states], should this appear to him necessary in order to help in filling any vacuum that may appear in the systems which the Charter and traditional diplomacy provide for the safeguarding of peace and security.
>
> (CF III: 664–5)

Initially, these statements went unquestioned. Hammarskjöld at any rate regarded developments that went beyond the original perspective as steps in something akin to constitutional evolution. Despite his regular protestations that he did not wish to create precedents, he created one precedent after another (Interview Lind 1998) – while emphasizing the practical value and necessary flexibility of such steps. Only once did he refer to Art. 99 directly, while exploiting the political implications of Art. 99 to the limit – and perhaps beyond. Referring to the combination of division of labour and mandating between the General Assembly and the Security Council on the one hand and the autonomous authority of the Secretary-General on the other, he himself spoke of Article 98½ (Cordier 1964: 264). To describe this process, Thomas M. Franck used the slogan 'The Secretary-General invents himself' (1985: 117–33). This process went so far that in the Suez Crisis, for instance, Hammarskjöld acted 'essentially as the foreign minister of the United Nations' (Schlüter 1978: 915). But Hammarskjöld never sought this capacity to shape and act for its own sake: 'He was, in a sense, a guardian of the Charter and its principles; governments could abstain from voting, but he could not abstain from acting' (Bailey 1962a: 39).

Walter Lippmann came to a similar assessment: 'He was not an innovator because he had an itch to change things. He was a political innovator because there was no decent alternative' (1961: 547). Narasimhan, too, describes Hammarskjöld as a 'cautious innovator' (1973: 10). Hammarskjöld's understanding of Art. 99 in this context is characteristic. He did not think the Article itself was significant: 'That instrument is a somewhat violent and dramatic one. It is a kind of political H-bomb, and for that reason it has more importance in principle than it can possibly have in practice' (PC 12 February 1956, in CF II: 678; see also CF IV: 350). Rather the most significant implication of Art. 99 was, to his mind, the creation of a 'detached element' in international politics:

> [T]his Article does imply that Governments of the United Nations expect the Secretary-General to take the independent responsibility, irrespective of their attitude, to represent the detached element in the international life of the peoples.'
>
> (From the transcript of Remarks to a Meeting of International Nongovernmental Organizations, 19 March 1954, in CF II: 278)

This detached element is also present in the annual reports, and in this context, Dicke, for instance, terms the Secretary-General the 'spokesman of a genuinely international interest that is more than the sum of the interest of the members and is rooted in the principles of the UN Charter' (1994: 122, see also Virally 1961: 380).

This approaches an area of personal autonomy that Franck calls 'ethical autonomy': '[The Secretary-General] has invented for himself a role as guardian of the principles of the UN Charter. ... None of these activities are envisioned by the Charter. Rather they manifest the creativity, ethical autonomy and activism of successive Secretaries-General' (1984: 431). The existence of such a detached element – apart from, beyond, or above the national interests – that operates solely on the basis of the Charter and the freedom of action granted by the member states is the cornerstone of the possibility of international organization. It was precisely on this point that the conflict with Khrushchev over the foundations of international organization erupted. In a view diametrically opposed to Hammarskjöld's approach, Khrushchev told the General Assembly: 'We cannot rely on the conscience of the Secretary-General, for each of us has his own idea of conscience, his own code of ethics. The capitalist world has its own code of ethics, the communist world another, and the neutral countries a third' (Khrushchev, Speech, 3 October 1960: para. 48). Perhaps Hammarskjöld would have agreed – though adding that precisely this circumstance underscored the requirement and the possibility of a detached element of international organization beyond these conflicting codes of ethics. As Hammarskjöld made clear, the ethical autonomy of the detached element in international politics, which is based on the principles of the Charter, is both an opportunity and an obligation:

Because he [the Secretary-General] has no pressure group behind him, no territory, and no parliament in the ordinary sense of the word, he can talk with much greater freedom, much greater frankness, and much greater simplicity in approaching governments than any government representative can do. In summing up, I would say that the lack of a superior body to which to refer does not matter if there is a clear-cut policy line laid down by the main bodies here. The lack of means of 'pressure' – if the word is not misunderstood – is in a certain sense a weakness which, however, is compensated for, and in some respects perhaps more than compensated for, by the freedom of action, the freedom of expression, which the Secretary-General can grant himself and which, I am happy to note, governments do grant him.

(PC, 4 April 1957, in CF III: 545)

The *sine qua non*, in turn, is independence and impartiality. According to Hammarskjöld, in this context it ultimately depends on the character of the incumbent, as he explained in a press conference on the reorganization of the Secretariat in 1953: '… I think that the possibility of a Secretary-General to resist pressure is not in any way dependent on this or that kind of administrative arrangement. I hate talking in personal terms, but it finally boils down to the man' (CF II: 182). At first glance, this statement contradicts Hammarskjöld's own claim on assuming office that in his new capacity the private man would have to disappear. In August 1957 he formulated this point more precisely, taking into account particularly the ethical views of the private person:

In my case, on one side I wear the hat of the Secretary-General, and on the other hand I am a human being like anybody else. In the first capacity I may try to convert my fellowmen. You see that I keep the two functions apart. The second element, the human element, is the one which I think can reconcile you to my general statement that the Secretary-General should not try to be a moral prophet.

(PC, 8 August 1957, in CF III: 618)

Seen in this way, the 'detached element' in international politics also reads – over and above echoes of the mystic concept of detachment[22] – as a concrete expression of that quality of judgement and dissociation that, once again referring to Max Weber, together with passion and a sense of responsibility, marks the professional politician. The corresponding passage in Weber strikes one as a basic explanation of Hammarskjöld's thoughts:

As a matter of fact, mere passion, however genuine, does not count for much. Whenever it serves a cause without for that matter making out of the corresponding sense of responsibility the guiding star of its action, the passion does not turn an individual into a politician. For that, one needs the ability of an all-encompassing eyesight which is the decisive psychological feature of the politician. In other words, he needs to have the faculty of letting the facts act upon him in inner calmness and quiet, and as a result, to know how to hold people and things at a distance. ... That sensible taming of the soul is possible only by turning detachment, in all the meanings of that term, into a habit. It is this detachment that marks the professional politician and distinguishes him from the mere political dilettante with his barren excitement.

(1989: 62–3)

In this context, political ethics becomes the source of the faculty of judgement in the daily political routine. Hammarskjöld's achievements were essentially the consequence of his ability to develop principles that became guidelines for action: 'Before acting, he went to the roots of a problem and established in his mind the principles on which he would base his actions. This gave him confidence and an apparent easiness, which was both impressive and inspiring. I know of no other political leader who so effectively turned his intellectual gifts to the solution of practical problems' (Urquhart 1987b: 12). Birnbaum takes the view that the speed and determination of Hammarskjöld's political actions can only be explained by the solid ethical underpinnings of his personality (Interview 1998).[23] Strict orientation by such principles is also a precondition for impartiality: 'Only through principled behaviour could he fulfill his obligation of impartiality and avoid the risks of partisan and special pleading' (Schachter 1962: 3). The practical problems this raised for Hammarskjöld conditioned in turn his contemplation of the underlying values and questions; in other words, this contemplation took place 'right in the thick of active life' (Snow 1968b: 165). This is not to say that Hammarskjöld was never frustrated or fatigued. In his last letter to Erik Lindegrén, Hammarskjöld aptly described the reciprocal interpenetration of politics and contemplation: 'At the present phase, events on all levels and the basic stone-age psychology of men make it rather difficult to translate contemplation into action and to make action the source material for contemplation. However, we do not ourselves choose the shelf on which we are placed' (quoted in Urquhart 1972: 544).

5 The Hammarskjöld tradition

In the preceding chapters we have tried to answer the questions asked at the beginning by identifying political ethics as one of the Secretary-General's instruments of power, reconstructing Hammarskjöld's specific political ethics and verifying their realization in concrete political concepts and instruments. This approach has covered the institutional, personal and applied dimensions of Hammarskjöld's political ethics. The respective results were summarized at the end of each chapter and need not be repeated here. This final chapter will examine the relevance and limits of Hammarskjöld's political ethics and the associated instruments (in effect an extension of the applied dimension). Second, it will deal with the question of a 'Hammarskjöld tradition' and its reception by his successors. By way of conclusion and with reference to the current Secretary-General Kofi Annan, the relevance of Hammarskjöld's political ethics for the challenges facing international relations and the United Nations at the beginning of the twenty-first century will be discussed.

Relevance and limits of Hammarskjöld's political ethics

Hammarskjöld's defence before the General Assembly during the dramatic events in the last months of his incumbency, the Congo Crisis and the simmering conflict over the troika proposal illustrated his difficult position. He must have realized that if this confrontation continued he would be doomed to failure. Some authors (Luard 1994: 110) maintain that at the time of his plane crash near Ndola he had already outlived his usefulness as Secretary-General. Bauer (1982: 4), for instance, sums up: 'Many felt that the Swede's physical end anticipated his political demise.' Cox (1969: 227) uses similar words: 'He became a political casualty before his tragic death in the air crash of September 1961.' Even Urquhart, whose appreciation of Hammarskjöld is beyond question, sums up: 'Today everybody thinks that Hammarskjöld was an enormous success. In reality he was crippled. The Russians and the French were no longer speaking with him, and a number of other people wanted nothing more to do with him. Towards the end of his term of office he was finished' (quoted in Bauer 1982: 4). Rivlin comes to the sober conclusion:

... Hammarskjöld had ideas about transforming the United Nations from a 'static conference machinery' to a more 'dynamic instrument', in which the role of the Secretary-General could be significantly enhanced. There were no takers of these ideas among the major world powers. Hammarskjöld's groping for a more meaningful role for the Secretary-General provided some moments of moral and political heroism.

(1993: 11)

Hammarskjöld's legacy: some moments of moral and political heroism? This would confirm James' thesis that the Secretary-General does not have an important autonomous role:

At the time of his death in September 1961 ... Hammarskjöld was well past the peak of his usefulness to the UN. ... And this fall from grace was not despite his trustful and imaginative personality. It was because of it. To a large extent Hammarskjöld went his own way, and found that the UN would not follow him. ... [H]e was *not*, superficial appearances to the contrary, the UN's leader. ... Hammarskjöld's experience, therefore, gives a severe knock to the idea that personality is the all important factor in a Secretary-General's success or failure in high political matters.

(1985: 44)

Hammarskjöld in this perspective is only a 'partial exception' (ibid.: 39) to this rule. Yet even as he delivers this categorical judgement, James, too, poses the question: 'Why, to put it harshly, was he allowed to get away with so much for so long?' (ibid.: 46). Hammarskjöld's approach, his political innovations and their ethical foundations enabled him to establish an extremely constructive role for the United Nations in some conflicts. Thus, within the limits imposed by the Cold War, Hammarskjöld created for the UN a new field of activity that he summed up as follows: 'In a world so deeply and dangerously divided as ours today the United Nations cannot be regarded as an agency for the *enforcement* of peace. But this does not mean that its role in the *maintenance* of peace has lost significance' (from Address at luncheon at the Empire Club, 25 February 1954, in CF II: 261). Many of his achievements were possible only because of changes in the global political environment. The international climate had grown friendlier since Stalin's death, a point Hammarskjöld himself noted in a radio statement shortly after his nomination (CF II: 28). US support had been crucial to the Peking mission and UNEF (see also Morgenthau 1965: 32). This reflects the composition of the UN: in the early years of Hammarskjöld's term the West dominated the General Assembly, a situation that began to change in the late 1950s. Thus, while big power politics determined the shape and frequency of the Secretary-General's activities, they did not determine how the UN or the Secretary-General exploited this scope for action or even expanded it. Crucial in this context was the mix of pragmatism and principles. This was supported by the complementary character of various forms of UN action, which Hammarskjöld employed in order to promote the triangle of objectives for world organization as outlined above. Hammarskjöld's ethics are unequivocally ethics of responsibility in that he was always aware of the specific conditions of his office and the long- and medium-term consequences of his actions: 'He ... had an eye on history and strove to place his work and his ideas in a framework that would endure. Therefore, he frequently spoke in a doctrinal vein, so as to give continuing meaning to actions which were improvised for the moment' (Gordenker 1967a: 135). He was there to promote the idea of the United Nations; for this goal alone, Hammarskjöld was prepared to make sacrifices – for instance in the form of momentary restraint and self-restriction so as to preserve the functioning and credibility of an institution that he wanted to see develop into the central medium of peaceful relations between states and people. As head of this organization, he felt responsible for this long-term goal. To this extent, Hammarskjöld met a goal that he set himself relatively early: 'I cannot find any part of my present task more challenging than the one which consists in trying to develop all the potentialities of that unique diplomatic instrument which the Charter has created in the institution called the Secretary-General of the United Nations' (Address at luncheon given by the American Political Science Association, 11 September 1953, in CF II: 84).

The choice of case studies presented above should not obscure the fact that his period in office included a number of failures, missions that broke down and political initiatives that fell flat. On several occasions, despite all his personal efforts, Hammarskjöld failed to bring in the UN. The situation after the CIA-supported *coup d'état* in Guatemala in June 1954 demonstrated the Secretary-General's impotence, if just one permanent member of the Security Council is determined to prevent discussion of a conflict at the UN. The American delegation made it quite clear that this was not a question for the United Nations; despite strong arguments in international law, the US blocked any substantial treatment of the matter in the Security Council until the facts on the ground were established and made irrelevant any efforts in support of the overthrown government (Urquhart 1972: 88–94). Urquhart mentions other cases: 'In the end he failed to find the way to a peaceful solution of the problems of Laos, and perhaps even Indochina, because his good intentions and his ingenuity were not high enough cards to play in a competition for influence between superpowers' (ibid.: 367). In the Bizerte Crisis he was humiliated by the French (CF V: 527–37). His limitations were demonstrated even more clearly during the Hungarian Crisis, where even attempts to apply the Peking Formula (CF III: 430) failed to open up an opportunity for the UN. Despite the consideration of possible damage to the UN as a whole (Urquhart 1972: 238), Hammarskjöld was prepared to become involved personally. But several requests to visit or to send fact-finding missions were rejected by the new Hungarian government (on the orders of the Soviet Union). Hungary is the best example of the difficulties and the concessions to political reality that permeate ethical practice. In November 1956 Hammarskjöld writes to Per Lind: 'Hungary is more or less forgotten. For moral reasons I react against this tendency. Politically it may be wise to go a bit soft for the moment when so much else is at stake. Anyway, nothing very much could be done ...' (quoted in Urquhart 1972: 244). Here, too, the imperative is to keep out the big powers. Hammarskjöld recognized these limits and shied away from directly interposing himself between the superpowers (Schachter 1962: 7; Zacher 1970: 242).

Towards the end of his term it was almost impossible to uphold his aim 'to insulate ... problem[s] from great power involvement' (Bailey 1962a: 13). The Congo mission caused Hammarskjöld greater difficulties than any other. Here the limits of his office became obvious. He undertook tasks that exceeded the Secretary-General's authority and robbed him of the support of the big powers. As a result, he was confronted with decisions that were the Security Council's to make, not the Secretary-General's (Goodrich 1967: 136). Hammarskjöld himself had warned of the dangers of just such a constellation:

> I do not conceive the role of the Secretary-General and the Secretariat as representing what has been called a 'third line' in the international debate. Nor is it for him to try and initiate 'compromises' that might encroach upon areas that should be exclusively within the sphere of responsibility of the respective national governments. ... He should not permit himself to become a cause of conflict unless the obligations of his office under the Charter and as an international civil servant leave him no alternative.
>
> (Address at dinner, 14 September 1953, in CF II: 93–4)

After the Suez Crisis he had formulated the same view more drastically in a letter to Max Ascoli, an American journalist (see also Zacher 1970: 114–15; Cox 1969: 227):

> I am perfectly willing to risk being a political casualty if there is an outside chance of achieving positive results. But if the Secretary-General is forced into a similar role through sheer escapism from those who should carry the responsibility, there is a place for solid warning.
>
> (KB DHS: Dag Hammarskjöld, Letter to Max Ascoli, 29 November 1956)

Hammarskjöld was well aware of the dangers of his actions – nevertheless he saw no alternative, especially as at the start of the Congo Crisis he was responding to an unambiguous request by the Security Council and the General Assembly. He gave a sombre account of this dilemma in a letter to Undén at the time of the Congo mission: 'It may be said that in the Congo case I have always had to choose between the risk that the Organization would break down and die out of inertia and inability, and the risk that it might break up and die because I overstretched its possibilities in relation to what the cold war situation permitted' (quoted in Urquhart 1972: 511). He openly discussed the option of withdrawing ONUC – though pointing out that the consequence would be unbridled civil war (CF V: 283).

The longer the mission continued, the wider the circle of Hammarskjöld's critics became. James takes the view: 'Conveniently for the West, it was the

Soviet Union who took the major anti-Hammarskjöldian line. But the Western states were not always happy with the way things were going, and must have been glad that this unpopular dirty work had been done for them' (1985: 46). Now, with failure looming, the steady expansion of the Secretary-General's room to manoeuvre was seen as a pattern of overstretching his competence and authority. The spiral of trust began to turn downwards (see also Åhman 1958: 12). In this situation, Hammarskjöld sought the support of the small and medium-sized UN member states. He recognized that they had the potential to break through the dividing line between East–West in the sense of Buber's concept of the crossfront. Linnér (Interview 1998) believes that he was particularly aware of the significance of the young African states in this respect: 'In the African Nations he saw the chance of building such a big central balancing block and he believed that maybe something new could be created that would transcend the left and right divisions thus opening the perspective of world community as a whole.' But there were clear limits to this strategy. In this sense Grewe (1986: 98) diagnoses a 'weakness in the Hammarskjöldian realism': 'He irritated the big powers by too openly setting himself up as the "protector of the small and the weak" in the UN.' Trevelyan takes the same view: 'He [Hammarskjöld] believed wrongly that he could do without the support of the great powers in his diplomacy and could rest on the new smaller powers, but their support was neither sufficient nor sure enough for his purpose' (1980: 36). Within the UN a coalition between the small and medium-sized states and the Secretary-General did not constitute 'some third line in world policy' (Lash 1961: 194).

To defend the independence of the Secretariat and stress the role of the small and medium-sized states Hammarskjöld employed a new style of argumentation: 'In defending these two basic concepts his style changed radically, and he hit back against his critics and detractors with a spirit, frankness and single-mindedness that bore little resemblance to the cautious and cryptic utterances of earlier years' (Urquhart 1972: 260). This decisiveness was not reserved only for the Soviet Union. In September 1961 Bunche reported that on account of fears that the UN actions in the Congo could lead to a communist takeover the US would withdraw their support. A representative of the American delegation had informed Bunche: '[T]he British are very upset, the Irish are considering withdrawal of their troops, [Belgian Foreign Minister] Spaak has decided that Hammarskjöld is a liar and the US position, while not like the others, is at least equivocal' (KB DHS: Ralph Bunche, Cable to Dag Hammarskjöld, 16 September 1961). Hammarskjöld sent a cable in reply: '[I]t is better for the UN to lose the support of the US because it is faithful to law and principles than to survive as an agent whose activities are geared to political purposes never avowed or laid down by the major organs of the UN' (quoted in Urquhart 1993a: 343).

Hence, Hammarskjöld was relatively defenceless as the allegations of the big powers rained down on him. The extent of his former success now mirrored the scope and intensity of criticism. After Lumumba's death, Gromyko warned that Hammarskjöld might picture himself as 'prime minister of a world government' if he were allowed to continue his course (in a speech of 21 March 1961, which

Hammarskjöld himself quotes; see CF V: 424). The fact that Morgenthau uses the same label to characterize Hammarskjöld's achievements underscores its ambivalence:

> First the weight of political decision shifted from an impotent Security Council to the General Assembly, and then it shifted from an unwieldy General Assembly to the Secretary-General.
>
> Yet the second shift would not have been possible without the fortuitous circumstance that during the decisive period, from 1953 to 1961, the office of Secretary-General was occupied by a man endowed with unsurpassed qualities of wisdom, skill, and courage: Dag Hammarskjöld. Without him, the United Nations could never have become what it is today and might well have followed the League of Nations into oblivion as an operating political institution. Hammarskjöld became a kind of prime minister of the United Nations, assuming through his office political functions that the Security Council and the General Assembly should have performed but could not.
>
> (1963: 122)

Previously, in difficult situations the national representatives – including those of the Soviet Union – were silently pleased that Hammarskjöld took such a position. Nelan (1995: 70) even writes: 'The activist role was forced on him in part by the cold-war paralysis of the Security Council, but with brilliant improvisation he made the most of his position.' Now he is accused of exercising that very degree of responsibility that the member states had transferred to him. Once again, it is Gromyko who overstates the case by accusing Hammarskjöld that he will end up one day asserting: 'Les Nations Unies, c'est moi!' (quoted in Lash 1961: 297). Aside from the criticism it entails, such a remark also involuntarily attests political relevance to the Secretary-General. Undén, Hammarskjöld's former superior, put it in a nutshell in a letter shortly after Khrushchev's attack in the General Assembly:

> He [Khrushchev] has become aware of your being a power-factor in international politics, which he is not able to manage. It must be unbearable for Khrushchev to know that the right of veto cannot be used when the Secretary-General is applying the directives of the Security Council. This shows that the mechanism of the UN can function under the leadership of an effective Secretary-General, also in important questions, without unanimity in the Security Council or when the Assembly cannot muster the sufficient majority.
>
> (quoted in Urquhart 1972: 470)

This quotation also clarifies once again the reasons for Hammarskjöld's principled defence of an international civil service and the Secretary-General's independence. Even at the risk of personal failure, he wanted to underscore the importance of this question. Indeed, questioning the Secretary-General's international loyalty would ultimately undermine his particular authority and negotiating position (Zacher 1966: 735). Removing the basis for his actions raises doubts about the entire system and operational repertoire of the UN, for 'an independent civil service in this sense becomes a sine qua non of an international organization of the type advocated by Hammarskjöld' (Langrod 1963: 267). Owing to his early death, it is impossible to give a definitive answer to the question of whether he was successful or unsuccessful in this respect. But, one may assume that his steadfastness prevented the creation of a troika-like system. Urquhart, who provides reasons enough for Hammarskjöld's political failure, comments in this respect: 'Perhaps most important of all, he showed that one man, if sufficiently spirited and courageous, could stand up for principle against even the greatest powers and that in doing so he might sometimes have an influence on important events' (1972: 596). This is not to say that Hammarskjöld was without flaws in his conduct of the office. Two examples (one procedural and one substantial) may illustrate this point.[1]

Overconfidence about his own position

Urquhart is not the only person who felt that this was one of Hammarskjöld's weaknesses: '[H]e [Hammarskjöld] displayed a certain overconfidence born out of successes of previous years – an overconfidence that disturbed many governments in addition to those which actively opposed him' (ibid.). In another passage he writes: 'For a time Hammarskjöld overestimated the extent to which some governments would tolerate his activism. … To more than one government Hammarskjöld's independence, if not his integrity, was in the end to become entirely unacceptable' (Urquhart 1972: 258). Barudio goes even further: 'There are undeniable signs of a degree of autosuggestion that his life had meaning as self-sacrifice for peace among men' (1989: 137). In his autobiography Urquhart (1987: 142) reports in this connection: 'As a rational, international Whig, I was sometimes uneasy at the possibility that Hammarskjöld might be beginning to hear voices.' Asked about this interpretation he later said: 'I'm afraid that in the end this was true. He began to hear voices. He made rather shrill remarks and he seems to have had the feeling of being engaged in a fight against Evil. He was very upset because of the Russians' (Interview 1997). Sture Linnér, who accompanied Hammarskjöld on his last trip to Africa and spent the previous weekend with him in Brewster, did not notice such a marked change (Interview 1998). Both agree, however, that Hammarskjöld's enormous output and power of political conviction were possible only thanks to a 'unity of purpose' (Address at a public meeting organized by the United Nations Association at the Royal Albert Hall, 17 December 1953, in CF II: 200) that he strove for and largely achieved. In the end, personal willpower was not enough to overcome blatant disinformation campaigns in the conflict over the role of the UN and the Secretary-General in the Congo. But he could only do so much with the support of small and medium-sized states, even with threats of votes of confidence, which Hammarskjöld resorted to habitually towards the end.

Human rights policy

Among the UN political initiatives and actions associated with Hammarskjöld's term of office, there is no notable achievement in the field of human rights. Although Hammarskjöld continually referred to the importance of human rights in his speeches, in political practice he tended to neglect it (King and Hobbins 2003). This is no coincidence, but closely tied up with the Hammarskjöldian 'diplomacy of reconciliation', which contains some indisputable voids. The avoidance of reproach or condemnation meant that his assessments of human rights practices in various conflicts and by different parties to these conflicts were non-committal. On taking office, Hammarskjöld gave the Director of the Human Rights Division, John P. Humphrey, instructions to avoid public assertiveness on the topic. Humphrey (1989: 194–5) subsequently reported that the Secretary-General commented that if he had his way he would throw the two human rights covenants (drawn up during his incumbency) out of the window. According to Hammarskjöld, the – partially ideological – controversies over the two human rights covenants did no service to the issue of rapprochement between East and West; in his view, mediation should avoid any public humiliation of any party (Zacher 1970: 128).

Internal administrative steps soon followed. Humphrey (1984: 174–262) records that Hammarskjöld wanted to downplay the topic of human rights and, by downgrading the Human Rights Division to an Office in the administrative division of USG Humphrey Trevelyan (on par with the Narcotics Office), curtail its organizational standing and staff. Even if Cordier (1964: 149) defends Hammarskjöld by remarking that he did not particularly care for the missionary zeal of the staff in the Human Rights Division, the conclusion is unavoidable that Hammarskjöld pursued his imperative of alleviating and calming Cold War tensions at the expense of an active human rights policy. As much as he was at pains to establish a philosophical, even universal basis of a politics based on standards of human rights (see his discussion of Kant and his distinction between ends and means), when it came to a concrete human rights policy and active condemnation of human rights violations, he was very ambivalent.[2] Despite the circumstances of the time and the importance he attached to preventing a clash between the superpowers, his record on human rights is still a weakness.

Thus, Hammarskjöld's strengths go hand in hand with his weaknesses. As mentioned several times in this study, much of his success was owing to his firm judgement based on his ethical convictions. The reverse of this was a certain tendency to overestimate the strength of his position and to mistake the political realities of a situation. In this context, the good-faith agreement concluded during the Suez Crisis is a symptomatic bundling of the strengths and weaknesses of the Secretary-General's and the UN's political options. Linnér expressed this aspect of Hammarskjöld's character as follows:

> Hammarskjöld's ethical capacity was both his strength and his weakness. Integrity, honesty and character were the basis for all his work. But at the

same time he could not understand some procedures of power politics. He could not understand and would not believe that people should be dishonest on very sincere matters and he got indignant about lying. So in a way he was too trusting. The technical and cynical game of power was not his. He kept himself at a distance to this and would not let himself be swallowed up by these procedures but in the end he was right in the middle of it all. This process is reflected in his diary.

(Interview 1998)

Yet his diary also shows that Hammarskjöld was not at all naïve, rather, sometimes utterly aware of the stratagems and intrigues of international politics. The personal frustration and bitterness experienced in office also coloured his view. In summer 1961, for the first time, Hammarskjöld replied with resignation to his friend Bo Beskow's regular question of whether he still believed in people: 'No, I never thought it possible, but lately I have come to understand that there are really evil persons – evil right through – only evil' (Beskow 1969: 181). Hammarskjöld had realized that his effectiveness and usefulness for the organization was being questioned, which discouraged him from running for a third term. Urquhart recorded his impression: 'There is some evidence that he intended to resign as soon as the Katanga question was settled' (1983: 145). Before he flew to meet Tshombe he told Mongi Slim that this would be his last personal mission and he would resign if the mission failed (Urquhart 1972: 565). As it turned out, the unresolved air crash on the night of 17 September 1961 ended Hammarskjöld's life and tenure in office. While the official investigations tend to treat a 'simple' pilot error as the most likely explanation of the crash, they can not definitely rule out other explanations. This has inspired a number of different and sometimes strange theories of the air crash.[3] In the context of this study, it is interesting to note that almost all of the major secret services in the world are at least suspects in one or another theory. In retrospect, Hammarskjöld's death becomes singular evidence of the Secretary-General's independence.

The Hammarskjöld tradition and its adoption by his successors

Taking the results of the analysis of Hammarskjöld's political ethics as our starting point, we shall now outline the development in the Secretary-Generalship after Hammarskjöld, the reception of his concept of the UN and his successors' utilization of the instruments he developed. This endeavour, too, opens with sceptical assessments of the possibility of continuing with Hammarskjöld's approach. In an article written in the 1980s, Grewe (1986: 96) called Hammarskjöld the greatest of the Secretaries-General up to that time and expressed doubts whether elements of his style of work and leadership could have become UN practice anyway, as they were too much part of his unique personality. Similarly, Trachtenberg writes: '… Hammarskjöld was probably the exception rather than the rule, a unique individual who took full advantage of the period in which he worked. It is unlikely that Hammarskjöld could have functioned in the same capacity as he did, or achieved what he did, in any other period since his death in 1961' (1982: 634). In this respect, Barros' assessment is pessimistic, although he does speak of a Hammarskjöld model: 'Much of this attitude emphasizing the public use of the office can be traced to what I like to call the "Hammarskjöld model" of Secretary-General. But Hammarskjöld's adroit use of the office was exceptional and does not reflect the norm. ... [T]he personal qualities that made Hammarskjöld an unusual Secretary-General are not likely to be repeated in most people selected for the office' (1983: 34). James, once again, articulates the strongest doubts, even stating that attempts to emulate Hammarskjöld's approach would be dangerously 'indulging in wooly internationalism' (1985: 47). In another passage (1959: 632) he writes: 'Whoever became Secretary-General in succession of Lie would have had before him considerable opportunities for an active and fruitful term of office.' And already in 1959, thinking of Hammarskjöld's successors, he comments: 'Whoever follows Hammarskjöld as Secretary-General is unlikely to make very much greater success of this enormously exacting office than he is achieving' (ibid.: 637). These views illustrate the problem of Hammarskjöld's 'legacy' and what it meant for his successors.[4] Any such comparison should consider Claude's caveat (1993: 255) that no Secretary-General 'will be an exact duplicate of any other'. Regardless of the assessment of the individual officeholders, one can assume that their performance is – negatively as well as positively – influenced by that of their predecessors.

Brian Urquhart, who worked for five Secretaries-General, observes:

> Each of the five Secretaries-General brought to the office his own personal view and his personal ideas and developed them through experiment on the basis of the vaguely defined principles of the Charter. The circumstances are always changing, new opportunities and sometimes new obstacles arise. Activities that were possible for one Secretary-General are impossible for his successor, and vice versa. The work of the office has inevitably developed through trial and error.'
>
> (Urquhart 1985: 255–6)

Against this backdrop, we shall examine each of Hammarskjöld's successors in terms of and whether they continued or rejected a 'Hammarskjöld tradition' (Jordan 1983b: 3–13). This tradition is defined by the fundamental characteristics of Hammarskjöld's conception of his office as established in this study, his political ethics as well as his political concepts and instruments. To do proper justice to this subject would require equally detailed analyses of Hammarskjöld's successors, which, of course, is beyond the scope of this work. Nevertheless, the answers to a short questionnaire should establish significant outlines of how Hammarskjöld's successors referred to and dealt with him. The four groups of questions are as follows:

1   Does the Secretary-General have a static or dynamic concept of the world organization? To what extent does he understand the Charter as an expression of international ethics? Does the Secretary-General try to find a universal argument for the unity of mankind?
2   Can the Secretary-General's actions be subsumed under the 'diplomacy of reconciliation'? Does he use quiet diplomacy? To what extent are his actions guided by ethics? How does he employ the moral force of the office? What importance does he attach to the concept of cooperation? What is his mix of pragmatism and principle?
3   Does the Secretary-General try to fill vacuums in international politics? Does he see his role as 'neutral' or 'impartial'? What image of the 'international civil servant' underlies his activities? Does he pursue an independent political role as 'detached element' amidst the interests of the nation-states?
4   Does he refer directly or indirectly to Dag Hammarskjöld? Has the Secretary-General tried to develop a doctrine of the United Nations?

Sithu U Thant

In describing his conception of the office, U Thant, Hammarskjöld's immediate successor, referred to President Roosevelt's proposal during the deliberations on the Charter to title the Secretary-General 'Moderator': 'I know of no better word to describe my own conception of this office' (1978: 31). In his biography he writes of the Secretary-General's 'singular perspective': 'I was called upon to view each dispute, not from one side or the other of the argument, but as a deeply concerned moderator standing in an absolutely unique position. Because of this perspective, the Secretary-General can see what is happening so much more objectively than those who confront each other' (ibid.: xvi). U Thant defines this 'detached view' (Saksena 1975: 345), which resonates in the title of his memoirs, in terms of the distinction between 'neutrality' and 'impartiality', exactly in Hammarskjöld's sense. In a television interview before his election he stated:

> In reply to a question … I said that whoever occupies the office of Secretary-General must be impartial but not necessarily neutral. In regard to moral issues, the Secretary-General cannot, and should not, remain neutral or passive. I cited the function of a judge who must try to be impartial, but who cannot be neutral when it comes to the question of 'who is the criminal and who is the person on whom a crime has been committed'.
>
> (1978: 17)

U Thant discussed his predecessor in greatest detail in an address to the Dag Hammarskjöld Memorial Fund. He quoted the rules of quiet diplomacy from Hammarskjöld's diary and continued:

> He felt a sense of total vocation in the Secretary-Generalship and devoted all of his strength and skill to its problems. Although he was anything but a

moralist and disliked moral judgments on public matters, he had an unshakable integrity and a clear and determined view of what was right. He knew that in public life there is no substitute for individual courage and conviction, and he demanded of himself far more than he expected of others. Though sensitive to public opinion, he steadfastly refused to compromise his principles for the sake of popularity.

(1971: 588–9)

U Thant gave a great deal of attention to the moral implications of his office. In his autobiography he devoted a whole chapter to this topic. He approaches it by considering the ethical implications of Buddhism and how this influenced his conception of the office:

> To understand my feelings – and my conception of the role of the Secretary-General – the nature of my religious and cultural background must first be understood. … As a Buddhist, I was trained to be tolerant of everything except intolerance. I was brought up not only to develop the spirit of tolerance, but also to cherish moral and spiritual qualities, especially modesty, humility, compassion, and, most important, to attain a certain degree of emotional equilibrium. … [A] brief explanation of certain ethical aspects of Buddhism will be necessary. Among the teachings of the Buddha are four features of meditation, the primary purpose of which is the attainment of moral and spiritual excellence: *metta* (good will or kindness), *karuna* (compassion), *mudita* (sympathetic joy), and *upekka* (equanimity or equilibrium).
>
> (Thant 1978: 21)

At times, U Thant was accused of being passive and dispassionate. Given his Buddhist background, these characteristics appear in a different light, in which personal meditation and a Buddhist view of suffering contribute to the attainment of inner equilibrium. These moral and spiritual qualities are immediately reminiscent of Hammarskjöld, whose thoughts revolved in part around the same words. In U Thant's case, the influence is specifically Buddhist, which confirms Hammarskjöld's conviction that his ethical principles could be found in all major religions and cultures. U Thant remarks:

> It is true that the spiritual and ethical values of Buddhism provide serenity, strength, tolerance, and humility. I believe that similarly the ethical values of any of the world's great faiths – Hinduism, Christianity, Judaism, or Islam, for instance – would likewise strengthen anyone [who] is [in] a position of high responsibility who draws on spiritual values in difficult moments.[5]

Just how close the goals of personal self-examination and development that U Thant mentions are to Hammarskjöld's concepts is illustrated by his more detailed definition of *metta*: 'Metta is the impersonal love or good will, the opposite of sensuous craving or a burning, sensual fire that can turn into wrath, hatred, or revenge when not requited. A true Buddhist has to practice metta to friends and foes alike' (Thant 1978: 21). Such an interpretation of the concept of 'love' is very close to the concept of 'love' that Hammarskjöld found among the Christian medieval mystics. In another passage U Thant explains: 'What above all helps to promote this sense of tolerance in a people is that universal and all-embracing kindness and love which, I believe, is the key to all great religions, and which is the foundation on which all moral and social progress is based' (Statement at the Consecration Ceremony of the Church Center for the United Nations, 22 September 1963, in CH VI: 465). The parallels between Hammarskjöld and U Thant go further. U Thant stresses that apart from his ethical and religious convictions, his view of the state of the world and mankind also influenced his conception of his office and his definition of the goals of the UN. He then refers to Albert Schweitzer. From the latter he derives almost the same ethical principles as Hammarskjöld did. The relevant passage in his autobiography reads:

> First of all, I am always conscious of the fact that I am a member of the human race, and I am very jealous of my membership. This consciousness prompts me to work for a great human synthesis, which is the implicit goal of the World Organization I had the privilege of serving.
>
> The ideal of human synthesis has been developed by almost all great religions. In regard to the ethical concepts of life that help bring such an ideal to realization, Albert Schweitzer and Pierre Teilhard de Chardin, among Western thinkers, had powerful ideas and have been important influences on me.
>
> In his Philosophy of Civilization, Schweitzer first presented the ethic of 'reverence for life' ... Man, he said, must not limit life to the affirmation of man alone; man's ethics must not end with man, but should extend to the universe. He must regain the consciousness of the great chain of life from which he cannot be separated. Schweitzer preached the necessity of the 'will to live an ethical life', which should be the primary motivation of man, and he said life should be for a higher value and purpose – not spent in merely selfish and thoughtless actions.
>
> (Thant 1978: 24)

As U Thant himself reports, at his first meeting with Hammarskjöld, when he presented his credentials as representative for Burma at the UN, they conversed about Buddhist philosophy and Hammarskjöld discussed, among other things, the concept of 'karma' in some detail (From Statement on the Tenth Anniversary of the Death of Dag Hammarskjöld, 17 September 1971, in CH VIII: 601).

U Thant described the 'global' challenge even more forcefully than Hammarskjöld. Some of his formulations are reminiscent of Buber's thinking: '[T]he realities of the present-day world call for a new quality of planetary imagination; they call for a global mentality that takes account of the nature of interdependence and the imperative need to change' (1978: 441). U Thant developed these ideas as far as the demand for world citizenship and global solidarity

(1978: 53–4; CH VIII: 421). In his last annual report this demand was linked with the vision that the individual should be the measure of international politics.[6] He even proposed giving to the Secretary-General a mandate under an Article 99a that would enable him to present to the Security Council not only resolutions on threats to peace and security, but also on other threats such as population growth and environmental pollution (thus the proposal in Thant 1971: 597). The significance of these new topics for U Thant also explains his commitment to the creation of the United Nations University. Echoing Hammarskjöld's reflection on Buber, in his first annual report U Thant also talked about a 'crisis of confidence' (AR 1962 in CH VI: 212) as the crucial challenge in international politics.

Speaking of U Thant's involvement in the Vietnam conflict, Urquhart (Interview 1984: 9) remarks: '[H]e had a very strong moral sense, perhaps the strongest moral sense of any Secretary-General.' He understood himself as a 'spokesman of the world conscience' (Leichter 1966: 105). U Thant's moral steadfastness was notorious among heads of delegations. In the words of a Soviet diplomat: 'convincing Mr. Thant is like fighting your way forward in a room full of mashed potatoes' (quoted in Franck 1987: 5.13). Nevertheless, Franck certifies that U Thant also tended to 'over-eager optimism' (ibid.), which upset his political calculations (as noted above in respect of Hammarskjöld).

U Thant – like Hammarskjöld – also underlined his dislike of moralism in politics and his reservations about public moral judgements: 'The luxury of judgments and moral declarations, so freely engaged in by national politicians and by the press in troubled times, must be foresworn by the Secretary-General if he is to maintain that degree of cooperation from governments through which alone he may be able eventually to get some results' (1971: 591). Integrity was as important for U Thant as for Hammarskjöld when he talked about the interpretations of General Assembly and Security Council resolutions: 'His only guide here is his judgment as to the intentions of the majority which voted the resolution, his application of the principles of the Charter to the situation at hand, and the confidence that his integrity will be respected even if his conclusions are disputed' (ibid.: 593). At the same time, he made it unambiguously clear that he shared Hammarskjöld's dynamic concept of the UN:

> The United Nations, to me, does not represent a vague ideal of universal peace and brotherhood which has its appeal only to starry-eyed idealists and moralists. Far from it. It is hardheaded, enlightened self-interest, the stake that all humanity has in peace and progress and, most important of all, survival, that dictates the need for the United Nations as a practical, institutional embodiment of the needs of nations on a shrinking planet, as a potent and dynamic instrument at the service of all nations, east and west, north as well as south.
>
> (Address at Johns Hopkins University, 2 December 1962, in CH VI: 265)

Paraphrasing Hammarskjöld's distinction between static and dynamic concepts, he stated in an interview: 'Needless to say, I subscribe to the second school.'[7]

Yet he was as conscious of the restrictions on shaping political developments as Hammarskjöld was: 'We live in an imperfect world, and have to accept imperfect solutions, which become more acceptable as we learn to live with them and as time passes by.'[8]

In addition to these general comparisons, U Thant also referred directly to Hammarskjöld. To clarify his role during the Cuba Crisis (see texts and documents in CH VI: 234–50; Rikhye 1991: 72–80), he quoted verbatim from Hammarskjöld's declaration on the Suez Crisis (Åhman 1963: 8). In his statement of 24 October 1962 U Thant directly quoted Hammarskjöld's defence on the principles of the Charter of 31 October 1956 (CH VI: 239). Nayar comments: '... U Thant cited, and thereby associated himself with, Dag Hammarskjöld's famous statement' (1974: 67). This is surely the most obviously identifiable 'birth' of the Hammarskjöld tradition. Just as significant is U Thant's reference to Hammarskjöld on taking office for a full term in 1962, when he quoted his predecessor and his emphasis on duty and humility (Statement, 30 November 1962, in CH VI: 251–4).

At the same time, U Thant had to cope with conflicts left unresolved by Hammarskjöld death. Initially appointed as acting Secretary-General, he was given a 'cabinet' (Kägi 1962) of several advisors as a concession to the Soviet Union, which was still insisting on a troika. Yet, through his actions – in particular his good offices and quiet diplomacy (another reference to Hammarskjöld) – he succeeded in preserving the Secretary-Generalship as an independent organ. The reserved Asian diplomat, whom many observers thought as 'inscrutable as a sphinx' (Gerwin 1972: 13) and accused of non-involvement in the outside world, was the same person who (with a somewhat modified mandate) uncompromisingly ordered offensive actions by ONUC against Katanga in the Congo in 1962 and 1963 (Hoffmann 1962; Meisler 1996).

U Thant felt his fundamental mission in accordance with the principles of the Charter was 'harmonization': this had the same importance for him as the concept of reconciliation for Hammarskjöld: '... I have always felt that the most important political duty of the Secretary-General is to concentrate on the harmonizing function of the United Nations, as set out in Article 1 (4) of the Charter. It defines one of the purposes of the United Nations "to be a centre for harmonizing the actions of nations"' (1978: 31). Precisely because most governments, despite the nuclear threat, stuck to 'pre-atomic and pre-global traditions that prevent them from taking fresh, new approaches on a planetary basis', the United Nations had to preserve the 'spirit of unity' (ibid.: xvii). It was clear that his origins in a small, 'neutral' country shaped his conception of his office as much as such origins had shaped Hammarskjöld's (ibid.: 36). In his first major speech at the University of Uppsala, U Thant stated: 'I am in complete agreement with my distinguished predecessor Mr. Dag Hammarskjöld when he said that it is the small nations, rather than the great powers, which need the protection the United Nations can give' ('The Small Nations and the Future of the United Nations, 6 May 1962', in CH VI: 107–8).

Nevertheless, U Thant and Hammarskjöld were often perceived as opposites. Unlike Hammarskjöld, U Thant played an unobtrusive role in the UN bodies and almost never spoke at meetings of the Security Council (Luard 1994: 111). He also acknowledged that there were limits to the Secretary-General's independence of action. In 1966 he pointed out that he lacked the authority to send election observers to South Vietnam. Only the Security Council or the General Assembly could make the decision to send such a mission (Leichter 1966: 106). However, on other occasions he scrupulously defended the Secretary-General's rights and emphasized the authority of his office with great self-confidence. Franck reports U Thant's initiative to establish an observer mission on the Yemeni–Saudi border in 1963. Here the Secretary-General personally took the initiative; however, the Soviet Union subsequently persuaded the Security Council that before the mission could be despatched it had to authorize the Secretary-General to send it (the Soviet Union abstained). Franck summarizes: 'Thant, more interested in getting the observers to work than in the precedent being set, agreed. Hammarskjöld might not have done so' (1987: 5.10).

The withdrawal of UNEF in 1967 is often used to highlight the differences between the two. This action revealed the limits of the good-faith formula devised by Hammarskjöld. U Thant was much criticized for agreeing to the withdrawal. However, it should be pointed out that the political reality and the Secretary-General's legal options practically left him no alternative (CH VII: 416–89; James 1972: 60–3). Nevertheless, he could have taken the question of withdrawing UNEF to not only the advisory committee, but also the full General Assembly. Under Art. 99, the Security Council could conceivably also have been consulted. One must agree with Tandon that in such a situation it would have been more helpful to point out the lack of alternatives than to argue largely in terms of the Secretary-General's 'rights' (Tandon 1968: 553).

On the basis of U Thant's first speech Morgenthau accused him of breaking with Hammarskjöld's conception of the Secretary-General and of favouring a policy of neutrality. He felt U Thant, unlike Hammarskjöld, had turned away from the basis of the will of the member states and was attempting to be a sort of 'superego in the conduct of foreign policy' (Morgenthau 1963: 123). In addition, the blurring of ideological differences in favour of the assumption that ultimately all states – including the superpowers – wanted peace went too far for Morgenthau. He saw this as playing down the differences in international relations, which could get the UN into serious difficulties. By measuring U Thant against Hammarskjöld, Morgenthau was helping to reinforce the 'Hammarskjöld tradition' from another perspective. Yet, U Thant also established the tradition of using commemorative addresses and lectures on Hammarskjöld as an opportunity to talk about his own conception of office. On the occasion of the tenth anniversary of Hammarskjöld's death, for instance, he summed up: 'In my ten years as Secretary-General I have, of course, been considerably influenced by my predecessor's ideas and actions. Most of all I have been impressed by the personal qualities which upheld him in a formidably difficult task' (CH VIII: 603). He phrased his similarity to Hammarskjöld even more clearly in his last annual report, which, like his predecessor, he wanted to be taken as his political testament: 'During my tenure of office, I have greatly benefited from the legacy of Dag Hammarskjöld, his historic vision of our Organization and his conception of the world of tomorrow' (AR 1971: 605). And, finally: 'My own experience has confirmed in every way Dag Hammarskjöld's philosophy concerning the powers of the Organization and, in particular, the role of the Secretary-General' (ibid.: 641). He felt he was part of a tradition, and characteristically stressed this at the unveiling of the Hepworth sculpture dedicated to Hammarskjöld in front of the UN headquarters in New York: '[L]ayer by layer, a tradition is built up' (from the 'Statement at The Unveiling of the Hepworth Sculpture, 11 June 1964', in CH VI: 595).

Kurt Waldheim

Significantly, U Thant's successor Kurt Waldheim stated his conception of the office in his own appreciation of Hammarskjöld (Waldheim 1983: 15–23). Yet, already in the first sentence there is a note of dissociation: 'We look back to the time of Dag Hammarskjöld's Secretary-Generalship with nostalgia for a simpler world now gone forever' (ibid.: 15). Waldheim recognizes Hammarskjöld's efforts – and then defines the latter's conception of the office in his, Waldheim's, terms: 'Hammarskjöld did not, I think, regard the Secretary-General primarily as a "force" in world politics but rather as an honest broker, a catalyst, and someone to whom governments could go for help in critical situations' (ibid.: 16). As shown above, Hammarskjöld saw his office in this light only at the start of his term. Waldheim understood the Secretary-General to be primarily a 'unique channel of communication' (ibid.: 18) and elaborates:

> The Secretary-General is not a sovereign force in world politics. I believe, however, that in the torturous and complicated development of human affairs he can provide something perhaps in the long run more valuable, a quiet centre for finding solutions, an honest go-between who can bear signals to anyone in the world even from the worst enemies and still maintain their confidence, and a caretaker of the delicate but essential idea of world community.
>
> (ibid.: 21).

Using this definition, Waldheim then proceeds to relativize, if not reject, Hammarskjöld's approach, which he felt lacked pragmatism:

> Dag Hammarskjöld died at the height of a crisis over the nature and principles of peace-keeping operations particularly as regards the authority of the Secretary-General. His successor, U Thant, was well suited both by temperament and by his third-world standing, to moderate that crisis and to bring the United Nations back to a more pragmatic course in the world.
>
> (ibid.: 20)

In his autobiography he writes:

And another thing was absolutely clear for me when I started working as Secretary-General, which fortunately suited my nature: this office did not need an otherworldly visionary intellectual, but a solid practical person who had the patience to seek contact and dialogue with everybody. I was and am convinced that the solution to political problems can not be found in theories of political science but only in dialogue and the unflagging search for compromise.

(Waldheim 1985: 76)

This quotation is all the more interesting in connection with another passage in which he explicitly describes Hammarskjöld as an intellectual and visionary.[9] Waldheim rejected some aspects of the Hammarskjöld tradition. Yet he, too, wanted to exploit the connection to Hammarskjöld – partly by pretty blatant redefinitions. Similarly, Waldheim was obviously disillusioned about the value of political ethics for his office:

If a government … is not prepared to react to moral pressure, what can we at the United Nations do, what can I do as Secretary-General? I have no executive authority, no power, I can only try to convince, try to persuade, I can write letters to governments, (send) appeals, cables, but when they do not react – the states themselves are responsible for morality.

(quoted in Bauer 1982: 1)

Ceding responsibility for 'morality' exclusively to states is hardly in the tradition of the active detached element that Hammarskjöld's reading of the Charter calls for. The two would probably have agreed on rejecting public moral judgements (Waldheim 1983: 20). Various assessments of Waldheim, however, address a number of 'moral' inactivities. According to Bauer (1982: 2), his silence on the General Assembly resolution equating Zionism with racism incurred 'a loss of moral authority in the eyes of at least democratically governed UN member states.' After Waldheim's retirement as Secretary-General, documents – incidentally available to all permanent members of Security Council (bar China) – were published about his activities as an officer in the German army during World War II (Finger and Saltzman 1990). These have raised doubts and criticism about his integrity, but do not appear to have affected his performance as Secretary-General. Even Urquhart (1987a: 227), who felt disappointed in Waldheim and called him a 'living lie' that did great damage to the office produces a reasonably balanced judgement: '[H]e did rather better than I had anticipated and demonstrated determination and even, on occasion, courage, but he lacked the qualities of vision, integrity, inspiration, and leadership that the United Nations so desperately needs' (ibid.: 228).

Waldheim attached importance to political initiatives that highlighted his authority, such as the successful efforts to persuade members of the Saharawi Liberation Movement (POLISARIO) to free their French hostages (Franck 1987: 5.14–15). In much the same way as Hammarskjöld, he indirectly influenced resolutions, for instance in the Teheran Affair, in which he referred to Art. 99, and was a background co-author of the resolution that requested him to use his good offices (Franck 1984: 485). He also resorted to quiet diplomacy between Iraq and the USA in 1981 after Israel destroyed the Osirak reactor (Waldheim 1985: 301–3). Yet, by the time Waldheim assumed office, the Secretary-General's activities of early warning and good offices were more or less part of the 'standard institutional practice' (Gordenker 1967a: 134) of the United Nations.

It was not only Urquhart who noted a dearth of more far-reaching activities and originality: '[H]e saw the United Nations as a glorified version of the Austrian Foreign Office, which it certainly is not. … [H]e certainly didn't formulate concepts which he then pursued into action, as Hammarskjöld did' (Interview 1984: 16). The opinions of many observers tend to be negative. Daniel Patrick Moynihan, a former US ambassador to the UN, saw Waldheim's role as that of a post office that exchanged messages between the delegations (Nelan 1995: 71). Waldheim also changed the tone in the Secretariat by ordering the guards in front of the headquarters to salute him; he also reserved one of the lifts to the thirty-eighth floor for his personal use, insisted on being addressed as Doctor, and on luxurious fittings in the aircraft he used. Practices such as these may also have produced the feeling among UN staff such as Rémy Gorgé 'that Waldheim, unlike Hammarskjöld and U Thant, was not a Secretary-General one would go through fire and water for' (1988: 13).

Waldheim was not interested in theoretically justifying and developing his authority. In this connection Jackson writes: 'Unlike Hammarskjöld and Thant, Waldheim has not used the introduction to the Annual Report as a vehicle for the promulgation of a doctrine of activism on the part of the Secretary-General' (1978: 240). Rather, Waldheim's demand of the UN reflected disillusionment: 'The United Nations are not a union of idealistic do-gooders, but a sober action group of sovereign states whose task it is to deal with problems, not ignore them' (1979: 3). Thus, he also cautioned against an activist Secretary-General: 'A Secretary-General who is too much of an activist will not last a year' (quoted in Bauer 1982: 4). Elsewhere he stated: 'People usually expect too much from the Secretary-General' (quoted in Nelan 1995: 71). James welcomes this scaling down of expectations placed in the Secretary-General as a necessary development of the office: 'In fact, it is arguable that most states now have a more realistic understanding of the kind of role the UN Secretary-General can usefully play – a limited one – and that this view is likely to be increasingly shared by future candidates for the office' (1985: 45). Although he quoted Hammarskjöld now and then (Waldheim 1978: 184), and, like him, was influenced by the neutrality of his homeland (ibid.: 37–51), Waldheim's approach was generally very different. Newman (1998: 53) comments: 'Waldheim was conscious, perhaps envious, of Hammarskjöld's almost legendary reputation'. Franck (1995: 364), comparing Waldheim to Hammarskjöld, concludes that he was 'less innovative by nature'. James (1981: 14), who gives a notably positive assessment of Waldheim's term, is obviously happy to conclude that: '… Hammarskjöld may at last be losing his spell'. Does Pérez de Cuéllar's term of office confirm this?

Javier Pérez de Cuéllar

Thanks to the abrupt improvement in the global political climate during his incumbency, Pérez de Cuéllar's period in office consists of a rather unproductive first term and a far more successful second term, whose high point was the award of the Nobel Peace Prize to the UN Blue Helmets in 1988. De Cuéllar, therefore, is a good example of how international politics can influence the scope for action of the United Nations and the Secretary-General. In their own ways, his two terms of office are illustrative of the 'spiral of trust': initially, de Cuéllar was sidelined in a number of conflicts, including the Falklands War. Already in his first annual report he diagnosed a crisis of multilateralism and admonished: 'We are perilously close to a new international anarchy' (AR 1982, in Cuéllar 1991: 6). This atmosphere and the series of negative results dogged his entire first five-year term. In consequence, he had little latitude and no major negotiation mandates (Shannon 1992: 2). The thaw in international relations and the election of Gorbachev, who introduced a paradigmatic change in Soviet politics, created new opportunities for the world organization. Gradually the spiral of trust began to move in the other direction, and in his second term a rather unprepossessing Secretary-General mutated into an extremely self-confident actor. This is reflected in his annual reports. In 1982 he stated: 'The Organization was intended to present to the world the highest common denominator of international behaviour and, in doing so, to develop a binding sense of international community' (AR 1982: 17). In 1987 he was able to talk of the growing importance of the 'commonality factor in international affairs' (AR 1987: 135) and a new pragmatism. In describing the UN's mission, de Cuéllar's emphasis on the function of harmonization (e.g. AR 1982: 3) most immediately recalls U Thant.

De Cuéllar expressed his conception of the office on various occasions. By choosing a lecture at the University of Oxford – and referring to Hammarskjöld's address in the same location – to make his clearest statements on the role of the Secretary-General, he placed himself in the Hammarskjöld tradition initiated by U Thant (Cuéllar 1995: 125–42). He was unequivocal in stressing the ethical content of the Charter and the consequences of this for the Secretary-General: 'He [the Secretary-General] is a world citizen because all world problems are *his* problems; the Charter is his home and his ideology, and its principles are his moral creed' (ibid.: 142). Like U Thant, de Cuéllar took novel problems as grounds to call for an 'earth patriotism' (AR 1990, in Cuéllar 1991: 300). This insight went hand in hand with the view, clearly in the Hammarskjöld tradition, that political ethics is a constitutive element of how the Secretary-General exercises his office:

> [T]he Secretary-General does not have the option of being partial or of being discouraged. In saying that, however, I do not claim that the Secretary-General has at his disposal moral resources greater than his fellow men. What I do assert is that he cannot shoulder the burden of his office without unlimited patience, and an unfailing sense of justice and humanity.'
>
> (Cuéllar 1995: 134)

De Cuéllar noted on various occasions that this moral force both limited and legitimized his scope for action. Thus, about his role after the Iraqi invasion of Kuwait he stated: '[I]t is my moral duty as Secretary-General to do everything in order to avoid war. My only strength is a moral strength' (Newman 1998: 102). This view was combined with the conviction and assertion of his independent negotiating authority, which he utilized during the First Gulf War between Iran and Iraq (Hume 1992: 173–84) and for his mediation in Cyprus. At the same time, he made a point of keeping the Security Council regularly informed about the course of these efforts (Bourloyannis 1990: 641–69). The list of conflicts to which the Secretary-General brought a new perspective is considerable: Afghanistan, Iraq–Iran, Angola/Namibia, Western Sahara, Cyprus and Cambodia (Urquhart 1989: 388–400). Since de Cuéllar, the Secretary-General's 'right' to seek to mediate in conflicts such as the Falklands War or to conduct negotiations between Venezuela and Guyana has become normality: 'No eyebrows are any longer raised by the fact that he neither requested nor received authorization from the Council or Assembly' (Franck 1987: 5.15).

Hence, it is not surprising that de Cuéllar also sought to standardize or further safeguard the Secretary-General's activities and flexibility. This concern was most pronounced in the field of fact-finding missions. Significantly, Ramcharan (1989: 315) says that de Cuéllar inherited the right to appoint such missions from his predecessors – and wanted to expand them. Referring to the humanitarian and moral responsibility of his office under the Charter, he suggested appointing so-called preparatory fact-finding missions (ibid.: 322). He felt fact-finding should not have to wait for conflicts to build up or erupt (AR 1982: 12). This proposal took form in 1987 as the Office of Research and the Collection of Information (ORCI), which was intended as a type of autonomous planning and analysis unit for the Secretary-General (Boudreau 1991; Dicke 1994: 151). For various reasons, including the critical stance of member states, ORCI failed to establish itself and was disbanded by Boutros-Ghali.

Besides structural evidence for the persistence of the Hammarskjöld tradition, de Cuéllar also made explicit reference to Hammarskjöld. For instance, he justified part of his efforts in mediating the withdrawal of Soviet troops from Afghanistan not with decisions of other UN bodies, but with his authority as Secretary-General (Franck 1995: 367; Newman 1998: 75–9) – in effect his application of the Peking Formula. Similarly, when he visited Iraq shortly before Operation Desert Storm to mediate in Iraq's invasion of Kuwait in 1990, de Cuéllar did not officially identify himself with the Security Council's condemnation of the annexation of Kuwait (Skjelsbaek and Fermann 1996: 85). He felt that this was his only chance of being accepted as mediator. Nonetheless, his mission to Baghdad ended in humiliation at the hands of Saddam Hussein, who did not even receive him. De Cuéllar, whose experiences in his first term had taught him the limitations of his office, explicitly echoed Hammarskjöld's vacuum theory.

No authority delegated to the Secretary-General, and no exercise by him of this authority, can fill the existing vacuum in collective security. This vacuum is due to the dissension among the Permanent Members of the Security Council, to the failure of member states to resort to the Charter's mechanisms for the settlement of disputes, and to their lack of respect for the decisions of the Security Council.

(1995: 132–3)

In this connection he underlined the importance of UN preventive actions (see in particular AR 1989: 228–32) and the UN's unacceptable financial situation. Although de Cuéllar does not once mention the name Hammarskjöld in his memoirs – in contrast to his speeches – many observers have compared the two (Kondracke 1990: 21): 'Pérez de Cuéllar already is widely considered by most UN-watchers to be the second-most-effective Secretary-General ever (after Dag Hammarskjöld)'. Moynihan sums up: 'Hammarskjöld was Secretary-General of the postwar UN, when it was an effective organization and there was a Western majority in the General Assembly. Pérez de Cuéllar took an organization that had almost self-destructed and become irrelevant, and found a role for it that no one expected. He's turned out to be the first Secretary-General of the post-cold war era' (ibid.). He competes for this title with his successor Boutros-Ghali.

Boutros Boutros-Ghali

Boutros-Ghali, too, consciously followed Hammarskjöld's and de Cuéllar's examples and used a lecture in Oxford to elucidate his conception of office. But there are also a number of biographic parallels. Boutros-Ghali is the scion of an aristocratic family with a tradition of public service (Meisler 1995) that produced a prime minister, Boutros-Ghali's grandfather – who, like Hjalmar Hammarskjöld, was extremely controversial. Indeed, in 1910 he was assassinated, an act that even found approval in various corners of the domestic political spectrum. Boutros-Ghali comments: 'For a small boy to see such things creates an impact. I felt that I must have a political career, that I would betray the tradition of our family if I didn't play a political role' (quoted in ibid.: 183). Initially, he pursued an academic career in international law, in the course of which he also lectured at the University of Uppsala. Then, like Hammarskjöld, the widely known expert in international law was appointed a minister of state in the Ministry of Foreign Affairs. Through the political events surrounding Sadat's rapprochement with Israel, Boutros-Ghali advanced to became one of the Egyptian president's main advisors; shortly afterwards he was appointed acting foreign minister. The highpoint of his diplomatic career was his role as chief Egyptian negotiator at the Camp David Accords.

He assumed the office of Secretary-General at a time of euphoric hopes in the UN. In contrast to Hammarskjöld, Boutros-Ghali 'campaigned' strongly for the office of Secretary-General: he wanted to achieve something in this office. In this connection, at the summit meeting of Security Council members initiated by various heads of government in 1992, he remarked: 'Whoever proposed the meeting first, I wanted it to result in a more effective role for the UN Secretary-General'

(1999: 23). The most immediate result of this meeting was the mandate to draw up a new 'Agenda for Peace' (UN Doc. A/47/277–S/24111, 17 June 1992), that would deal with the dramatic changes of international politics since 1989. Presenting a new phase model of conflict resolution (preventive diplomacy, peacemaking, peacekeeping and peace-building), Boutros-Ghali again stated an unmistakable claim, which must be seen against the background of the extraordinary politicking that preceded his election: 'I had won my post through politics, and now I was being asked to become a political leader' (1999: 26).

In his Oxford address he emphasized, contrary to his image of a very publicity-conscious Secretary-General, the importance of quiet, preventive diplomacy: 'As an impartial figure with a global mandate, relatively unencumbered by political or bureaucratic pressures and without the desire or compulsion to publicize his role, the Secretary-General can achieve a great deal behind the scenes to help parties settle their differences before their confrontation becomes public' (1996a: 91). Boutros-Ghali also repeatedly referred to – his view of – the ethical dimension of his office:

> Deciding when to act and when to refrain presents a profound ethical dilemma, but at present these choices are informed not by ethics but solely by power politics. … As the international community works its way toward a consensus on these intellectual and moral questions, the Secretary-General must take a central role in resolving the conflict between realism and responsibility.
>
> (ibid.: 93–4)

Here Boutros-Ghali presents the conception of global leadership that he pursued in his term: in the age of globalization, the Secretary-General, in accordance with his mandate is obliged by the Charter to actively lead the community of states to shift their focus from national politics to international concerns. Hence, it is not surprising that, given this perception of his mission, Boutros-Ghali emphasizes the Secretary-General's independence as a crucial factor:

> The key to the future is credibility. Nothing is more precious to the United Nations than its reputation. That reputation rests on four pillars: impartiality, equity, efficiency, and achievement. A fifth, indispensable principle is independence. If one word above all is to characterize the role of the Secretary-General, it is independence. The holder of this office must never be seen as acting out of fear of, or in an attempt to curry favour with, one state or group of states. Should that happen, all prospects for the United Nations would be lost.
>
> (ibid.: 98)

This emphasis on independence, which goes beyond impartiality, presumes that the Secretary-General and the United Nations have their point of view on the political and moral questions facing the international community. With Boutros-Ghali the harmonization stressed by U Thant acquires an objective that goes beyond reaching an understanding between existing forces and tendencies: it now has a definite idea of the direction in which the community of states must move – also in terms of concrete issues at hand. This view is predicated on the end of the Cold War; it is Boutros-Ghali's answer to the redefinition of international relations. Elsewhere he underlines this by highlighting the different functions of the Security Council and the Secretary-General within the UN:

> [S]ans doute est-il vrai de dire que chacun de ces organs incarne, à sa manière, une certaine conception de l'intérêt général dans la société internationale. Le Conseil de sécurité le traduit sous la forme réaliste d'un compromis politique. Le Secrétaire-Général tente de lui donner un contenu plus impartial et je serais tenté de dire aussi parfois moral.
>
> (1996b: 410)

In this description, Boutros-Ghali in principle claims parity – in the form of a division of labour – between the Security Council and the Secretary-General. This view is a clear break with unambiguous subordination to the Security Council, or even Hammarskjöld's description in his early annual reports of the UN as an instrument of the member states. Rather, it is a development of the idea of the 'detached element' in international politics, also expressed by Hammarskjöld. However, taking into account the new global political situation, Boutros-Ghali describes his claim to global leadership in notably activist language:

> … j'estime que le Secrétaire-Général n'a pas seulement un devoir d'exécution, il a aussi un devoir de vérité, et en particulier celui de mettre les Etats face à leurs responsabilités et de les amener à prendre les décisions qu'il estime conforme à l'intérêt général de la communauté internationale. C'est dans cet esprit que je veux exercer ma fonction. Cela m'a amené, ces dernières années, non seulement à adapter les compétences traditionnelles du Secrétaire-Général, mais aussi à prendre en charge des fonctions nouvelles.
>
> (ibid.: 408)

Despite the novel nature and tone of Boutros-Ghali's approach, this activist perception of office, the emphasis on independence and the attempt to find new fields of activity for the Secretary-General fall well within the Hammarskjöld tradition (Nelan 1995: 71). Yet, Hammarskjöld would most probably not have stated in such an insistent tone that he defined the general interest of the international community.

Boutros-Ghali's version of the 'detached element' goes further than Hammarskjöld's in that his conception for the UN includes not only an 'action préventive', but also a so-called 'action prospective' (Boutros-Ghali 1996b: 411). Whereas under the former he subsumes further developments by whatever channels and means in the forms of preventive diplomacy devised by Hammarskjöld, under 'action prospective' he includes efforts at predictive analysis and conceptual guidelines for the future structuring of international relations. '[Á] mes yeux, le rôle du Secrétaire-Général des Nations unies est non seulement d'impulser un rythme à l'activité multilatérale des Etats, mais aussi des principes d'action' (ibid.: 413). In particular, he linked these efforts with the series of international conferences held during his term of office (Boutros-Ghali 1996a: 88–9) and above all with the Agenda for Peace, in which, one year later, under the pressure of events, he included a number of additions and modifications.[10]

Along with Boutros-Ghali's activist and self-confident conception of office went a pronounced personalization, e.g. when he speaks as a matter of course of 'ma politique de sécurité' (1996b: 412). Ajami (1996: 162) draws attention to the inflationary use of 'I' in Boutros-Ghali's texts. In Newman's view: 'He [Boutros-Ghali] had a vision of the Office as the zenith of the global ethos, almost detached from the intergovernmental forces which appoint and control it ...' (1998: 5). This assessment also explains why Boutros-Ghali consciously spoke of global, and not international leadership. The concepts of 'global' and 'international leadership' define the similarities and differences between Hammarskjöld and Boutros-Ghali. Hammarskjöld – bound by the realities of the Cold War – worked on the principle of at best cautious, protracted changes in relations between the member states, whereas Boutros-Ghali started from different assumptions.

In this connection, Jones (1994: 1047–50) contrasts Hammarskjöld's idea of a UN growing organically with Boutros-Ghali's conception, which was marked by a mechanical vocabulary and greater impatience. Moreover, Hammarskjöld did not waste time complaining about the actual situation of the UN; he focused consistently on the future. Using the Agenda for Peace, Jones shows that Boutros-Ghali's tone is that of a teacher 'who is much tried by the recalcitrance and general thick-headedness of his students' (ibid.: 1047). Such rhetoric tends to quickly sap the sympathy and support of the member states. They were as sensitive after the Cold War as before, and Boutros-Ghali lacked Hammarskjöld's appreciation of the need to respect this. Here, Hammarskjöld's strategy was just the opposite:

> The somewhat deceptive open leadership style of Hammarskjöld was flexible enough to include considerable closed-room bargaining. He was always careful to gather support behind the scenes before going public, and then to disguise his own boldness as deference to the wishes of the member states.
>
> (ibid.: 1050)

Boutros-Ghali's approach was underscored by his treatment of the Security Council, in which he broke with de Cuéllar's practice of close cooperation with the body (Meisler 1995: 196). Ultimately, this became a crucial argument against Boutros-Ghali when he came up for re-election. In addition, he lacked the standing in the UN administration to 'earth' the enormous growth in his competencies within the Secretariat. On the contrary: his management was at times labelled arrogant and he had disagreements with staff; in conjunction with reform efforts and job cuts, these undermined staff motivation and the standing of the Secretary-General (Rivlin 1994: 65). The two Secretaries-General also differ with regard to the moral dimension of the office. Despite his appeal to the moral authority of his task, Boutros-Ghali managed to damage it too, for instance by defining the conflict in Bosnia as 'a war of the rich' (Ajami 1996: 162–4). Here, too, his claims to more extensive activities and authority – especially in his dealings with member states – were inadequately substantiated by political ethics.

Despite these obvious distinctions, there were parallels in the way their respective terms ended. In both cases, the Secretary-General's authority in respect of peacekeeping operations became a bone of contention. The similarity is underscored by the fact that with hindsight, the dilemmas that Boutros-Ghali faced in Bosnia and Somalia (Matthies 1993) seem like a re-run of the problems in the Congo. In both cases the Secretary-General increasingly assumed or had to assume personal responsibility for far-reaching political and military initiatives as well as for others' mistakes. Under the pressure of events, as the respective conflicts persisted and the international community dithered about mandates, both Hammarskjöld and Boutros-Ghali were caught in the crossfire of political controversies. The parallel is even more striking when one compares Meisler's assessment that Boutros-Ghali arrogated executive powers 'as if he were a kind of chief minister of the Security Council' (Meisler 1995: 192) with contemporary statements, say Gromyko's, about Hammarskjöld. A slightly amended version of Boutros-Ghali's Oxford address appeared in *Foreign Affairs* and Jesse Helms (1996), chairman of the Foreign Affairs Committee of the US senate, promptly wrote an extremely critical rejoinder. This circumstance defines the almost tragic nature of Boutros-Ghali's term of office: he retired from office, partly, because of the concept of leadership that had previously been demanded of him (Rivlin 1994: 57–61).

Boutros-Ghali himself called Hammarskjöld the 'epitome of a United Nations Secretary-General' and added: 'His accomplishments, his innovations, and his vision are a great inspiration. I have sought, within the framework of my own experience and of this moment in time, to uphold the standards he put into place'.[11] Meisler sums up: 'When historians make their assessments, Boutros-Ghali will surely rank as at least as active as Hammarskjöld in crises and just as effective at expanding the role of the office. But he will never be given the same reverence and affection' (1995: 180). He continues: 'Boutros-Ghali ... has proven the most stubbornly independent Secretary-General in the half-century history of the United Nations. He has made the Secretary-General an international player in a way that has not been seen since the days of the Congo crisis' (ibid.: 181). In his autobiography, however, the Egyptian labelled his term of office a 'loss of an opportunity to construct an agreed-upon post-cold war structure for international peace and security' (1999: 336). Newman differentiates: 'In sending envoys on his own initiative, talking to Security Council members and the Council informally, making normative public statements, and assuming political-military control and authority, Boutros-Ghali has imposed an activist stamp upon his Office which has set the tone for the post-Cold War model' (1998: 189).

The notion that Hammarskjöld's concrete political ideas could simply be transferred to others is unrealistic in the light of the diverse determinants of the office. Moreover, simple worship would have gone against Hammarskjöld's grain, who in his assessment of future developments of the world organization openly acknowledged the role of uncertainty. The content of concepts such as preventive diplomacy can change depending on the global political context (Petrolia-Ammaniti 1976: 367–8). But our review of the Hammarskjöld tradition and his successors has verified that 'Hammarskjöld's personal style and his authority … shaped the development of the Secretary-General's political role' (Urquhart 1985: 257).

A quotation from a statement by Hammarskjöld, a reference to one of his reports or a concrete action in the spirit of his leadership counts as a political argument with an almost canonical quality. Hammarskjöld's name is code for an active, dynamic interpretation of the provisions of the Charter. To this extent, though, his 'legacy' can also be a burden. Rovine, reviewing Hammarskjöld's remarkable expansion of executive authority notes: '[T]he development of an independent role for global institutions, symbolized so magnificently by Hammarskjöld, would henceforth be questioned and restrained, and it appeared unlikely that the Secretary-General's successor would be permitted the freedom to strengthen executive capacities' (1970: 324). With U Thant in mind, Petrolia-Ammaniti states: 'It might be considered possible that if the record of his predecessor had not been quite outstanding, his critics might have been less strict' (1976: 358). According to Meron (1977: 27), the confrontation with Khrushchev led the next Secretaries-General (U Thant and Waldheim) to act more guardedly in respect of the executive authority of the office. Regardless of the respective differences, all incumbents agreed their power was closely related to political ethics as a prerequisite and obligation of their office. In respect of ethical reflection, U Thant is closest to Hammarskjöld.[12] De Cuéllar made greatest use of good offices, and Boutros-Ghali emphasized the independence of the Secretary-General. The greatest difference is between the conceptions of Hammarskjöld and Waldheim. This comparative perspective has offered a wealth of evidence for the evolution of the office amidst the interplay of personality, institutional structure and international developments. From this standpoint, we shall present some concluding remarks on the contemporary relevance of the Hammarskjöld tradition today.

Kofi Annan and the contemporary relevance of the Hammarskjöld tradition

This final section will discuss the relevance of the Hammarskjöld tradition for challenges facing international politics and the UN at the beginning of the twenty-first century as reflected by the seventh UN Secretary-General, Kofi Annan (Annan 2004; Bauer 2005). In many respects, Hammarskjöld is no longer 'up to date', for instance, on the environment, the influence of NGOs and even his reticence on human rights. Moreover, his conception of office was rooted in Cold War premises that, even if still latent, no longer predominate as in Hammarskjöld's time. On the other hand, many of Hammarskjöld's novel statements and ideas are now commonplace – proof of how innovative these concepts were in the 1950s and 1960s. In this sense, many of Hammarskjöld's contemporaries held him for a man of the 'next generation'

(Ward quoted in Zacher 1970: 249; Cordier 1960: 1271). This judgement needs to be examined by comparing his term with that of Kofi Annan's.

In keeping with an unwritten law of phases, Annan, following a very activist Secretary-General, started off noticeably low-key – much as Hammarskjöld started after Lie, and U Thant after Hammarskjöld. The appointment of the experienced UN staff member was itself taken as 'a reaction against the Secretary-General's high profile status' (Newman 1998: 126). A distinct contrast to his predecessor in temperament and personality, Annan, too, is in many ways part of the Hammarskjöld tradition. This was indicated early by the newly elected Secretary-General's choice of words before the General Assembly:

> ... I shall neither overstep nor minimize my role as head of one of the six principle organs of this Organization. I intend to present my independent views to Member States for their considerations. I intend to offer my services and good offices as mediator and intermediary whenever and wherever I feel it can be helpful. I intend to lead an international civil service that will be honest, efficient, independent and proud of its honorable contribution to the improvement of life on this planet. Finally, I intend to stress not only our legal obligations, not only our fiscal limitations, not only our political and diplomatic considerations, but above all, the moral dimension of our work in this Organization.
>
> (UN Doc. GA/9211, 17 December 1996: 2–3)

By emphasizing the moral dimension, Annan was following in Hammarskjöld's footsteps. This is underlined by reference to a 'time of healing' and his appeal to member states: '[W]e cannot succeed without your political, moral, financial and material support and participation. Applaud us when we prevail; correct us when we fail; but, above all, do not let this indispensable, irreplaceable institution wither, languish or perish as a result of Member State indifference, inattention or financial starvation' (ibid.: 3). If one compares this with Hammarskjöld's words in the same place: 'It is for you to judge how I succeed, and it is for you to correct me if I fail. Ours is a work of reconciliation and realistic construction' (Statement 10 April 1953, in CF II), one cannot but assume a deliberate reference. In an interview, Annan also names Hammarskjöld as the predecessor he most admires: 'I think I liked his fortitude, his vision, his principled and moral stand on issues. And also that fact that he was quite active and tackled the issues, regardless of the forces that were at play.'[13] On the occasion of his re-election, Annan quoted Hammarskjöld's words from 1957, and at a press conference talked about similarities between Hammarskjöld and himself.[14]

Besides these sporadic statements, Annan also held an 'Oxford address', as it were, to explain his conception of office, though to the Council on Foreign Relations in the USA as he was concerned with rebuilding US confidence in the organization. In this speech Annan stresses that moral authority was the specific attribute of the Secretary-General. But this should not tempt him to express moral judgements and personal convictions in public: 'It is a luxury I cannot afford. The integrity, impartiality and independence of the office of Secretary-General are too important to be so easily sacrificed' (Annan 1998c: 19). On the other hand, he is aware that he has greater scope for action than some of his predecessors: '[T]he end of the cold war transformed the moral promise of the role of the Secretary-General. It allowed him to place the United Nations at the service of the universal values of the Charter, without the constraints of ideology or particular interests' (ibid.: 19). In this connection, he notes the distinction between impartiality and neutrality which was so crucial to Hammarskjöld (ibid.: 19): 'Impartiality does not – and must not – mean neutrality in the face of evil. It means strict and unbiased adherence to the principles of the Charter – nothing more, and nothing less'. Against the experience of UN and member state failure in Bosnia and Rwanda, Annan initiated a broad conceptual debate about the UN's peacekeeping capacity. This included a rather self-critical investigation into the Srebrenica massacre and the Rwandan genocide but also various reform proposals in the so-called Brahimi report (Fröhlich 2001b).[15] Reconsidering Hammarskjöld's principles, it is clear than none can remain unquestioned (Roberts 1994; Thakur 1995; Kühne 1999). Annan summed up: '[T]he prerequisites of traditional peacekeeping will not exist in the majority of cases' (1998a: 171). If that is the case, then the perennial tension between sovereignty and intervention, a topic that Hammarskjöld already had explicitly taken up (see, for example, his Commencement Address, 13 February 1954, in CF II) is highlighted once more. In a cable after the Baluba massacre in the Congo, Hammarskjöld had written: 'Prohibition against intervention in internal conflicts cannot be considered to apply to senseless slaughter of civilians or fighting arising from tribal hostilities' (quoted in Urquhart 1972: 438; see also Bring 2003). Annan, for his part, contrasted two concepts of sovereignty: 'The Charter protects the sovereignty of peoples. It was never meant as a license for governments to trample on human rights and human dignity. Sovereignty implies responsibility, not just power' (UN Doc. SG/SM/6613/Rev. 1, 3). This 'face the alternative' is the same method that Hammarskjöld used when outlining the static versus dynamic concept of the UN.[16] For the time being, the careful adoption and reference to the 'responsibility to protect' marks this crucial shift in the UN's action (ICISS 2001; Annan 2005).

The terrorist attacks of 11 September 2001 mark yet another event in world politics that goes beyond the scope of Hammarskjöld's time. But Annan, in his various efforts to promote dialogue among cultures, can once more claim to be treading in Hammarskjöld's footsteps.[17] Much the same as Hammarskjöld, Annan highlighted the spiritual basis underlying the UN's work.[18] It is worth noting that a portrait of Annan cites five traditional African virtues (Enyimyam/dignity; Awerehyemu/trust; Akokoudor/courage; Ehumbobor/sympathy and Gyedzi/faith) (Ramo 2000), similar to Hammarskjöld's basic harmony of love, patience, justice and humility or U Thant's Buddhist concepts of metta, karuna, mudita and upekka. Annan, an Anglican Christian, has no qualms about interrupting his management vocabulary to stress the 'power of prayer' (UN Doc. SG/SM/6541, 7), which he consciously includes among the success factors in his negotiations in Baghdad in 1998. Annan's argument is similar to Hammarskjöld's: 'All the great religions and traditions overlap when it comes to the fundamental principles of human conduct: charity, justice, compassion, mutual respect, the equality of human beings in the sight of God' (UN Doc. SG/SM/7048, 8).

The Secretary-Generalship has changed considerably since Hammarskjöld's days. Apart from the challenges of peacekeeping, intervention and the dialogue among cultures and civilizations in the face of global terrorism, the tenure of Kofi Annan was in many ways determined by various problems connected to the situation in Iraq. The bypassing of the United Nations during the war in 2003 was a considerable setback to the world organization as a whole and its Secretary-General who – like Dag Hammarskjöld – had been awarded the Nobel Prize for Peace in 2001. And yet, various aspects of the Iraqi question illustrate Kofi Annan's particular place in the Hammarskjöld tradition while at the same time highlighting the special nature of international leadership by the Secretary-General.

First, Iraq (at various instances) confronted the Secretary-General with the question if and how he should personally take the initiative and involve himself in diplomatic manoeuvres. In this context, Hammarskjöld's Peking Formula still seems to have particular relevance. When virtually all diplomatic channels have been exhausted, the Secretary-General must be prepared in 'fallback position' (Lash 1959: 49) to act exclusively on the authority of his office (and possibly at a remove to condemnatory resolutions of other UN organs). Based on both the authority of his office and his personal integrity, the Secretary-General as the ultimate negotiating resource even has to be prepared to intervene and negotiate with dictators or ostracized regimes. This is what Hammarskjöld did in Peking and Kofi Annan did in Baghdad in 1998 (on the background see Shawcross 2000: 249–79; Gordon and Sciolino 1998: 11; Fröhlich 1998: 19). In such situations he of necessity lays himself open to ethically motivated criticism. However, in view of his responsibility for world peace, the Secretary-General must accept such charges of apparent moral indifference. At the same time, Kofi Annan – as Dag Hammarskjöld – did not see his role as an isolated force of its own, but rather in contact with other forces and influences at work. In connection with his successful 1998 negotiations in Iraq (which Iraqi actions subsequently wrecked) he recognized that it was not only his intervention that persuaded Saddam Hussein to temporarily relent: '[I]f diplomacy is to succeed, it must be backed both by force and by fairness' (UN Doc. SG/SM/6613/Rev. 1, 5). In this he clearly paid tribute to the US-led military build-up in the region lent considerable support to his activities.

Second, the Iraqi challenge also underlined the crucial administrative responsibilities, integrity and standing of the international civil service. Annan's efforts to introduce reforms and a new code of conduct for UN staff – in his view a 'calling' – directly link up to Hammarskjöld's perspective on this component of the office's relevance.[19] Although Annan introduced a series of unprecedented management reforms that substantially changed the work of the UN Secretariat (Fröhlich 2005), his administrative and political standing have been severely contested by the scandals surrounding the Oil-For-Food programme, initially aimed at alleviating the strains on the Iraqi people during the time of international sanctions.[20] The programme turned out to be manipulated by Saddam Hussein's regime which, for example, was able to gain illicit revenues by smuggling oil in contradiction of the programme's intentions. Highlighting serious mismanagement and failure of oversight on part of the Secretariat and its chief administrative officer, the Independent Inquiry Committee that examined the programme – rather symptomatically – also stressed that 'responsibility for what went wrong with the Programme cannot be laid exclusively at the door of the Secretariat'.[21] The Security Council and member states, which held at least part of the administrative control of the programme, also did not sufficiently provide direction and oversight of the programme. The criticism directed personally against Kofi Annan from various sides also brings back two lessons from Hammarskjöld's time: it is the special moral authority of the Secretary-General that results in a special scrutiny on his personal integrity. Even minor details or the mere possibility rather than fact of unethical conduct have the capacity to damage his personal and political standing. The second lesson is that there seems to be hardly any criticism of the person that does not aim at the office and there is no criticism of the office that is not embedded in critical views of the UN's overall role in international relations. Taken together, these two lessons illustrate, first, how careful the Secretary-General has to guard his personal integrity and, second, how tempting it may be for his opponents to use personal and moral criticism instead of political argumentation. While exclusively assigning blame for failure may be a difficult task, the Oil-for-Food Programme (covering financial transactions of more than $100 billion in only seven years, which undoubtedly saved lives among the Iraqi population) is also an expression of the enlargement – and possibly limitation – of possible UN roles and duties in current international affairs.

Third, the war in Iraq undoubtedly challenged the very concept of collective security as spelled out in the Charter in 1945. In his speech to the General Assembly on 23 September 2003, Annan argued:

> Since this Organization was founded, States have generally sought to deal with threats to the peace through containment and deterrence, by a system based on collective security and the United Nations Charter. Article 51 of the Charter prescribes that all States, if attacked, retain the inherent right of self-defence. But until now it has been understood that when States go beyond that, and decide to use force to deal with broader threats to international peace and security, they need the unique legitimacy provided by the United Nations. Now, some say this understanding is no longer tenable, since an "armed attack" with weapons of mass destruction could be launched at any time, without warning, or by a clandestine group. Rather than wait for that to happen, they argue, States have the right and obligation to use force pre-emptively, even on the territory of other States, and even while weapons systems that might be used to attack them are still being developed. According to this argument, States are not obliged to wait until there is agreement in the Security Council. Instead, they reserve the right to act unilaterally, or in ad hoc coalitions. This logic represents a fundamental challenge to the

principles on which, however imperfectly, world peace and stability have rested for the last 58 years. My concern is that, if it were to be adopted, it could set precedents that resulted in a proliferation of the unilateral and lawless use of force, with or without justification. But it is not enough to denounce unilateralism, unless we also face up squarely to the concerns that make some States feel uniquely vulnerable, since it is those concerns that drive them to take unilateral action. We must show that those concerns can, and will, be addressed effectively through collective action. Excellencies, we have come to a fork in the road. This may be a moment no less decisive than 1945 itself, when the United Nations was founded.

(UN Doc. SG/SM/8891 23 September 2003)

Annan's reaction is similar to Hammarskjöld's method, who, in times of challenge presented member states with alternatives on the future development of the organization as a whole: the Secretary-General does not try to 'lead' by simply trying to force his will on member states, but rather he tries to ask questions,[22] offer alternative directions, mobilize support and refresh the consensus of the Charter in the light of new experiences. Annan did this with the establishment of a High-Level Panel whose subsequent report on threats, challenges and change offered him the chance to infuse proposals and elements of reform beyond vested or national interest (High-Level Panel on Threats, Challenges and Change 2004). He relied on the diverse composition of the 'independent experts' representing the major constituent parts of UN member states and took their recommendations as the basis for presenting his own report 'In Larger Freedom' (Annan 2005) which can, in effect, be taken as his comprehensive view of the organization's role in the twenty-first century. It is, however, too simple to confine Annan's tenure to the Iraqi problem and it is also too simple to say that Iraq, for Annan, was his Peking, his Congo and his troika at the same time. The examples taken from Hammarskjöld's time nonetheless open an instructive perspective on current problems while also underlying that the UN and its role in world affairs have profoundly changed.

Hammarskjöld was not unaware of the persistent change that is a characteristic feature of the UN's existence. He tried to account for it with a reference to 'constitutional development'. In his speech at the University of Chicago Law School in May 1960, he had argued that on the international level – much the same as on the national level – the self-consciousness of people (or peoples) manifests itself in the form of a constitution. This constitution emerges as a legal expression of the decision by individuals (or individual states and peoples) that they feel themselves bound together as a 'society' and that they have decided to live together under common rules. Taking note of various difficulties in such an analogy, Hammarskjöld describes the United Nations Charter as being the manifestation of self-consciousness by the international society, a society of states. The UN Charter – in his terms – then logically resembles something like a 'constitution' on the international level: representing basic rules of international ethics without in any way constituting a kind of 'super-state' – rather (in the words of his annual report in 1961) 'a first step in the direction of an organized international community' (AR 1961: 543). Tentative and insufficient as this first step may be, it has brought about a change in international law and relations from coexistence to cooperation (Friedman 1964). Referring to this constitutional aspect, Hammarskjöld, in his address to the University of California in June 1955, elaborated: 'When a new social organism is created, we give it a constitution. Inside the framework of that constitution the first vital urges begin to stir, but as its life develops towards fullness the constitution is adjusted, so to say, from within, to new and changing needs which even the wisest legislator and statesman could only partly foresee' (CF II: 518). One may argue that Kofi Annan's efforts to find and implement common principles and standards of action beyond state actors is a prolongation of Hammarskjöld's constitutional perspective. By including NGOs and transnational corporations into the work of the United Nations[23] he not only enlarged the appeal of the UN's ethical foundations but also introduced a new mode of cooperation in international affairs. Going beyond 'coexistence' and 'cooperation' in the traditional sense, 'trilateral' alliances – by way of 'coalition' – nowadays emerge as important actors in fighting global challenges, from HIV/ AIDS to blood diamonds (Annan 2004: 47–52). The United Nations Organization in this context does not represent a mere imitation of national government at the world level: its organs do not fit into any static system of powers and competences. Improvisation thus emerges as an essential *modus operandi*. There is no automatic mechanism operating towards world organization and no guarantee for steady progress. The capacity to cope with setbacks and unpredictable impediments is the measure of success. The fact that for the Secretary-General there are 'fewer "no-go"-areas for the Office than ever before' (Newman 1998: 3) is also a burden. In the 1960 Chicago speech Hammarskjöld expressed this in the following words:

> Working at the edge of the development of human society is to work on the brink of the unknown. Much of what is done will one day prove to be of little avail. That is no excuse for the failure to act in accordance with our best understanding, in recognition of its limits but with faith in the ultimate result of the creative evolution in which it is our privilege to cooperate.
>
> (CF IV: 592)

The comparison with his successor Kofi Annan shows that Hammarskjöld's political ethics are extraordinarily topical. They are neither an easy manual for conflict resolution nor blind to the political and material limitations of the office of the Secretary-General and the work of the United Nations. But they are a valuable orientation in that they point to a potential that can – through the catalyst of the institutional structure of the United Nations and its Secretary-General as an 'exceptionally-situated individual actor' (Murphy 1970: 165) – be transformed into political effectiveness and reality. De Cuéllar had stated that to understand international relations it helps to study the UN, and to understand the UN it helps to study the office of the Secretary-General. One can go further: to understand the office of the Secretary-General it certainly helps to study Hammarskjöld. His very personal approach to the office and his concept of political ethics and the United Nations is still applicable and relevant today.

Forty years after Hammarskjöld's death, Kofi Annan honoured his predecessor with a lecture in Uppsala (UN Doc. SG/SM/7941, 6 September 2001), where he stated: 'There can be no better rule of thumb for a Secretary-General, as he approaches each new challenge or crisis, than to ask himself, 'how would Hammarskjöld have handled this?' The 'formula' that Hammarskjöld sought to find during his term of office can still be used to deal with complicated equations of global politics. Their ultimate solution, however, is dependent on the perennial challenge to achieve that '*quantum satis*' in the conflict between politics and ethics towards which not only the Secretary-General or the United Nations, but a variety of other actors must work.

Notes

1 Introduction

1 See Burns 1978; Blondel 1987; Stuart 1983; Etzersdorfer 1997 and Helms 2000 on the concept of leadership in general.
2 As for example outlined in George Bush's remarks at Maxwell Air Force Base on 13 April 1991 (in *EA* 1991, Vol. 46: D254–D258). See also Haass (1995: 43–58); Cooper (1993: 507–16).
3 This part has been considerably shortened in comparison to the German edition (see Fröhlich 2002: 15–29).
4 The standard work is Urquhart 1972. For an interesting perspective on Hammarskjöld in private life, see the book by the Swedish painter Beskow (1969), a friend of Hammarskjöld, who also draws on their intense correspondence. Other personal accounts include the biographies by Stolpe (1964a), and the former head of the television department of the UN and cartoonist Kelen (1966, 1969). The pictorial biography by Söderberg (1962) provides a concise overview.
5 Besides Urquhart 1972, others who focus on the politician include Lash 1957; Levine 1962; Simon 1967; Henderson 1969; Gillett 1970; Montgomery 1975. The first collection of Hammarskjöld's speeches was prepared by Foote 1963. Edited volumes include Jordan 1983a and Cordier and Foote 1965. For a thorough discussion of Hammarskjöld's conceptions as UN Secretary-General see Zacher 1970.
6 Fore example, Stolpe 1964a; Sundén 1967; Dusen 1969; Aulén 1969; Stephan 1983; Hoffmann-Herreros 1991; Specker 1999; Kania 2000. See also 'The only true profile' in Chapter 3.
7 Most accounts on Buber and Schweitzer simply ignore the contact between these three people. The only notable exceptions are the biographies of Buber by Hodes (1971: 136–52) and Friedman (1999: 490–501).
8 I have adopted the method of citation that Bernhard Erling uses in his new English translation of the Swedish text. Each year (or period of years) is followed by the entries for that period numbered consecutively; this method is more helpful than just the page number (Erling 1999). Thus, citations read *Markings* [year]: [number], [page of the English edition].
9 From a letter to his friend Leif Belfrage, to whom he left the decision of whether to publish the diary or not (*Markings*: v).
10 From this only his correspondence with Alexis Leger, a French diplomat and poet, who wrote under the nom de plume of Saint-John Perse, has been published in its entirety with a commentary. See Leger 1993; Little 2001. Other correspondence is documented in Grace 1987; Hovde 1997 and Fröhlich 2001a.
11 See the list of interviews in the Bibliography.

2 The office of the UN Secretary-General

1 On the following see the standard works by Schwebel 1952; Bailey 1962a; Gordenker 1967a; Rovine 1970; Smouts 1971; Fosdick 1972; Boudreau 1991; Rivlin and Gordenker 1993; Göller 1995; Newman 1998.

2 On the international service of the League of Nations see Ranshofen-Wertheimer 1945; Schwebel 1951.

3 On his period of office see Rovine (1970: 17–103); Fosdick (1972: 19–46); Bailey (1962a: 16–21); Drummond 1931.

4 See, for instance, the biography of his assistant Phelan 1936; Ramcharan (1990: 103).

5 On the history see Gordenker (1967a: 3–33); Fröhlich 1997b; Schwebel (1983: 341–5). Urquhart (1967: 50) speaks of Art. 99 as a 'complete innovation'.

6 On the history and the interests reflected in the different drafts at the conference in Dumbarton Oaks, see Russell and Muther 1958; Gordenker (1967a: 3–33). For a splendid account of the UN's origins see also Schlesinger 2003.

7 On the legal interpretation of Arts. 97–99 see Fiedler (1994: 1019–57); for Art. 100 Schreuer (1994: 1057–76); and for Art. 101 Göttelmann (1994: 1076–101). The French commentary by Cot and Pellet 1991 contains commentaries on the relevant articles by Bettati 1991 (Art. 97), Smouts 1991 (Arts. 98–99), Ruzie 1991 (Art. 100) and Dubouis 1991 (Art. 101). See also Kelsen 1964 (296–318); Goodrich *et al.* (1969: 572–609) and Szasz 1991.

8 The preparatory commission of the UN distinguished between at least six functions of the Secretary-General: '1) general administrative and executive functions; 2) technical functions; 3) financial functions; 4) organization and administration of the International Secretariat; 5) political functions; and 6) representational functions' (Goodrich *et al.* 1969: 574).

9 Gordenker (1967a: 114–21). See also Bailey (1962a: 63): 'It is only in books that a neat distinction can be made between policy and administration.'

10 For an overview see Bottenberg 1959; Pak 1963; Goodrich 1967; Jessen 1975; Barros 1983; Urquhart 1985; Boudreau (1991: 8–24); Rivlin 1994.

11 Schwebel (1951: 376) points out that in San Francisco Uruguay proposed that the Secretary-General should have the right to bring all matters to the attention of the Security Council that constitute a violation of the Charter's provisions (even in a country's internal affairs). The proposal failed to pass by just three votes.

12 Examples include Hammarskjöld's application of Art. 99 on 13 July 1960 in the context of the Congo Crisis and Waldheim's in the context of the occupation of the US embassy in Teheran in 1979. Most commentators do not interpret Lie's actions in the Korean War as a direct application of Art. 99 (Fiedler, 1994: 1049–52). Nevertheless, in several situations the Secretary-General has mentioned Art. 99, but, owing to other circumstances (e.g. the simultaneous discussion of the topic in the Security Council), his action is not interpreted as a direct application of Art. 99. For instance, on 28 July 1961 Hammarskjöld cited Art. 99 in connection with the French bombing of Tunisia. In 1994, the concrete options that Boutros-Ghali submitted to the Security Council on how to proceed in Rwanda call Art. 99 to mind, although the Secretary-General did not mention the Article in his report (UN Doc. S/1994/470, 20 April 1994). See also Newman (1998: 148) and Morr (1995: 1136–42).

13 See Goodrich *et al.* (1969: 586) for various examples.

14 See also Lentner (1965: 537); Morse (1972:87); Rovine (1972: 80) and Trachtenberg (1982: 615).

15 Incidentally, this profile bears an astonishing resemblance to the conditions listed by Holsti (1976: 30).

16 Even James (1993: 27), who is sceptical about the Secretary-General's abilities to act independently, is unequivocal when he states: 'He [the Secretary-General] is not an

independent international actor, in the sense of being formally free to choose his own policies. And, particularly with respect to political issues, he is a man under authority. … Nonetheless, the Secretary-General is undoubtedly an international player and it would be a great mistake to assume that in this capacity he is entirely without independence.'

17 Lung-Chu Chen quoted in Overland (1992: 321).
18 In this connection special mention must be made of Zacher 1970; Schachter 1962; Stein 1962; Virally 1962; Lash 1962; Lentner 1965 and Dicke 1994: 132–8, who analysed the annual reports from the viewpoint of efficiency and effectiveness. Hüfner 1982 studies the annual reports in terms of their significance for economic policy.
19 This finds expression in, among other things, use of quotations from the Secretary-General's report during the debate to legitimize national positions. See also Szasz (1991: 189).
20 For 1954 see DAG-1/5.0. Box 3 Secretary-General's Private Meeting, 25 June 1954.
21 The quantitative content analysis has been left out. For details see Fröhlich (2002: 66–70).
22 See also Aulén (1969: 91); Sundén (1967: 53–4) and Lipsey (1996: 16). There are also echoes of Bergson in Hammarskjöld's diary. Bergson, too, took an intense interest in mysticism, and there is a link between his view of the 'elan vital' born of universal life and Schweitzer. For details see the sections on 'Christian mysticism' and the summary in Chapter 3. On Bergson see Bergson (1994: 3–357) and 1993. For background see Deleuze 1997 and Plug 1985. Hammarskjöld's private library contained Bergson 1932 and 1921.
23 Address at University of California Convocation, 13 May 1954, in CF II: 294–301, in which he speaks of the 'slow and painful growth of all human institutions' (ibid.: 301). See also the Address at Special United Nations Convocation of the University of California, 25 June 1955, in CF II: 518–24, and the Address at the University of Chicago, 1 May 1960, in CF IV: 583–93.
24 See Hauriou 1965, in particular 'Die Theorie der Institution und der Gründung (Essay über den sozialen Vitalismus)', (27–66). On Hauriou see Schild 1974.
25 See two statements during a visit to the Congo in 1960, in CF V: 51/54.
26 Thus, Arendt's concept of power has often been criticized (e.g. Kaiser 1979).
27 For detailed examples see Chapter 4.
28 Dicke (1994: 126) uses the word 'conflicts' in the same context.

3 Principal elements of Dag Hammarskjöld's political ethics

1 An August 1959 entry in his diary is a poem titled 'From Uppsala' containing the following lines: 'A box on the ear taught the boy / that Father's name / was odious to them' (*Markings* 1959: 35, 180).
2 To Stolpe he said: 'You know me and also know that I cannot say I knew my father particularly well when he was still alive …' (Stolpe 1964a: 18). In the aforementioned letter to Beskow he wrote: 'But that picture tells more about me than about him and is in this connection outside the lighted area' (quoted in Beskow 1969: 33).
3 The German edition (Fröhlich 2002: 112–17) at this point offers further material on the influence of Hammarskjöld's mother as well as archbishop Nathan Söderblom, a friend of the family. For the special Uppsala atmosphere of these days see Hammarskjöld 1971.
4 Formally, the British continued to support Lester Pearson and therefore could not officially nominate Hammarskjöld (Lash 1961: 17). In his interview Gross (1964) suspected that the British and French delegations had come to an arrangement beforehand.
5 Incidentally, Lie had strong reservations about Hammarskjöld, against whom he tried to curry opposition in the General Assembly. See Cordier (1964: 2), and Barros

(1989: 341), who reports that Lie spread the rumour in the General Assembly that Hammarskjöld was homosexual.

6 The oath reads: 'I, Dag Hammarskjöld, solemnly swear to exercise in all loyalty, discretion and conscience the functions entrusted to me as Secratary-General of the United Nations, to discharge these functions and regulate my conduct with the interests of the United Nations only in view, and not to seek or accept instructions in regard to the performance of my duties from any government or other authority external to the Organization' (Dusen 1965: 169).

7 The original Swedish edition, Hammarskjöld 1966b has no commentary; the order and graphic design of the entries follows the diary closely. The most comprehensive edition, with a commentary on each entry, is Erling 1999, with detailed explanations of religious references, a subject index, and, for the first time, numbered citations. The English translation used in this study, Hammarskjöld 1964, is translated from the Swedish by Leif Sjöberg and W. H. Auden. There are sometimes major discrepancies, even disagreements, between translations (Falkman 1999: 14–15). Erling 1999, a completely new English translation, is a useful alternative, but has not yet appeared in book form. For further references on Hammarskjöld's sources see also the newly edited German edition Hammarskjöld 2005.

8 Although doubts have been voiced, the classification of Hammarskjöld as a mystic appears to be justified. See in this sense Hardy 1978; Schäfer 1970; Beyschlag 1980a; Stolpe 1964b; McClendon 1973.

9 Of course, one must bear in mind Auden's warning that no one can draw his own profile truly (1964: ix).

10 See the overview in Wehr 1995a; Borchert 1997; Dinzelbacher 1998 and Ruhbach and Sudbrack 1984. For a classic attempt to categorize mystical experience, see James (1982); Hammarskjöld had a copy of the English edition in his private library.

11 Interestingly, Hammarskjöld gave Ben Gurion a copy of de Chardin's 'The Phenomenon of Man' (Dusen 1965: 121).

12 Various authors have attempted to classify Hammarskjöld's diary by specific phases, e.g. Dusen (1965: 44), who distinguishes between the following seven phases: '1. The Starting Point: 1925–1930; 2. The Silent Decade: 1930–1940; 3. The 'Middle Years': 1941–1950; 4. The Darkest Night: 1950–1952; 5. The Turning Point: 1952–1953; 6. The Fulfilment: 1953–1958; 7. The Terminus: 1958–1961.'

13 The American and British editions incorrectly attribute these lines to Meister Eckhart.

14 Following remarks of Uno Willers, Hammarskjöld's friend and director of the Swedish National Library, Sundén (1967: 42) limits the time to the months of May and June 1957. The Suez Crisis could have been the external motivation for this step.

15 Auden (1964: xii) questions the authenticity of some early entries, which he assumes have been substantially revised at a later date. Falkman (1999:14), referring to Birnbaum, asserts that given the consistence between the entries from Hammarskjöld's youth and those in Auden, it cannot be assumed that Hammarskjöld made major rearrangements, subsequent additions or changes in the sequence of the entries.

16 In style and substance, the vicinity to Ekman 1923 is particularly remarkable.

17 Dusen (1965: 66) assumes that Hammarskjöld had become a witness to suicides.

18 See Urqhart (1964: 233) and Sölle (1997: 283).

19 In this context, McClendon (1973: 232) points out the influence on Hammarskjöld's thinking of Axel Hägerström and logic positivism, which he had studied at university. In the Murrow interview he discusses his critical attitude to conventional religious beliefs.

20 Dusen (1965: 110) points out that this passage on the day of great joy appears almost verbatim in his speech to UN staff in 1958 – another indication of the reciprocal influence between Hammarskjöld's inner and outer life.

21 See also Urquhart (1964: 232).

22 Erling (1999: 2) points out that the last entry in this style comes back to the image of the first entry in the diary.

23 See on biography and background Haas 1984; Ruh 1985; Wehr 1994; Haas 1995; Winkler 1997. On the reception by Hammarskjöld, see Brandt 1995; Specker (1999: 97–103).

24 Hammarskjöld's private library also contains a Swedish translation of the sermons: Meister Eckehart 1922, and a monograph on Eckhart: Lönborg 1931 (Brandt 1995: 222).

25 See the text on detachment, in Meister Eckhart (1991: 138–50). On the concept of detachment in Eckhart, see also Haas (1995: 44–8).

26 With this in mind, Sölle (1997: 286) writes: 'This cooperation between God and man liberated from the ego is a fundamental certainty of mystic life.'

27 Hammarskjöld's private library contained St John of the Cross 1951, 1947, 1955; Muños-Garnicia 1875. On his person and work, see Boldt 1990. On Hammarskjöld's reception see Huls 1991; Specker (1999: 103–8).

28 This is even more true of the song 'Love's Flame' (St John of the Cross 1989).

29 A discussion of a 'Dark Night' goes beyond the scope of the present work. On this see Huls 1991 and Wojtyla (1998: 127–39).

30 However, the passage in Chapter III of the 2nd Book of 'The Ascent of Mount Carmel' is very close to the diary: 'Faith, so say the theologians, is an attitude of the soul, secure and dark' (quoted in Huls 1991: 887).

31 Huls therefore speaks of 'union by similarity' (1991: 891) (English translation following the online edition on http://www.ecatholic2000.com/stjohn/ascent26.sthml).

32 On the similarity between the images see Specker (1999: 106) (English translation following the online edition on http://www.ecatholic2000.com/stjohn/ascent26.sthml).

33 For the only investigation see Erling (1987: 343–57), who identifies seven passages in which Hammarskjöld quotes Thomas and in this context points out the mistaken attribution of one quotation by Auden, who gives Thomas Aquinas as the source.

34 Hughes (1995: 178) regards Thomas à Kempis as a counterweight to what he sees as Eckhart's speculative quest for pure being.

35 See the edition Kant (1920: 44–5; 54). The entry and his speeches contain – like Schweitzer's – simplifications that do not appear in Kant. See, for instance, Statement at the Human Rights Day Concert, 10 December 1960, in CF V: 296: '[A] great German philosopher formulated the underlying principle when he said that the basic rule of ethics is never to treat man as a means but always as an end. In less paradoxical forms the same thought is common to all the great religions represented in this Organization.' Kant reads: 'Act in such a way that at all times you treat man, both in your person and in the person of each and every person, *also* as an end, never *only* as a means' and 'For reasonable beings are all subject to the law that each being should treat himself and all others never *only* as a means, but at all times *also* as an end in itself' (1785: 66).

36 Erling (1981: 905) translates 'sanctification' instead of salvation and, in response to allegations of blasphemy, adds: '"Santification", a technical theological term refers to the process of growth and development in the Christian life.'

37 In recent decades, this common element has been widely discussed in the literature on theology. See, among others, Schimmel 1996; Johnston 1974; Bock 1991; Waldenfels 1990 and James (1982: 419).

38 This also holds for Nathan Söderblom. Dusen (1964: 23), points out that Sundar Singh, an Indian mystic, visited Uppsala while Hammarskjöld was living there.

39 Hammarskjöld used the English edition Confucius 1951 (Brandt 1995: 230).

222   *Notes*

40   The library contains, for instance: Schweitzer 1924; 1930; 1933; 1950a; 1950b, 1951a
     1951b; and a first edition of Schweitzer's Nobel Peace Prize acceptance speech,
     obviously a gift from an admirer of Hammarskjöld.
41   See also his Address at the Annual Dinner of the Advertising Council 17 November
     1954, in CF II: 384: 'In the words of Albert Schweitzer, in his recent Nobel Peace
     Prize speech, man has become superman – in the field of technology. In other respects
     we may feel that he is less than worthy in his behaviour of being described even as
     man.'
42   The English newspaper is the *British Weekly*, in which an abridged version of the
     Murrow interview appeared (Dusen 1965: 45).
43   In this context, see also Schweitzer (1987: 321), which could be lifted directly from
     Hammarskjöld's diary: 'Whatever more than others you have received in health,
     natural gifts, working capacity, success, a beautiful childhood, harmonious family
     circumstances, you must not accept as being a matter of course. You must pay a price
     for them. You must show more than average devotion of life to life.'
44   See *Markings* (1951: 29, 68–9) 'A young man, adamant in his committed life. ...

     He had assented to a possibility in his being, of which he had had his first inkling
     when he returned from the desert. If God required anything of him, he would not
     fail. Only recently, he thought, had he begun to see more clearly, and to realize
     that the road of possibility might lead to the Cross. He knew, though, that he had
     to follow it still uncertain as to whether he was indeed "the one who shall bring it
     to pass", but certain that the answer could only be learned by following the road
     to the end. The end might be a death without significance – as well as being the
     end of the road of possibility. ...
         A young man, adamant in his commitment, who walks the road of possibility
     to the end without self-pity or demand for sympathy, fulfilling the destiny he has
     chosen – even sacrificing affection and fellowship when the others are unready
     to follow him – into a new fellowship.'

     See also Dusen (1965: 181) and McClendon (1973: 236).
45   Buber shares this conviction (see the next section, 'Martin Buber: genuine dialogue
     as a precondition of peace'). See also Weizsäcker 1967 and Schwartländer (1984a:
     28–47).
46   Hammarskjöld had the following books by Buber in his private library: 1947, 1948,
     1949, 1955, 1957, 1958 and the book by Friedman1956.
47   On his biography and work, see the contribution in the anthology by Schilpp and
     Friedman 1963, to which Buber himself 'replies' (589–639). See further Schaeder
     1966; Hodes 1971; Friedman 1999; Werner 1994; Wehr 1995b, 1996; Buber 1975 and
     Wolf 1992. Buber describes some aspects of his relationship with the UN Secretary-
     General in his memoir of Hammarskjöld, in Buber 1965.
48   See, for instance, Buber (1906: 74).
49   The dates: Hammarskjöld 1905–61; Martin Buber 1878–1965; Albert Schweitzer
     1875–1965; John Steinbeck (whom Hammarskjöld includes in this 'generation')
     1902–68.
50   See also Bartosch (1995: 181–6) refering to Karl Jasper.
51   The German edition at this point offers an excursion on Carl Friedrich von Weizsäcker's
     theory of peace (Fröhlich 2002: 224–8).

4 Connections between ethical thought and political action

1   For a more comprehensive account of working methods and structures see Fröhlich
    (2002: 232–53).
2   Lind states: 'We discovered the United Nations together' (Interview 1990: 3).

3 See also Urquhart (1987a: 125–6).
4 On the following see Urquhart (1972: 94–131); Trachtenberg 1983; Gordenker (1967a: 152–6); Smouts (1971: 66–71, 98–115); Lash (1961: 71–81); CF II: 415–59.
5 See also Cordier's appeal (1967: 19): 'His skillful negotiations with Chou En-Lai at the end of 1954 for the release of the American fliers represented the first major use of quiet diplomacy. The building of a weak case into strength, and the tactics that he employed in the successive conversations, will one day be used as an important case-study in diplomacy. This, like so many other successes in quiet diplomacy, has not yet been fully revealed to the world. It is important to the cause of peace, as well as the proper image of the man, that the whole story of his efforts should be presented to a reading world as soon as possible.'
6 The resolution talks only of 11 people, as among the 13 detained, two were civilians travelling in one of the aircraft and therefore not under UN command; they were removed from the list. Unofficially it was clear to all parties that these two were involved in some sort of undercover operation (CF II: 416). These were, however, tacitly included in the context of the resolution.
7 See his reserved approval in reply to a question on the necessity of China's Representation at the United Nations at the National Press Club, 14 April 1954, in CF II: 286–7.
8 Hammarskjöld used an Anglican edition published in 1762.
9 See *Markings* (1955: 30, 110): 'He broke fresh ground – because and only because, he had the courage to go ahead without asking whether others were following or even understood. He had no need for the divided responsibility in which others seek to be safe from ridicule, because he had been granted a faith which required no confirmation.'
10 See for instance the Address at Commencement Exercises of Amherst College, 13 June 1954, in CF II: 303–5 and the Speech to the Foreign Policy Association at a dinner given in his honour, 21 October 1953, in CF II: 100–6.
11 The full background of the crisis goes beyond the scope of this study; for details see Thomas 1967; Kyle 1991; Eden (1962: 475–657, in particular 552–629); Heikal (1973: 158–83); Urquhart (1972: 159–94); Urquart (1987a: 131–44); Ghali 1993; Volger (1995: 101–8); Schild *et al.* 1995; Heinemann and Wiggershaus 1999. For principal documents, see CF II: 304–404.
12 Incidentally, Hammarskjöld repeated these comments on 4 November in connection with the situation in Hungary (CF III: 313). For further texts on Hungary, see ibid.: 412–52. For detailed background see Urquhart (1972: 231–48) and, 'Relevance and limits of Hammarskjöld's political ethic' in Chapter 5.
13 Among the abstentions were the Soviet bloc, Egypt, the UK, France, Israel, Austria, Laos, Portugal, South Africa, Australia and New Zealand (CF III: 322).
14 See Bunche's remarks in AC UNEF 14 November 1956: 27: 'I might say, in conclusion, that we are trying to give some kind of common identification to the Force so that it can be readily identified as a United Nations Force. In addition to the arm bands and shoulder patches, we are purchasing a considerable supply of what are known as helmet liners – the liners that go in the steel helmets. These were considered by the military group yesterday. They will be painted in United Nations blue. They are light in weight, they are made of plastic, and they will look quite nice when painted with United Nations blue, with the letters "UN" in white on each side and the UN seal in front. In addition we are having UN blue helmets made so that the national units, while wearing their own uniforms, will have a common headdress.'
15 In 1959 Hammarskjöld used the simple argument of chronological priority: the Secretariat was fully occupied by the Suez Crisis, which had broken out shortly before. Moreover, the General Assembly determined the Secretary-General's priorities and scope of action (PC 21 May 1959, in CF IV: 398).

16 Pearson (1973: 260–1) reports expressing his reservations to Hammarskjöld about Egypt's rights on the withdrawal of UNEF, which Hammarskjöld and Nasser discussed on 12 November. Nasser insisted that Egypt have the unrestricted authority to order withdrawal: 'I remember reacting quite strongly, but not violently. I said, "This is going to cause trouble in the future." Hammarskjöld said: "Oh, don't worry about it, because I told him [Nasser] that condition was quite inadmissable." It did not turn out to be inadmissable eleven years later.' See 'The Hammarskjöld tradition and its adoption by his successors' in Chapter 5.

17 On the history and development of international service see Langrod 1963; Siotis 1963; Bailey 1962a; Meron 1983; Weiss 1975; Graham and Jordan 1980; Aghnides 1953.

18 On the Congo, see Franck and Carey 1963; Amirie 1967; Dayal 1976; Birnbaum 1962; Hoffmann 1962; Saksena 1978; Nolte 1995a; Meisler 1996; Gibbs 1993; Urquhart (1993a: 299–335); Lash (1961: 243–82) and Bunche 1965.

19 For different accounts of this scene see Grinevskij (1996: 483) and Taubman (2003: 475–6).

20 For a more detailed discussion of the Oxford speech see Fröhlich 2002: 322–9.

21 Peaceful coexistence as used here differs from, say, the Soviet concept with its undertones of competitiveness and other strategic considerations (Khrushchev 1959).

22 On the concept of 'detached', which evokes the mystics' specific understanding of detachment, see also Kania (2000: 259–65).

23 See also Morgenthau (1963: 122–3): 'That his conception prevailed is above all a tribute to the extraordinary qualities of the man. The triumph of one man – powerfully supported, it is true, by the universal fear of war – has served to conceal the inner weakness of the organization on behalf of which he spoke and acted. He walked on the most brittle of grounds. It was only the sureness of his step that made those grounds seem less brittle than they actually were.'

5 The Hammarskjöld tradition

1 The German edition (Fröhlich 2002: 367–72) offers further examples.

2 King and Hobbins (2003: 384) conclude: 'Dag Hammarskjöld actively deflated the role of the human rights programme of the United Nations while he served as Secretary-General. Initially he was hostile, and later merely neglectful.'

3 See Fröhlich 2002: 372–8 for a discussion of various theories.

4 For an overview see also Rovine 1970; Fosdick 1972: 77–180; Barros 1983; Grewe 1986: 93–107; Franck 1985: 117–60; Boudreau 1991: 25–101; Dicke 1998: 77–85; Dicke 1994: 127–55; Urquhart 1987a; Rivlin 1994: 49–70; Göller 1995; and Newman 1998: 37–194.

5 From an interview with David Sureck in *The Saturday Evening Post*, 21 September 1963, in CH VI: 441.

6 See AR (1971: 648–9): 'I feel more strongly than ever that the worth of the individual human being is the most unique and precious of all our assets and must be the beginning and the end of all our efforts. Governments, systems, ideologies, and institutions come and go, but humanity remains.'

7 From the transcript of Cooke on '"International Zone" – A Conversation with U Thant, September 1963', in CH VI: 427.

8 'Statement in the General Assembly accepting a full term as Secretary-General, 30 November 1962', in CH VI: 254.

9 See Waldheim (1978: 26–7): '... Dag Hammarskjöld was an unusual person, an intellectual, a visionary, a reputable economist.'

10 See UN Doc. A/50/60–S/1995/1 Supplement to an Agenda for Peace. See also 'An Agenda for Development', in UN Doc. A/48/935 and the 'Agenda for Democratization', UN Docs. A/50/332 and A/51/512.

11 See the speech on the occasion of an exhibition on Hammarskjöld, UN Doc. SG/SM 6058, of 18 September 1996: 1–2.

12 In addition to his autobiography, U Thant also wanted to write a book titled *An Ethic for our Time*. See Muller (1985: 137).

13 Institute of International Studies, University of California, Kofi Annan, Interview, April 1998, at http://www.globetrotter.berkeley.edu/UN/Annan/annan-con2.html.

14 See 'Press encounter following reappointment for a further five year term as Secretary-General', 29 June 2001: 'I think if there is a similarity I believe that we both believe firmly in the principles of the Charter. We both believe in this Organization and what it stands for. We both believe that there is an obligation to speak and stand out for the weak and to have a certain understanding and compassion for the human condition. But it is not enough to recognize that, you should not stop there but go out and do something about it, and encourage others to join you in trying to make a difference.'

15 The German edition (Fröhlich 2002: 412–19) at this point offers a more detailed discussion of the peacekeeping debate in the 1990s.

16 See Schachter (1983: 49), according to which Hammarskjöld typically expressed 'basic principles in terms of opposing tendencies'.

17 See the lecture at the Centre for Islamic Studies at Oxford University, UN Doc. SG/SM/7048, 28 June 1999 and see his speech at the University of Teheran, UN Doc. SG/SM/6419, 9 December 1997. Fröhlich 2002: 420–3 offers a more detailed chapter on the dialogue among civilizations.

18 See his speech at the Tanenbaum Center for Interreligious Understanding, UN Doc. SG/SM/6541, 27 April 1998 as well as Birnbaum (1997: 300).

19 See his reform programmes UN Doc. A/51/950, 14 July 1997 and UN Doc. A/57/387, 9 September 2002 as well as the measures proposed in the Report of the High-level Panel on Threats, Challenges and Change; A/59/565, 2 December 2004. See also UN Doc. SG/SM/6410, 9 January 1997: 'Service with the United Nations is more than just a job. It is a calling. No one joins the Secretariat to become rich and famous, to be appreciated and applauded, to live a life of ease and conduct.'

20 See the comprehensive report of the Independent Inquiry Committee into the United Nations Oil-for-Food-Programme, *The Management of the United Nations Oil-for-Food Programme*, New York 7 September 2005 (www.iic-offp.org).

21 Press Release of the Independent Inquiry Committee into the United Nations Oil-for-Food Programme, 7 September 2005: 2 (www.iic-offp.org).

22 Leadership in that sense may simply mean asking questions, as Hammarskjöld pointed out in an address at Lund university: 'Leadership – the word I have used to designate what may come instead of superior power – is a dangerous word if one does not keep in mind that the most influential leaders in the European cultural tradition were askers of questions like Socrates or the carpenter's son from Nazareth' (Address at Lund University, 4 May 1959, in CF IV: 385).

23 See, for instance, the two speeches at the World Economic Forum in Davos: UN Doc. SG/SM/6153 and UN Doc. SG/SM/6881/Rev. 1, 1 February 1999, which formed the basis of the Global Compact initiative.

Bibliography

Documents from the United Nations archives are referred to as UNA (...). Documents from Hammarskjöld's private archives in Sweden are referred to KB DHS (...). Individual documents of the United Nations, the Preparatory Commission, etc. and other official documents are cited as UN Doc. (...) followed by the appropriate details. Resolutions of the General Assembly are cited as GA Res. (...) and minutes of the General Assembly meetings as GAOR (...) (Stölken, 1991).

Abbreviations used:

AJIL	American Journal of International Law
ASIL	American Society of International Law
AVR	Archiv des Völkerrechts
EA	Europa-Archiv
EPIL	Encyclopaedia of Public International Law
FA	Foreign Affairs
FAZ	Frankfurter Allgemeine Zeitung
FP	Foreign Policy
GYIL	German Yearbook of International Law
IA	International Affairs
IO	International Organization
IPG	Internationale Politik und Gesellschaft
PVS	Politische Vierteljahresschrift
VN	Vereinte Nationen
ZParl	Zeitschrift für Politikwissenschaft
ZPol	Zeitschrift für Politikwissenschaft

Aghnides, T. (1953), 'Standards of Conduct of the International Civil Servant', *International Review of Administrative Sciences*, Vol. 19, pp. 179–87.
Åhman, S. (1958), 'Mr. Hammarskjöld's Not-So-Quiet Diplomacy', *The Reporter*, 4 September, p. 12.
—— (1963), *Impressions of Dag Hammarskjöld*, Columbia University: Oral History Research Office.

Ajami, F. (1996), 'The Mark of Bosnia: Boutros-Ghali's Reign of Indifference', *FA*, Vol. 75, No. 3, pp. 62–4.

Albrecht, U. (ed.) (1998), *Die Vereinten Nationen am Scheideweg: Von der Staaten-organisation zur internationalen Gemeinschaftswelt?*, Hamburg: Lit.

Amirie, A. (1967), *The United Nations Intervention in the Congo Crisis 1960–1961: With Special Emphasis on the Political Role of the Late Secretary-General, Dag Hammarskjöld*, (Diss.). Carbondale, IL: S.N.

Annan, K. (1997), '"Ich bin ein Glücklicher Narr": Interview mit dem UN-Generalsekretär', *Die Zeit*, 25 July, p. 9.

—— (1998a), 'Challenges of the New Peacekeeping', in Otunnu and Doyle (1998: 169–87).

—— (1998b), Interview, *Time Magazine*, 9 March, p. 24.

—— (1998c), 'Walking the International Tightrope', *The New York Times*, 19 September, p. 19.

—— (1999), 'Two Concepts of Sovereignty', *The Economist*, 18 September, pp. 49–50.

—— (2004), *Die Vereinten Nationen im 21. Jahrhundert: Reden und Beiträge 1997–2003*, edited by Manuel Fröhlich, Wiesbaden: VS Verlag.

—— (2005), *In Larger Freedom: Towards Development, Security and Human Rights for all. Report of the Secretary-General*; A/59/2005, 21 March, New York: United Nations.

Anzenbacher, A. (2001), *Einführung in die Ethik*, Düsseldorf: Patmos.

Arendt, H. (1958), *The Human Condition*, Chicago, IL: University of Chicago Press.

—— (1969), *On Violence*, New York: Harcourt, Brace & World.

—— (1994), *Über die Revolution*, 4th edn, Munich, Zurich: Piper.

Ascoli, M. (1956), 'The Price of Peace Mongering', *The Reporter*, 29 November, p. 10.

—— (1965), 'On Reading Hammarskjöld', *The Reporter*, 20 May, pp. 37–40.

Auden, W.H. (1964), 'Foreword', in Hammarskjöld (1964: vii–xxiv).

Aulén, G. (1969), *Dag Hammarskjöld's White Book: An Analysis of Markings*, Philadelphia, PA: Fortress Press.

Austin, J.L. (1962), *How to do Things with Words*, 2nd edn, Cambridge, MA: Harvard University Press.

Axelrod, R. (ed.) (1976a), *Structure of Decision: The Cognitive Maps of Political Elites*, Princeton, NJ, New York: University Press.

—— (1976b), 'The Analysis of Cognitive Maps', in Axelrod (1976a: 55–73).

Baehr, P.R. and Gordenker, L. (1994), *The United Nations in the 1990s*, 2nd edn, Basingstoke, London: Macmillan.

Bähr, H.-W. (ed.) (1987), *Albert Schweitzer: Leben, Werk und Denken 1905–1965 mitgeteilt in seinen Briefen*, Heidelberg: Schneider.

Bailey, S. D. (1962a), *The Secretariat of the United Nations*, United Nations Study 11, New York: Carnegie Endowment for International Peace.

—— (1962b), *The Troika and the Future of the UN*, International Conciliation, New York: Carnegie Endowment for International Peace.

—— (1966), 'The United Nations Secretariat', in Luard (1966: 92–103).

Barnes, D. (1985), *Antiphon*, 2nd edn, Frankfurt a.M.: Suhrkamp.

Barros, J. (1983), 'The Importance of Secretaries-General of the United Nations', in Jordan (1983a: 25–37).

—— (1989), *Trygve Lie and the Cold War: The UN Secretary-General pursues Peace 1946–1953*, DeKalb, IL: Northern Illinois University Press.

Bartosch, U. (1995), *Weltinnenpolitik: Zur Theorie des Friedens von Carl Friedrich von Weizsäcker*, Beiträge zur politischen Wissenschaft 86, Berlin: Duncker & Humblot.

Barudio, G. (1989), 'Dag Hammarskjöld – dem Frieden auf der Spur', in Neumann (1989b: 96–177).

Bauer, F. (2005), *Kofi Annan: Ein Leben*, Frankfurt: S. Fischer.

Bauer, G. (1982), 'Der unterschätzte Generalsekretär. Zur Amtszeit Kurt Waldheims (1972–1981)', *VN*, Vol. 30, pp. 1–5.

Beck, W. and Schmid, R. (eds) (1967), *Streit um den Frieden*, Mainz, Munich: Matthias-Grünewald-Verlag.

Becker, M. (1998), 'Die Eigensinnigkeit des Politischen. Hannah Arendt über Macht und Herrschaft', in Imbusch (1998: 167–81).

Becker, W. and Oelmüller, W. (eds) (1987), *Politik und Moral: Entmoralisierung des Politischen?*, Paderborn: Schöningh.

Beigbeder, Y. (1988), *Threats to the International Civil Servant*, London, New York: Pinter.

Benton, B. (ed.) (1996), *Soldiers for Peace: Fifty Years of United Nations Peacekeeping*, New York: Facts on File.

Bercovitch, J. (1996), *Resolving International Conflicts: The Theory and Practice of Mediation*, London: Lynne Rienner Publishers.

Berendsohn, W.A. (1962), 'Dag Hammarskjöld und sein Leben für die Humanität', *Universitas*, Vol. 9, pp. 977–90.

—— (1964), *Dag Hammarskjöld und sein Werk*, Dortmunder Vorträge Reihe A Heft 66, Dortmund: Kulturamt.

Bergson, H. (1921), *Essai sur les données immédiates de la conscience*, Paris: Alcan.

—— (1932), *Les deux sources de la morale et de la religion*, Paris: Alcan.

—— (1954), *The Two Sources of Morality and Religion*, New York: Doubleday Anchor Books.

—— (1992), *Die beiden Quellen der Moral und der Religion*, Frankfurt: Fischer.

—— (1993), *Denken und schöpferisches Wollen: Aufsätze und Vorträge*, Hamburg: Europäische Verlagsanstalt.

—— (1994), *Schöpferische Entwicklung*, Nobelpreis für Literatur 27, Zurich: Coron-Verlag.

Berridge, G.R. and Jennings, A. (eds) (1985), *Diplomacy at the UN*, Basingstoke, London: Macmillan.

Beskow, B. (1969), *Dag Hammarskjöld: Strictly Personal*, Garden City, NY: Doubleday.

Bettati, M. (1991), 'Art. 97', in Cot, J.-P. and Pellet, A. (eds), *La Charte des Nations Unies: Commentaire article par article*, Paris: Economica, pp. 1307–15.

Bettauer, R.J (1972), 'A More Powerful Secretary-General for the United Nations?', *ASIL Proceedings*, Vol. 66, pp. 78–89.

Beyschlag, K. (1980a), 'Dag Hammarskjöld – ein protestantischer Mystiker unserer Tage', in Reller and Seitz (1980: 21–53).

—— (1980b), 'Was heißt mystische Erfahrung?', in Reller and Seitz (1980: 169–96).

—— (1984), 'Dag Hammarskjöld', in Ruhbach and Sudbrack (1984: 317–37).

Bindschedler, R.L. (1981), 'Good Offices', *EPIL*, Vol. 1, pp. 67–9.

Birnbaum, K.E. (1962), 'Hammarskjöld und die Funktionen der Vereinten Nationen während der Kongo-Krise', *EA*, Vol. 17, pp. 533–48.

—— (1997), 'Towards Cooperative World Politics: Utopian Realism and the Requirements of Political Leadership', in Leifland *et al.* (1997: 289–305).

—— (2000), *Die innere Welt des jungen Dag Hammarskjöld: Einblicke in den Werdegang eines Menschen*, Münster: Agenda-Verlag.

Blondel, J. (1987), *Political Leadership: Towards a General Analysis*, London: Sage.

Bock, E. (1991), *Meine Augen haben dich geschaut: Mystik in den Religionen der Welt*, Zurich: Benziger.

Boekle, H., Rittberger, V. and Wagner, W. (1999), *Normen und Außenpolitik: Konstruktivistische Außenpolitiktheorie*, Tübinger Arbeitspapiere zur internationalen Politik und Friedensforschung 34, Tübingen: Abteilung Internationale Beziehungen/Friedens- und Konfliktforschung, Institut für Politikwissenschaft.

Boldt, J. (1990), *Johannes vom Kreuz: Sein Leben in Kontemplation und Aktion*, Mainz: Matthias-Grünewald-Verlag.

Booth, K. (1995), 'Human Wrongs and International Relations', *IA*, Vol. 71, pp. 103–26.

Borchert, B. (1997), *Mystik. Das Phänomen – Die Geschichte – Neue Wege*, Freiburg, Basel, Vienna: Herder.

Bottenberg, P. (1959), *Die politischen Leitungsfunktionen der Generalsekretäre internationaler Organisationen*, Göttingen: Diss.

Boudreau, T.E. (1991), *Sheathing the Sword: The U.N. Secretary-General and the Prevention of International Conflict*, New York: Greenwood Press.

Bourantonis, D. and Wiener, J. (eds) (1995), *The United Nations in the New World Order: The World Organization at Fifty*, Basingstoke, London: Macmillan.

Bourloyannis, M.-C. (1990), 'Fact-finding by the Secretary-General of the United Nations', *New York Journal of International Law and Politics*, Vol. 23, pp. 641–69.

Boutros-Ghali, B. (1996a), 'Global Leadership after the Cold War', *FA*, Vol. 75, No. 2, pp. 86–98.

—— (1996b), 'Le Secrétaire général des Nations unies: Entre l'urgence et la durée', *Politique Étrangère*, Vol. 61, pp. 407–14.

—— (1999), *Unvanquished. A U.S.–U.N. Saga*, New York: Random House.

Brandt, R. v. d. (1995), 'Schicksalsmäßiges und schöpferisches Wollen. Dag Hammarskjöld und Meister Eckhart', *Studies in Spirituality*, Vol. 5, pp. 220–31.

Bring, O. (2003), 'Dag Hammarskjöld and the Issue of Humanitarian Intervention', in Petman and Klabbers (2003: 485–517).

Brown, C. (1994), 'International Ethics: Fad, Fantasy or Field?', *Paradigms*, Vol. 8, pp. 1–12.

Buber, M. (1906), 'Elements of the Interhuman', in Buber (1998: 62–78).

—— (1909), 'Die Lehre vom Tao', in Buber (1953: 44–83).

—— (1918), 'Mein Weg zum Chassidismus', in Buber (1953: 179–96).

—— (1929), 'Dialogue', in Buber (1979: 17–52).

—— (1936), 'The Question to the Single One', in Buber (1979: 60–108).

—— (1938), 'What is Man?', in: Buber (1979: 148–248).

—— (1947), *Tales of the Hasidim: The Early Masters*, New York: Schocken Books.

—— (1948), *Tales of the Hasidim: The Late Masters*, New York: Schocken Books

—— (1949), *Die Erzählungen des Chassidim*, Zurich: Manesse Verlag.

—— (1952), 'Hoffnung für diese Stunde', in Buber (1953: 313–26).

—— (1953), *Hinweise, Gesammelte Essays*, Zurich: Manesse Verlag.

—— (1955), *Die Legende des Baalschem*, Zurich: Manesse Verlag.

—— (1957), *Pointing the Way*, New York: Harper.

—— (1958), *Hasidism and Modern Man*, edited and translated by Maurice Friedman, New York: Horizon Press.

—— (1962), 'Erinnerung an Hammarskjöld', in Buber (1965: 33–6).

—— (1963a), *Pointing the Way*, New York, Evanston, IL: Harper Torchbooks.

—— (1963b), 'The Demand of the Spirit and Historical Reality', in Buber (1963a: 177–91).

—— (1963c), 'The Validity and Limitation of the Political Principle', in Buber (1963a: 208–19).

—— (1963d), 'What is to be Done?', in Buber (1963a: 109–11).

—— (1963e), 'Genuine Dialogue and the Possibilities of Peace', in Buber (1963a: 232–9).

—— (1963f), 'Hope for this Hour', in Buber (1963a: 220–9).

—— (1963g), 'Abstract and Concrete', in Buber (1963a: 230–1).

—— (1963h), 'Gandhi, Politics, and Us', in Buber (1963: 126–38).

—— (1963i), 'With a Monist', in Buber (1963a: 25–30).

—— (1965), *Nachlese*, Heidelberg: Schneider.

—— (1966), *I and Thou*, translated by R.G. Smith, 2nd edn, Edinburgh: T. & T. Clark.

—— (1975), *Briefwechsel aus sieben Jahrzehnten*, Vol. II: 1938–65/Vol. III: 1938–65, edited by G. Schraeder, Heidelberg: Schneider.

—— (1979), *Between Man and Man*, translated and introduced by R.G. Smith, Glasgow: Collins Fount Paperbacks.

—— (1985), *Pfade in Utopia: Über Gemeinschaft und deren Verwirklichung*, 3rd edn, Heidelberg: Schneider.

—— (1994a), *Das dialogische Prinzip*, 7th edn, Darmstadt: Wissenschaftliche Buchgesellschaft.

—— (1994b), *Mystische Zeugnisse aller Zeiten und Völker*, edited by P. Sloterdijk, 2nd edn, Munich: Eugen Diederichs.

—— (1994c), 'Zur Geschichte des dialogischen Prinzips', in Buber (1994a: 301–20).

—— (1998), *The Knowledge of Man. Selected Essays*, Amherst, New York: Humanity Books.

Buchheim, H. (1957), 'Ernst Niekischs Ideologie des Widerstands', *Vierteljahreshefte für Zeitgeschichte*, Vol. 5, No. 4, pp. 332–61.

—— (1991), *Politik und Ethik*, Otto von Freising Lectures, Vol. 3, Munich: Oldenbourg.

Bunche, R.J. (1965), 'The United Nations Operation in the Congo', in Cordier and Foote (1965: 119–38).

—— (1995), *Selected Speeches and Writings*, edited by Charles P. Henry, Ann Arbor, MI: University of Michigan Press.

Bundesakademie für Sicherheitspolitik (ed.) (2004), *Sicherheitspolitik in neuen Dimensionen*, Hamburg: Verlag E.S. Mittler & Sohn.

Burns, J.M. (1978), *Leadership*, New York: Harper and Row.

Bush, G. (1991), 'Remarks at Maxwell Air Force Base', *EA* Vol. 46, pp. D 254–8.

Buzan, B. (1991), *People, States and Fear: An Agenda for International Security Studies in the Post-Cold War Era*, Boulder, CO: Rienner.

Byman, D.L. and Pollack, K.M. (2001), 'Let Us Now Praise Great Men: Bringing the Statesman Back In', *International Security*, Vol. 25, No. 4, pp. 107–46.

Caldwell, D. and McKeown, T.J. (eds) (1993), *Diplomacy, Force, and Leadership. Essays in Honor of Alexander L. George*, Boulder, CO, San Francisco, CA, Oxford: Westview Press.

Canovan, M. (1983), 'A Case of Distorted Communication: A Note on Habermas and Arendt', *Political Theory*, Vol. 11, pp. 105–16.

Chatami, M. (1999), 'Dialog der Zivilisationen', *Die literarische Welt*, 7 August, pp. 3–4.

Chekel, J.T. (1998), 'The Constructivist Turn in International Relations Theory', *World Politics* Vol. 50, pp. 324–48.

Clark, H. (1962), *The Ethical Mysticism of Albert Schweitzer: A Study of the Sources and Significance of Schweitzer's Philosophy of Civilization*, Boston, MA: Beacon Press.

Claude, I.L. (1964), *Swords into Plowshares: The Problems and Progress of International Organization*, 3rd edn, New York: Random House.
—— (1993), 'Reflections on the Role of the UN Secretary-General', in Rivlin and Gordenker (1993: 249–60).
—— (1966), 'Collective Legitimization as a Political Function of the United Nations', in Goodrich and Kay (1973: 209–21).
Clausen, O. (1964), 'Clues to the Hammarskjold Riddle', *The New York Times Magazine*, 28 June, pp. 18, 37.
Commission on Global Governance (1995), *Our Global Neighbourhood: The Report of the Commission on Global Governance*, Oxford: Oxford University Press.
Confucius (1951), *The Unwobbling Pivot, The Great Digest, The Analects*, translation and commentary by E. Pound, New York: New Directions Publishing Corp.
Cooper, R. (1993), 'Gibt es eine neue Welt-Ordnung?', *EA*, Vol. 48, pp. 507–16.
Cordier, A.W. (1960), 'The Role of the Secretary-General', in Swift (1960: 1–14).
—— (1961), 'Dag Hammarskjöld', *The Christian Century*, 25 October, p. 1271.
—— (1964), *Recollections of Dag Hammarskjöld and the United Nations*, New York: Columbia University.
—— (1967), 'Motivations and Methods of Dag Hammarskjöld', in Cordier and Maxwell (1967), pp. 1–21.
—— (1972), *Commemoration Talk on the Tenth Anniversary of the Death of Dag Hammarskjöld*, mimeo, Uppsala: Dag Hammarskjöld Foundation.
Cordier, A.W and Foote, W. (eds) (1965), *The Quest for Peace: The Dag Hammarskjöld Memorial Lectures*, New York, London: Columbia University Press.
—— (1969), *Public Papers of the Secretaries-General of the United Nations: Volume I: Trygve Lie 1946–1953*, New York, London: Columbia University Press.
—— (1972–5), *Public Papers of the Secretaries-General of the United Nations: Volumes II–V: Dag Hammarskjöld 1953–1961*, New York, London: Columbia University Press.
Cordier, A.W and Harrelson, M. (eds) (1976–7), *Public Papers of the Secretaries-General of the United Nations. Volumes VI–VIII: U Thant 1961–1971*, New York, London: Columbia University Press.
Cordier A.W. and Maxwell, K.L. (eds) (1967), *Paths to World Order*, New York, London: Columbia University Press.
Cot, J.-P. and Pellet, A. (1991), *La Charte des Nations Unies: Commentaire article par article*, Paris: Economica.
Cox, R.W. (1969), 'The Executive Head: An Essay on Leadership in International Organizations', *IO*, Vol. 23, pp. 205–30.
Cox, R.W. and Jacobson, H.K. (1974), *The Anatomy of Influence: Decision Making in International Organizations*, New Haven, CT, London: Yale University Press.
Cuéllar, J.P. de (1991), *Anarchy or Order: Annual Reports 1982–1991*, New York: United Nations.
—— (1995), 'The Role of the UN Secretary-General', in Roberts and Kingsbury (1995: 125–42).
D'Amato, A. (1984), 'Good Faith', *EPIL*, Vol. 7, pp. 107–9.
Dahlgren, S. (ed.) (1992), *Nathan Söderblom as a European*, Uppsala: Church of Sweden Research Dept.
Davies, J.G.W. (1953), 'The Work of the Secretariat', in Eagleton and Swift (1953: 135–56).
Dayal, R. (1976), *Mission for Hammarskjold. The Congo Crisis*, Princeton, NJ: Oxford University Press.

Delbrück, J. (1964), *Die Entwicklung des Verhältnisses von Sicherheitsrat und Vollversammlung der Vereinten Nationen*, Kiel: Diss.

—— (ed.) (1997), *New Trends in International Lawmaking – International 'Legislation' in the Public Interest*, Berlin: Duncker & Humblot.

Deleuze, G. (1997), *Henri Bergson zur Einführung*, 2nd edn, Hamburg: Junius.

Dicke, K. (1993), 'Internationale Kooperation als politikwissenschaftliche Kategorie', *Christiana Albertina*, Vol. 36, pp. 5–16.

—— (1994), *Effizienz und Effektivität internationaler Organisationen. Darstellung und Kritik eines Topos im Reformprozeß der Vereinten Nationen*, Berlin: Duncker & Humblot.

—— (1998), 'Der "starke Generalsekretär" – Was bewirkt der Mann an der Spitze der UN-Administration?', in Albrecht (1998: 70–88).

Dicke, K. and Fröhlich. M. (eds) (2005), *Wege multilateraler Diplomatie: Politik, Handlungsmöglichkeiten und Entscheidungsstrukturen im UN-System*, Baden-Baden: Nomos.

Dinzelbacher, P. (ed.) (1998), *Wörterbuch der Mystik*, 2nd edn, Stuttgart: Kröner.

Dixon, P. (1967), 'Diplomacy at the United Nations', in Kay (1967a: 81–91).

Dobhan, U. and Körner, R. (1995), 'Einführung', in Johannes vom Kreuz (1995: 9–18).

Drummond, E. (1931), 'The Secretariat of the League of Nations', *Public Administration*, Vol. 9, pp. 228–35.

Dubouis, L. (1991), 'Art. 101', in Cot and Pellet (1991: 1349–63).

Dunne, T. (1988), *Inventing International Society: A History of the English School*, London: Macmillan.

Durch, W.J. (ed.) (1993), *The Evolution of UN Peacekeeping*. Case Studies and Comparative Analysis, New York: St Martin's Press.

Dusen, H.P. van (1965), 'Dag Hammarskjöld's Spiritual Pilgrimage', *Theology Today*, Vol. 22, pp. 433–47.

—— (1967), 'Dag Hammarskjöld: The Inner Person', in Cordier and Maxwell (1967: 22–44).

—— (1969), *Dag Hammarskjöld: The Man and his Faith*, New York, London: Harper & Row.

Dworkis, M.B. (1955), 'Administrative Matters', Eagleton and Swift (1955: 174–208).

Eagleton, C. and Swift, R.N. (1955), *1954 Review of United Nations Affairs*, New York: Oceana.

Eckert, P.W. (1981), 'Meister Eckhart. Spekulative Mystik', in Sudbrack (1981: 95–112).

Eden, A. (1962), *Memoirs*. Vol. 2, London: Cassell & Company Ltd.

Eisenhower, D.D. (1964), *Die Jahre im Weißen Haus 1953–1956*, Düsseldorf, Vienna: Econ-Verlag.

Ekman, B. (1923), *Strödda blad ur Bertil Ekmans efterlämnade papper*, Stockholm: P. A. Norstedt & Söners.

Elaraby, N. (1987), 'The Office of the Secretary-General and the Maintenance of International Peace and Security', in UNITAR (1987: 177–209).

Erling, B. (1981), 'Discipleship at the United Nations: Hammarskjöld's Religious Commitment', *The Christian Century*, 16 September, pp. 902–6.

—— (1987), 'Dag Hammarskjold's Use of Thomas à Kempis', *Lutheran Quarterly*, Vol. 1, pp. 343–57.

—— (1999), *A Reader's Guide to Dag Hammarskjöld's Waymarks*, St Peter, MN: Gustavus Adolphus College.

Etzersdorfer, I. (1997), '"Persönlichkeit" und "Politik": Zur Interaktion politischer und seelischer Faktoren in der interdisziplinären "Political Leadership"-Forschung', *Österreichische Zeitschrift für Politikwissenschaft*, Vol. 26, pp. 378–80.

Falk, R. (1999), 'Hans Küng's Crusade: Framing a Global Ethic', *International Journal of Politics, Culture and Society*, Vol. 13, No. 1, pp. 63–81.

Falkman, K. (1999), 'Signposts in the Wrong Direction. W.H. Auden's Misinterpretations of Dag Hammarskjöld's Markings', *Times Literary Supplement*, 10 September, pp. 14–15.

Fassmann, K. (ed.) (1978), *Die Großen der Weltgeschichte: Vol. XI Einstein bis King*, Munich: Kindler Verlag.

Fiedler, J. (1994), 'Art. 97–99', in Simma (1994: 1019–57).

Finger, S.M. and Saltzman, A.A. (1990), *Bending with the Winds: Kurt Waldheim and the United Nations*, New York: Praeger.

Finnemore, M. and Sikkink, K. (1998), 'International Norms Dynamics and Political Change', *IO*, Vol. 52, pp. 887–917.

Foote, W. (ed.) (1963), *Servant of Peace: A Selection of the Speeches and Statements of Dag Hammarskjold*, New York: Harper & Row.

Fosdick, R.B. (1972), *The League and the United Nations after Fifty Years. The Six Secretaries-General*, Newtown, CT: Raymond B. Fosdick.

Franck, T.M. (1984), 'Finding a Voice: How the Secretary-General makes himself heard in the Councils of the Nations', in Makarczyk (1984: 482–91).

—— (1985), *Nation against Nation. What Happened to the U.N. and What the US can do About it*, New York: Oxford: Oxford University Press.

—— (1987), 'The prerogative powers of the Secretary-General', in Norton (1987: 5.1–5.20).

—— (1995), 'The Secretary-General's Role in Conflict Resolution: Past, Present and Pure Conjecture', *European Journal of International Law*, Vol. 6, pp. 360–87.

Franck, T.M. and Carey, J. (1963), *The Legal Aspects of the United Nations Action in the Congo*, New York: Oceana Publications.

Franck, T.M. and Nolte, G. (1995), 'The Good Offices of the UN Secretary-General', in Roberts and Kingsbury (1995: 143–82).

Friedman, M. (1956), *Martin Buber*, Chicago, IL: University of Chicago Press.

—— (1999), *Begegnung auf dem schmalen Grat. Martin Buber – ein Leben*, Münster: Agenda-Verlag.

Friedman, W.G. (1964), The Changing Structure of International Law, London: Stevens.

Friedrichs, J. (1985), *Methoden der empirischen Sozialforschung*, 13th edn, Opladen: Westdeutscher Verlag.

Fröhlich, M. (1997a), *Sprache als Instrument politischer Führung: Helmut Kohls Berichte zur Lage der Nation im geteilten Deutschland*, Munich: Forschungsgruppe Deutschland.

—— (1997b), 'Der alte und der neue UNO-Generalsekretär', *Außenpolitik*, Vol. 48, pp. 301–9.

—— (1998), 'Zur Friedensmission von UN-Generalsekretär Kofi Annan in Bagdad: Gewagte Pirouetten auf sehr dünnem Eis', *Das Parlament*, 3 April, p. 19.

—— (2001a), 'A Fully Integrated Vision. Politics and the Arts in the Dag Hammarskjöld – Barbara Hepworth Correspondence', *Development Dialogue*, No. 1, pp. 17–57.

—— (2001b), 'Keeping Track of UN Peacekeeping – Suez, Srebrenica, Rwanda and the Brahimi Report', in *Max Planck Yearbook of United Nations Law 5*, pp. 185–248.

234   *Bibliography*

—— (2002), *Dag Hammarskjöld und die Vereinten Nationen: Die politische Ethik des UNO-Generalsekretärs*, Paderborn: Schöningh.

—— (2005), 'Zwischen Verwaltung und Politik: Die Arbeit des UN-Sekretariats', in Dicke and Fröhlich (2005: 41–63).

Früh, W. (1991), *Inhaltsanalyse: Theorie und Praxis*, 3rd edn, Munich: Ölschläger.

Gadamer, H.-G. (1972), 'Hermeneutik als praktische Philosophie', in Riedel (1972: 325–44).

George, A.L. and George, J.L. (1964), *Woodrow Wilson and Colonel House: A Personality Study*, New York: Dover.

Gerhardt, V. (1995), *Immanuel Kants Entwurf 'Zum ewigen Frieden': Eine Theorie der Politik*, Darmstadt: Wissenschaftliche Buchgesellschaft.

Gerwin, E. (1972), 'Zehn Jahre U Thant', *VN*, Vol. 20, pp. 12–15.

Ghali, M. (1993), 'United Nations Emergency Force', in Durch (1993: 104–30).

Gibbs, D. N. (1993), 'Dag Hammarskjöld, the United Nations, and the Congo Crisis of 1960–1. A Reinterpretation', *Journal of Modern African Studies*, Vol. 31, pp. 163–74.

Gillett, N. (1970), *Dag Hammarskjöld*, The Great Nobel Prizes, Geneva: Edito-Service.

Goldstein, J. and Keohane, R.O. (eds) (1993a), *Ideas and Foreign Policy. Beliefs, Institutions, and Political Change*, Ithaca, NY, London: Cornell University Press.

—— (1993b), 'Ideas and Foreign Policy: An Analytical Framework', in Goldstein and Keohane (1993a: 3–30).

Göller, J.-T. (1995), *Anwälte des Friedens. Die UNO und ihre sechs Generalsekretäre*, Bonn: Dietz.

Goodrich, L.M. (1967), 'The Political Role of the Secretary-General', in Goodrich and Kay (1967: 127–41).

Goodrich, L.M. and Kay, D.A. (eds) (1973), *International Organization. Politics and Process*, London: University of Wisconsin Press.

Goodrich, L.M., Hambro, E.I. and Simons, A.P. (1969), *Charter of the United Nations*. Commentary and Documents, 3rd edn, New York, London: Columbia University Press.

Gordenker, L. (1967a), *The UN Secretary-General and the Maintenance of Peace*, Columbia University Studies in International Organization 4, New York, London: Columbia University Press.

—— (1967b), 'U Thant and the Office of U.N. Secretary-General', *International Journal*, Vol. 22, pp. 1–16.

—— (1993a), 'The UN Secretary-General: Limits, Potentials, and Leadership', in Rivlin and Gordenker (1993: 261–82).

—— (1993b), 'The UN Secretary-General. Intellectual Leadership and Maintaining Peace', *International Spectator*, Vol. 47, pp. 634–8.

Gordon, M.R. and Sciolino, E. (1998), 'How the U.S. got What it Wanted from Iraq and Resolved its Own Internal Debate', *The New York Times*, 25 February, p. 11.

Gorgé, R. (1988), '"Wie ich ihn erlebte": Zur Causa Waldheim', *VN*, Vol. 36, pp. 11–13.

Göttelmann, W. (1994), 'Art. 101', in Simma (1994: 1076–101).

Goulding,M. (1993) 'The Evolution of United Nations Peacekeeping', *IA*, Vol. 69, pp. 451–64.

Grace, S.E. (1987), 'About a Tragic Business: The Djuna Barnes–Dag Hammarskjöld Letters', *Development Dialogue*, Vol. 2, pp.1–117.

Graevenitz, J. von (1967), 'Persönliche Voraussetzungen der Friedfertigkeit', in Beck and Schmid (1967: 11–30).

Graham, N.A. and Jordan, R.S. (eds) (1980), *The International Civil Service Changing Roles and Concepts*, New York: Pergamon in association with UNITAR.

Gräßer, E. (1997a), *Studien zu Albert Schweitzer*. Gesammelte Aufsätze, edited by Andreas Mühling, Beiträge zur Albert-Schweitzer-Forschung 6, Bodenheim: Philo.

—— (1997b), 'Zum Stichwort "Interimsethik": Eine notwendige Korrektur', in Gräßer (1997a: 51–63).

—— (1997c), 'Mystik und Ethik: Ihr Zusammenhang im Denken Albert Schweitzers (Thesen)', in Gräßer (1997a: 91–4).

Gray, K.R. (1987), 'United Nations Notebook. The Relationship of Dag Hammarskjöld with the Press', *Development Dialogue*, No. 1, pp. 33–58.

Greenwood, C. (1993), 'Gibt es ein Recht auf humanitäre Intervention?', *EA*, Vol. 48, pp. 93–106.

Greschat, M. (ed.) (1985), *Gestalten der Kirchengeschichte, Vol. 10: Die neueste Zeit 3.1.*, Bonn: Kohlhammer.

Grewe, W.G. (1986), 'Dag Hammarskjöld und seine Nachfolger', in Opitz and Rittberger (1986: 93–107).

Grinevskij, O. (1996), *Tauwetter: Entspannung, Krisen und Neue Eiszeit*, Berlin: Siedler.

Gross, E. (1964), *Dag Hammarskjöld as Secretary-General*, New York: Columbia University, Oral History Research Office.

—— (1969), *The Reminiscences of Ernest Gross*, New York: Columbia University, Oral History Research Office.

Günzler, C. (ed.) (1990), *Albert Schweitzer heute: Brennpunkte seines Denkens*, Tübingen: Katzmann.

—— (1996), *Albert Schweitzer: Einführung in sein Denken*, Munich: Beck.

Haas, A.M. (1984), 'Meister Eckhart', in Ruhbach and Sudbrack (1984: 156–70).

—— (1995), *Meister Eckhart als normative Gestalt geistlichen Lebens*, 2nd edn, Freiburg: Johannes Verlag.

—— (1996), *Mystik als Aussage. Erfahrungs-, Denk- und Redeformen christlicher Mystik*, Frankfurt a.M.: Suhrkamp.

Haass, R.N. (1995), 'Paradigm Lost', *FA*, Vol. 74, No. 1, pp. 43–58.

Habermas, J. (1991), *Philosophisch-politische Profile*, 2nd edn, Frankfurt a. M.: Suhrkamp.

Hall, M.H. (1969), 'A Conversation with Ralph Bunche: The Psychology of Humanity', *Psychology Today*, April, pp. 48–58.

Hamilton, T.J. (1950), 'The U.N. and Trygve Lie', *FA*, Vol. 19, No. 1, pp. 67–77.

—— (1962), 'Dag Hammarskjoelds letzter Flug: Das Untersuchungsergebnis der Vereinten Nationen', *VN*, Vol. 10, pp. 139–45.

Hammarskjöld, Å. (1930), 'The Permanent Court of International Justice and its Place in International Relations', *Journal of the Royal Institute of International Affairs*, Vol. 9, pp. 567–97.

—— (1935), 'Persönliche Eindrücke aus Walther Schückings Richtertätigkeit', *Die Friedenswarte*, Vol. 35, pp. 214–17.

—— (1937), *Les Immunités des Personnes Investies de Fonctions Internationales*, Paris: Académie de Droit Internationale.

—— (1938), *Jurisdiction Internationale*, Leiden: Sijthoff.

Hammarskjöld, D. (1933), *Konjunkturspridningen: En teoretisk och historisk undersökning*, Stockholm: P.A. Norstedt.

—— (1945a), 'From Bretton Woods to Full Employment', *Svenska Handelsbanken's Index*, December, Suppl. A, pp. 1–24.

—— (1945b), 'Sweden's International Credit Accomodation in 1944 and 1945', *Svenska Handelsbanken's Index*, December, Suppl. B, pp. 1–24.

—— (1951a), 'Statstjänstemannen och samhället', *Tiden*, Vol. 43, pp. 391–6.

—— (1951b), 'Att välja Europa', *Svensk Tidskrift*, Vol. 38, pp. 442–59.

—— (1952), 'Politik och ideologi', *Tiden*, Vol. 44, pp. 6–17.

—— (1961), 'The International Civil Servant in Law and in Fact. Lecture delivered in Congregation at Oxford University, 30 May 1961', in Cordier and Foote (1974: 471–89).

—— (1962), *Från Sarek till Haväng*, Stockholm: Svenska turistföreningen.

—— (1963), *Vägmärken*, Stockholm: A. Bonniers Förlag.

—— (1964), *Markings*, translated from Swedish by L. Sjöberg and W.H. Auden, New York: Alfred A. Knopf.

—— (1965), *Zeichen am Weg*, edited with an introduction by A. Graf Knyphausen, Munich, Zurich: Droemer, Knaur.

—— (1966a), *Merkstenen*, Brugge, Utrecht: Brouwer.

—— (1966b), *Vägmärken*, Dutch edn, Stockholm.

—— (1966c), 'Dag Hammarskjöld om Martin Buber', *Judisk Tidskrift*, Vol. 2, pp. 18–21.

—— (1967), *Jalons*, Paris: Plon.

—— (1971), *Castle Hill*, Uppsala: Dag Hammarskjöld Foundation

—— (1987) 'Landmarks', Photographs by Dag Hammarskjöld, *Development Dialogue*, No. 1, pp. 17–33.

—— (2005), *Zeichen am Weg: Das spirituelle Tagebuch des UN-Generalsekretärs*, revised edition with an introduction by Manuel Fröhlich, Munich: Knaur.

Hammarskjöld, D., Selander, S. and Arnick, C. (eds) (1943), *Svensk Natur*, Stockholm: Svenska turistföreningens förl.

Hammarskjöld, H. (1923), 'La Neutralité en Général: Leçons données à l'Academie de Droit International de la Haye', in *Bibliotheca Visseriana Dissertationum Ius Internatonale Illustrantium* (1924) Tomus Tertius, Lugundi Batavorum: Brill, pp. 53–141.

Hardy, R.P. (1978), 'Hammarskjold, the Mystic', *Ephemerides Carmeliticae*, Vol. 29, pp. 266–77.

Hartman, S.S. (1966), 'Dag Hammarskjöld and the Religions', in *Acta Orientalia Vol. XXX 1966. Iranian Studies presented to Kaj Barr on his 70th birthday*, Hauniae, pp. 103–15.

Hasenclever, A. (2001), *Die Macht der Moral in der internationalen Politik: Militärische Interventionen westlicher Staaten in Somalia, Ruanda und Bosnien-Herzegowina*, Frankfurt a. M., New York: Campus.

Hauriou, M. (1965), *Die Theorie der Institution und zwei andere Aufsätze*, edited by R. Schnur, Berlin: Duncker & Humblot.

Hawden, J.G. and Kaufmann, J. (1962), *How United Nations Decisions are Made*, 2nd edn, Leiden, New York: Sijthoff.

Heikal, M. (1973), *The Cairo Documents*, New York: Doubleday.

Heinemann, W. and Wiggershaus, N. (eds) (1999), *Das internationale Krisenjahr 1956: Polen, Ungarn, Suez, Beiträge zur Militärgeschichte 48*, Munich: Oldenbourg.

Heinrich, H.-G. (1989), *Einführung in die Politikwissenschaft*, Vienna, Cologne: Böhlau.

Helms, J. (1996), 'Saving the U.N.: A Challenge to the Next Secretary-General', *FA*, Vol. 75, No. 5, pp. 3–7.

Helms, L. (2000), '"Politische Führung" als politikwissenschaftliches Problem', *PVS*, Vol. 41, No. 3, pp. 411–34.

Henderson, J.L. (1969), *Hammarskjöld: Servant of a World Unborn*, London: Methuen Educational.

Henkel, M. (1999), *Frieden und Politik: Eine interaktionistische Theorie*, Berlin: Duncker & Humblot.

Hermann, M.G. and Hagan, J.D. (1998), 'International Decision Making: Leadership Matters', *FP*, Vol. 102, No. 1, pp. 124–37.

Hermann, M.G. and Milburn, T.W. (eds) (1977), *A Psychological Examination of Political Leaders*, New York, London: Free Press, Collier Macmillan.

Hershey, B. (1961), *Dag Hammarskjold: Soldier of Peace*, Britannica Bookshelf – Great Lives for Young Americans, Chicago, IL: Encyclopaedia Britannica Press.

High-Level Panel on Threats, Challenges and Change (2004), *Report of the High-Level Panel on Threats, Challenges and Change*, A/59/565, 2 December, New York: United Nations.

Hocevar, R.K., Maier, H. and Weinacht, P. (eds) (1971), *Politiker des 20. Jahrhunderts, Vol. II: Die geteilte Welt*, Munich: Beck.

Hodes, A. (1971), *Martin Buber: An Intimate Portrait*, New York: Viking Press.

Hoek, K. van (1953), 'Dag Hammarskjoeld', *Europa: Magazin für Wirtschaft, Politik und Kultur*, Vol. 41, pp. 13–14.

Höffe, O. (ed.) (1985), *Klassiker der Philosophie. Vol. II*, 2nd edn, Munich: Beck.

—— (1991), 'Eine entmoralisierte Moral: Zur Ethik der modernen Politik', *PVS*, Vol. 32, No. 2, pp. 302–16.

Hoffmann, E.P. and Fleron, F.J. Jr. (eds) (1971), *The Conduct of Soviet Foreign Policy*, Chicago, IL, New York: Aldine.

Hoffmann, S. (1962), 'In Search of a Thread: The UN in the Congo Labyrinth', in Kay (1967: 230–60).

Hoffmann-Herreros, J. (1991), *Dag Hammarskjöld. Politiker – Schriftsteller – Christ*, Mainz: Matthias-Grünewald-Verlag.

Holsti, O. (1970), 'The "Operational Code" Approach to the Study of Political Leaders: John Foster Dulles' Philosophical and Instrumental Beliefs', *Canadian Journal of Political Science*, Vol. 3, pp. 123–57.

—— (1976), 'Foreign Policy Formation Viewed Cognitively', in Axelrod (1976a: 18–54).

Hoppenot, H. (1961), 'Dag Hammarskjoeld', *Le Monde diplomatique*, October, pp. 1, 6.

Hovde, C.F. (1997), 'The Dag Hammarskjöld–John Steinbeck Correspondence', *Development Dialogue*, No. 1–2, pp. 97–122.

Hubel, H. (1995), 'Regionale Krisenherde der Weltpolitik', in Kaiser and Schwarz (1995: 347–57).

Huber, M. (1938), 'In memoriam Åke Hammarskjöld', in Hammarskjöld (1938: 9–32).

—— (1955), 'Prolegomena und Probleme eines internationalen Ethos', in Strohm and Wendland (1969: 352–82).

Hüfner, K. (1982), 'Vorzeitige Gedanken eines Generalsekretärs. Dag Hammarskjöld als politischer Entwicklungsökonom', *VN*, Vol. 30, pp. 5–9.

—— (ed.) (1994), *Die Reform der Vereinten Nationen: Die Weltorganisation zwischen Krise und Erneuerung*, Opladen: Leske & Budrich.

Hughes, E.J. (1995), 'On Naming the Crack in the Wall: The Ethical Mysticism of Dag Hammarskjöld', *Studia Mystica*, Vol. 16, pp. 164–92.

Huls, J. (1991), 'Dag Hammarskjöld als Interpret des hl. Johannes vom Kreuz', in Steggink (1991: 883–905).

Hume, C.R. (1992), 'Pérez de Cuéllar and the Iran–Iraq War', *Negotiation Journal*, Vol. 8, pp. 173–84.

Humphrey, J.P. (1984), *Human Rights and the United Nations: A Great Adventure*, Dobbs Ferry, NY: Transnational Publ.
—— (1989), 'Inaugural Lecture on Human Rights', *McGill Law Journal*, Vol. 34, pp. 193–202.
Imbusch, P. (ed.) (1998), *Macht und Herrschaft: Sozialwissenschaftliche Konzeptionen und Theorien*, Opladen: Leske & Budrich.
Imhof, P. (ed.) (1990), *Gottes Nähe: Religiöse Erfahrung in Mystik und Offenbarung. Festschrift Josef Sudbrack zum 65. Geburtstag*, Würzburg: Echter.
Italiaander, R. (ed.) (1967), *Frieden in der Welt – aber wie? Gedanken der Friedens-Nobelpreisträger*, Stuttgart: Fink.
Jackson, E. (1957), 'The Developing Role of the Secretary-General', *IO*, Vol. 11, pp. 431–45.
Jackson. W.D. (1978), 'The Political Role of the Secretary-General under U Thant and Kurt Waldheim: Development or Decline?', in *World Affairs* Vol. 140 (1978), pp. 230–44.
James, A. (1959), 'The Role of the Secretary-General of the United Nations in International Relations', *International Relations*, October, pp. 620–38.
—— (1972), 'U Thant and his Critics', in *The Year Book of World Affairs* 26, pp. 43–64.
—— (1981), 'Why Dag's Name no Longer Casts a Spell', *The Times*, 14 September, p. 14.
—— (1985), 'The Secretary-General: A comparative Analysis', in Berridge and Jennings, (1985: 31–47).
—— (1993), 'The Secretary-General as an Independent Political Actor', in Rivlin and Gordenker (1993: 22–39).
James, W. (1982), *The Varieties of Religious Experience. A Study in Human Nature*, The Gifford Lectures 1901/2, Lectures XI and XVII, New York: Penguin.
Janowski, H.N. (ed.) (1978), *Geert Groote, Thomas von Kempen und die Devotio moderna*, Olten, Freiburg: Walter.
Jaspert, B. (ed.) (1992a), *Leiden und Weisheit in der Mystik*, Paderborn: Bonifatius.
—— (1992b), 'Leid und Trost bei Heinrich Seuse und Dag Hammarskjöld', in Jaspert (1992a: 167–205).
Jensen, E. (1985), 'The Secretary-General's Use of Good Offices and the Question of Bahrain', *Millennium*, Vol. 14, No. 3, pp. 335–48.
Jessen, J.C. (1975), *Eigenständige friedliche Streitbeilegung durch den Generalsekretär der Vereinten Nationen*, Kiel: Diss.
Jessup, P.C. (1956), 'Parliamentary Diplomacy: An Examination of the Legal Quality of the Rules of Procedure of Organs of the United Nations', *Recueil des Cours*, Vol. 89, pp. 181–320.
Johannes vom Kreuz (1987), *Aufstieg zum Berge Karmel*, 8th edn, Darmstadt: Wissenschaftliche Buchgesellschaft (Collected Works, Vol. 1).
—— (1989), *Glut der Liebe: Kommentar zu den Werken Geistlicher Gesang, Lebendige Liebesflamme*, edited by C. Lapauw, Innsbruck, Vienna: Tyrolia-Verlag.
—— (1995), *Die Dunkle Nacht*, edited and translated by U. Dobhan, E. Hense and E. Peeters, Freiburg: Herder.
Johnston, W. (1974), *Der ruhende Punkt. Zen und christliche Mystik*, 2nd edn, Freiburg: Herder.
Jones, D.V. (1991), *Code of Peace. Ethics and Security in the World of Warlord States*, Chicago, IL, London: University of Chicago Press.
—— (1992), 'The Declaratory Tradition in Modern International Law', in Nardin and Mapel (1992: 42–61).

—— (1994), 'The Example of Dag Hammarskjöld: Style and Effectiveness at the UN', *The Christian Century*, 9 November, pp. 1047–50.

—— (1995), 'The World Outlook of Dag Hammarskjöld', in Nolan (1995: 135–49).

Jordan, R.S. (ed.) (1983a), *Dag Hammarskjöld Revisited: The UN Secretary-General as a Force in World Politics*, Durham, NC: Carolina Academic Press.

—— (1983b), 'The Legacy which Dag Hammarskjöld Inherited and his Imprint on it', in Jordan (1983a: 3–13).

Juan de la Cruz (1947), *Poesias completas*, Santiago de Chile: Cruz del Sar.

—— (1951), *The Poems of St. John of the Cross*, New York: Pantheon Books.

—— (1955), *Vida y obras de San Juan de la Cruz*, Madrid.

Kägi, U. (1962), 'Der Generalsekretär und sein Kabinett', *VN*, Vol. 10, pp. 60–2.

Kaiser, K. and Schwarz, H.-P. (eds) (1995), *Die neue Weltpolitik*, Bonn: Bundeszentrale für Politische Bildung.

Kaiser, J. (1979), 'Der Stärkste ist am ohn-mächtigsten allein: Zu Hannah Arendts Thesen über "Macht und Gewalt"', in Reif (1979: 307–15).

Kania, A.T. (2000), *The Art of Love: A Study of Dag Hammarskjöld's Mystical Theology*, Uppsala: Uppsala University.

Kanninen, T. (1995), *Leadership and Reform: The Secretary-General and the UN Financial Crisis of the late 1980s*, Legal Aspects of International Organization 22, The Hague: Kluwer Law International.

Kant, I. (1785), *Grundlegung zur Metaphysik der Sitten*, in Kant (1983: 9–102).

—— (1795), Perpetual Peace: A Philosophical Sketch, in Kant (1984: 107–43).

—— (1920), *Grundlegung zur Metaphysik der Sitten*, 5th edn, Leipzig: Meiner.

—— Kant, I. (1983), *Werke in zehn Bänden*, Vol. 6, edited by W. Weischedel, Darmstadt: Wissenschaftliche Buchgesellschaft.

—— (1984), *Perpetual Peace and Other Essays*, Indianapolis, IN, Cambridge: Hacket Publishing Inc.

Kay, D.A. (ed.) (1967a), *The United Nation's Political System*, New York: Wiley.

—— (1967b), 'Instruments of Influence in the United Nations Political Process', in Kay (1967a: 92–107).

Kelen, E. (1966), *Hammarskjöld*, New York: Putnam.

—— (ed.) (1968), *Hammarskjöld: The Political Man*, New York: Funk & Wagnall.

—— (1969), *Dag Hammarskjöld. A Biography*, New York: Meredith Press.

Kelsen, H. (1964), *The Law of the United Nations: A Critical Analysis of Its Fundamental Problems*, London: Stevens.

Khrushchev, N.S. (1959), 'On Peaceful Coexistence', *FA*, Vol. 38, No. 1, pp. 1–18.

King, E. (1982), 'Dag Hammarskjold's Befriending Death: A Case Study in Theological Reflection', *Pastoral Sciences*, Vol. 1, pp. 91–112.

King, J. and Hobbins, A.J. (2003), 'Hammarskjöld and Human Rights: the Deflation of the UN Human Rights Programme 1953–1961', *Journal of the History of International Law 5*, pp. 337–86.

Knapp, M. (1997), '50 Jahre Vereinte Nationen: Rückblick und Ausblick im Spiegel der Jubiläumsliteratur', *ZPol*, Vol. 7, pp. 423–81.

Knyphausen, A. Graf (1965), 'Introduction', in Hammarskjöld (1965).

Kondracke, M. (1990), 'Javier of the U.N.', *The New Republic*, 13 August, pp. 20–3.

Körtner, U.H.J. (1988), 'Ehrfurcht vor dem Leben – Verantwortung für das Leben: Bedeutung und Problematik der Ethik Albert Schweitzers', *Zeitschrift für Theologie und Kirche*, Vol. 85, pp. 329–48.

Kranz, G. (1973a), *Sie lebten das Christentum: Achtundzwanzig Biographien*, Augsburg: Verlag Winfried-Werk.

—— (1973b), 'Dag Hammarskjöld', in Kranz (1973a: 15–26).

Kriesberg, L. and Thorson, S.J. (eds) (1991), *Timing the De-Escalation of International Conflicts*, New York: Syracuse University Press.

Kromrey, H. (1991), *Empirische Sozialforschung: Modelle und Methoden der Daten-erhebung und Datenauswertung*, 5th edn, Opladen: Westdeutscher Verlag.

Kühne, W. (ed.) (1993), *Blauhelme in einer turbulenten Welt*, Baden-Baden: Nomos-Verlagsgesellschaft.

—— (1999), 'Peace Support Operations: How to Make them Succeed', *IPG*, Vol. 4, pp. 358–67.

Küng, H. (1998), *Projekt Weltethos*, 4th edn, Munich, Zurich: Piper.

Kyle, K. (1991), *Suez*, London: Weidenfeld & Nicolson.

Lall, A. (1966), *Modern International Negotiation. Principles and Practice*, New York, London: Columbia University Press.

Langrod, G. (1963), *The International Civil Servant. Its Origins, its Nature, its Evolution*, Dobbs Ferry, NY: Oceana.

Larus, J. (ed.) (1965), *From Collective Security to Preventive Diplomacy. Readings in International Organization and the Maintenance of Peace*, New York: Wiley.

Lash, J.P. (1957), 'The U.N.'s Hammarskjold', *The Progressive*, January, pp. 17–20.

—— (1959), 'The Man on the 38th Floor', *Harper's Magazine*, October, pp. 47–52.

—— (1961), *Dag Hammarskjöld. Custodian of the Brush-fire Peace*, New York: Doubleday.

—— (1962), 'Dag Hammarskjöld's Conception of His Office', *IO*, Vol. 16, pp. 542–66.

Lavalle, R. (1990), 'The "Inherent" Powers of the UN Secretary-General in the Political Sphere: A Legal Analysis', *Netherlands International Law Review*, Vol. 37, pp. 22–36.

Lefever, E.W. (1993), 'Reining in the U.N. Mistaking the Instrument for the Actor', *FA*, Vol. 72, No. 3, pp. 17–20.

Leger, A. (1993), *Correspondance 1955–1961*, Texts collected and edited by M.-N. Little, Paris: Gallimard.

Leichter, O. (1966), 'Wahl des Generalsekretärs und andere UN-Probleme', *VN*, Vol. 14, pp. 105–11.

Leifland, L., Wahlbäck, K., Wallin, G. and Sundelius, B. (eds) (1997), *Brobyggare: En vänbok till Nils Andrén*, Stockholm: Nerenius & Santérus.

Leites, N. (1953), *A Study of Bolshevism*, Glencoe, IL: Free Press.

Lentner, H.H. (1965), 'The Diplomacy of the United Nations Secretary-General', *The Western Political Quarterly*, Vol. 18, pp. 531–50.

Leppin, V. (1997), 'Die Komposition von Meister Eckharts Maria-Martha-Predigt', *Zeitschrift für Theologie und Kirche*, Vol. 94, pp. 69–83.

Levine, I.E. (1962), *Dag Hammarskjold: Champion of World Peace*, New York: Julian Messner.

Lie, T. (1954), *In the Cause of Peace: Seven Years with the United Nations*, New York: Macmillan.

Lindegren, E. (1971), *Gedenkrede auf Dag Hammarskjöld von seinem Nachfolger in der schwedischen Akademie*, translated by Agda Lundgren, Berlin: Dag-Hammarskjöld-Oberschule (duplicated manuscript).

Link, W. (1999), *Die Neuordnung der Weltpolitik: Grundprobleme globaler Politik an der Schwelle zum 21. Jahrhundert*, 2nd edn, Munich: Beck.

Linnér, S. (1989), 'Dag Hammarskjöld', in Schultz (1989: 127–35).

Lippert, E. and Wakenhut, R. (eds) (1983), *Handwörterbuch der Politischen Psychologie*, Studienbücher zur Sozialwissenschaft 46, Opladen: Westdeutscher Verlag.

Lippmann, W. (1961), 'Dag Hammarskjöld, United Nations Pioneer', *IO*, Vol. 15, pp. 547–8.

Lipsey, R. (1996), 'For the Other Mahatma', *Parabola*, Vol. 21, pp. 12–17.

—— (1997), 'Blessed Uneasiness: Dag Hammarskjöld on Conscience', *Parabola*, Vol. 22, pp. 47–56.

Little, M.-N. (ed.) (2001), *The Poet and the Diplomat. The Correspondence of Dag Hammarskjöld and Alexis Leger*, Syracuse, NY: Syracuse University Press.

Lönborg, S. (1931), *Ekkehart*, Stockholm: Wahlström & Widstrand.

Luard, E. (ed.) (1966), *The Evolution of International Organizations*, London: Thames & Hudson.

—— (1994), *The United Nations. How it Works and What it Does*, 2nd edn, Basingstoke, London: Macmillan.

Maloney, S.M. (1999), 'Die Schaffung der United Nations Emergency Force I, November 1956 bis März 1957', in Heinemann and Wiggershaus (1999: 257–79).

Marcel, G. (1963), 'Ich und Du bei Martin Buber', in Schilpp and Friedman (1963: 35–41).

Matthies, V. (1993), 'Zwischen Rettungsaktion und Entmündigung: Das Engagement der Vereinten Nationen in Somalia', *VN*, Vol. 41, pp. 45–51.

Maurina, Z. (1965), *Die Aufgabe des Dichters in unserer Zeit: Essays mit literarischen Porträts von Dag Hammarskjöld, Giorgos Seferis, Alexander Solschenizyn*, Munich: Jolis Verlag Lenz.

McClendon, J. (1973), 'The Twice-Born Religion of Dag Hammarskjöld', *Review and Expositor*, Vol. 70, pp. 223–38. Meadow, M.J. (1984), 'The Dark Side of Mysticism: Depression and "The Dark Night"', *Pastoral Psychology*, Vol. 33, pp. 105–25.

Meisler, S. (1995), 'Dateline U.N.: A New Hammarskjöld?', *FP*, Vol. 98, No. 1, pp. 189–97.

—— (1996), 'Crisis in Katanga', in Benton (1996: 101–19).

Meister Eckhart (1922), *Undervisande tal jämte andra predikningar av Mäster Eckehart, övers. och inledn av Richard Hejll, förörd av Hans Larsson*, Stockholm.

—— (1934), *Schriften zur Gesellschaftsphilosophie*, Jena: Fischer.

—— (1979a), *Texte*, Olten, Freiburg: Walter-Verlag.

—— (1979b), *Deutsche Predigten und Traktate*, edited and translated by J. Quint, Zurich: Diogenes.

—— (1991), *Mystische Schriften*, translated by G. Landauer, Frankfurt a. M.: Insel-Verlag.

—— (1996), *Vom Wunder der Seele. Eine Auswahl aus den Traktaten und Predigten*, edited by F. A. Schmid Noerr, Stuttgart: Reclam.

Meron, T. (1983), 'Civil Service, International', *EPIL*, Vol. 5, pp. 4–8.

Merten, K. (1983), *Inhaltsanalyse. Einführung in Theorie, Methode und Praxis*, Opladen: Westdeutscher Verlag.

Mieth, D. (1969), *Die Einheit von vita activa und vita contemplativa in den deutschen Predigten und Traktaten Meister Eckharts und bei Johannes Tauler*, Studien zur katholischen Moraltheologie 15, Regensburg: Verlag Friedrich Pustet.

Mohr, R. (1998), 'Autobiographie', in Dinzelbacher (1998: 42).

Montgomery, E.R. (1975), *Dag Hammarskjold: Peacemaker for the U.N.*, Champaign, IL: Garrard Publishing Co.

Morgenthau, H. (1963), 'U Thant', in Morgenthau (1970: 121–6).

—— (1965), 'The U.N. of Dag Hammarskjold is Dead', *The New York Times*, 14 March, pp. 32, 40.

—— (1970), *Truth and Power. Essays of a Decade 1960–1970*, New York: Praeger.

—— (1973), *Politics among Nations: The Struggle for Power and Peace*, 5th edn, New York: Alfred A. Knopf.

Morr, H. (1991), 'Generalsekretär', in Wolfrum (1991: 220–5).

—— (1995), 'Secretary-General', in Wolfrum (1995b: 1136–46).

Morse, D.A. (1972), 'Remarks at Roundtable "A More Powerful Secretary-General for the United Nations?"', *ASIL Proceedings*, Vol. 66, pp. 84–7.

Muller, R. (1985), *Ich lernte zu leben: Eine Autobiographie*, Munich: Dianus-Trikout

Muños-Garnicia, M. (1875), *San Juan de la Cruz*, Jaen: Rubio.

Murphy, J.D. (1970), 'The Papacy and the Secretary-Generalship: A Study of the Role of the Exceptionally-situated Individual Actor in the International System', *Co-existence*, Vol. 7, pp. 165–81.

Narasimhan, C.V. (1973), *Dag Hammarskjöld Interview*, New York: Columbia University, Oral History Research Office.

—— (1988), *The United Nations: An Inside View*, New Dehli: UNITAR in association with Vikas Publishing House.

Nardin, T. and Mapel, D.R. (eds) (1992), *Traditions of International Ethics*, Cambridge, New York: Cambridge University Press.

Nawaz, M.K. (ed.) (1976), *Essays on International Law in Honour of Krishna Rao*, Leiden: Sijthoff.

Nayar, M.G.K. (1974), 'Dag Hammarskjöld and U Thant: The Evolution of Their Office', *Case Western Reserve Journal of International Law*, Vol. 36, pp. 36–83.

Nelan, B.W. (1995), 'The World's Toughest Job', *Time*, 23 October, pp. 70–1.

Neumann, F. (ed.) (1985), *Handbuch Politische Ethik*, Baden-Baden: Signal Verlag.

Neumann, M. (ed.) (1989a), *Der Friedens-Nobelpreis von 1926 bis 1932*, Zug: Ed. Pacis.

—— (ed.) (1989b), *Der Friedensnobelpreis von 1953 bis 1962*, Zug: Ed. Pacis.

Newman, E. (1998), *The UN Secretary-General from the Cold War to the New Era: A Global Peace and Security Mandate*, Basingstoke, London: Macmillan.

Nicholas, H.G. (1975), *The United Nations as a Political Institution*, 5th edn, London: Oxford University Press.

Nolan, C.J. (ed.) (1995), *Ethics and Statecraft. The Moral Dimension of International Affairs*, Foreword by J.H. Rosenthal, Westport, CT, London: Greenwood Press.

Nolte, B. (1995a), 'Conflicts: Congo', in Wolfrum (1995a: 225–32).

—— (1995b), 'Uniting for Peace', in Wolfrum (1995b: 1341–8).

Norton, J.J. (ed.) (1987), *Public International Law and the Future World Order: Liber Amicorum in Honour of A.J. Thomas Jr.*, Littleton, CO: F.B. Rothman.

Nye, J. (1991), *Bound to Lead. The Changing Nature of American Power*, New York: Basic Books.

O'Brien, C.C. (1961), 'My Case', *The Observer*, 17 December, p. 17.

Onuf, N.G. (1989), *World of Our Making. Rules and Rule in Social Theory and International Relations*, Columbia, SC: University of South Carolina Press.

Opitz, P.J. and Rittberger, V. (eds) (1986), *Forum der Welt: 40 Jahre Vereinte Nationen*, Bonn: Bundeszentrale für Politische Bildung.

Oren, M.B. (1992), 'Ambivalent Adversaries: David Ben-Gurion and Israel vs. the United Nations and Dag Hammarskjold, 1956–1957', *Journal of Contemporary History*, Vol. 27, pp. 89–127.

Otunnu, O.A. and Doyle, M.W. (eds) (1998), *Peacemaking and Peacekeeping for the New Century*, Lanham, MD: Rowman & Littlefield.

Overland, A. (1992), 'Discussion Report "The Changing Role of the UN Secretary-General"', *ASIL Proceedings*, Vol. 86, pp. 321–3.

Pak, C.Y. (1963), *The Political Role of the Secretary-General of the United Nations in Theory and Practice*, Ann Arbor, MI: Diss.

Partsch, K.-J. (1981), 'Fact-finding and Inquiry', *EPIL*, Vol. 1, pp. 61–2.

Pearson, L. (1957a), 'Force for U.N.', *FA*, Vol. 36, No. 3, pp. 395–404.

—— (1957b), 'The Four Faces of Peace. Nobel Prize Lecture', in Pearson (1959: 89–114).

—— (1959), *Diplomacy in the Nuclear Age*, Cambridge, MA: Harvard University Press.

—— (1973), *Mike: The Memoirs of the Right Honourable Lester B. Pearson. Volume 2: 1948–1957*, edited by J.A. Munro and A.I. Inglis, New York: Quadrangle, NY Times Book Co.

Pechota, V. (1972), *The Quiet Approach: A Study of the Good Offices Exercised by the United Nations Secretary-General in the Cause of Peace*, UNITAR Papers No. 6, New York: UNITAR.

—— (1976), 'Good Offices of the Secretary-General of the United Nations: Contemporary Theory and Practice', in Nawaz (1976: 191–205).

Perse, S.-J. (1960), *Chronik*, translated from French by F. Kemp, Darmstadt: Luchterhand.

—— (1989), *Œuvres complètes*, Paris: Gallimard.

Petman, J. and Klabbers J. (eds) (2003), *Nordic Cosmopolitanism: Essays in International Law for Martti Koskenniemi*, Leiden: Nijhoff.

Petrolia-Ammaniti, M. (1976), 'The Position of the Secretary-General of the United Nations in the Organization in the International Community', in *Thesaurus Acroasium Vol. II*, Thessaloniki: Institute of International Public Law and International Relations, pp. 353–68.

Phelan, E.J. (1933), 'The new international civil service', *FA*, Vol. 11, No. 2, pp. 307–14.

—— (1936), *Yes and Albert Thomas*, London: Cresset Press Limited.

Plug, G. (1985), 'Henri Bergson (1859–1941)', in Höffe (1985: 298–314).

Preparatory Commission of the United Nations (1945), *Report of the Preparatory Commission of the United Nations (PC/20)*, 23 December, New York: United Nations.

Progoff, I. (1965), 'The Integrity of Life and Death', in *Eranos Jahrbuch 1964: Das menschliche Drama in der Welt der Ideen*, Zurich: Rhein-Verlag, pp. 200–43.

Puchala, D.J. (1993), 'The Secretary-General and his Special Representatives', in Rivlin and Gordenker (1993: 81–97).

Pzillas, F. (1966), 'Dag Hammarskjölds geistliches Vermächtnis', *VN*, Vol. 14, pp. 26–8.

Ramcharan, B.G. (1982), 'The Good Offices of the United Nations Secretary-General in the Field of Human Rights', *AJIL*, Vol. 76, pp. 130–41.

—— (1989), *The Concept and Present Status of the International Protection of Human Rights: Forty Years after the Universal Declaration*, Dordrecht: Nijhoff.

—— (1990), 'The History, Role and Organization of the "Cabinet" of the United Nations Secretary-General', *Nordic Journal of International Law*, Vol. 59, pp. 103–16.

Ramo, J.C. (2000), 'The Five Virtues of Kofi Annan', *Time*, 4 September, pp. 40–7.

Ranshofen-Wertheimer, E.F. (1945), *The International Secretariat. A Great Experiment in International Administration*, Washington, DC: Carnegie Endowment for International Peace.

Reif, A. (ed.) (1979), *Hannah Arendt: Materialien zu ihrem Werk*, Munich: Europaverlag.

Reller, H. and Seitz, M. (eds) (1980), *Herausforderung: Religiöse Erfahrung. Vom Verhältnis evangelischer Frömmigkeit zu Meditation und Mystik*, Göttingen: Vandenhoeck & Ruprecht.

Riedel, M. (ed.) (1972), *Rehabilitierung der praktischen Philosophie. Band I: Geschichte, Probleme, Aufgaben*, Freiburg: Rombach.

Riedmaier, M. (1966), 'Friedensreligiösität in den Vereinten Nationen', *VN*, Vol. 14, pp. 177–82.

Riehle, W. (1984), 'Die Wolke des Nichtwissens', in Ruhbach and Sudbrack (1984: 172–3).

Righter, R. (1995), *Utopia Lost: The United Nations and World Order*, New York: Twentieth Century Fund Press.

Rikhye, I.J. (1991), 'Critical Elements in Determining the Suitability of Conflict Settlement Efforts by the United Nations Secretary-General', in Kriesberg and Thorson (1991: 58–82).

Riklin, A. (1994), 'Politische Ethik', *Österreichische Zeitschrift für Politikwissenschaft*, Vol. 23, pp. 105–20.

Rivlin, B. (1993), 'The Changing International Political Climate and the Secretary-General', in Rivlin and Gordenker (1993: 4–21).

—— (1994), 'The UN-Secretary-Generalship at Fifty', *Paradigms*, Vol. 8, pp. 49–70.

—— (1997), 'Leadership in the UN, 1997: The Secretary-General and the U.S. – a symbiotic relationship under stress', *International Journal*, Vol. 52, pp. 197–218.

Rivlin, B. and Gordenker, L. (eds) (1993), *The Challenging Role of the UN Secretary-General: Making "The Most Impossible Job in the World" Possible*, Westport, CT, London: Praeger.

Roberts, A. (1994), 'The Crisis in UN Peacekeeping', *Survival*, Vol. 36, No. 3, pp. 93–120.

Roberts, A. and Kingsbury, B. (eds) (1995), *United Nations, Divided World: The UN's Roles in International Relations*, 2nd edn, Oxford: Clarendon Press.

Rosenthal, J.H. (1995), 'Biography, Ethics, and Statecraft', in Nolan (1995: xi–xvii).

Rösiö, B. (1993), 'The Ndola Crash and the Death of Dag Hammarskjöld', *The Journal of Modern African Studies*, Vol. 31, pp. 661–71.

Rovine, A.W. (1970), *The First Fifty Years: The Secretary-General in World Politics 1920–1970*, Leyden: Sijthoff.

—— (1972), 'Remarks at Roundtable "A More Powerful Secretary-General for the United Nations"', *ASIL Proceedings*, Vol. 66, pp. 78–81.

Ruh, K. (1985), *Meister Eckhart: Theologe, Prediger, Mystiker*, Munich: Beck.

Ruhbach, G. (1987), 'Dag Hammarskjöld: UNO-Generalsekretär und geistlich lebender Mensch', *Theologische Beiträge*, Vol. 18, pp. 305–15.

Ruhbach, G. and Sudbrack, J. (eds) (1984), *Große Mystiker: Leben und Wirken*, Munich: Beck.

Rupps, M. (1997), *Helmut Schmidt: Politikverständnis und geistige Grundlagen*, Bonn: Bouvier.

Rusk, D. (1955), 'Parliamentary Diplomacy vs. Negotiation', *World Affairs Interpreter*, Vol. 26, pp. 121–38.

Russell, R.B. and Muther, J.E. (1958), *A History of the United Nations Charter: The Role of the United States 1940–1945*, Washington, DC: Brookings Institution.

Russett, B. and Sutterlin, J.S. (1991), 'The U.N. in a New World Order', *FA*, Vol. 70, No. 1, pp. 69–83.

Ruzie, D. (1991), 'Art. 100', in Cot and Pellet (1991: 1337–48).

Saksena, K.P. (1975), 'Secretary-General U Thant', *India Quarterly*, Vol. 31, pp. 342–61.

—— (1978), 'Hammarskjold and the Congo Crisis: A Review Article', *India Quarterly*, Vol. 34, pp. 193–210.

Sauvage, L. (1960), 'M. Hammarskjoeld quitte la séance de l'O.N.U. et nous parle des bienfaits de la Poésie en diplomatie', *Le Figaro Litteraire*, 5 November, pp. 1, 5.

Schachter, O. (1948), 'The Development of International Law through the Legal Opinion of the United Nations Secretariat', in *British Yearbook of International Law 25*, pp. 91–132.

—— (1962), 'Dag Hammarskjold and the Relation of Law to Politics', *AJIL*, Vol. 56, pp. 1–8.

—— (1963), 'The Relation of Law, Politics and Action in the United Nations', *Recueil de Cours*, Vol. 109, pp. 165–256.

—— (1972), 'Preface', in Pechota (1972: i–ii).

—— (1983), 'The International Civil Servant: Neutrality and Responsibilty', in Jordan (1983: 39–63).

—— (1993), 'Sovereignty and Threats to Peace', in Weiss (1993: 19–44).

Schaeder, G. (1966), *Martin Buber. Hebräischer Humanismus*, Göttingen: Vandenhoeck & Ruprecht.

Schäfer, R. (1970), 'Glaube und Werk – ein Beispiel aus der Gegenwart: Beobachtungen zu Dag Hammarskjölds geistlichem Tagebuch', *Zeitschrift für Theologie und Kirche*, Vol. 67, pp. 348–93.

Schild, A.L., Tscheulin, M., Schillhorn, K. and Kenny, K. (1995), 'Conflicts: Middle East', in Wolfrum (1995a: 286–310).

Schild, W. (1974), 'Die Institutionentheorie Maurice Haurious', *Österreichische Zeitschrift für öffentliches Recht*, Vol. 25, pp. 3–21.

Schiller, E. (1990), 'Dialog als Gottesnähe: Die Sicht des jüdischen Philosophen Martin Buber (1878–1965)', in Imhof (1990: 282–306).

Schilling, T. (1995), 'Die "neue Weltordnung" und die Souveränität der Mitglieder der Vereinten Nationen', *AVR* 33, pp. 67–106.

Schilpp, P. A. and Friedman, M. (eds) (1963), *Martin Buber*, Stuttgart: Kohlhammer.

Schimmel, A. (1996), *Wie universal ist die Mystik? Die Seelenreise in den großen Religionen der Welt*, Freiburg: Herder.

Schlenke, M. and Matz, K.-J. (eds) (1984), *Frieden und Friedenssicherung in Vergangenheit und Gegenwart*, Munich: Fink.

Schlesinger, S.C. (2003), *Act of Creation: The Founding of the United Nations – A Story of Superpowers, Secret Agents, Wartime Allies and Enemies and Their Quest for a Peaceful World*, Boulder, CO: Westview Press.

Schlüter, H. W. (1978), 'Trygve Lie, Dag Hammarskjöld, Sith U Thant, Kurt Waldheim: Aufgaben und Probleme einer Weltorganisation', in Fassmann (1978: 909–15).

Schreuer, C. (1994), 'Art. 100', in Simma (1994: 1057–76).

Schultz, H.J. (ed.) (1989), *Liebhaber des Friedens*, Munich: Deutsche Taschenbuch-Verlag.

Schwartländer, J. (ed.) (1984a), *Die Verantwortung der Vernunft in einer friedlosen Welt*: *Philosophisch-pädagogisches Kolloquium aus Anlaß des 80. Geburtstages von Otto Friedrich Bollnow*, Tübingen: Attempto.

—— (1984b), 'Die Verantwortung der Vernunft in einer friedlosen Welt', in Schwartländer (1984a: 28–47).

Schwebel, S.M. (1951), 'The Origins and Development of Article 99 of the Charter', in *British Yearbook of International Law 28*, pp. 371–82.

—— (1952), *The Secretary-General of the United Nations: His Political Powers and Practice*, Cambridge, MA: Harvard University Press.

Schweitzer, A. (1923), *Christianity and the Religions of the World: Lectures delivered at the Selly Oak Colleges Birmingham, February 1922*, London: George Allen & Unwin.

—— (1924), *Aus meiner Kindheit und Jugendzeit*, Munich: Beck.

—— (1930), *Selbstdarstellung*, Leipzig: Meiner.

—— (1933), *Geschichte der Leben-Jesu-Forschung*, Tübingen: Mohr.

—— (1945), *The Quest for the Historical Jesus. A Critical Study of its Progress from Remarus to Wrede*, London: Adam & Charles Black.

—— (1950a), *Aus meinem Leben und Denken*, Hamburg: Meiner.

—— (1950b), *Une anthologie*, Paris: Payot.

—— (1951a), *Verfall und Wiederaufbau der Kultur*, Munich: Beck.

—— (1951b), *Kultur und Ethik*, Munich: Beck.

—— (1951c), 'Humanität und Frieden', in Schweitzer (1991b: 95–101).

—— (1952), 'Was der Menschheit zur Zeit am meisten not tut', in Schweitzer (1991b: 102–5).

—— (1957), *Indian Thought and Its Development*, Boston, MA: The Beacon Press.

—— (1962), 'Friedensartikel für Dr. Wilhelm Kayser', in Schweitzer (1991b: 175–6).

—— (1984), *Geschichte der Leben-Jesu-Forschung*, 9th edn, Tübingen: Mohr.

—— (1986), *Was sollen wir tun? 12 Predigten über ethische Probleme*, 2nd edn, Heidelberg: Schneider.

—— (1987), *The Philosophy of Civilization: Part I, The Decay and the Restoration of Civilization / Part II, Civilization and Ethics*, Amherst, MA, New York: Prometheus Books.

—— (1991a), *Die Ehrfurcht vor dem Leben: Grundtexte aus fünf Jahrzehnten*, edited by H. W. Bähr, 6th edn, Munich: Beck.

—— (1991b), *Menschlichkeit und Friede: Kleine philosophisch-ethische Texte*, collected and edited by G. Fischer, Berlin: Verlag-Anstalt Union.

—— (1991c), 'Die Entstehung der Lehre der Ehrfurcht vor dem Leben und ihre Bedeutung für unsere Kultur', in Schweitzer (1991a: 13–31).

—— (1991d), 'Das Problem des Friedens in der heutigen Welt', in Schweitzer (1991a: 113–28).

—— (1992a), *Letters 1905–1965*, edited by H.W. Bähr, New York: Macmillan.

—— (1992b), *Das Christentum und die Weltreligionen*, Munich: Beck.

—— (1998a), *The Mysticism of the Apostle Paul*, Baltimore, MD, London: Johns Hopkins University Press.

—— (1998b), *Out of my Life and Thought. An Autobiography*, Baltimore, MD, London: Johns Hopkins University Press.

—— (2001), *The Quest for the Historical Jesus*, Minneapolis, MN: Fortress Press.

Senghaas, D. and Zürn, M. (1992), 'Kernfragen für die Friedensforschung der neunziger Jahre', *PVS*, Vol. 33, pp. 455–62.

Seynes, P. de (1983), 'An Informal Retrospection on Dag Hammarskjöld's Commitment to Economic and Social Development', in Jordan (1983: 65–75).

Shannon, D.B. (1992), 'Ernüchterung, Erfolg, Erleichterung. Zur Amtszeit von Pérez de Cuéllar (1982–1991)', *VN*, Vol. 40, pp. 1–4.

Shawcross, W. (2000), *Deliver Us from Evil: Peacekeepers, Warlords and a World of Endless Conflict*, New York: Simon & Schuster.

Shlaim, A. (ed.) (1976), *International Organisations in World Politics Yearbook 1975*, London: Croom Helm.

Simma, B. (ed.) (1994), *The Charter of the United Nations: A Commentary*, Munich: Beck.

Simmonds, K.R. (1959), '"Good Offices" of the Secretary-General', *Nordisk Tidskrift for International Ret og Jus Gentium*, Vol. 29, pp. 330–45.

Simon, C.M. (1967), *Dag Hammarskjöld*, New York: Dutton.

Singer, M. and Wildavsky, A. (1993), *The Real World Order: Zones of Peace/Zones of Turmoil*, London: Chatham House.

Siotis, J. (1963), *Essai sur le Secrétariat International*, Paris: Minard.

Skjelsbaek, K. (1991), 'The UN Secretary-General and the Mediation of International Disputes', *Journal of Peace Research*, Vol. 28, pp. 104–9.

Skjelsbaek, K. and Fermann G. (1996), 'The UN Secretary-General and the Mediation of International Disputes', in Bercovitch (1996: 75–104).

Smith, G. (1980), 'Hammarskjold was Killed by Mercenaries', *Daily Nation* (Nairobi), 22 May, p. 17.

Smith, G. and O'Brien, C.C. (1992), 'Hammarskjold Plane Crash "No Accident"', *The Guardian*, 9 November, p. 18.

Smouts, M.-C. (1971), *Le Secrétaire Général des Nations Unies: Son Rôle dans la Solution des Conflicts Internationaux*, Travaux et Recherches de Sciences Politiques 16, Paris: Armand Colin.

—— (1991), 'Art. 98–99', in Cot and Pellet (1991: 1317–35).

Snow, C.P. (1968a), *Variety of Men*, London, Melbourne, Toronto: Macmillan.

—— (1968b), 'Dag Hammarskjöld', in Snow (1968a: 151–68).

Sobosan, J.G. (1974), 'Politics and Spirituality: A Study of Dag Hammarskjold', *Cithara*, Vol. 14, pp. 3–12.

Söderberg, S. (1962), *Hammarskjöld: A Pictorial Biography*, New York: The Viking Press.

Söderblom, N. (1914), *Beruf und Berufstreue*, Leipzig: Hinrichs.

Sölle, D. (1997), *Mystik und Widerstand: 'Du stilles Geschrei'*, Hamburg: Hoffmann & Campe.

Spear, O. (1978), *Albert Schweitzers Ethik: Ihre Grundlinien in seinem Denken und Leben*, Hamburg: Evangelischer Verlag.

Specker, A. (1999), *Leben als Opfer? Die geistliche Entwicklung Dag Hammarskjölds auf Grundlage seines Tagebuchfragmentes 'Zeichen am Weg'*, Augsburg: Wißner.

Steffahn, H. (1996), *Albert Schweitzer in Selbstzeugnissen und Bilddokumenten*, 12th edn, Reinbek: Rowohlt.

Steggink, O. (1991), *Espiritu de Llama: Estudios con occasion del cuarto centenario de su muerte (1591–1991)*, (Studies in Spirituality Suppl. 1), Kampen: Edizione Carmelitane.

Stein, E. (1962), 'Mr. Hammarskjöld, The Charter Law and the Future Role of the United Nations Secretary-General', *AJIL*, Vol. 56, pp. 9–32.

Stephan, L. (1983), *Der einsame Weg des Dag Hammarskjöld*, Munich: Kaiser.

Sternberger, D. (1979), 'Auch Reden sind Taten', in Sternberger (1991: 52–68).

—— (1991), *Schriften XI: Sprache und Politik*, Frankfurt a. M.: Insel-Verlag.

Stevenson, A. E. (1965), 'From Containment to Cease-Fire and Peaceful Change', in Cordier and Foote (1965: 51–66).

Stockholm International Peace Research Institute (ed.) (1989), *Rüstung und Abrüstung*, SIPRI-Jahrbuch 1989, Baden-Baden: SIPRI.

Stölken, I. (1991), 'Dokumentenführer Vereinte Nationen', in Wolfrum (1991: 1159–71).

Stolpe, S. (1964a), *Dag Hammarskjölds geistiger Weg*, Frankfurt a. M.: Knecht.

—— (1964b), 'Dag Hammarskjölds geistiges Testament', *Stimmen der Zeit*, pp. 384–7.

—— (1965), 'Zu den Angriffen auf Hammarskjöld', *VN*, Vol. 13, pp. 170–2.

Strohm, T. and Wendland, H.-D. (eds) (1969), *Politik und Ethik*, Wege der Forschung CXXXIX, Darmstadt: Wissenschaftliche Buchgesellschaft.

Stuart, D.T. (1983), 'Führung', in Lippert and Wakenhut (1983: 103–12).

Sudbrack, J. (ed.) (1981), *Zeugen christlicher Gotteserfahrung*, Mainz: Matthias-Grünewald-Verlag.

—— (1990), *Mystische Spuren: Auf der Suche nach der christlichen Lebensgestalt*, Würzburg: Echter.

Sundén, H. (1967), *Die Christusmeditationen Dag Hammarskjölds*, Frankfurt a. M.: Knecht.

Sundkler, B. (1968), *Nathan Söderblom: His Life and Work*, London: Lutterworth Press.

Sundstrom, E. (1962), 'Why Hammarskjöld was Silent', *Frontier Spring*, pp. 313–18.

Susser, B. (1984), 'Peace and Dialogue in the Thought of Martin Buber', in Schlenke and Matz (1984: 57–65).

Sutor, B. (1991), *Politische Ethik: Gesamtdarstellung auf der Basis der Christlichen Gesellschaftslehre*, Paderborn: Schöningh.

Sutterlin, J.S. (1991), 'Foreword', in Boudreau (1991: ix–xii).

—— (1993), 'The UN Secretary-General as Chief Administrator', in Rivlin and Gordenker (1993: 43–59).

Swift, R.N. (ed.) (1960), *Annual Review of United Nations Affairs 1960–1961*, New York: Oceana.

Szasz, P.C. (1991), 'The Role of the U.N. Secretary-General: Some legal aspects', *New York Journal of International Law and Politics*, Vol. 24, pp. 161–98.

Tandon, Y. (1968), 'UNEF, the Secretary-General, and International Diplomacy in the Third Arab-Israeli War', *IO*, Vol. 22, pp. 529–56.

Taubman, W. (2003), *Khrushchev: The Man and his Era*, New York, London: Norton.

Thakur, R. (1995), *A Crisis of Expectations: UN peacekeeping in the 1990s*, Boulder, CO: Westview Press.

Thant, S. U (1964), *Toward World Peace: Addresses and Public Statements 1957–1963*, selected by Jacob Baal-Teshuva, New York, London: Yoseloff.

—— (1971), 'From Speech at Luncheon for the Dag Hammarskjöld Memorial Scholarship Fund 16 September 1971', in Cordier and Harrelson (1977: 588–600).

—— (1978), *View from the UN*, New York: Doubleday.

Thaysen, U. (1996), 'Biographien im Jahrzehnt des Umbruchs: Vom Charisma in der aktuellen Politik', *ZParl*, Vol. 27, pp. 719–26.

Thelin, B. (1998), *Fostered to Internationalism and Peace: Biographical Notes on UN Secretary-General Dag Hammarskjöld*, Peace Education Miniprints 97, Malmö: School of Education.

—— (2001), *Dag Hammarskjöld*, Stockholm: Carlsson.

Thomas, H. (1967), *The Suez Affair*, London: Weidenfeld & Nicolson.

Thomas à Kempis (1952), *The Imitation of Christ*, London: Penguin.

Thompson, K.W. (1965), 'The New Diplomacy and the Quest for Peace', *IO*, Vol. 19, pp. 394–409.

Tinker, C. (1992), 'The changing role of the UN Secretary-General', *ASIL Proceedings*, Vol. 86, pp. 308–13.

Tomuschat, C. (1986), 'Ethos, Ethics, and Morality in International Relations', *EPIL*, Vol. 9, pp. 126–9.

Touval, S. (1982), *The Peace Brokers: Mediators in the Arab-Israeli Conflict 1948–1979*, Princeton, NJ: Princeton University Press.
—— (1994), 'Why the U.N. fails', *FA*, Vol. 73, No. 5, pp. 44–57.
Trachtenberg, L. (1982), 'Dag Hammarskjöld as Leader: a Problem of Definition', *International Journal*, Vol. 37, pp. 613–35.
—— (1983), 'A Bibliographic Essay on Dag Hammarskjöld', in Jordan (1983: 149–77).
Trevelyan, H. (1980), *Public and Private*, London: Hamilton.
UN Review (1962) 'Report on Fatal Crash of Mr. Hammarskjold's Plane. Cause of Tragedy Remains Undetermined' *UN Review* 1962, pp. 17–20.
UNITAR (ed.) (1987), *The United Nations and the Maintenance of International Peace and Security*, Dordrecht: Nijhoff.
Urquhart, B. (1963), 'United Nations Peace Forces and the Changing United Nations: An Institutional Perspective', in Goodrich and Kay (1973: 223–39).
—— (1964), 'The Point of Rest', *The New Yorker*, 31 October, pp. 232–44.
—— (1972), *Hammarskjold*, New York: Norton.
—— (1982), 'International Peace and Security: Thoughts on the Twentieth Anniversary of Dag Hammarskjold's Death', *FA*, Vol. 60, No. 1, pp. 1–16.
—— (1983), 'Dag Hammarskjöld: The Private Person in a Very Public Office', in Jordan (1983: 133–48).
—— (1984), *United Nations Oral History Programme*, 30 May.
—— (1985), 'Die Rolle des Generalsekretärs', *Außenpolitik*, Vol. 36, pp. 254–60.
—— (1987a), *A Life in Peace and War*, New York, London: Harper & Row.
—— (1987b), 'International Leadership: The Legacy of Dag Hammarskjöld', in *Development Dialogue*, No. l. 1, pp. 6–16.
—— (1989), 'Konfliktlösung 1988: Die Rolle der Vereinten Nationen', in Stockholm International Peace Research Institute (1989: 379–401).
—— (1993a), *Ralph Bunche: An American Life*, New York, London: Norton.
—— (1993b), 'For a UN Volunteer Military Force', *New York Review of Books*, 10 June, pp. 3–4.
—— (1995), 'Mut zur Vision: Zum Jubiläum der UNO – Erinnerung an den herausragendsten Generalsekretär', *Die Zeit*, 20 October, p. 12.
—— (2000), *Between Sovereignty and Globalisation: Where does the United Nations Fit In?*, The Second Dag Hammarskjöld Lecture, Uppsala: Dag Hammarskjöld Foundation.
Urquhart, B. and Childers, E. (1990), *A World in Need of Leadership: Tomorrow's United Nations*, Uppsala: Dag Hammarskjöld Foundation (Development Dialogue 1–2/1990).
—— (1992), *Towards a More Effective United Nations*, Uppsala: Dag Hammarskjöld Foundation (Development Dialogue 1–2/1991).
—— (1994), *Renewing the United Nations System*, Uppsala: Dag Hammarskjöld Foundation (Development Dialogue 1/1994).
—— (1996), *A World in Need of Leadership. Tomorrow's United Nations. A Fresh Appraisal*, Uppsala: Dag Hammarskjöld Foundation.
Valdés, E.G. (1987), 'Weitere Überlegungen zur These von der Trennung von Politik und Moral', in Becker and Oelmüller (1987: 92–5).
Vega, R. de la (1985), 'Grundpositionen der Ethik. Ethik und Politik in der Geschichte', in Neumann (1985: 9–43).
Vertzberger, Y.Y.I. (1990), *The World in Their Minds: Information Processing, Cognition, and Perception in Foreign Policy Decisionmaking*, Stanford, CA: Stanford University Press.

Virally, M. (1961), 'Le Testament Politique de Dag Hammarskjoeld', *Annuaire Francais de Droit International*, Vol. 76, pp. 355–80.

—— (1962), 'Das politische Testament Dag Hammarskjölds', *VN*, Vol. 10, pp. 45–9; 78–82; 111–13.

Volger, H. (1995), *Geschichte der Vereinten Nationen*, Munich, Vienna: Oldenbourg.

Waldenfels, H. (1990), 'Mystik und soziale Verantwortung in den Weltreligionen', in Imhof (1990: 382–400).

Waldheim, K. (1975), 'Die Rolle der Vereinten Nationen in der Weltpolitik', *VN*, Vol. 23, pp. 1–3.

—— (1978), *Der schwierigste Job der Welt*, Vienna: Molden.

—— (1979), 'Die Rolle der Vereinten Nationen in der Weltpolitik', *VN*, Vol. 27, pp. 41–5.

—— (1980), *Building the Future Order. The Search for Peace in an Interdependent World*, edited by R.L. Schiffer, New York, London: The Free Press.

—— (1983), 'Dag Hammarskjöld and the Office of United Nations Secretary-General', in Jordan (1983: 15–23).

—— (1985), *Im Glaspalast der Weltpolitik*, Düsseldorf, Vienna: Econ-Verlag.

Wallensteen, P. (1985), 'Routes to Peace – The Thoughts of Dag Hammarskjöld and the Models of Peace Research', *Current Research on Peace and Violence*, Vol. 8, pp. 161–4.

—— (1995), *Dag Hammarskjöld*, Stockholm: Svenska Institutet.

Wallensteen, P., Frederiksson, G., Kindskog, L. and Persson, S. (1996), *Sweden at the UN*, Stockholm: Svenska Institutet.

Weber, M. (1989), *The Profession of Politics*, Washington, DC: Plutarch Press.

Wege, H. (1976), 'Rechtliche Legitimation eigenständiger streitschlichtender Aktivitäten des UN-Generalsekretärs in friedensbedrohenden Konfliktsituationen', *GYIL*, pp. 352–78.

Wehr, G. (1994), *Meister Eckhart in Selbstzeugnissen und Bilddokumenten*, 3rd edn, Reinbek: Rowohlt.

—— (1995a), *Europäische Mystik zur Einführung*, Hamburg. Junius.

—— (1995b), *Martin Buber*, 12th edn, Reinbek: Rowohlt.

—— (1996), *Martin Buber: Leben, Werk und Wirkung*, revised edn, Zurich: Diogenes.

Weiss, T.G. (1975), *International Bureaucracy: An Analysis of the Operation of Functional and Global International Secretariats*, Lexington, VA: Lexington Books.

—— (ed.) (1993), *Collective Security in a Changing World. A World Peace Foundation Study*, Boulder, CO: Rienner.

Weizsäcker, C.F. von (1967), 'Friedlosigkeit als seelische Krankheit', in Weizsäcker (1983: 153–77).

—— (1983), *Der bedrohte Friede. Politische Aufsätze 1945–1981*, Munich: DTV.

Weltsch, R. (1963), 'Bubers politische Philosophie', in Schilpp and Friedman (1963: 384–97).

Werner, H.-J. (1990), 'Die Ethik Albert Schweitzers und die deutsche Mystik des Mittelalters', in Günzler (1990: 196–226).

—— (1994), *Martin Buber*, Frankfurt a. M., New York: Campus Verlag.

Wheeler, N.J. (2000), *Saving Strangers: Humanitarian Intervention in International Society*, Oxford: Oxford University Press.

Wiener, J. (1995), 'Leadership, the United Nations, and the New World Order', in Bourantonis and Wiener (1995: 41–63).

Wight, M. (1992), *International Theory: The Three Traditions*, edited by Brian Porter and Gabriele Wight, New York: Holmes & Meier.

Winkler, N. (1997), *Meister Eckhart zur Einführung*, Hamburg: Junius.

Wojtyla, K. (1998), *Der Glaube bei Johannes vom Kreuz (1948): Dissertation an der Theologischen Fakultät der Päpstlichen Universität Angelicum in Rom*, Vienna: Verlag Christliche Innerlichkeit.

Wolf, S. (1992), *Martin Buber zur Einführung*, Hamburg: Junius.

Wolfrum, R. (ed.) (1991), *Handbuch Vereinte Nationen*, 2nd edn, Munich: Beck.

—— (ed.) (1995a), *United Nations. Law, Policies, Practice. Vol. 1*, Munich: Beck.

—— (ed.) (1995b), *United Nations. Law, Policies, Practice. Vol. 2*, Munich: Beck.

—— (1995c), 'Consensus', in Wolfrum (1995a: 350–5).

Zacher, M.W. (1966), 'The Secretary-General and the United Nations' Function of Peaceful Settlement', *IO*, Vol. 20, pp. 724–49.

—— (1970), *Dag Hammarskjold's United Nations*, New York, London: Columbia University Press.

—— (1983), 'Hammarskjöld's Conception of the United Nations' Role in World Politics', in Jordan (1983: 111–32).

List of interviews

Birnbaum, Karl, Stockholm, 24 June 1998.

Frederick, Pauline, United Nations Oral History Programme, 20 June 1986/11 July 1986.

Hamrell, Sven, Uppsala, 26 June 1998.

Lind, Per, Yale University Hammarskjöld Project, 7 November 1990.

—— Stockholm, 16 June 1998.

Linnér, Sture, Yale University Hammarskjöld Project, 8 November 1990.

—— Stockholm, 26 June 1998.

Rikhye, Indar Jit, Yale University Hammarskjöld Project, 26 March 1990.

Schachter, Oscar, 'Dag Hammarskjöld Interview', Oral History Research Office, Columbia University, 1978.

—— United Nations Oral History Programme, 11 October 1985.

Thelin, Bengt, Stockholm, 17 June 1998/14 September 2000.

Urquhart, Brian, Oral History Research Office, Columbia University, 1978.

—— New York, 08 October 1997/15 October 1997.

Weizsäcker, Carl Friedrich von, Starnberg, 4 February 1999.

Yorck, Alexander Graf, Heidelberg, 28 November 1997.

Index

The initials DH are used to refer to Dag Hammarskjöld.